Merry Christmas
2009
Mama

>>> Table of Contents

D0001538

>>> Note from the Author

B usy People's Cookbooks have won numerous awards and have sold over one million copies, which is pretty amazing, because as a homemaker with only a high school education, I originally self-published these cookbooks to pay for my husband's cancer treatments, even though I didn't know how to type, use a computer, or anything about publishing! That, in and of itself, is what I call, "a God thing."

After a six-and-a-half year battle with brain cancer my husband became completely cancer free. However, after he became cancer free he fell, hit his head on the cement, and had a brain hemorrhage. At thirty-eight years old he died a hero. The research gathered from the experimental cancer treatment he underwent through Dr. Stanislaw Burzynski in Houston, Texas, is now helping many live; and because he was cancer free, he was able to be an organ and tissue donor.

As a single mother, writing Busy People's Cookbooks is now how I financially support my family. A percentage of my profits also helps poor inner-city outreach programs such as Solid Rock Ministries, Christian Health Ministries, and Vision Ministries.

I was born on a diet and have always struggled with my weight. The Bible says, "God will use our weaknesses as our strengths." I believe my cookbooks are evidence of that. Cancer, heart disease, obesity, diabetes, high blood pressure, and hypertension run in my family. All of these diseases thrive on a high-fat diet. That is why all of the recipes in my cookbooks are low in fat.

I used to think I was doomed because I would literally dream of recipes to create. I thought my obsession with food had been incorporated into my dreams and that surely something was wrong with me. Never in a million years did I think God would use my recipes not only to help others with their food issues but also as a means, as a single mother, to support my family.

I know that my purpose in life is not only to create fast and easy low-fat recipes for busy people but also to share the love of God. Many people will not listen to a preacher speak but will listen to me, the "Cookbook Lady," speak on TV or radio or at a large event. I can share the love of God with them in a nonthreatening way. I can encourage them not only to be healthier by eating low-fat but also to have an overall higher quality of life by putting God first in their lives.

I know this is highly unusual, and some people may even think it is strange, but now that you know the story behind Busy People's Cookbooks it seems only natural that I dedicate this book to God. I am hoping this book will be the first of many cookbooks in a series of Busy People's Super Simple Menu Cookbooks.

As with all of my Busy People's Cookbooks, I give God all the praise and glory for the gifts and talents He uses through me to create absolutely mouth-watering and delicious home-style recipes. Without a doubt, I know your entire family will enjoy them; and if you don't tell them that the recipes are low-fat and healthy, they'll never know.

For more information about Dawn Hall, the inner-city ministries, or Dr. Stanislaw Burzynski, go to her Web site at: www.DawnHallCookbooks.com.

>>> Special Thanks

First and foremost, I want to thank God and give Him all the praise and glory for the success Busy People's Cookbooks have had. I consider it an honor and a privilege to have my cookbooks published by Thomas Nelson Publishers. As an author, I think of my books as extensions of myself, just as children are extensions of parents. Who we choose as our spouse and, ultimately, the parent of our future children is an important decision. The same analogy can be used with publishing. As an author, my books are my babies and having Thomas Nelson Publishers as my publisher is a relationship that I cherish. We are an extension of each other and I am grateful to be published by a company of high integrity, a company I take pride in.

Larry Stone conceived the unique idea of creating this Busy People's Super Simple Menus Cookbook, which strategically organizes the entire meal preparation, incorporating a format of easy-to-read and comfortable-to-follow, step-by-step instructions for every recipe used. With all of my heart, thank you, Larry, for extending to me the opportunity to create the format and write the first cookbook using this unique menu cookbook concept.

Thank you to my literary agent, Coleen O'Shea. Coleen's feedback during the beginning stages of creating this book was very helpful. She encouraged me as I persistently kept rethinking and retesting ideas until I finally found one that worked. It was not easy!

Thanks to my editor, Geoff Stone, for undertaking the editing of this unique idea in cookbook writing. Thanks, too, for the extra time you gave me to iron out the wrinkles during the developmental and final stages of creating this book. I believe the format of this cookbook will be a model that many will follow.

To my assistants, Ashley Hall, LuAnne Surgeson, Mary Shaffer, Morgan Price, Lauren Meiring, and Brenda Crosser: I say thank you. I appreciate your hard work and efforts.

Thank you to Tammi Hancock, the registered dietician who performs the nutritional and diabetic exchanges analyses. Your work is such a blessing!

Last but not least, to you, the customer who keeps buying and asking for more of my books and telling your friends and family about them; thank you so very much! You are why I do what I do and I could not be more grateful!

May God bless us all as we try to bless others!

>>> Introduction

For healthy, home-cooked meals served at their best, time management is an absolute must. Let's get real. As an experienced cook and homemaker I know the frustration and uncertainties that often accompany trying to figure out the what's, when's and where's of meal preparations. There are a lot of elements to consider in preparing a multiple-course menu such as: appropriate portion sizes, complementing recipes, proper temperature of the food, and overall appearance. It is no wonder people feel overwhelmed and either eat high-fat, processed junk food or eat out.

I can't tell you how many times I have eaten at someone's home (who has spent a lot of time and effort preparing a beautiful meal) only to have the hot food served cold and the cold food served at room temperature. UGH!

The unique integrated time line incorporates instructions for every recipe of the dinner menu, ensuring maximum ease of preparation in thirty minutes or less. Cooks no longer have to try to figure out when to start each recipe so the entire meal will be ready at the same time. The home-style menus are heart smart, low fat, low calorie, and taste delicious. Each menu includes a grocery list, supplies list, and nutritional information.

SUPPLIES, GROCERY, AND PANTRY LISTS

A supplies list, grocery list, and pantry list are included in every menu so you can easily tell with a glance if you have everything you need to prepare the entire meal. The grocery list includes things you most likely will need to purchase. The pantry list includes items you may have on hand, but may need to buy. The supplies list includes items (that are not food) such as special cooking utensils, pans, etc. that you'll need. Standard items such as spatulas, knives, measuring cups, and cutting boards are not included.

PORTION SIZES

A lot of people don't have a clue what a portion size is or what a well-balanced meal is. Portion sizes follow the American Heart Association and the American Diabetic Association guidelines for portion sizes. They are smaller than what we normally think of as portion sizes in this day of supersizing everything. I've indicated what the portion size should be to match the nutrition information.

ABBREVIATIONS

Since the directions for all the recipes are integrated, sometimes the menu goes to three pages. For convenience I've included the quantities of the ingredients in the directions as well as in the ingredient lists. However, because we don't have a lot of room I abbreviated the measurements, using the following standard abbreviations (for singular and plural):

c = cup	T = tablespoon	oz = ounce	qt = quart
t = teaspoon	lb = pound	pt = pint	

TEAM TIME

If you're used to having to do everything else while also trying to prepare a meal, let me encourage you with this bit of insight from my personal experience. This could be as good a time as any to start implementing team effort within the family or household. There is no reason why older children can't keep an eye on the younger children for 30 minutes while you focus on preparing dinner. I suggest the following:

Implement a plan of who does what and stick to it! It doesn't matter that little Johnny doesn't feel like helping set the table. We all have to do things we don't feel like doing. That is what being part of a family or team is about.

Acknowledge everyone's efforts in front of the other family members. Express appreciation for a job well done and watch their self-confidence grow.

AFTER-MEAL CLEAN-UP

Make clean-up a family affair. There's no need for one person to have to take care of all the dishes all of the time. When you do it together, you will see your family's interaction with one another improve. There's no reason why everyone can't help by carrying his or her plate, silverware, and glass to the sink.

I have found sharing the responsibilities of after-meal clean-up works best when put in writing. Discuss the responsibilities as a group and decide what is most fair in regard to dividing up the duties. This helps children feel like they are a part of the process and in the long run will help to eliminate complaining. Explain how you are trying to be fair and how it is not fair within the household for one person to have to do all of the preparing and cleaning up. Even though as the parent, I did most of the cooking myself, I always tried to help with after-meal clean-up as a means of incorporating quality time with whomever else was responsible with helping clean up.

> Delegate different responsibilities that need to be completed after dinner, such as clearing the table, cleaning the table and counters, washing the dishes, or loading the dishwasher, and put it in the clean-up agreement.

> Include in the clean-up agreement the consequences that will follow if someone does not follow through with his or her responsibility.

> Have everyone who is participating with clean-up responsibilities sign the agreement stating that this is not a debatable topic and that they are all in agreement with the terms and will participate without complaining.

> After the clean-up agreement is signed, post it in a convenient place so everyone knows what his or her responsibilities are.

> Expect a few wrinkles to have to be ironed out in the beginning stages of this process, especially if your family is used to one parent having all of the responsibilities.

> Once a rhythm is established within the able-bodied members of the household, dinnertime preparation and clean-up will run smoothly and will become a way of life as a team effort. The key is to get in the practice of establishing and maintaining good habits.

TIME MANAGEMENT AND MONEY MANAGEMENT

When I first started creating this cookbook I cut time by purchasing precut lettuces. It didn't take long before I realized that if the precut lettuces weren't on sale I was spending an arm and a leg to save a few minutes. I'm too frugal for that, so I revamped things a bit. Unless I was under a major time restraint when preparing the menu (or if the precut salads were on sale), I opted to chop my own lettuce. It saved oodles of money and, for the most part, the salads could be freshly cut and comfortably prepared within the 30 minutes.

Note: A good place to purchase large quantities of precut romaine and iceberg lettuce along with spring lettuce mixes are wholesale clubs.

QUESTIONS AND ANSWERS

Do all menus take 30 minutes to make?

No, many menus take less than 30 minutes; however, all of the menus can be completely and comfortably made in 30 minutes or less. When a meal is completed in 22 minutes I did not add extra recipes to the menu to use up time because the entire menu already has everything it needs nutritionally for a well-balanced meal with healthy portions of carbohydrates, lean proteins, and vegetables.

Sometimes I added fresh-baked bread recipes of some kind to the menu, if it wasn't a high-calorie menu. In all honesty, most families do not need the extra carbohydrates with their pasta or rice entrées. I tried to be health conscious and take into consideration what most people need, which is more free time to enjoy life.

Watching your weight or want to lose weight?

If you are like me and were born watching your weight, and do not need or want the extra calories of eating every recipe in the menu, then I recommend eating the protein (meat, fish, chicken, vegetarian meat substitute, etc.) along with the vegetables and avoid eating the carbohydrates such as potatoes, rice, pasta, or bread. My menus comfortably fit within the guidelines of well-balanced diets. If an entrée has more calories than you want, then simply cut back on your portion size. Small reductions can add up to great weight losses. Often less is more.

I recommend the following support groups for weight loss: First Place, TOPS (Taking Off Pounds Sensibly), Weight Watchers, Body For Life, and Overeaters Anonymous. Check your phone book for local chapters.

The serving sizes in this cookbook are ones recommended by the American Heart Association and the American Diabetes Association's guidelines and are good amounts for those watching their weight.

Nutritional information and diabetic exchanges are listed with each menu. Ask your doctor for the recommended number of servings that you need daily.

Why do menus serve six?

Overall, most recipes in this book serve six because the average-size family will usually be able to eat six servings given that most men and growing boys will eat more than one serving. And for those with smaller families, leftovers are nice so that you don't have to cook every day.

What if I don't want to make a certain side dish or vegetable in a menu?

No big deal, not to worry. During the time allocated within the instructional timeline, simply substitute a precut salad for the vegetable or side dish. Use your favorite blend of lettuces and, if desired, garnish the salad with your favorite fresh vegetables, such as cucumbers, mushrooms, tomatoes, carrots, celery, onion, and bell peppers. Serve with salad dressing on the side.

If you want to save money by purchasing heads of lettuce instead of precut packaged salad blends, substitute one large head of romaine or iceberg lettuce, which averages about 9 cups after being washed and chopped.

If you don't want to make a certain bread recipe, again, no big deal. The bread is usually used as an extra side dish "filler-upper" for heartier appetites and for those whose metabolisms can afford the extra calories.

If you want to serve bread, but don't want the bread recipe in the menu, then serve your favorite store-bought bread instead.

Busy People's Super Simple 30-Minute Menus Cookbook takes the guess work out of planning your meal. The precise, easy-to-follow, step-by-step, timeline instructions tell you not just how to prepare a recipe but how to prepare the entire meal. It is just the answer busy people have needed. This unique way of explaining how to make the entire menu will help you get all the recipes on the table at the same time. I am confident you will be blessed by how much easier it is to put together a complete meal!

WHAT ELSE CAN I DO TO MAKE COOKING THESE MENUS EASIER?

Go to www.DawnHallCookbooks.com and print the downloadable grocery list to use while shopping.

In an easy-to-view location in your cooking area, place a 30-minute timer that you can watch as it counts down the minutes. Timers in the cooking supplies and tools aisle at your grocery stores are inexpensive and work great!

Use a cookbook stand to keep the book open on the counter in front of you while you prepare the meal.

Set out on the counter all of the groceries and supplies that you will need to prepare the meal *before* starting the menu.

Have a sink of hot soapy water ready before you begin cooking, so you can easily wash and rinse cooking utensils and supplies if you have any free time during preparation of the meal. Cleaning just-used utensils is a lot easier than cleaning ones that have been sitting around for hours. To save even more time, simply let them air dry and put them away after dinner.

DEFINITION OF SUPPLIES

These are just a few of the supplies I use in this book with which you may not be familiar.

Colander – A bowl with holes in the bottom that is used for draining water from an ingredient such as pasta or soup stock.

Dutch Oven – A 12- to 16-cup size pan that is used to boil pastas, potatoes, or make soups in.

Indoor Electric Grill –A grill that cooks both sides at once. It cooks at least two times faster than outdoor gas grills. I only use the large size, not the two-person size.

Jelly-Roll Pan – A baking sheet with at least a one-half-inch rim to prevent ingredients from going off the pan.

Nonstick Saucepan – A heavy-duty pan with 2- to 3-inch high sides that has been coated with a special material to prevent sticking and to allow for fat-free cooking. Investing in a good quality nonstick 12-inch saucepan would be very useful in using this cookbook.

Nonstick Skillet – The difference between a saucepan and a skillet (or a fry pan) is that a skillet is not usually as deep as a saucepan, doesn't have a lid, and doesn't hold as much as a saucepan.

Microwave Cooking – Microwaves vary in cooking time. All of the recipes in this book were tested in my own home with an assistant, a clock, and a timer. If for some reason your microwave cooks either faster or slower than mine, please adjust your future microwaving cooking times accordingly.

Range Temperatures – Most ranges have knobs regulating heat as such:

Low: 1–2   Medium Low: 3   Medium: 5   Medium High: 7   High: 9–10

DEFINITION OF INGREDIENTS

I sometimes mention brand names because I have found them to work best in my recipes. However, you may substitute other ingredients if you want. Please note: the brand names mentioned in this book are registered trademarks and are thus protected by law.

Imitation butter flavored sprinkles are an all natural, fat- and cholesterol-free butter-flavored substitute found in the spice section of most grocery stores. A common brand name is Butter Buds.

Liquid egg substitute is a generic term for the Egg Beaters brand.

Splenda is a calorie-free sugar substitute that tastes like sugar but does not have the fattening carbohydrates of sugar. I've used Splenda granular in many recipes. It is not the same as the condensed versions of Splenda sold in packet form. Equal amounts of Splenda packets can not be substituted for Splenda granular; the different forms measure differently and are not interchangeable. Sugar can be substituted for Splenda granular in any of my recipes. Remember, using sugar instead of Splenda will increase the calories. No conversions are needed to substitute sugar for Splenda granular.

Splenda Brown Sugar Blend is a reduced calorie brown sugar substitute that tastes like brown sugar but does not have the fattening carbohydrates of brown sugar. I've used Splenda Brown Sugar Blend in many recipes. You can use regular brown sugar instead of Splenda Brown Sugar Blend, just keep in mind that the recipe will contain more calories. No conversions are needed to substitute brown sugar for Splenda Brown Sugar Blend.

CHILLED MEALS

>>> Spicy Shrimp Soup

Two-Step Cucumber Salad • Marble Rye Bread

If you like shrimp cocktail, nonalcoholic Bloody Marys, cool refreshing cucumbers from the garden, and cold beverages on a hot summer day, then this is the menu for you! It's an original that will satisfy your taste buds and refresh you after a long, hot day.

SPICY SHRIMP SOUP

Yield: 7 servings (1 cup per serving)

Calories: 138 (7% fat); Total Fat: 1g; Cholesterol: 190mg; Carbohydrate: 9g; Dietary Fiber: 2g; Protein 22g; Sodium: 857mg; Diabetic Exchanges: 2 vegetable, 2 1/2 very lean meat

TWO-STEP CUCUMBER SALAD

Yield: 6 servings (3/4 cup per serving)

Calories: 41 (0% fat); Total Fat: 0g; Cholesterol: 0mg; Carbohydrate: 9g; Dietary Fiber: 1g; Protein 1g; Sodium: 203mg; Diabetic Exchanges: 1/2 other carbohydrate

SPICY SHRIMP SOUP

1 1/2   pounds cocktail shrimp, cooked, peeled, and deveined (40 to 50-count per pound)
3   cups Bloody Mary mix (nonalcoholic), chilled
1/2   cup finely chopped celery
1   (14 1/2-ounce) can diced stewed tomatoes, chilled
1/2   teaspoon dried parsley

TWO-STEP CUCUMBER SALAD

1/2   cup fat-free French salad dressing, chilled
1/2   teaspoon prepared horseradish
2   large cucumbers, chilled

Instructions

17 MINUTES BEFORE DINNER, start the soup. In a large bowl, stir together 1¹/₂ lb shrimp, 3 c Bloody Mary mix, ¹/₂ c celery, 1 can stewed tomatoes, and ¹/₂ t dried parsley until well mixed. Cover with plastic wrap and keep chilled in refrigerator.

7 MINUTES BEFORE DINNER, start the salad. In a medium bowl, stir together ¹/₂ c French salad dressing and ¹/₂ t horseradish until well mixed. Set aside. Slice the 2 cucumbers into thin slices and stir into the salad dressing until well coated.

2 MINUTES BEFORE DINNER, ladle the soup into individual bowls and place on the table. Put the cucumber salad on the table along with bread if desired.

NOTE: *Buy shrimp already precooked, peeled, and deveined. It costs the same as uncooked and it will save you a lot of time. Also save time by putting the Bloody Mary mix, the can of tomatoes, cucumbers, and French salad dressing in the refrigerator to chill before using.*

Supplies List

Timer
Large mixing bowl
Medium mixing bowl
Ladle to serve

Grocery List

PACKAGED

3 cups Bloody Mary mix
    (nonalcoholic)
1 (14¹/₂-ounce) can diced
    stewed tomatoes
1 (8-ounce) bottle
    French salad dressing
Prepared horseradish
Marble rye bread (optional)

PRODUCE

2 large cucumbers
Celery

FROZEN

1¹/₂ pounds cooked and
    peeled cocktail shrimp
    (40 to 50-count per
    pound)

Pantry List

Dried parsley

>>> Buffalo Chicken Salad Soft Tacos

Fresh Green Bell Pepper Strips with French Honey Dip • Frosted Watermelon Wedges
with Fresh Blueberries

This is a terrific summertime menu using ingredients fresh from the garden.

BUFFALO CHICKEN SALAD SOFT TACOS
Yield: 6 servings (1 taco per serving)

Calories: 242 (7% fat); Total Fat: 2g; Cholesterol: 34mg; Carbohydrate: 28g; Dietary Fiber: 3g; Protein 24g; Sodium: 989mg; Diabetic Exchanges: 1¹/₂ starch, 1 vegetable, 3 very lean meat

FRESH GREEN BELL PEPPER STRIPS WITH FRENCH HONEY DIP
Yield: 6 servings (¹/₂ pepper and 2 tablespoons dip per serving)

Calories: 54 (0% fat); Total Fat: 0g; Cholesterol: 0mg; Carbohydrate: 13g; Dietary Fiber: 2g; Protein 1g; Sodium: 203mg; Diabetic Exchanges: 1 vegetable, ¹/₂ other carbohydrate

FROSTED WATERMELON WEDGES WITH FRESH BLUEBERRIES
Yield: 6 servings (1 wedge per serving)

Calories: 111 (0% fat); Total Fat: 0g; Cholesterol: 3mg; Carbohydrate: 24g; Dietary Fiber: 1g; Protein 4g; Sodium: 99mg; Diabetic Exchanges: 1¹/₂ fruit, ¹/₂ very lean meat

BUFFALO CHICKEN SALAD SOFT TACOS

1	(8-ounce) package fat-free cream cheese
2	tablespoons plus 1 teaspoon buffalo chicken wing sauce
1	(13-ounce) can chicken breast in water, drained
¹/₂	cup shredded fat-free cheddar cheese
1	cup finely chopped celery
2	large tomatoes
6	flour tortillas (from a 16-ounce package)

FRESH GREEN BELL PEPPER STRIPS WITH FRENCH HONEY DIP

3	large green bell peppers, cut into strips
¹/₂	cup fat-free French salad dressing
2	teaspoons honey

FROSTED WATERMELON WEDGES WITH FRESH BLUEBERRIES

¹/₄	seedless watermelon
¹/₄	cup marshmallow crème
4	ounces fat-free cream cheese
1	tablespoon Splenda granular
1	cup fresh blueberries

Instructions

30 MINUTES BEFORE DINNER, set out the cream cheese to soften.

Begin making the bell pepper tray with dip. In a small bowl, stir together $^1/_2$ c French salad dressing and 2 t honey until well mixed. Place the bowl in the center of a large dinner plate. Arrange the bell pepper strips around the dip. Cover with plastic wrap and refrigerate until dinner is ready to be served.

20 MINUTES BEFORE DINNER, start the frosted watermelon. Cut the watermelon into 6 (1-inch) wedges, and place on a platter.

In a small bowl, mix together $^1/_4$ c marshmallow crème, 4 oz cream cheese, and 1 T Splenda granular until well mixed. Spread a rounded tablespoon of cream mixture on top of each wedge of watermelon, and then evenly divide the blueberries on top of each of the frosted watermelons. Place on the dinner table.

10 MINUTES BEFORE DINNER, begin the chicken salad. In a medium bowl, stir together 1 package cream cheese, 2 T plus 1 t buffalo chicken wing sauce, 1 can drained chicken breast chopped, $^1/_2$ c shredded cheddar cheese, and 1 c chopped celery until well mixed.

Spread $^1/_3$ c chicken mixture on half of each flour tortilla.

Cut the tomatoes into 6 ($^1/_2$-inch) slices. Cut the slices in half and place 2 half slices of tomato on top of each chicken salad taco. Fold the flour tortilla over the tomato slices to make a taco.

1 MINUTE BEFORE DINNER, place the tacos on the table along with the bell pepper tray and dip.

NOTE: *For added crunch, add shredded iceberg lettuce on each taco.*

Supplies List

Timer
2 small bowls
Medium bowl
Large dinner plate
Platter

Grocery List

PACKAGED

Buffalo chicken wing sauce
1 (13-ounce) can chicken breast in water
6 flour tortillas
Marshmallow crème
4 ounces fat-free cream cheese

PRODUCE

Celery
2 large tomatoes
3 large green bell peppers
$^1/_4$ seedless watermelon
1 cup fresh blueberries

DAIRY

4 ounces fat-free cream cheese
$^1/_2$ cup shredded fat-free cheddar cheese

Pantry List

Honey
Splenda granular

>>> Hawaiian Chicken Salad Sandwich

Melon Medley Kebabs

The presentation of the colorful orange and green fruit kebabs along with the unique super-sized sandwich is every bit as refreshing and delicious as it looks.

HAWAIIAN CHICKEN SALAD SANDWICH
Yield: 8 servings
(⅛ sandwich per serving)

Calories: 307 (14% fat); Total Fat: 5g; Cholesterol: 47mg; Carbohydrate: 39g; Dietary Fiber: 1g; Protein 24g; Sodium: 1185mg; Diabetic Exchanges: 2 starch, ½ fruit, 3 lean meat

MELON MEDLEY KEBABS
Yield: 8 servings
(3 mini kebabs per serving)

Calories: 58 (0% fat); Total Fat: 0g; Cholesterol: 0mg; Carbohydrate: 14g; Dietary Fiber: 1g; Protein 1g; Sodium: 28mg; Diabetic Exchanges: 1 fruit

HAWAIIAN CHICKEN SALAD SANDWICH

2	(13-ounce) cans chicken breast in water, drained	1	(16-ounce) round loaf Hawaiian sweet bread
1	(8-ounce) can sliced pineapple in pineapple juice, drained	2	thin slices red onion
⅔	cup Teriyaki Baste & Glaze	6	leaves red leaf lettuce
		3	kebab skewers

MELON MEDLEY KEBABS

4	cups cantaloupe (about ½ of a large melon)	12	kebab skewers
4	cups honeydew melon (about ½ of a large melon)		

Instructions

25 MINUTES BEFORE DINNER, prepare the melon kebabs. Remove the seeds and rind from $^1/_2$ of a large cantaloupe and $^1/_2$ of a large honeydew melon. Cut the melons into bite-sized pieces. Thread the pieces of honeydew and cantaloupe alternately on wooden kebab skewers. Cut the kebab skewers in half. Place the kebabs on a platter, cover with plastic wrap, and refrigerate.

10 MINUTES BEFORE DINNER, start the sandwich. In a medium bowl, shred the chicken using a fork. Place in a mixing bowl. Cut the pineapple slices into small pieces. Stir the pineapple and $^2/_3$ c Teriyaki Baste & Glaze into the chicken until well mixed.

Cut 1 round loaf Hawaiian sweet bread in half horizontally. With a spatula, spread the chicken salad on the bottom layer of the bread, pressing firmly into the bread. Separate 2 thin slices red onion into rings and arrange on top of the chicken salad. Place the lettuce on top of the onion slices and place the top layer of bread on the sandwich.

2 MINUTES BEFORE DINNER, cut the sandwich into 8 large, pie-shaped pieces. Secure each wedge with a skewer that has been cut in half and put on the dinner table.

1 MINUTE BEFORE DINNER, place the melon kebabs on the table.

Supplies List

Timer
2-quart pitcher
Medium bowl
Mixing bowl
12 wooden kebab skewers

Grocery List

PACKAGED

2 (13-ounce) cans chicken breast in water
1 (8-ounce) can sliced pineapple in pineapple juice
Teriyaki Baste & Glaze
1 (16-ounce) round loaf Hawaiian sweet bread

PRODUCE

Red onion
1 head red leaf lettuce
$^1/_2$ large honeydew melon
1 medium cantaloupe

>>> Not Just Another Chicken Salad Sandwich

Watermelon Sandwiches • Baby Carrot Sticks

Don't worry, you don't have to eat two of the same kind of sandwich. This fun menu includes a unique watermelon sandwich filled with a thick, sweet, rich, and creamy filling I know you'll love.

NOT JUST ANOTHER CHICKEN SALAD SANDWICH

Yield: 6 servings

(1 sandwich per serving)

Calories: 209 (11% fat); Total Fat: 2g; Cholesterol: 32mg; Carbohydrate: 27g; Dietary Fiber: 1g; Protein 17g; Sodium: 612mg; Diabetic Exchanges: 2 starch, 2 very lean meat

WATERMELON SANDWICHES

Yield: 6 servings

(1 sandwich per serving)

Calories: 106 (0% fat); Total Fat: 0g; Cholesterol: 7mg; Carbohydrate: 19g; Dietary Fiber: 1g; Protein 6g; Sodium: 191mg; Diabetic Exchanges: 1 1/2 fruit, 1 very lean meat

NOT JUST ANOTHER CHICKEN SALAD SANDWICH

1	(13-ounce) can chicken breast in water, drained
1	(8-ounce) container fat-free sour cream
3/4	cup finely chopped celery
1	teaspoon fat-free Italian dressing mix
1/2	teaspoon Italian seasoning
2	tablespoons fat-free mayonnaise
1	(8-ounce) loaf French bread
	Lettuce and tomato (optional)

WATERMELON SANDWICHES

1	(8-ounce) package fat-free cream cheese, softened
1/4	cup marshmallow crème
1/4	cup Splenda granular
12	(1/2-inch thick) slices watermelon

Instructions

30 MINUTES BEFORE DINNER, set the cream cheese out to soften.

Make the chicken salad. In a medium bowl, mix together 1 container sour cream, $^3/_4$ c finely chopped celery, 1 t Italian dressing mix, $^1/_2$ t Italian seasoning, and 2 T mayonnaise until well blended. Add the canned chicken to the mixture. Stir until the chicken is well coated. Cover the chicken salad and place in the refrigerator.

23 MINUTES BEFORE DINNER, prepare the watermelon sandwiches. In a small bowl, mix together 1 package cream cheese, $^1/_4$ c marshmallow crème, and $^1/_4$ c Splenda granular until well blended.

Remove the rind from the watermelon slices. Using a 4-inch round cookie cutter, cut each watermelon slice into a circle; these circles will act as slices of "bread" for our watermelon sandwiches. In order not to waste these tasty leftover pieces, I suggest cutting the scraps into bite-size pieces and placing them in a large bowl to use for snacks.

Spread the crème mixture over the 6 watermelon slices. Place the remaining slices of watermelon on top of the cream mixture. Arrange on a platter with a lip so the juice from the watermelon will not run off the platter.

5 MINUTES BEFORE DINNER, assemble the chicken salad sandwiches by cutting the loaf of bread in half horizontally. Spread the chicken salad mixture onto the bottom half of the bread. Add lettuce and tomato slices, if desired. Place the remaining half of the bread on top to complete the sandwich. Cut into 6 individual sandwiches and arrange on a platter on the dinner table.

1 MINUTE BEFORE DINNER, place the watermelon sandwiches and carrot sticks on the dinner table.

Supplies List
Timer
Medium bowl
Small bowl

Grocery List

PACKAGED
1 (13-ounce) can chicken
   breast in water
Fat-free Italian dressing mix
Marshmallow crème
1 (8-ounce) loaf French bread

PRODUCE
Celery
Lettuce and tomato
   (optional)
$^1/_2$ watermelon

DAIRY
1 (8-ounce) container
   fat-free sour cream
1 (8-ounce) package fat-free
   cream cheese

Pantry List
Italian seasoning
Fat-free mayonnaise
Splenda granular

>>> Freckled Cucumber & Ham Salad

Ruby Fruit Salad • Reduced-Fat Buttered Crackers

This refreshing menu is light, yet filling and satisfying.

FRECKLED CUCUMBER & HAM SALAD
Yield: 6 servings
(1⅓ cups per serving)

Calories: 220 (22% fat); Total Fat: 4g; Cholesterol: 43mg; Carbohydrate: 13g; Dietary Fiber: 1g; Protein 23g; Sodium: 1245mg; Diabetic Exchanges: 1 vegetable, ½ other carbohydrate, 3 lean meat

RUBY FRUIT SALAD
Yield: 6 servings (1 cup per serving)

Calories: 65 (0% fat); Total Fat: 0g; Cholesterol: 0mg; Carbohydrate: 15g; Dietary Fiber: 1g; Protein 2g; Sodium: 49mg; Diabetic Exchanges: 1 fruit

FRECKLED CUCUMBER & HAM SALAD

½ cup fat-free French vanilla nondairy creamer, chilled

1½ teaspoons ranch salad dressing mix

1 teaspoon dried dill weed

2 large cucumbers, unpeeled, sliced thin, chilled

½ cup finely chopped Vidalia onion, chilled

1 pound extra-lean smoked ham, cut into bite-size pieces

1 cup fat-free mild cheddar cheese, shredded

RUBY FRUIT SALAD

2 cups seedless watermelon, cut into small bite-size pieces (or about ⅛ of a seedless watermelon), chilled

2 cups cantaloupe, cut into small bite-size pieces (about ½ of a small cantaloupe), chilled

2 cups fresh pineapple, cut into small bite-size pieces (about ½ of a small pineapple), chilled

1 (0.3 ounce) box sugar-free raspberry-flavored gelatin dessert mix

Instructions

30 MINUTES BEFORE DINNER, prepare the ham salad. In a large bowl stir together $^1/_2$ c nondairy creamer, $1^1/_2$ t ranch salad dressing mix, and 1 t dried dill weed until well blended. Set aside.

28 MINUTES BEFORE DINNER, thinly slice 2 cucumbers. Finely chop $^1/_2$ of a Vidalia onion. Cut 1 lb extra-lean smoked ham into bite-size pieces. Add to the dressing mixture and stir until well mixed. Stir in 1 c shredded cheddar cheese. Cover and keep refrigerated until ready to eat.

15 MINUTES BEFORE DINNER, make the Ruby Fruit Salad. Combine the fruit in a large serving bowl. Sprinkle with 1 box sugar-free raspberry-flavored gelatin dessert mix and gently stir together until the fruit is well coated. Place on the dinner table.

1 MINUTE BEFORE DINNER, place the crackers on a serving plate and put on the dinner table next to the ham salad and the fruit salad.

NOTE: *Put the creamer, cucumbers, onion, and fruit in the refrigerator when you get home from the store to chill them for this menu.*

Supplies List
Timer
2 large serving bowls
Serving plate

Grocery List
PACKAGED
Ranch salad dressing mix
1 (0.3 ounce) box sugar-free raspberry-flavored gelatin dessert mix
Reduced-fat butter-flavored or whole wheat crackers

PRODUCE
1 Vidalia onion
1 seedless watermelon
1 cantaloupe
1 fresh pineapple
2 large cucumbers

MEAT
1 pound extra-lean smoked ham

DAIRY
1 cup shredded fat-free mild cheddar cheese
$^1/_2$ cup fat-free French vanilla nondairy creamer

Pantry List
Dried dill weed

>>> Barbequed Chicken Salad

Grape Salad • Whole Wheat Low-Fat Crackers

Barbeque sauce is used instead of salad dressing in this entrée-salad that is perfect for days when you don't want to turn on any heat to prepare dinner. For super-fast preparation, purchase prewashed and cut romaine or iceberg lettuce in the produce section.

BARBEQUED CHICKEN SALAD
Yield: 6 servings
(3 cups per serving)

Calories: 329 (8% fat); Total Fat: 3g; Cholesterol: 55mg; Carbohydrate: 38g; Dietary Fiber: 3g; Protein 32g; Sodium: 1136mg; Diabetic Exchanges: 2 vegetable, 2 other carbohydrate, 4 very lean meat

GRAPE SALAD
Yield: 6 servings (1 cup per serving)

Calories: 104 (0% fat); Total Fat: 0g; Cholesterol: 0mg; Carbohydrate: 27g; Dietary Fiber: 1g; Protein 1g; Sodium: 3mg; Diabetic Exchanges: 2 fruit

BARBEQUED CHICKEN SALAD

2	(13-ounce) cans chicken breast in water, undrained and chilled	3	medium heads iceberg lettuce (about 18 cups chopped)
1	cup shredded fat-free cheddar cheese	1/2	medium sweet onion
1 1/2	cups sweet barbeque sauce, chilled	1	pint grape or cherry tomatoes
		1	cup fat-free croutons

GRAPE SALAD

1	pound fresh red seedless grapes (3 cups)	1/4	cup Splenda granular (optional)
1	pound fresh green seedless grapes (3 cups)		

Instructions

30 MINUTES BEFORE DINNER, start the chicken salad. In a very large bowl, combine 2 cans undrained, chilled chicken breast and liquid, 1 c shredded cheddar cheese, and $1^1/_2$ c chilled barbeque sauce until well mixed.

26 MINUTES BEFORE DINNER, cut 3 heads lettuce into bite-size pieces to make 18 c. Chop $^1/_2$ sweet onion to make $^1/_2$ c. Place the lettuce and onion on top of the barbequed chicken mixture. Do not combine or the lettuce will become soggy. Cover and place in the refrigerator to keep chilled.

16 MINUTES BEFORE DINNER, make the grape salad. Remove the grapes from the stems, rinse under cold water, and place in a trifle bowl or glass serving bowl. Gently stir in $^1/_4$ c Splenda. Place the grape salad on the dinner table.

4 MINUTES BEFORE DINNER, put whole wheat low-fat crackers in a basket and place on the dinner table.

3 MINUTES BEFORE DINNER, toss the barbequed chicken mixture with the lettuce and onion. Add 1 pint grape tomatoes, mix well, and put on the table.

1 MINUTE BEFORE DINNER, top the salad with 1 cup croutons and place on the dinner table.

NOTE: Prechill the chicken and barbeque sauce by refrigerating them as soon as you get home from the grocery store.

Although the grape salad looks prettier in a tall trifle dish, any glass dish will show off the contrasting colors.

Supplies List

Timer
Very large bowl
Trifle bowl or glass serving
   bowl
Basket

Grocery List

PACKAGED

$1^1/_2$ cups sweet barbeque
   sauce
2 (13-ounce) cans chicken
   breast in water
Fat-free croutons
Whole wheat low-fat crackers

PRODUCE

3 medium heads iceberg
   lettuce
Medium sweet onion
1 pint grape or cherry
   tomatoes
1 pound fresh red seedless
   grapes
1 pound fresh green seedless
   grapes

DAIRY

1 cup shredded fat-free
   cheddar cheese

Pantry List

Splenda granular (optional)

>>> Chilled Tex-Mex Black Bean Soup

South of the Border Taco Dip • Salsa Salad • Baked Tortilla Chips

The slightly spicy South of the Border Taco Dip is filling and satisfying and is the perfect side dish with this refreshing chilled soup on a hot day. If you like Gazpacho and other Mexican foods, then you'll like this unique soup combining both of these flavors and textures. The Salsa Salad rounds the meal off nicely.

CHILLED TEX-MEX BLACK BEAN SOUP

Yield: 7 servings (1 cup per serving)

Calories: 118 (0% fat); Total Fat: 0g; Cholesterol: 0mg; Carbohydrate: 23g; Dietary Fiber: 6g; Protein 5g; Sodium: 755mg; Diabetic Exchanges: 1 starch, 1^1/$_2$ vegetable

SOUTH OF THE BORDER TACO DIP

Yield: 16 servings (2½ tablespoons per serving)

Calories: 35 (0% fat); Total Fat: 0g; Cholesterol: 4mg; Carbohydrate: 4g; Dietary Fiber: 0g; Protein 3g; Sodium: 148mg; Diabetic Exchanges: ^{1}/$_2$ other carbohydrate

SALSA SALAD

Yield: 6 servings (1½ cups per serving)

Calories: 87 (0% fat); Total Fat: 0g; Cholesterol: 2mg; Carbohydrate: 17g; Dietary Fiber: 2g; Protein 4g; Sodium: 493mg; Diabetic Exchanges: ^{1}/$_2$ starch, 1^1/$_2$ vegetable

CHILLED TEX-MEX BLACK BEAN SOUP

1	(11^1/$_2$-ounce) bottle V-8 juice, chilled	1	(11-ounce) can Mexicorn, chilled
1	(14-ounce) can diced chili-style tomatoes, chilled	1	cup mild chunky salsa, chilled
1	(15-ounce) can black beans, chilled		

SOUTH OF THE BORDER TACO DIP

1	cup fat-free sour cream	^{1}/$_2$	cup shredded fat-free cheddar cheese
4	ounces fat-free cream cheese		
1	tablespoon taco seasoning	^{1}/$_4$	cup chopped green onions
^{1}/$_2$	cup sliced black olives		

SALSA SALAD

1	head of iceberg lettuce	6	teaspoons fat-free sour cream
1^1/$_2$	cups salsa	6	tablespoons fat-free French salad dressing
6	tablespoons shredded fat-free cheddar cheese	12	baked tortilla chips

Instructions

25 MINUTES BEFORE DINNER, make the black bean soup by stirring together in a large bowl 1 bottle V-8 juice, 1 can diced chili-style tomatoes, 1 can black beans, 1 can corn, and 1 c mild chunky salsa until well mixed. Cover and place the soup in the refrigerator to keep chilled until dinner is ready.

19 MINUTES BEFORE DINNER, make the dip. In a medium bowl, use an electric mixer on low speed to beat together 1 c sour cream, 4 oz cream cheese, and 1 T taco seasoning for 1 minute, or until smooth.

15 MINUTES BEFORE DINNER, stir $^1/_2$ c sliced black olives, $^1/_2$ c shredded cheddar cheese, and $^1/_4$ c chopped green onions into the sour cream mixture. Stir until well mixed.

12 MINUTES BEFORE DINNER, put the dip on the dinner table.

9 MINUTES BEFORE DINNER, make the salad. Cut 1 head of iceberg lettuce into bite-size pieces to make 9 c. Put $1^1/_2$ c of lettuce into 6 individual serving bowls. Top each serving of lettuce with $^1/_4$ c of salsa, 1 T shredded cheddar cheese, 1 t sour cream, and 1 T French salad dressing.

3 MINUTES BEFORE DINNER, retrieve the soup from the refrigerator and place on the dinner table with a ladle to serve.

2 MINUTES BEFORE DINNER, place the tortilla chips (either in the bag or in a basket or bowl) on the dinner table near the dip.

1 MINUTE BEFORE DINNER, crush 2 tortilla chips over each salad. Place the salads on the dinner table at individual place settings.

NOTE: Prechill ingredients by storing them in the refrigerator as soon as you get home from the grocery store so they are ready to use when you need them.

Supplies List

Timer
Large bowl
Medium bowl
Electric mixer

Grocery List

PACKAGED
$^1/_2$ cup sliced black olives
1 ($11^1/_2$-ounce) bottle
  V-8 juice
1 (14-ounce) can diced
  chili-style tomatoes
1 (15-ounce) can black beans
1 (11-ounce) can Mexicorn,
$2^1/_2$ cups mild chunky salsa
Fat-free French salad dressing
Baked tortilla chips

PRODUCE
1 bunch green onions
1 head iceberg lettuce

DAIRY
1 (16-ounce) container
  fat-free sour cream
4 ounces fat-free cream
  cheese
1 cup shredded fat-free
  cheddar cheese

Pantry List

Taco seasoning

>>> Bold & Spicy Gazpacho

Chilled Veggie Bruschetta

This meal has the taste and appeal of a meal from an expensive restaurant but is easy and inexpensive to prepare right at home. Your family and guests will be very impressed.

BOLD & SPICY GAZPACHO
Yield: 6 servings
(1$1/3$ -cup per serving)
Calories: 69 (0% fat); Total Fat: 0g; Cholesterol: 0mg; Carbohydrate: 13g; Dietary Fiber: 2g; Protein 3g; Sodium: 910mg; Diabetic Exchanges: 2$1/2$ vegetable

CHILLED VEGGIE BRUSCHETTA
Yield: 6 servings
(2 slices per serving)
Calories: 171 (10% fat); Total Fat: 2g; Cholesterol: 0mg; Carbohydrate: 33g; Dietary Fiber: 2g; Protein 6g; Sodium: 428mg; Diabetic Exchanges: 2 starch, 1 vegetable

BOLD & SPICY GAZPACHO

1$1/2$ medium cucumbers, chopped (about 3 cups)
1 yellow or orange bell pepper, chopped (about 2 cups)
3 cups Bold and Spicy Bloody Mary Mix (nonalcoholic)
2 (14$1/2$-ounce) cans diced tomatoes with basil, garlic, and oregano
1 small green onion, finely chopped (about 2 tablespoons)

CHILLED VEGGIE BRUSCHETTA

1 medium tomato, finely chopped ($2/3$ cups)
$1/2$ cucumber, peeled and finely chopped (1$1/2$ cups)
$1/2$ tablespoon dried basil
12 ($1/2$-inch-thick) slices sourdough French bread
2 tablespoons low-fat blue cheese crumbles
1 tablespoon fat-free Italian salad dressing

Instructions

30 MINUTES BEFORE DINNER, make the gazpacho. In a large mixing bowl, stir together until well mixed 3 c cucumbers, 2 c bell pepper, 3 c Bloody Mary mix, and 2 cans diced tomatoes. Cover and put in the refrigerator.

23 MINUTES BEFORE DINNER, start making the Chilled Veggie Bruschetta. In a small mixing bowl, stir together $2/3$ c tomato, $1^1/2$ c cucumber, and $1/2$ T dried basil. Set the mixture aside.

20 MINUTES BEFORE DINNER, slice the loaf of bread into 12 ($1/2$-inch-thick) slices. Arrange the slices of bread on a large serving plate. Spoon 1 heaping tablespoon of the cucumber and tomato mixture on top of each bread slice.

16 MINUTES BEFORE DINNER, sprinkle 2 T blue cheese crumbles on top of the cucumber and tomato mixture. Very lightly drizzle 1 T Italian salad dressing on top of blue cheese crumbles. Put bruschetta in refrigerator to keep chilled before dinner.

10 MINUTES BEFORE DINNER, remove the gazpacho from the refrigerator. Ladle $1^1/3$ c soup into each of 6 serving bowls.

7 MINUTES BEFORE DINNER, sprinkle 1 t finely chopped green onion on top of each bowl of gazpacho as a garnish.

4 MINUTES BEFORE DINNER, place the bowls of gazpacho on dinner table.

1 MINUTE BEFORE DINNER, remove the bruschetta from the refrigerator and set on the dinner table.

NOTE: Bloody Mary mix is found in the alcohol or mixer aisle but is a virgin drink.

Supplies List

Timer
Large mixing bowl
Small mixing bowl
Large serving plate

Grocery List

PACKAGED
3 cups Bold and Spicy Bloody Mary Mix (nonalcoholic)
2 (14$1/2$-ounce) cans diced tomatoes with basil, garlic, and oregano
Sourdough French bread
Fat-free Italian salad dressing

PRODUCE
2 medium cucumbers
1 yellow or orange bell pepper
1 small green onion
1 medium tomato

DAIRY
Low-fat blue cheese crumbles

Pantry List

Dried basil

>>> Beef & Spinach Salad with Sweet Lime Dressing

Bacon & Green Onion Cheese Spread • Low-Fat Bagel Chips

Here's a wonderful source of lean proteins and healthy carbohydrates that taste every bit as delicious as they are good for you!

BEEF & SPINACH SALAD WITH SWEET LIME DRESSING
Yield: 6 servings (3 cups spinach, 4 ounces beef, 3 strawberries, and dressing per serving)
Calories: 271 (9% fat); Total Fat: 3g; Cholesterol: 47mg; Carbohydrate: 38g; Dietary Fiber: 4g; Protein 26g; Sodium: 955mg; Diabetic Exchanges: 2 fruit, 1 1/2 vegetable, 3 very lean meat

BACON & GREEN ONION CHEESE SPREAD
Yield: 10 servings (2 tablespoons per serving)
Calories: 38 (30% fat); Total Fat: 1g; Cholesterol: 6mg; Carbohydrate: 2g; Dietary Fiber: 0g; Protein: 4g; Sodium: 185mg; Diabetic Exchanges: 1/2 lean meat

BEEF & SPINACH SALAD WITH SWEET LIME DRESSING

2 (15-ounce) cans mandarin oranges in light syrup, drained, chilled
1 cup fat-free sour cream
4 teaspoons lime juice concentrate
2 tablespoons Splenda granular

2 (10-ounce) bags fresh spinach, large stems removed
1 1/2 pounds extra-lean deli-style roast beef, cut into small strips
18 large strawberries, sliced

BACON & GREEN ONION CHEESE SPREAD

1/4 cup reduced-fat real bacon bits
1/4 cup fat-free sour cream
4 ounces fat-free cream cheese, softened
2 tablespoons blue cheese crumbles

1/4 cup chopped green onions

Low-fat bagel chips (100 calories or less—not in nutrition information)

Instructions

30 MINUTES BEFORE DINNER, make the spread. In a medium bowl, combine ¹/₄ c bacon bits, ¹/₄ c sour cream, 4 oz cream cheese, 2 T blue cheese crumbles, and ¹/₄ c green onions. Stir with a spatula until well mixed. Transfer to a serving bowl and place in the middle of a serving plate. Place the bagel chips around the bowl of spread and put on the dinner table. As it rests until dinner time it will become softer.

27 MINUTES BEFORE DINNER, prepare the salad. Drain and discard the juice from 2 cans mandarin oranges. Set aside.

25 MINUTES BEFORE DINNER, in a medium bowl, stir together 1 c fat-free sour cream, 4 t lime juice concentrate, and 2 T Splenda until well-blended.

Gently, stir the mandarin oranges into the dressing, until well coated, trying not to break the mandarin oranges. Cover and put in the refrigerator to keep chilled.

20 MINUTES BEFORE DINNER, tear off and discard the stems from 2 bags spinach.

15 MINUTES BEFORE DINNER, divide the spinach among 6 dinner plates.

11 MINUTES BEFORE DINNER, cut 1¹/₂ lb of deli style roast beef into ¹/₂-inch strips. Arrange 4 oz of roast beef on top of each salad.

7 MINUTES BEFORE DINNER, slice 18 strawberries and arrange the slices on top of the salads.

3 MINUTES BEFORE DINNER, divide the Sweet Lime Dressing mixture on top of each of the prepared salads. Place the Beef & Spinach Salads with Sweet Lime Dressing at individual place settings on the dinner table.

1 MINUTE BEFORE DINNER, place the bagel chips in a serving bowl.

NOTE: Have the mandarin oranges already chilled by storing them in the refrigerator as soon as you unload your groceries.

Supplies List
Timer
Medium bowl

Grocery List

PACKAGED
Low-fat bagel chips
2 (15-ounce) cans mandarin oranges in light syrup
Lime juice concentrate
Reduced-fat real bacon bits

PRODUCE
2 (10-ounce) bags fresh spinach
18 large strawberries
1 bunch green onions

MEAT
1¹/₂ pounds extra-lean deli-style roast beef, cut into small strips
¹/₄ cup reduced-fat real bacon bits

DAIRY
1 (16-ounce) container fat-free sour cream
4 ounces fat-free cream cheese
Low-fat blue cheese crumbles

Pantry List
Splenda granular

>>> Crunchy Crab Salad

Raspberry Cream Spread ● Honeydew Melon Bowls ● Whole Wheat Crackers

This salad is delicious, and a fun way to serve it is in edible melon bowls. The bowls not only have a lot of eye appeal, but they are very yummy as well, especially when honeydew is fresh and in season.

CRUNCHY CRAB SALAD

Yield: 6 (1¼-cup) servings

Calories: 213 (5% fat); Total Fat: 1g; Cholesterol: 56mg; Carbohydrate: 25g; Dietary Fiber: 1g; Protein 16g; Sodium: 219mg; Diabetic Exchanges: 1 vegetable, 1½ other carbohydrate, 2 very lean meat

RASPBERRY CREAM SPREAD

Yield: 10 servings

(1 tablespoon spread)

Calories: 42; Total Fat: 0g (0% fat); Cholesterol: 2mg; Carbohydrate: 7g; Dietary Fiber: 0g; Protein: 3g; Sodium: 110mg; Diabetic Exchanges:

CRUNCHY CRAB SALAD

1	medium red bell pepper
2	large cucumbers
1	green onion
½	cup fat-free French vanilla nondairy creamer
1½	teaspoons ranch salad dressing mix

1½	teaspoons fresh dill weed
3	(8-ounce) packages imitation crabmeat
3	small honeydew melons (optional)

RASPBERRY CREAM SPREAD

1	(8-ounce) package fat-free cream cheese, softened
¼	cup raspberry jam

2	teaspoons Splenda granular

Low-fat whole wheat crackers

Instructions

30 MINUTES BEFORE DINNER, chop 1 red bell pepper, 2 large cucumbers, and 1 green onion. Set aside.

23 MINUTES BEFORE DINNER, start making the salad. In a blender process on high $^1/_2$ c French vanilla nondairy creamer, $1^1/_2$ t ranch salad dressing mix, and $1^1/_2$ t fresh dill weed until well blended.

20 MINUTES BEFORE DINNER, in a large bowl, combine the dressing, the chopped red bell pepper, the chopped cucumber, the chopped green onion, and 3 packages imitation crabmeat chunks. Cover and keep refrigerated until ready to eat.

17 MINUTES BEFORE DINNER, make the honeydew bowls if desired. Cut each melon in half. With a spoon, scoop out and discard the seeds from the inside of the honeydew. Remove about $^1/_2$ inch from the bottom of each melon half to make a melon bowl.

6 MINUTES BEFORE DINNER, set each melon bowl on an individual dinner plate.

Place $1^1/_4$ c crab salad into the center of each honeydew bowl. Put the plates on the dinner table.

4 MINUTES BEFORE DINNER, prepare the spread for crackers. Combine the 1 package cream cheese, $^1/_4$ c jam, and 2 t Splenda granular in a medium bowl. Stir with a spatula or wooden spoon until well mixed and smooth. Transfer to a serving bowl and place on a serving plate.

1 MINUTE BEFORE DINNER, place the crackers on the serving plate and place on the dinner table.

NOTE: *If desired, $^3/_4$ t dried dill weed can be substituted for $1^1/_2$ t fresh dill weed. If serving in melon bowls add 165 calories, 42 g carbohydrates, 4 g dietary fiber, 2 g protein, and 82 mg sodium per half melon serving.*

Supplies List

Timer
Blender
Large bowl
Medium bowl
Serving bowl
Individual dinner plates

Grocery List

PACKAGED

3 (8-ounce) packages
   imitation crabmeat
Ranch salad dressing mix
Raspberry jam
Low-fat whole wheat crackers

PRODUCE

1 medium red bell pepper
2 large cucumbers
1 green onion
3 small honeydew melons
   (optional)
Fresh dill weed

DAIRY

1 (8-ounce) package fat-free
   cream cheese
Half pint French vanilla
   nondairy creamer

Pantry List

Splenda granular

>>> Little Italy Chicken Salad

Cantaloupe Slices • Seasoned Crusty French Bread • Dill Pickle Spears

The mild seasonings in this light salad dressing enhance the flavor of the rotisserie chicken, which I use as the base. If you like chicken, but don't like the heaviness of traditional mayonnaise-based salad dressings used in most chicken salads, then I encourage you to try this very light version. Not only is it good stuffed in a pita, it is also terrific as an open-faced sandwich piled on top of fresh-baked French bread.

LITTLE ITALY CHICKEN SALAD
Yield: 6 servings
(²/₃ cup per serving)
Calories: 119 (24% fat); Total Fat: 3g; Cholesterol: 42mg; Carbohydrate: 7g; Dietary Fiber: 1g; Protein 16g; Sodium: 367mg; Diabetic Exchanges: 1¹/₂ vegetable, 2 lean meat

SEASONED CRUSTY FRENCH BREAD
Yield: 6 servings
(7-inch long slice per serving)
Calories: 163 (10% fat); Total Fat: 2g; Cholesterol: 0mg; Carbohydrate: 31g; Dietary Fiber: 2g; Protein 5g; Sodium: 506mg; Diabetic Exchanges: 2 starch

LITTLE ITALY CHICKEN SALAD

2	chicken breasts from a rotisserie chicken (2 cups chopped)	1	large red bell pepper
		¹/₂	cup fat-free Italian salad dressing
1	medium tomato	2	tablespoons light Miracle Whip
1	medium cucumber	¹/₂	tablespoon dried sweet basil

SEASONED CRUSTY FRENCH BREAD

1	(16-ounce) loaf crusty French bread	1¹/₂	teaspoons Italian seasoning
6	tablespoons fat-free Italian salad dressing		

Instructions

30 MINUTES BEFORE DINNER, start the chicken salad by removing the skin from the rotisserie chicken. Slice the chicken breasts from the chicken. Using your fingers, shred the meat. Set aside. Finely chop the tomato, peel and chop the cucumber, and finely chop the bell pepper. Combine with the shredded rotisserie chicken breasts in a medium bowl, along with $1/2$ c Italian salad dressing, 2 T Miracle Whip, and $1/2$ T dried basil. Stir until well mixed. Set aside.

14 MINUTES BEFORE DINNER, cut a large cantaloupe in half. With a spoon, remove and discard the seeds. Cut each melon half into 6 slices. If desired, sprinkle slices very lightly with Splenda granular to sweeten.

10 MINUTES BEFORE DINNER, make the crusty French bread. Cut 1 loaf of French bread in half horizontally and then into thirds, making 6 pieces of bread.

Spread 1 T Italian salad dressing on each piece of bread and sprinkle with $1/4$ t Italian seasoning.

6 MINUTES BEFORE DINNER, assemble each of the 6 dinner plates with $2/3$ cup chicken salad, 2 slices cantaloupe, and 1 slice crusty French bread.

1 MINUTE BEFORE DINNER, place the dinner plates on the table.

NOTE: For a first-class presentation on each dinner plate, place one scoop of the chicken salad in the center and put 1 slice of seasoned crusty French bread under it. Garnish the plate with the slices of cantaloupe and dill pickle.

Supplies List

Timer
Medium bowl
6 dinner plates

Grocery List

PACKAGED
1 (16-ounce) loaf crusty
   French bread
Dill pickle spears
1 (8-ounce) bottle fat-free
   Italian salad dressing

PRODUCE
1 medium tomato
1 medium cucumber
1 large red bell pepper
1 large cantaloupe

POULTRY
2 chicken breasts from a
   rotisserie chicken

Pantry List

Dried sweet basil
Italian seasoning
Light Miracle Whip
Splenda granular (optional)

>>> Honey Dijon Chicken Salad Sandwiches

Baby Carrot Sticks with Zesty Poppy Seed Vegetable Dip • Tangy Watermelon Wedges

Everyone went crazy over this sandwich. This is one of those sandwiches that I can't imagine anyone not liking. It's just that good. The entire menu feeds eight and is great for entertaining and parties. It is a finger food menu, so no silverware is needed.

HONEY DIJON CHICKEN SALAD SANDWICHES

Yield: 8 servings

($1/8$-sandwich per serving)

Calories: 270 (13% fat); Total Fat: 4g; Cholesterol: 27mg; Carbohydrate: 42g; Dietary Fiber: 2g; Protein 15g; Sodium: 723mg; Diabetic Exchanges: 3 starch, 1 very lean meat

BABY CARROT STICKS WITH ZESTY POPPY SEED VEGETABLE DIP

Yield: 8 servings (4 ounces carrots and 2 tablespoons dip per serving)

Calories: 101 (8% fat); Total Fat: 1g; Cholesterol: 0mg; Carbohydrate: 22g; Dietary Fiber: 3g; Protein 2g; Sodium: 325mg; Diabetic Exchanges: $1^1/2$ vegetable, 1 other carbohydrate

TANGY WATERMELON WEDGES

Yield: 8 servings (2 wedges per serving)

Calories: 39 (0% fat); Total Fat: 0g; Cholesterol: 0mg; Carbohydrate: 9g; Dietary Fiber: 0g; Protein 1g; Sodium: 25mg; Diabetic Exchanges: $1/2$ fruit

HONEY DIJON CHICKEN SALAD SANDWICHES

1	(16-ounce) round loaf Hawaiian sweet bread
1	(13-ounce) can chicken breast in water, drained, chilled
1	tablespoon honey
$3/4$	cup fat-free honey Dijon salad dressing, chilled
$1/4$	cup finely chopped celery
$1/4$	cup dried cranberries, chopped
6	lettuce leaves or 1 cup chopped lettuce

BABY CARROT STICKS WITH ZESTY POPPY SEED VEGETABLE DIP

1	teaspoon poppy seeds
$3/4$	cup fat-free honey Dijon salad dressing
2	tablespoons honey
2	tablespoons fat-free mayonnaise
2	pounds baby carrots

TANGY WATERMELON WEDGES

1	(4 pound) seedless watermelon
1	(0.3-ounce) box sugar-free strawberry gelatin mix

Instructions

25 MINUTES BEFORE DINNER, make the vegetable dip. In a small bowl, stir together 1 t poppy seeds, $^3/_4$ c honey Dijon salad dressing, 2 T honey, and 2 T mayonnaise until well blended. Place the dip on the center of a serving plate and arrange 2 lb of baby carrots around the dip. Place on the dinner table.

20 MINUTES BEFORE DINNER, make the chicken salad sandwiches. Cut 1 round loaf of Hawaiian bread in half horizontally. Place bread on a cake plate and set aside.

Drain and discard the liquid from 1 can chicken breast. In a medium bowl, combine the chicken, 1 T honey, $^3/_4$ c honey Dijon salad dressing, $^1/_4$ c celery, and $^1/_4$ c dried cranberries until well mixed.

15 MINUTES BEFORE DINNER, begin assembling the sandwich. Spread the chicken salad on the bottom half of the Hawaiian bread. Top with the lettuce. Place the top half of the bread on the lettuce. Using a long serrated knife, cut the sandwich into 8 wedges. If desired, stick a long pretty, frilly toothpick through the center of each sandwich wedge. Place the sandwiches on the dinner table.

10 MINUTES BEFORE DINNER, make the watermelon wedges. Cut off the ends of 1 watermelon. Cut the watermelon into 1-inch-thick slices, and then cut each slice into quarters. Place the watermelon slices on a large serving platter. Sprinkle both sides of the watermelon lightly with 1 box sugar-free strawberry gelatin mix.

1 MINUTE BEFORE DINNER, place the watermelon wedges on the dinner table.

NOTE: Store the canned chicken and honey Dijon salad dressing in refrigerator as soon as you unload groceries so these ingredients are already chilled when needed.

Supplies List

Timer
Small bowl
Serving plate
Cake plate
Medium bowl
Large serving platter

Grocery List

PACKAGED

1 (16-ounce) round loaf Hawaiian sweet bread
1 (13-ounce) can chicken breast in water
$^1/_4$ cup dried cranberries
1 (8-ounce) bottle fat-free honey Dijon salad dressing
1 (0.3-ounce) box sugar-free strawberry gelatin mix

PRODUCE

Celery
2 pounds baby carrots
1 head romaine or iceberg lettuce
1 (4-pound) seedless watermelon

SEASONINGS

Poppy seeds

Pantry List

Honey
Fat-free mayonnaise
Toothpicks (optional)

>>> Tabbouleh Tuna Pockets

Greek Seasoned Tomato Slices • Green Grape Bunches

Here's a creative way to use Tabbouleh that delivers a lot of flavor and color to this delicious meal.

TABBOULEH TUNA POCKETS
Yield: 6 servings
(1 sandwich per serving)

Calories: 222 (7% fat); Total Fat: 2g; Cholesterol: 26mg; Carbohydrate: 26g; Dietary Fiber: 3g; Protein 26g; Sodium: 674mg; Diabetic Exchanges: 1^1/$_2$ starch, 3 very lean meat

LOW-CARB TABBOULEH TUNA POCKETS
Yield: 6 servings
(1 sandwich per serving)

Calories: 146 (6% fat); Total Fat: 1g; Cholesterol: 26mg; Carbohydrate: 10g; Dietary Fiber: 1g; Protein 23g; Sodium: 514mg; Diabetic Exchanges: 2 vegetable, 3 very lean meat

GREEK SEASONED TOMATO SLICES
Yield: 6 servings
(1 small tomato per serving)

Calories: 20 (0% fat); Total Fat: 0g; Cholesterol: 0mg; Carbohydrate: 4g; Dietary Fiber: 1g; Protein 1g; Sodium: 81mg; Diabetic Exchanges: 1 vegetable

TABBOULEH TUNA POCKETS

3	(6-ounce) cans chunk light tuna in water, drained
6	tablespoons tabbouleh salad (found in deli)
3	tablespoons fat-free feta cheese, finely crumbled
6	tablespoons reduced-fat red wine vinaigrette
^{1}/$_2$	teaspoon dried oregano
6	leaves from 1 head romaine lettuce
3	whole wheat pita bread rounds, cut in half

GREEK SEASONED TOMATO SLICES

6	small vine-ripened tomatoes
^{1}/$_2$	teaspoon lemon pepper
^{1}/$_2$	teaspoon dried oregano
2	tablespoons fat-free feta cheese, finely crumbled

Instructions

30 MINUTES BEFORE DINNER, start the tuna pockets. In a medium mixing bowl, stir together the 3 cans drained tuna, 6 T tabbouleh salad, 3 T feta cheese, 6 T red wine vinaigrette, and $^1/_2$ t dried oregano until well mixed. Cover the tuna salad and place in the refrigerator.

24 MINUTES BEFORE DINNER, prepare the tomato slices. Slice 6 tomatoes into $^1/_2$-inch-thick slices and arrange on a dinner plate. Lightly sprinkle the tomato slices with $^1/_2$ t lemon pepper seasoning and $^1/_2$ t dried oregano leaves. Then sprinkle with 2 T feta cheese on top. Cover and place the tomatoes in refrigerator.

19 MINUTES BEFORE DINNER, wash and rinse $1^1/_2$ lb green grapes under cold water in the sink. Place the grapes in a colander to dry.

15 MINUTES BEFORE DINNER, slice the 3 pita rounds in half. Set aside.

12 MINUTES BEFORE DINNER, break off 6 leaves from 1 head of romaine lettuce. Rinse leaves under running water and pat dry. Cut off and discard any discolored pieces of leaves. Cut the leaves in half. Set aside.

10 MINUTES BEFORE DINNER, assemble sandwiches. Retrieve the tuna salad from refrigerator. Put $^1/_4$ c of tuna salad in each half of the pita pockets. Put two half-leaves of lettuce in each pocket and place the sandwiches on a serving tray.

4 MINUTES BEFORE DINNER, place serving platter of sandwiches on dinner table.

3 MINUTES BEFORE DINNER, cut the $1^1/_2$ lb washed green grapes into 6 individual bunches. Place the 6 bunches of grapes into a serving bowl and place on the dinner table.

1 MINUTE BEFORE DINNER, retrieve the tomato slices and place on the dinner table.

NOTE: *To make Low-Carb Tabbouleh Tuna Pocket Sandwiches, spread the tuna salad in the center of a large leaf of romaine lettuce instead of pita bread. Fold the lettuce leaf in half like a soft taco.*

Supplies List

Timer
Medium mixing bowl
Dinner plate
Serving platter
Colander
Serving bowl

Grocery List

PACKAGED

3 (6-ounce) cans chunk light
    tuna in water
$^1/_2$ cup tabbouleh salad
1 (8-ounce) bottle
    reduced-fat red wine
    vinaigrette
3 whole wheat pita bread
    rounds

PRODUCE

6 small vine-ripened tomatoes
1 head romaine lettuce

DAIRY

4 ounces fat-free feta cheese

Pantry List

Dried oregano
Lemon pepper

>>> Smoked Salmon Caesar Salad

Dilly-Ranch Blue Cheese Spread • Reduced-Fat Butter-Flavored Crackers • Clementines

I first ate Smoked Salmon Caesar Salad while traveling on the Alaska Railway. When creating this recipe my goal was to have my fast and easy low-fat version taste as great as theirs. I'm elated to say, mine is every bit as good as theirs, if not better.

SMOKED SALMON CAESAR SALAD

Yield: 6 (large entrée-sized) salads

Calories: 127 (20% fat); Total Fat: 3g; Cholesterol: 14mg; Carbohydrate: 11g; Dietary Fiber: 2g; Protein 13g; Sodium: 1607mg; Diabetic Exchanges: 1 vegetable, $1/2$ other carbohydrate, $1^1/2$ lean meat

DILLY-RANCH BLUE CHEESE SPREAD

Yield: 6 servings (3 tablespoons per serving)

Calories: 35 (30% fat); Total Fat: 1 gm; Cholesterol: 7 mg; Carbohydrate: 5 gm; Dietary Fiber: 0 gm; Protein: 2 gm; Sodium: 125 mg; Diabetic Exchanges: $1/2$ other carbohydrate

SMOKED SALMON CAESAR SALAD

3	ounces fat-free cream cheese, softened
3	large heads romaine lettuce
1	cup fat-free Caesar Italian salad dressing
3	(3-ounce) foil packages smoked Alaskan Pacific salmon*
6	teaspoons reduced-fat Parmesan-style grated topping
	Freshly ground black pepper

DILLY-RANCH BLUE CHEESE SPREAD

$1/2$	teaspoon dried dill
1	tablespoon Ranch dip mix (I use Hidden Valley)
1	cup fat-free sour cream
$1/4$	cup skim milk
$1/4$	cup low-fat crumbled blue cheese

Instructions

30 MINUTES BEFORE DINNER, set 3 oz cream cheese on the counter to soften.
    Make the spread. Combine $^1/_2$ t dried dill, 1 T Ranch dip mix, 1 c sour cream, $^1/_4$ c milk, and $^1/_4$ c crumbled blue cheese together in a bowl. Cover and place in the refrigerator.

25 MINUTES BEFORE DINNER, start making the salads. Place 6 large dinner plates on the counter. Wash and rinse 3 heads of romaine lettuce under running water. Shake the lettuce dry. Remove and discard the core of the lettuce. Remove the leaves from the heads of the lettuce. Lay 3 large lettuce leaves on each dinner plate in a fan pattern, allowing the tops of the leaves to extend over the plate's edge. Chop the remaining lettuce leaves into bite-size pieces and put in a large salad bowl.

15 MINUTES BEFORE DINNER, in a medium mixing bowl, using a whisk, stir together 1 c Caesar Italian salad dressing and 3 oz cream cheese until well mixed.

12 MINUTES BEFORE DINNER, using a whisk stir in 3 packages salmon to the dressing mixture.

9 MINUTES BEFORE DINNER, toss the bite-size pieces of lettuce into large bowl. Divide the salad among the prepared plates.

7 MINUTES BEFORE DINNER, sprinkle 1 t Parmesan on each salad.

5 MINUTES BEFORE DINNER, cut 12 clementines into quarters and place 8 wedges around the perimeter of each plate of the salads.

2 MINUTES BEFORE DINNER, sprinkle freshly ground pepper on top of each salad. Place the dinner plates on the dinner table.

1 MINUTE BEFORE DINNER, place the spread on a serving plate with butter-flavored crackers and place on the dinner table.

NOTE: Do not substitute canned salmon. Although this meal is pricey, it is worth every penny!

Supplies List

Timer
Small serving bowl
Large salad bowl
Medium mixing bowl
6 large dinner plates
Whisk
Serving plate

Grocery List

PACKAGED

1 (8-ounce) bottle fat-free Caesar Italian salad dressing
Reduced-fat Parmesan-style grated topping
Ranch dip mix (Hidden Valley)
Reduced-fat butter-flavored crackers

PRODUCE

3 large heads romaine lettuce
12 clementines

FISH

3 (3-ounce) foil packages Smoked Alaskan Pacific salmon

DAIRY

Skim milk
3 ounces fat-free cream cheese
1 (8-ounce) container fat-free sour cream
$^1/_4$ cup low-fat crumbled blue cheese

Pantry List

Freshly ground black pepper
Dried dill

ONE-PAN STOVE-TOP CASSEROLES

>>> Ham & Yam Casserole

French Cauliflower

Here's a unique entrée that will curb both your sweet tooth and cravings for something salty without adding a lot of unhealthy fat. My secret ingredients are the sugar-free maple syrup and just a tad of steak salt. Mmmm!

HAM & YAM CASSEROLE

Yield: 7 servings (1 cup per serving)

Calories: 308 (14% fat); Total Fat: 5g; Cholesterol: 35mg; Carbohydrate: 49g; Dietary Fiber: 6g; Protein 17g; Sodium: 1064mg; Diabetic Exchanges: 3^1/$_2$ starch, 2 very lean meat

FRENCH CAULIFLOWER

Yield: 6 servings

(^{2}/$_3$ cup per serving)

Calories: 81 (0% fat); Total Fat: 0g; Cholesterol: 2mg; Carbohydrate: 15g; Dietary Fiber: 4g; Protein 4g; Sodium: 345mg; Diabetic Exchanges: 1^1/$_2$ vegetable, ^{1}/$_2$ other carbohydrate

HAM & YAM CASSEROLE

4	large sweet potatoes		^{1}/$_2$	tablespoon light butter
10	reduced-fat butter-flavored crackers		2	(8-ounce) packages fully cooked extra-lean diced ham
1^1/$_2$	tablespoons Spenda Brown Sugar Blend		^{1}/$_2$	cup sugar-free maple syrup
^{1}/$_2$	teaspoon plus ^{1}/$_4$ teaspoon steak seasoning			

FRENCH CAULIFLOWER

2	(16-ounce) bags frozen cauliflower		^{1}/$_4$	teaspoon light salt
^{1}/$_2$	cup fat-free French salad dressing		1	tablespoon 30%-less-fat bacon pieces

Instructions

30 MINUTES BEFORE DINNER, start the casserole. In a 12-inch ovenproof, nonstick saucepan, bring 6 c water to boil over medium-high heat.

28 MINUTES BEFORE DINNER, peel 4 large sweet potatoes and cut them into 1-inch pieces to make about 10 c.

23 minutes before dinner, add the sweet potatoes to the boiling water and return to a boil. Boil for 4 minutes.

22 minutes before dinner, prepare the cauliflower. Put 1 c water and 2 bags frozen cauliflower in a 12-inch nonstick saucepan. Cover and cook over high heat.

19 minutes before dinner, turn off the sweet potatoes. Cover and let sit on the hot burner.

17 minutes before dinner, crush 10 crackers with a rolling pin. Combine the cracker crumbs with $1^1/_2$ T Spenda Brown Sugar Blend, $^1/_4$ t steak seasoning, and $^1/_2$ T butter in a microwavable bowl. Microwave for 10 seconds, just enough to melt the butter. Stir together until crumbly and well mixed. Set aside.

10 minutes before dinner, preheat the broiler to high.

9 minutes before dinner, place 2 packages fully cooked extra-lean diced ham into a medium bowl. Cover with waxed paper and cook in the microwave for $1^1/_2$ to 2 minutes, or until fully heated. Let the ham remain in the microwave until needed.

8 minutes before dinner, drain the sweet potatoes. Pour the sweet potatoes into a large mixing bowl. Add $^1/_2$ c maple syrup and $^1/_2$ t steak seasoning. Beat with an electric mixer until the potatoes become soft and creamy.

With a spatula, stir the cooked ham into the sweet potatoes.

Rinse and dry the 12-inch nonstick saucepan used for the sweet potatoes. Coat the saucepan with nonfat cooking spray. Spread the ham and sweet potato mixture into the prepared nonstick saucepan. Sprinkle with the cracker crumb mixture.

3 minutes before dinner, broil the casserole in the oven on the top rack until golden brown, watching very closely.

2 minutes before dinner, drain the water from the cauliflower. Put into a large serving bowl and gently stir with $^1/_2$ c fat-free French dressing and $^1/_4$ t light salt. Sprinkle 1 T bacon pieces on top.

1 minute before dinner, take the casserole out of the oven and set on a hot pad on the dinner table.

Supplies List

Timer
12-inch ovenproof, microwavable nonstick saucepan
Small bowl
Medium bowl
Large serving bowl
Large mixing bowl
Electric mixer
Rolling pin
Colander

Grocery List

PACKAGED
30%-less-fat bacon pieces
10 reduced-fat butter-flavored crackers
$^1/_2$ cup sugar-free maple syrup
$^1/_2$ cup fat-free French salad dressing

PRODUCE
4 large sweet potatoes

FROZEN
2 (16-ounce) bags frozen cauliflower

DAIRY
Light butter

MEAT
2 (8-ounce) packages fully cooked extra-lean diced ham

Pantry List

Light salt
Nonfat cooking spray
Splenda Brown Sugar Blend
Steak seasoning

>>> Tuna Tabbouleh Rice Casserole

Asparagus Spears with Honey Mustard Sauce

Tabbouleh is a Mediterranean salad made up of finely chopped parsley, garlic, tomato, and seasonings. It is found in the deli. One of my assistants, Lauren Meiring, kept saying over and over again, "I really like this. I really like this." I have to agree; it is very good. The sweetness of the Honey Mustard Sauce on the asparagus accentuates the flavorful tuna entrée.

TUNA TABBOULEH RICE CASSEROLE

Yield: 7 servings (1 cup per serving)

Calories: 290 (14% fat); Total Fat: 4g; Cholesterol: 32mg; Carbohydrate: 39g; Dietary Fiber: 4g; Protein 22g; Sodium: 1116mg; Diabetic Exchanges: 2 starch, 2 vegetable, 2^1/$_2$ very lean meat

ASPARAGUS SPEARS WITH HONEY MUSTARD SAUCE

Yield: 6 servings (4 ounces per serving)

Calories: 63 (0% fat); Total Fat: 0g; Cholesterol: 0mg; Carbohydrate: 14g; Dietary Fiber: 3g; Protein 3g; Sodium: 251mg; Diabetic Exchanges: 1 vegetable, ^{1}/$_2$ other carbohydrate

TUNA TABBOULEH RICE CASSEROLE

1^1/$_2$ cups water

1 (14^1/$_2$-ounce) can diced tomatoes with green pepper, celery, and onion

1 cup tabbouleh salad

1^1/$_2$ teaspoons seasoned salt

1^1/$_2$ cups instant whole grain brown rice

3 (6-ounce) cans tuna in water, undrained

1 (10^3/$_4$ ounce) can 98% fat-free cream of celery soup

ASPARAGUS SPEARS WITH HONEY MUSTARD SAUCE

1^1/$_2$ pounds fresh asparagus spears

^{1}/$_2$ teaspoon light salt

^{1}/$_4$ cup fat-free honey Dijon salad dressing

2 tablespoons honey

Instructions

30 MINUTES BEFORE DINNER, start the casserole. In a 12-inch nonstick saucepan, combine $1^1/_2$ c water, 1 can diced tomatoes, 1 c tabbouleh salad, and $1^1/_2$ t seasoned salt. Bring to a boil over medium-high heat.

27 MINUTES BEFORE DINNER, once the liquid and tomatoes are to a boil, stir in $1^1/_2$ c brown rice, 3 cans undrained tuna in water, and 1 can cream of celery soup. Stir until well mixed. Reduce the heat to medium low and simmer.

24 MINUTES BEFORE DINNER, stir and cover the casserole.

23 MINUTES BEFORE DINNER, start the asparagus. Trim the tough ends of the asparagus and discard. In a $2^1/_2$-quart saucepan, put $1^1/_2$ lb asparagus spears in 1 c of water. Add $^1/_2$ t light salt to the water. Cook, covered, over high heat.

18 MINUTES BEFORE DINNER, reduce the heat to low on the casserole. Stir the rice, and continue cooking on low, covered.

17 MINUTES BEFORE DINNER, start making the honey mustard sauce. In a small bowl, put $^1/_4$ c honey Dijon salad dressing. Stir in 2 T honey until well mixed. Set aside.

15 MINUTES BEFORE DINNER, turn off the heat to the asparagus. Keep covered and let sit on the hot burner.

11 MINUTES BEFORE DINNER, stir the casserole. Turn off the heat and let sit on the hot burner.

4 MINUTES BEFORE DINNER, heat the sauce in the microwave for 15 to 20 seconds, just enough to warm it; stir.

3 MINUTES BEFORE DINNER, drain and discard the water from the asparagus spears and place the asparagus on a large serving dish with sides. Pour the sauce over the asparagus spears. Place on the dinner table.

1 MINUTE BEFORE DINNER, put the saucepan of casserole on a hot pad on the dinner table.

NOTE: The thinner the asparagus spears the more tender they are. Avoid thick spears as they tend to be tough.

Supplies List

Timer
12-inch nonstick saucepan with lid
$2^1/_2$-quart saucepan with lid
Large serving dish with sides
Small bowl

Grocery List

PACKAGED

1 ($14^1/_2$-ounce) can diced tomatoes with green pepper, celery, and onion
1 cup tabbouleh salad
Instant whole grain brown rice
3 (6-ounce) cans tuna in water
1 ($10^3/_4$ ounce) can 98% fat-free cream of celery soup
Fat-free honey Dijon salad dressing

PRODUCE

$1^1/_2$ pounds fresh asparagus spears

Pantry List

Light salt
Seasoned salt
Honey

>>> Three-Pepper, Four-Cheese Chicken Pasta

Super Simple Spinach Salad with Sweet Homemade Dressing • Garlic & Parsley Bread Knots

This meal reminds me of something that would be served at a fine Italian restaurant.

THREE-PEPPER,
FOUR-CHEESE CHICKEN PASTA
**Yield: 6 servings (1 cup pasta and
4 ounces chicken breasts per serving)**
*Calories: 380 (11% fat); Total Fat: 5g;
Cholesterol: 77mg; Carbohydrate: 46g;
Dietary Fiber: 5g; Protein 36g;
Sodium: 651mg; Diabetic Exchanges:
2¹/₂ starch, 1¹/₂ vegetable,
4 very lean meat*

GARLIC & PARSLEY BREAD KNOTS
**Yield: 10 servings
(1 knot per serving)**
*Calories: 63 (31% fat); Total Fat: 2g;
Cholesterol: 2mg; Carbohydrate: 10g;
Dietary Fiber: 0g; Protein 2g; Sodium:
290mg; Diabetic Exchanges: 1 starch*

SUPER SIMPLE SPINACH SALAD
WITH SWEET HOMEMADE DRESSING
**Yield: 6 servings
(1¹/₂ cups per serving)**
*Calories: 50 (0% fat); Total Fat: 0g;
Cholesterol: 0mg; Carbohydrate: 6g;
Dietary Fiber: 1g; Protein: 6g; Sodium:
237mg; Diabetic Exchanges:
1 vegetable, ¹/₂ very lean meat*

THREE-PEPPER, FOUR-CHEESE CHICKEN PASTA

3 (8-ounce) frozen boneless, skinless chicken breasts, cut in half
1 cup hot water
1 (26-ounce) jar three-cheese pasta sauce
1 (16-ounce) bag frozen three-pepper and onion blend vegetables
4 cups No-Yolk extra-broad noodles
¹/₂ cup low-fat ricotta cheese
¹/₂ cup shredded fat-free mozzarella cheese

GARLIC & PARSLEY BREAD KNOTS

1 (7¹/₂-ounce) roll buttermilk biscuits
1 tablespoon light butter
1 tablespoon minced garlic (in jar)
¹/₂ plus ¹/₂ teaspoon garlic salt
2 teaspoons parsley
1 tablespoon reduced-fat Parmesan-style grated topping

SUPER SIMPLE SPINACH SALAD WITH SWEET HOMEMADE DRESSING

1 (9-ounce) bag prewashed fresh spinach
1 cup pasteurized liquid egg substitute
1 cup sliced fresh mushrooms
¹/₄ cup ketchup
¹/₂ cup skim milk
1 tablespoon Splenda granular

Instructions

30 MINUTES BEFORE DINNER, start the chicken. In a 12-inch nonstick saucepan, cook 3 frozen, boneless, skinless chicken breasts on high heat for 4 to 6 minutes, covered, or until there is no pink in the middle. Press the chicken firmly into the pan to help absorb some of the juices. Flip the chicken so it is well coated with the juices. Remove the chicken from pan and set aside.

24 MINUTES BEFORE DINNER, add 1 c hot water to the saucepan with the chicken drippings and scrape bottom of the pan with a spatula to loosen the pan drippings.

Stir in 1 jar pasta sauce and 1 bag frozen vegetables and bring to a boil. Once to a boil, add 4 c noodles; coat the noodles with the sauce and cover with a lid. Reduce the heat to medium and cook for 10 minutes.

17 MINUTES BEFORE DINNER, stir the pasta.

Start making the bread knots out of the biscuit dough by rolling each biscuit into a rope and shaping the rope into a knot.

12 MINUTES BEFORE DINNER, reduce the heat of the pasta to low and cook uncovered. Stir in $1/2$ c ricotta cheese and cook for 2 more minutes stirring occasionally.

10 MINUTES BEFORE DINNER, preheat the oven to 400 degrees.

Start making the butter mixture for the bread knots by melting 1 T butter in a zip-top bag in the microwave for 10 seconds, or until butter is melted. Add 1 T minced garlic, $1/2$ t garlic salt, and 2 t parsley to the bag. Place the bread knots in the bag and shake until well coated. Coat a baking sheet with nonfat cooking spray and place the bread knots on the baking sheet. Sprinkle the top of the bread knots with 1 T Parmesan topping and $1/2$ t garlic salt. Set aside

9 MINUTES BEFORE DINNER, bake the bread knots in the preheated oven for 8 minutes.

Turn off the heat to the pasta. Add the chicken breasts to the pasta so that each breast is surrounded with pasta and the tops of the chicken breasts are still visible. Sprinkle $1/2$ c fat-free mozzarella cheese over the top of the entire entrée, and spray the cheese with cooking spray. Cover, keeping the entrée in the saucepan on the warm burner.

Supplies List

Timer
12-inch nonstick saucepan with lid
Baking sheet
Microwave-safe bowl
Large bowl
Small mixing bowl
Zip-top bag

Grocery List

PACKAGED
1 (26-ounce) jar three-cheese pasta sauce
1 (12-ounce) bag No-Yolk extra-broad noodles

PRODUCE
1 cup sliced mushrooms
1 (9-ounce) bag prewashed fresh spinach

FROZEN
1 (16-ounce) bag frozen three-pepper and onion blend vegetables
3 (8-ounce) frozen boneless, skinless chicken breasts

DAIRY
light butter
$1/2$ cup low-fat ricotta cheese
$1/2$ cup shredded fat-free mozzarella cheese
$1/2$ cup skim milk
1 cup pasteurized liquid egg substitute
Reduced-fat Parmesan-style grated topping
1 ($7 1/2$-ounce) package refrigerated buttermilk biscuits

Pantry List on page 38

CONTINUED ON NEXT PAGE >>>

>>> Three-Pepper, Four-Cheese
Chicken Pasta
CONTINUED FROM PREVIOUS PAGE

Pantry List

Garlic
Garlic salt
Parsley
Nonfat cooking spray
Ketchup
Splenda granular

5 MINUTES BEFORE DINNER, make the salad. Cook 1 c liquid egg substitute in a microwave-safe bowl for 1 to $1^{1}/_{2}$ minutes, or until fully cooked. Chop the cooked egg into tiny pieces. Place a few ice cubes in the bowl and stir to help the eggs cool quickly.

While eggs are cooking, place 1 bag spinach in a large bowl. Top the spinach with 1 c sliced mushrooms and the chopped eggs. Set aside.

In a small mixing bowl, mix $^{1}/_{4}$ c ketchup, $^{1}/_{2}$ c skim milk, and 1 T Splenda granular until well blended. Drizzle over the spinach salad and place the salad on the dinner table.

1 MINUTE BEFORE DINNER, remove the bread knots from oven, place on a plate, and set them on the dinner table. Place the chicken pasta on a hot pad on the table.

NOTE: *Cutting the chicken breast while it is still frozen is easier than when the chicken is thawed. I began this entire meal while the chicken was still frozen. And spraying fat-free cheese with nonfat cooking spray allows the cheese to be creamy instead of rubbery.*

>>> Philly Cheese Steak Macaroni Casserole

Fresh Strawberry Spinach Salad with Sweet Bacon & Blue Cheese Vinaigrette • Dinner Rolls

Preparing the salad ahead of time really saves time. However, be sure to wait until you are ready to serve it before adding the dressing. Otherwise, the salad will wilt and become soggy.

PHILLY CHEESE STEAK MACARONI CASSEROLE

Yield: 6 servings (1 cup per serving)

Calories: 192 (13% fat); Total Fat: 3g; Cholesterol: 34mg; Carbohydrate: 23g; Dietary Fiber: 1g; Protein 19g; Sodium: 499mg; Diabetic Exchanges: 1 1/2 starch, 2 very lean meat

FRESH STRAWBERRY SPINACH SALAD WITH SWEET BACON & BLUE CHEESE VINAIGRETTE

Yield: 6 servings (1 2/3 cups per serving)

Calories: 64 (25% fat); Total Fat: 2g; Cholesterol: 6mg; Carbohydrate: 9g; Dietary Fiber: 2g; Protein 4g; Sodium: 580mg; Diabetic Exchanges: 1 vegetable, 1/2 other carbohydrate, 1/2 fat

PHILLY CHEESE STEAK MACARONI CASSEROLE

1 (14-ounce) can 99% fat-free beef broth

1 medium onion

1/2 tablespoon light butter

1 1/2 cups elbow macaroni pasta, uncooked

3/4 pound thinly sliced deli roast beef

1/2 cup fat-free mozzarella cheese

FRESH STRAWBERRY SPINACH SALAD WITH SWEET BACON & BLUE CHEESE VINAIGRETTE

1 cup fresh strawberries, cut into thin slices

1 (10-ounce) bag prewashed fresh baby spinach

1/2 cup Italian croutons

1 plus 1 tablespoons blue cheese crumbles

1 plus 1 tablespoons 30%-less-fat real bacon pieces

3/4 cup fat-free zesty Italian salad dressing

1 tablespoon Splenda granular

CONTINUED ON NEXT PAGE >>>

Supplies List

Timer
Large salad bowl
12-inch nonstick saucepan
    with lid
12-inch nonstick skillet

Grocery List

PACKAGED
Dinner rolls
1 (14-ounce) can 99%
    fat-free beef broth
Elbow macaroni pasta
Splenda granular
30%-less-fat real bacon
    pieces
Italian croutons
1 (8-ounce) bottle fat-free
    zesty Italian Salad
    dressing

PRODUCE
1 medium onion
1 cup fresh strawberries
1 (10-ounce) bag prewashed
    fresh baby spinach

MEAT
$^3/_4$ pound thinly sliced
    deli sliced roast beef

DAIRY
$^1/_2$ cup fat-free mozzarella
    cheese
Light butter
Blue cheese crumbles

Instructions

30 MINUTES BEFORE DINNER, make the vinaigrette. In the bottom of a large salad bowl, stir together 1 T blue cheese crumbles, 1 T bacon pieces, $^3/_4$ c zesty Italian salad dressing, and 1 T Splenda granular until well mixed. Cover and keep in the refrigerator.

26 MINUTES BEFORE DINNER, start the casserole. In a 12-inch nonstick saucepan, bring 1 can beef broth to a boil over medium heat. Chop 1 medium onion into bite-size pieces, set aside.

In a separate 12-inch nonstick skillet melt the $^1/_2$ T butter over medium heat.

23 MINUTES BEFORE DINNER, add the chopped onion to the melted butter and cook for 10 minutes, or until tender.

20 MINUTES BEFORE DINNER, add the $1^1/_2$ c uncooked elbow macaroni pasta to the boiling beef broth. Cover and cook 10 minutes, stirring occasionally.

18 MINUTES BEFORE DINNER, cut the $^3/_4$ lb sliced roast beef into bite-size pieces; set aside.

Place dinner rolls in a basket and put on the table.

13 MINUTES BEFORE DINNER, remove the cooked onion from the burner. Set aside $^1/_4$ c of the onion to use later.

10 MINUTES BEFORE DINNER, add the roast beef and the remaining onion to the skillet of cooked macaroni; mix well. Reduce the heat to low and cover. Cook for 5 minutes, or until the roast beef is warm.

5 MINUTES BEFORE DINNER, turn off the burner under the casserole and sprinkle the top of the casserole with $^1/_2$ c mozzarella cheese. Spray with non-fat cooking spray to help it melt better. Cover and let sit until time for dinner.

Thinly slice 1 c fresh strawberries. Set aside 10 slices of strawberries to use as garnish.

2 MINUTES BEFORE DINNER, retrieve the salad dressing from the refrigerator. Using a large spatula, gently stir in the remaining fresh strawberry slices, 1 bag prewashed fresh baby spinach, and $^1/_2$ c Italian croutons until the salad is well coated with the dressing.

Arrange the reserved 10 slices of strawberries on top of the salad and sprinkle the top of the salad with 1 T blue cheese crumbles and 1 T real bacon pieces.

1 MINUTE BEFORE DINNER, put the skillet with the casserole in it on a hot pad and place on the dinner table. Place the salad on the table and serve dinner immediately.

NOTE: *Only stir the salad dressing into the spinach just before you are ready to serve dinner. Otherwise, if you do it too soon before eating, the salad will wilt and/or become soggy.*

>>> One-Pan Italian Chicken Noodle Casserole

Italian Squash Medley • Italian Buttons

The blend of fresh garden squash and zucchini is wonderful with this delicious Italian chicken casserole. It is a great spin-off of the traditional chicken casserole seasoned with Italian herbs. LuAnne Surgeson, a big thank-you to you for this idea. We were able to come up with a simple, time-saving, home-style casserole with only a fraction of the calories that your momma would have made. You're going to love it.

ONE-PAN ITALIAN CHICKEN NOODLE CASSEROLE

Yield: 6 servings (1 cup per serving)

Calories: 260 (11% fat); Total Fat: 3g; Cholesterol: 53mg; Carbohydrate: 30g; Dietary Fiber: 3g; Protein 25g; Sodium: 808mg; Diabetic Exchanges: 2 starch, 2 1/2 very lean meat

ITALIAN SQUASH MEDLEY

Yield: 6 servings (2/3 cup per serving)

Calories: 22 (0% fat); Total Fat: 0g; Cholesterol: 0mg; Carbohydrate: 4g; Dietary Fiber: 1g; Protein 1g; Sodium: 328mg; Diabetic Exchanges: 1 vegetable

ITALIAN BUTTONS

Yield: 4 servings (6 buttons per serving)

Calories: 81 (24% fat); Total Fat: 2g; Cholesterol: 0mg; Carbohydrate: 14g; Dietary Fiber: 0g; Protein 2g; Sodium: 403mg; Diabetic Exchanges: 1 starch

ONE-PAN ITALIAN CHICKEN NOODLE CASSEROLE

1	pound stir-fry chicken breasts*	1	(7-ounce) can sliced mushrooms, drained
2 3/4	cup chicken broth	1	tablespoon Italian seasoning
1	(10 3/4 -ounce) can 98% fat-free condensed cream of chicken soup	1/4	cup reduced-fat Parmesan-style grated topping
4	cups No-Yolk noodles, uncooked		

ITALIAN SQUASH MEDLEY

2	small zucchini	1	teaspoon steak seasoning
2	small yellow squash	1/4	teaspoon seasoned salt
10	grape tomatoes		
1/4	cup fat-free Italian salad dressing		

ITALIAN BUTTONS

1	(7 1/2-ounce) can refrigerated buttermilk biscuits	1	teaspoon garlic powder
1	teaspoon Italian seasoning	1	teaspoon garlic salt

Instructions

30 MINUTES BEFORE DINNER, start the casserole by coating a 12-inch non-stick saucepan with nonfat cooking spray. Brown 1 lb chicken stir-fry breasts over high heat for 5 minutes.

25 MINUTES BEFORE DINNER, remove the chicken from the pan and set aside. Using the same pan, combine $2^3/4$ c chicken broth and 1 can chicken soup. Bring to a boil and cook for about 2 minutes. Add 4 c No-Yolk noodles to the boiling mixture and return to a boil. Cook, covered, over medium heat for 10 minutes, stirring frequently.

20 MINUTES BEFORE DINNER, start the squash by spraying a 12-inch nonstick skillet with nonfat cooking spray. Preheat the pan over medium heat. Slice the 2 zucchini and 2 yellow squash and add to the skillet. Add $1/4$ c Italian salad dressing, 1 t steak seasoning, and $1/4$ t seasoned salt. Cover and cook for 10 minutes.

15 MINUTES BEFORE DINNER, reduce the heat under the pasta to low. Add the cooked chicken, 1 can sliced mushrooms, and 1 T Italian seasoning. Cover and simmer for 5 minutes.

13 MINUTES BEFORE DINNER, preheat the oven to 350 degrees. Generously coat a baking sheet with nonfat cooking spray. Set aside.

Stir 10 grape tomatoes into the squash medley. Cover and continue cooking
Start the Italian Buttons by cutting each of the 10 biscuits into 4 equal parts. Roll each piece into a ball and place on the prepared baking sheet. Spray each biscuit ball with nonfat cooking spray and sprinkle with 1 t Italian seasoning, 1 t garlic powder, and 1 t garlic salt.

9 MINUTES BEFORE DINNER, turn off the heat under the pasta and stir one more time. Sprinkle $1/4$ cup Parmesan topping over the pasta. Cover and keep warm on the burner until dinnertime.

Turn off the heat under the squash medley and stir one more time. Cover and keep warm on the burner until dinnertime.

Place the Italian Buttons in the oven and bake for 8 minutes. Place the casserole and the Italian Squash Medley on hot pads on the dinner table.

1 MINUTE BEFORE DINNER, remove the Italian Buttons from oven and place in a basket on the dinner table.

NOTE: *Stir-fry chicken breasts are prechopped for your convenience.*

Supplies List

Timer
12-inch nonstick saucepan
 with lid
12-inch nonstick skillet
Baking sheet
Basket

Grocery List

PACKAGED
$2^3/4$ cup chicken broth
1 ($10^3/4$-ounce) can 98%
 fat-free condensed cream
 of chicken soup
1 (12-ounce) bag No-Yolk
 noodles
1 (7-ounce) can sliced
 mushrooms
$1/4$ cup reduced-fat
 Parmesan-style grated
 topping
Fat-free Italian salad dressing

PRODUCE
2 small zucchini
2 small yellow squash
10 grape tomatoes

DAIRY
1 ($7^1/2$-ounce) can
 refrigerated buttermilk
 biscuits

POULTRY
1 pound chicken stir-fry
 breasts

Pantry List

Italian seasoning
Seasoned salt
Garlic powder
Garlic salt
Nonfat cooking spray
Steak seasoning

>>> Reuben Macaroni Casserole

Mandarin Orange Spinach Salad with Sweet Bacon & Blue Cheese Vinaigrette

If you like Reuben sandwiches with corned beef and sauerkraut, then you are sure to like this creative casserole version of that all-time favorite sandwich.

REUBEN MACARONI CASSEROLE
Yield: 9 servings
(1 cup per serving)

Calories: 179 (10% fat); Total Fat: 2g; Cholesterol: 14mg; Carbohydrate: 29g; Dietary Fiber: 2g; Protein 11g; Sodium: 773mg; Diabetic Exchanges: 2 starch, 1 very lean meat

MANDARIN ORANGE SPINACH SALAD WITH SWEET BACON & BLUE CHEESE VINAIGRETTE SALAD DRESSING
Yield: 6 servings
(1 $2/3$ cups per serving)

Calories: 70 (21% fat); Total Fat: 2g; Cholesterol: 6mg; Carbohydrate: 11g; Dietary Fiber: 2g; Protein 4g; Sodium: 439mg; Diabetic Exchanges: $1/2$ fruit, 1 vegetable, $1/2$ fat

REUBEN MACARONI CASSEROLE

2 (14-ounce) cans 99% fat-free beef broth
3 cups elbow macaroni, uncooked
3 (2-ounce) packages corned beef
1 (14-ounce) can sauerkraut, undrained
$1/2$ cup shredded fat-free mozzarella cheese
2 tablespoons fat-free Thousand Island salad dressing (optional)

MANDARIN ORANGE SPINACH SALAD
WITH SWEET BACON & BLUE CHEESE VINAIGRETTE

1 (15-ounce) can mandarin oranges, $1/4$ cup juice reserved, chilled
1 plus 1 tablespoons blue cheese crumbles
1 plus 1 tablespoons 30%-less-fat real bacon pieces
$1/2$ cup fat-free Italian salad dressing
2 teaspoons Splenda granular
1 (10-ounce) bag prewashed fresh baby spinach
$1/2$ cup zesty Italian croutons

Instructions

30 MINUTES BEFORE DINNER, begin making the casserole. In a 12-inch non-stick saucepan over medium heat, bring to a boil 2 cans beef broth.

25 MINUTES BEFORE DINNER, add to the saucepan 3 c uncooked elbow macaroni. Cover and cook for 10 minutes, stirring occasionally.

20 MINUTES BEFORE DINNER, slice 3 packages corned beef into small pieces and set aside.

15 MINUTES BEFORE DINNER, reduce the heat under the cooked macaroni to low. Add the pieces of corned beef and 1 can sauerkraut to the saucepan with the macaroni, mixing well. Cover and let cook 10 minutes.

13 MINUTES BEFORE DINNER, start making the salad. Drain 1 can chilled mandarin oranges, reserving $1/4$ cup juice. Reserve 12 slices mandarin oranges for a garnish. Cover and refrigerate them.

Prepare the vinaigrette by combining 1 T blue cheese crumbles and 1 T bacon pieces in a large salad bowl,

Stir in the reserved $1/4$ c of the mandarin orange juice, the remaining mandarin oranges, $1/2$ c Italian salad dressing, and 2 t Splenda granular until well mixed. Cover and keep in the refrigerator.

5 MINUTES BEFORE DINNER, turn off the heat under the casserole. Sprinkle $1/2$ c shredded mozzarella cheese on top of the pasta and spray with cooking spray. Cover and keep on the warm burner for 3 minutes, or until the cheese is melted.

2 MINUTES BEFORE DINNER, if desired drizzle 2 T dressing over the casserole and put the skillet on a hot pad on the dinner table.

Using a large spatula, gently stir in 1 bag fresh baby spinach and $1/2$ c zesty Italian croutons into the salad dressing until the salad is well coated with the dressing. Arrange the 12 reserved mandarin orange slices on top of the salad and sprinkle with 1 T blue cheese crumbles and 1 T real bacon pieces. Place the salad on the dinner table and serve dinner immediately.

NOTE: Only stir the spinach into the salad dressing just before you are ready to serve dinner, or the salad will wilt and become soggy.

Supplies List

Timer
12-inch nonstick saucepan with lid
Large salad bowl

Grocery List

PACKAGED
30%-less-fat real bacon pieces
2 (14-ounce) cans 99% fat-free beef broth
Elbow macaroni
1 (14-ounce) can sauerkraut
1 (15-ounce) can mandarin oranges
Zesty Italian croutons
1 (8-ounce) bottle fat-free Thousand Island salad dressing (optional)
1 (8-ounce) bottle fat-free Italian salad dressing

PRODUCE
1 (10-ounce) bag prewashed fresh baby spinach

MEAT
3 (2-ounce) packages corned beef

DAIRY
$1/2$ cup shredded fat-free mozzarella cheese
Blue cheese crumbles

Pantry List

Splenda granular

>>> Peppercorn Ranch Casserole

Garlic-Buttered Broccoli, Cauliflower & Carrot Medley

This is one of those super simple meals that people really like and request over and over again, which is great since it is so fast and easy to assemble!

PEPPERCORN RANCH CASSEROLE
Yield: 6 servings
(1¹/₃ cups per serving)
Calories: 282 (19% fat); Total Fat: 5g; Cholesterol: 56mg; Carbohydrate: 26g; Dietary Fiber: 1g; Protein 27g; Sodium: 1116mg; Diabetic Exchanges: 2 starch, 3 very lean meat

GARLIC-BUTTERED BROCCOLI, CAULIFLOWER & CARROT MEDLEY
Yield: 6 servings
(³/₄ cup per serving)
Calories: 58 (14% fat); Total Fat: 1g; Cholesterol: 3mg; Carbohydrate: 10g; Dietary Fiber: 4g; Protein 4g; Sodium: 400mg; Diabetic Exchanges: 2 vegetable

PEPPERCORN RANCH CASSEROLE

- 2 (13-ounce) cans 98% fat-free white chicken in water
- 2 cups water
- 1/2 tablespoon dried chopped chives
- 3 tablespoons Ranch salad dressing mix
- 1/4 teaspoon freshly ground black pepper
- 1 (12-ounce) bag No-Yolk noodles (only 4 cups needed)
- 1/3 cup light ranch salad dressing

GARLIC-BUTTERED BROCCOLI, CAULIFLOWER & CARROT MEDLEY

- 2 (16-ounce) bags frozen California blend vegetables
- 2 tablespoons imitation butter-flavored sprinkles
- 1 tablespoon light butter
- 1 teaspoon garlic salt

Instructions

30 MINUTES BEFORE DINNER, start the casserole. Drain the broth from 2 cans chicken into a 12-inch nonstick saucepan. Set the cans of drained chicken aside.

To the saucepan of chicken broth, add 2 c water, $1/2$ T dried chopped chives, 3 T ranch salad dressing mix, and $1/4$ t freshly ground black pepper. Bring to a boil over high heat.

22 MINUTES BEFORE DINNER, stir in 4 c No-Yolk noodles to the boiling broth. Return to a low boil, then reduce the heat to medium and simmer, covered, for 15 minutes, or until the pasta is tender.

20 MINUTES BEFORE DINNER, make the vegetable medley. Put 2 bags frozen California blend vegetables in a medium microwave-safe bowl. Cover with waxed paper and cook for 8 minutes.

12 MINUTES BEFORE DINNER, remove the vegetables from the microwave and stir. Recover and cook for an additional 8 minutes.

7 MINUTES BEFORE DINNER, turn off the heat to the pasta and stir in the reserved canned chicken and $1/3$ c light ranch salad dressing.

Cover the casserole and let sit for 3 to 4 minutes on the hot burner.

4 MINUTES BEFORE DINNER, remove the vegetables from the microwave. Add 2 T imitation butter-flavored sprinkles, 1 T light butter, and 1 T garlic salt and stir until well mixed.

2 MINUTES BEFORE DINNER, place the vegetable medley on the dinner table.

1 MINUTE BEFORE DINNER, place the casserole on a hot pad on the dinner table.

Supplies List

Timer
12-inch nonstick saucepan
   with lid
Medium microwave-safe bowl

Grocery List

PACKAGED

2 (13-ounce) cans 98%
   fat-free white chicken
1 (12-ounce) bag No-Yolk
   noodles
Light ranch salad dressing
Ranch salad dressing mix

FROZEN

2 (16-ounce) bags frozen
   California blend vegetables

DAIRY

Light butter

Pantry List

Dried chopped chives
Freshly ground black pepper
Garlic salt
Imitation butter-flavored
   sprinkles

>>> Pork Dijon & Brown Rice Casserole

Creamed Turnip Greens with Diced White Turnips • Honey Mustard Bread Crisps

> When I asked my friend Mary what she thought about this entrée, all she could do was shake her head in amazement and say, "I love that pork stuff!"

PORK DIJON & BROWN RICE CASSEROLE

Yield: 7 servings (1 cup per serving)

Calories: 297 (21% fat); Total Fat: 7g; Cholesterol: 56mg; Carbohydrate: 30g; Dietary Fiber: 3g; Protein 26g; Sodium: 858mg; Diabetic Exchanges: 1 starch, 1 other carbohydrate, 3 lean meat

HONEY MUSTARD BREAD CRISPS

Yield: 6 servings (1 slice per serving)

Calories: 111 (7% fat); Total Fat: 1g; Cholesterol: 2mg; Carbohydrate: 18g; Dietary Fiber: 1g; Protein 7g; Sodium: 278mg; Diabetic Exchanges: 1 starch, $^1/_2$ very lean meat

CREAMED TURNIP GREENS WITH DICED WHITE TURNIPS

Yield: 9 servings ($^1/_2$ cup per serving)

Calories: 59 (28% fat); Total Fat: 2g; Cholesterol: 8mg; Carbohydrate: 7g; Dietary Fiber: 3g; Protein 5g; Sodium: 839mg; Diabetic Exchanges: $1^1/_2$ vegetable, $^1/_2$ lean meat

PORK DIJON & BROWN RICE CASSEROLE

$1^1/_2$ pounds extra-lean pork loin, cut into bite-size pieces

$2^3/_4$ cup beef broth

$1^1/_4$ cup fat-free honey Dijon salad dressing

$1^1/_2$ cups whole grain instant brown rice

1 (15-ounce) can asparagus, drained

HONEY MUSTARD BREAD CRISPS

6 ($^1/_3$-inch thick) slices French bread

6 teaspoons honey mustard

$^3/_4$ cup shredded fat-free mozzarella cheese

3 tablespoons fresh chopped chives (or $1^1/_2$ tablespoons dried chives)

CREAMED TURNIP GREENS WITH DICED WHITE TURNIPS

3 ($14^1/_2$-ounce) cans turnip greens with diced white turnips, drained

1 teaspoon liquid smoke

1 teaspoon Splenda granular

$1^1/_2$ tablespoons imitation butter sprinkles

$^1/_4$ cup chopped onion

4 ounces diced ham ($^1/_2$ cup firmly packed)

1 ($10^3/_4$-ounce) can 98% fat-free cream of celery soup

Instructions

30 MINUTES BEFORE DINNER, start the casserole. In a 12-inch nonstick saucepan, bring to a boil over high heat $1^1/_2$ lb pork, $2^3/_4$ c beef broth, and $1^1/_4$ c honey Dijon salad dressing.

24 MINUTES BEFORE DINNER, once the liquid is to a boil, stir in $1^1/_2$ c instant brown rice. Return to a boil, then reduce the heat to medium low. Cover and cook for 12 minutes.

20 MINUTES BEFORE DINNER, make the creamed turnip greens. In a microwavable bowl, stir together until well mixed 3 cans drained turnip greens with diced white turnips, 1 t liquid smoke, 1 t Splenda granular, $1^1/_2$ T butter sprinkles, $^1/_4$ c chopped onion, 4 oz diced ham, and 1 can cream of celery soup. Set aside.

12 MINUTES BEFORE DINNER, turn off the heat and stir in 1 can drained asparagus. Cover and let sit on the warm burner until dinner is ready to be served.

11 MINUTES BEFORE DINNER, start making the bread crisps. Preheat the oven to 425 degrees. Spray both sides of 6 slices of French bread generously with butter-flavored cooking spray. Spread 1 t honey mustard on one side of each slice of bread and place on a baking sheet. Sprinkle $^3/_4$ c shredded mozzarella cheese and 3 T fresh chives over the honey mustard. Generously spray the cheese with cooking spray.

7 MINUTES BEFORE DINNER, bake the bread crisps for 5 minutes, or until the bottom of the bread is crispy and golden brown.

5 MINUTES BEFORE DINNER, cover the creamed turnips with waxed paper and microwave for 2 to 3 minutes, stirring halfway.

2 MINUTES BEFORE DINNER, place the casserole on a hot pad and put on the dinner table. Place the bread crisps on a hot pad on the dinner table.

1 MINUTE BEFORE DINNER, place the turnip greens on the dinner table.

Supplies List

Timer
12-inch nonstick saucepan
   with lid
Baking sheet
Microwavable bowl

Grocery List

PACKAGED

Whole grain instant
   brown rice
French bread
1 ($10^3/_4$-ounce) can
   98% fat-free cream of
   celery soup
1 (15-ounce) can asparagus
3 ($14^1/_2$-ounce) cans turnip
   greens with diced white
   turnips
1 (16-ounce) bottle fat-free
   honey Dijon salad
   dressing
Liquid smoke

PRODUCE

$^1/_4$ cup chopped onion

MEAT

$1^1/_2$ pounds extra-lean
   pork loin
4 ounces diced ham

DAIRY

$^3/_4$ cup shredded fat-free
   mozzarella cheese

Pantry List

$2^3/_4$ cups beef broth
fresh chopped chives or dried
   chives
Imitation butter sprinkles
Honey mustard
Fat-free butter-flavored spray
Splenda granular

>>> Mediterranean Chicken Pasta Casserole

Greek-Style Salad with Sweet & Tangy Salad Dressing

Even people who do not like artichokes really liked this casserole. The salad with this entrée is just the right blend of pizzazz to complement the entrée and not overpower it.

MEDITERRANEAN CHICKEN PASTA CASSEROLE

Yield: 6 servings (1 cup per serving)

Calories: 346 (9% fat); Total Fat: 3g; Cholesterol: 50mg; Carbohydrate: 43g; Dietary Fiber: 4g; Protein 32g; Sodium: 1673mg; Diabetic Exchanges: 2^1/$_2$ starch, 1 vegetable, 3 very lean meat

GREEK-STYLE SALAD WITH SWEET & TANGY SALAD DRESSING
Yield: 6 servings (1^1/$_2$ cups per serving)

Calories: 41 (18% fat); Total Fat: 1g; Cholesterol: 1mg; Carbohydrate: 7g; Dietary Fiber: 2g; Protein 1g; Sodium: 521mg; Diabetic Exchanges: ^{1}/$_2$ other carbohydrate

MEDITERRANEAN CHICKEN PASTA CASSEROLE

2^3/$_4$	cups chicken broth
^{1}/$_2$	cup tabbouleh
1^1/$_4$	cup fat-free Italian salad dressing
4	cups No-Yolk noodles
2	(12-ounce) cans 98% fat-free chicken in water, drained
1	(14-ounce) can artichokes, drained
^{1}/$_2$	cup fat-free crumbled Feta cheese

GREEK-STYLE SALAD WITH SWEET & TANGY SALAD DRESSING

6	green olives, cut into thin slices
3	mild cherry peppers, cut into thin slices
2	thin slices red onion, separated into rings
1	head iceberg lettuce
^{3}/$_4$	cup fat-free Italian salad dressing
1	teaspoon dried parsley

Instructions

30 MINUTES BEFORE DINNER, start the salad. Cut into thin slices, 6 green olives and 3 mild cherry peppers. Cut 2 thin slices of red onion and set aside with the olives and peppers. Cut the iceberg lettuce into bite-size pieces and place in a large salad bowl. Set aside.

25 MINUTES BEFORE DINNER, make the salad dressing. In a small bowl, combine $^3/_4$ c Italian salad dressing and 1 t dried parsley, mixing well. Stir in the sliced olives and peppers.

22 MINUTES BEFORE DINNER, start the casserole. In a 12-inch nonstick saucepan over high heat, bring $2^3/_4$ c chicken broth, $^1/_2$ c tabbouleh, and $1^1/_4$ c Italian salad dressing to a boil.

17 MINUTES BEFORE DINNER, once the liquid is boiling, stir in 4 c No-Yolk noodles. Return to a boil and then reduce the heat to medium. Cover and cook for 10 minutes, or until the pasta is tender.

14 MINUTES BEFORE DINNER, continue the salad. In the large salad bowl pour the salad dressing over the iceberg lettuce. Top with the red onion slices, sliced green olives, and sliced peppers. Cover and keep in the refrigerator.

7 MINUTES BEFORE DINNER, turn off the heat to the pasta and stir in 2 cans drained chicken and 1 can drained artichokes. Keep on hot burner, covered.

4 MINUTES BEFORE DINNER, sprinkle $^1/_2$ c crumbled Feta cheese on top of the casserole. Cover and let sit for 3 minutes.

1 MINUTE BEFORE DINNER, place the casserole on a hot pad and put on the dinner table. Retrieve the salad from the refrigerator and place on the dinner table.

Supplies List

Timer
Large salad bowl
Small bowl
12-inch nonstick saucepan
    with lid

Grocery List

PACKAGED
$^1/_2$ cup tabbouleh
Green olives
1 (12-ounce) bag No-Yolk
    noodles
2 (12-ounce) cans 98%
    fat-free chicken
1 (14-ounce) can artichokes
3 mild cherry peppers
1 (8-ounce) bottle fat-free
    Italian salad dressing

PRODUCE
1 red onion
1 head iceberg lettuce

DAIRY
Fat-free crumbled Feta cheese

Pantry List

$2^3/_4$ cups chicken broth
Dried parsley

>>> Barbequed Beef Pasta Casserole

Cheesy Cheddar Cauliflower • Wheat Rolls

Men especially like this hearty casserole. The Cheesy Cheddar Cauliflower is a special welcome for those thinking they had to avoid cheese sauces.

BARBEQUED BEEF PASTA CASSEROLE

Yield: 6 servings (1 cup per serving)

Calories: 293 (5% fat); Total Fat: 2g; Cholesterol: 30mg; Carbohydrate: 41g; Dietary Fiber: 1g; Protein 24g; Sodium: 1644mg; Diabetic Exchanges: 2 starch, 1 other carbohydrate, 3 very lean meat

CHEESY CHEDDAR CAULIFLOWER

Yield: 6 servings (³/₄ cup per serving)

Calories: 95 (5% fat); Total Fat: 1g; Cholesterol: 8mg; Carbohydrate: 12g; Dietary Fiber: 4g; Protein 10g; Sodium: 546mg; Diabetic Exchanges: 2¹/₂ vegetable, 1 very lean meat

BARBEQUED BEEF PASTA CASSEROLE

2³/₄	cups beef broth	1	pound extra-lean deli-style sliced roast beef
2	teaspoons liquid smoke	1	cup shredded fat-free cheddar cheese
1¹/₄	cups mesquite-flavored barbeque sauce		
4	cups No-Yolk noodles		

CHEESY CHEDDAR CAULIFLOWER

2	(16-ounce) bags frozen cauliflower	2	tablespoons reduced-fat Parmesan-style grated topping
4	plus 3 slices fat-free sharp cheddar cheese	1¹/₂	tablespoons imitation butter-flavored sprinkles
¹/₂	teaspoon dried parsley		

Instructions

30 MINUTES BEFORE DINNER, start the cauliflower. Place 2 bags frozen cauliflower in a microwavable bowl. Cover with waxed paper and cook for 6 minutes.

25 MINUTES BEFORE DINNER, start the casserole. In a 12-inch nonstick saucepan over high heat, bring $2^3/_4$ c beef broth, 2 t liquid smoke, and $1^1/_4$ c barbeque sauce to a boil.

22 MINUTES BEFORE DINNER, stir the cauliflower, return to the microwave, cover and cook for another 6 minutes.

20 MINUTES BEFORE DINNER, stir 4 c No-Yolk noodles into the boiling broth. Return the broth to a boil, then reduce the heat to medium. Cover and simmer for 10 minutes, or until the pasta is tender. While the pasta is cooking, cut 1 lb sliced roast beef into bite-size pieces.

15 MINUTES BEFORE DINNER, stir the cauliflower, cover and cook in the microwave for another 4 minutes.

11 MINUTES BEFORE DINNER, remove the cauliflower from the microwave and top with 4 slices sharp cheddar cheese. Cover and microwave for 2 minutes.

9 MINUTES BEFORE DINNER, remove the cauliflower from the microwave and stir in $^1/_2$ t parsley, 2 T Parmesan topping and $1^1/_2$ T butter sprinkles until well mixed. Lay the remaining 3 slices cheddar cheese on top of the cauliflower and cover with a plate. Keep covered so the cheese slices will melt. Wrap the bowl with a dish towel to keep warm.

7 MINUTES BEFORE DINNER, turn off the heat under the saucepan and stir in the roast beef. Sprinkle 1 c shredded cheddar cheese over the top. Spray the cheese with nonfat cooking spray. Cover and let sit on the hot burner until the cheese is melted.

5 MINUTES BEFORE DINNER, put the wheat rolls on the dinner table.

3 MINUTES BEFORE DINNER, microwave the cauliflower for 1 to 2 more minutes if needed to make sure it is still nice and hot. Place the cauliflower on a hot pad on the dinner table.

1 MINUTE BEFORE DINNER, place casserole on a hot pad on the dinner table.

NOTE: No water is added to this recipe to cook the cauliflower.

Supplies List

Timer
12-inch nonstick saucepan
   with lid
Large microwavable bowl

Grocery List

PACKAGED
1 (12-ounce) bag No-Yolk
   noodles
Reduced-fat Parmesan-style
   grated topping
Liquid smoke
Mesquite-flavored barbeque
   sauce

FROZEN
2 (16-ounce) bags frozen
   cauliflower

MEAT
1 pound extra-lean deli-style
   sliced roast beef

DAIRY
1 cup shredded fat-free
   cheddar cheese
7 slices fat-free sharp
   cheddar cheese slices

Pantry List

$2^3/_4$ cups beef broth
Dried parsley
Imitation butter-flavored
   sprinkles
Nonfat cooking spray

>>> Caesar Chicken Pasta Casserole

Super Simple Caesar Salad with Bacon • Cheesy-Stuffed Portobello Mushrooms

Special thanks for the Cheesy-Stuffed Portobello recipe from Connie Ramey in Delta, Ohio. They go very well in this menu and complement the Caesar Chicken Pasta Stove-Top Casserole nicely.

CAESAR CHICKEN PASTA CASSEROLE
Yield: 6 servings (1 cup per serving)

Calories: 353 (30% fat); Total Fat: 11g; Cholesterol: 69mg; Carbohydrate: 30g; Dietary Fiber: 2g; Protein 27g; Sodium: 1241mg; Diabetic Exchanges: 2 starch, 3 lean meat

CHEESY-STUFFED PORTOBELLO MUSHROOMS
Yield: 6 servings (1 mushroom per serving)

Calories: 49 (34% fat); Total Fat: 2g; Cholesterol: 3mg; Carbohydrate: 4g; Dietary Fiber: 1g; Protein 4g; Sodium: 135mg; Diabetic Exchanges: 1 vegetable, 1/2 lean meat

SUPER SIMPLE CAESAR SALAD WITH BACON
Yield: 6 servings (1 1/2 cups per serving)

Calories: 53 (13% fat); Total Fat: 1g; Cholesterol: 3mg; Carbohydrate: 8g; Dietary Fiber: 2g; Protein 3g; Sodium: 560mg; Diabetic Exchanges: 1/2 other carbohydrate

CAESAR CHICKEN PASTA CASSEROLE

- $2^3/4$ cups chicken broth
- $1^1/4$ cup fat-free Caesar salad dressing
- 4 cups No-Yolk noodles
- 2 (12-ounce) cans 98% fat-free chicken in water, drained
- 3 tablespoons reduced–fat grated Parmesan cheese topping

CHEESY-STUFFED PORTOBELLO MUSHROOMS

- 6 portobello mushroom caps
- 1/4 cup frozen chopped onion
- 1 tablespoon bottled minced garlic
- 2 tablespoons light mayonnaise
- 1/2 cup shredded fat-free cheddar cheese

SUPER SIMPLE CAESAR SALAD WITH BACON

- 9 cups precut romaine lettuce
- 3/4 cup fat-free Caesar Salad dressing
- 2 tablespoons 30%-less-fat real bacon pieces
- 1/2 cup fat-free croutons

Instructions

30 MINUTES BEFORE DINNER, start the mushrooms. Spray a jelly-roll pan with nonfat cooking spray. Set aside.

Using a paper towel, wipe off 6 mushroom caps and remove the stems, reserving the stems for later. Place the mushroom caps on the prepared jelly-roll pan. Set aside.

Spray a 12-inch skillet with nonfat cooking spray. Over medium heat, sauté $1/4$ c frozen chopped onion and 1 T minced garlic until the onion is tender.

25 MINUTES BEFORE DINNER, chop the reserved mushroom stems and add to the skillet. Cover and cook for 2 more minutes, stirring frequently. Turn off the burner and let the skillet sit on the warm burner.

22 MINUTES BEFORE DINNER, start the casserole. In a 12-inch nonstick saucepan over high heat, bring $2^3/_4$ c chicken broth and $1^1/_4$ c Caesar salad dressing to a boil. Preheat the oven to 450 degrees.

20 MINUTES BEFORE DINNER, place the sautéed onion, garlic, and mushroom stems in a small bowl. Add 2 T mayonnaise and $1/2$ c shredded cheddar cheese. Mix until well blended. Spoon 1 T of the onion mixture into the center of each portobello mushroom cap. Set aside.

17 MINUTES BEFORE DINNER, stir 4 c No-Yolk noodles into the boiling chicken broth. Return to a boil and then reduce the heat to medium. Simmer, covered, for 10 minutes, or until the pasta is tender.

15 MINUTES BEFORE DINNER, place the jelly-roll pan with the Stuffed Portobello Mushroom Caps in the preheated oven and bake for 12 minutes.

11 MINUTES BEFORE DINNER, begin making the salad. In a large bowl, stir together 9 c lettuce with $3/4$ c dressing. Sprinkle the salad with 2 T bacon pieces and top with $1/2$ c croutons. Place the salad on the table.

5 MINUTES BEFORE DINNER, turn off heat to the pasta and stir in 2 cans drained chicken. Sprinkle 3 T Parmesan topping over the casserole. Cover and let sit for 4 minutes.

3 MINUTES BEFORE DINNER, remove the mushroom caps from the oven and place them on a serving platter on the dinner table.

1 MINUTE BEFORE DINNER, place the casserole on a hot pad on the table.

Supplies List

Timer
Jelly-roll pan
12-inch nonstick skillet
12-inch nonstick saucepan
  with lid
Small bowl
Large bowl
Platter

Grocery List

PACKAGED
1 (12-ounce) bag No-Yolk
  noodles
2 (12-ounce) cans 98%
  fat-free chicken
Reduced-fat Parmesan-style
  grated topping
Fat-free croutons
1 (16-ounce) bottle fat-free
  Caesar salad dressing
30%-less-fat real bacon
  pieces

PRODUCE
9 cups precut romaine lettuce
6 Portobello mushrooms

FROZEN
$1/4$ cup frozen chopped onion

DAIRY
$1/2$ cup shredded fat-free
  cheddar cheese

Pantry List

$2^3/_4$ cups chicken broth
Light mayonnaise
Minced garlic
Nonfat cooking spray

>>> Beefy Ranch Stroganoff

Garlic Broccoli & Carrot Medley • Pumpernickel Dinner Rolls

You are not going to believe how fabulous this is. It is a wonderful combination of ranch seasonings united with an old-time comfort food favorite, Beef Stroganoff. It tastes like I slaved over it all day and it should be loaded with fats, but the reality is that this wonderful menu is done in thirty minutes and is very low fat!

Beefy Ranch Stroganoff

Yield: 6 servings (1 cup per serving)

Calories: 301 (16% fat); Total Fat: 5g; Cholesterol: 65mg; Carbohydrate: 31g; Dietary Fiber: 2g; Protein 30g; Sodium: 773mg; Diabetic Exchanges: 2 starch, 3 1/2 very lean meat

Garlic Broccoli & Carrot Medley

Yield: 7 servings (3/4 cup per serving)

Calories: 51 (8% fat); Total Fat: 1g; Cholesterol: 0mg; Carbohydrate: 10g; Dietary Fiber: 4g; Protein 4g; Sodium: 644mg; Diabetic Exchanges: 2 vegetable

BEEFY RANCH STROGANOFF

2 cups water
1 tablespoon ranch salad dressing mix
4 cups No-Yolk noodles
2 (12-ounce) cans 98% fat-free roast beef with gravy
1 (7-ounce) can sliced mushrooms, drained
1/4 plus 1/4 cup fat-free ranch salad dressing

GARLIC BROCCOLI & CARROT MEDLEY

2 (16-ounce) bags frozen broccoli cuts
1 tablespoon bottled minced garlic
1/4 cup imitation butter-flavored sprinkles
1 teaspoon light salt
1 (8 1/4-ounce) can sliced carrots, drained

Instructions

25 MINUTES BEFORE DINNER, start vegetable medley. In a medium microwave-safe bowl, put 2 bags frozen broccoli cuts. Cover with waxed paper and cook for 8 minutes in the microwave.

22 MINUTES BEFORE DINNER, start the stroganoff. In a 12-inch nonstick saucepan over high heat, bring 2 c water and 1 T Ranch salad dressing mix to a boil.

18 MINUTES BEFORE DINNER, stir 4 c No-Yolk noodles into the boiling water. Return to a boil, then reduce the heat to medium and simmer. Cover and cook for 8 minutes, or until pasta is tender.

16 MINUTES BEFORE DINNER, stir the broccoli. Cover with waxed paper and microwave for an additional 6 minutes.

14 MINUTES BEFORE DINNER, if you would like to serve dinner rolls, put them in a basket and place on the dinner table with light butter and jam, if desired.

10 MINUTES BEFORE DINNER, turn off the heat to the pasta and stir in 2 cans roast beef with gravy, 1 can drained sliced mushrooms, and $1/4$ c ranch salad dressing. Cover and let sit for 5 minutes to heat the roast beef and mushrooms.

8 MINUTES BEFORE DINNER, stir into the broccoli 1 T minced garlic, $1/4$ c butter sprinkles, 1 t salt, and 1 can drained sliced carrots. Stir until well mixed. Cook the broccoli and carrots 5 more minutes in the microwave, to heat the carrots.

5 MINUTES BEFORE DINNER, spread $1/4$ c ranch salad dressing over the cooked pasta. Cover and continue to let sit on the warm burner.

2 MINUTES BEFORE DINNER, remove the vegetable medley from the microwave. Stir and put on a hot pad on the dinner table.

1 MINUTE BEFORE DINNER, place the stroganoff on a hot pad on the dinner table.

Supplies List

Timer
Medium microwave-safe bowl
12-inch nonstick saucepan
   with lid

Grocery List

PACKAGED

1 (12-ounce) bag No-Yolk
   noodles
1 (8-¼-ounce) can sliced
   carrots
2 (12-ounce) cans 98%
   fat-free roast beef with
   gravy
1 (7-ounce) can sliced
   mushrooms
1 (8-ounce) bottle fat-free
   Ranch salad dressing

FROZEN

2 (16-ounce) bags frozen
   broccoli cuts

SEASONINGS

Ranch salad dressing mix

Pantry List

Minced garlic
Imitation butter-flavored
   sprinkles
Light salt

>>> Swiss Ranch Beef Pasta Casserole

Bundled Salads with Cucumber, Tomato & French Dressing • Broccoli, Mushroom & Onion Medley

This is incredibly awesome with the blended flavors of ranch seasoning, beef, gravy, and Swiss cheese. It's a unique dish the whole family will love!

SWISS RANCH BEEF PASTA CASSEROLE
Yield: 6½ servings
(1 cup per serving)

Calories: 286 (18% fat); Total Fat: 6g; Cholesterol: 63mg; Carbohydrate: 28g; Dietary Fiber: 1g; Protein 28g; Sodium: 692mg; Diabetic Exchanges: 2 starch, 3 very lean meat

BUNDLED SALADS WITH CUCUMBER, TOMATO & FRENCH DRESSING
Yield: 6 servings (
1 bundle per serving)

Calories: 81 (0% fat); Total Fat: 0g; Cholesterol: 0mg; Carbohydrate: 19g; Dietary Fiber: 4g; Protein 2g; Sodium: 309mg; Diabetic Exchanges: 2 vegetable, ½ other carbohydrate

BROCCOLI, MUSHROOM & ONION MEDLEY
Yield: 6 servings (⅔ cup per serving)

Calories: 45 (27% fat); Total Fat: 1g; Cholesterol: 4mg; Carbohydrate: 6g; Dietary Fiber: 3g; Protein 3g; Sodium: 298mg; Diabetic Exchanges: 1½ vegetable

SWISS RANCH BEEF PASTA CASSEROLE

2 cups water
1 tablespoon ranch salad dressing mix
4 cups No-Yolk noodles
2 (12-ounce) cans roast beef with gravy
¼ cup fat-free ranch salad dressing
2 slices reduced-fat natural Swiss cheese
½ teaspoon dried parsley

BUNDLED SALADS WITH CUCUMBER, TOMATO & FRENCH DRESSING

1 large head romaine lettuce, chilled
1 slice red onion
1 medium fresh tomato, chilled
1 medium cucumber, chilled
¾ cup fat-free French salad dressing, chilled

BROCCOLI, MUSHROOM & ONION MEDLEY

1 (16-ounce) bag frozen broccoli cuts
1 (7-ounce) can sliced mushrooms
5 Holland-style whole onions, quartered*
1 tablespoon light butter
1 tablespoon imitation butter-flavored sprinkles
1 tablespoon 30%-less-fat real bacon pieces

Instructions

30 MINUTES BEFORE DINNER, make the salad bundles. Break off 6 large romaine lettuce leaves and place each leaf on an individual salad plate. Separate the rings of 1 red onion slice. Slide each lettuce leaf through one ring of red onion. Chop 1 medium tomato and place in a medium bowl. Seed and chop 1 medium cucumber. Add the cucumber to the tomato. Stir in ³/₄ c French salad dressing. Spoon the tomato and cucumber mixture evenly among the salads. Refrigerate the salad bundles until dinner is ready.

22 MINUTES BEFORE DINNER, start the casserole. In a 12-inch nonstick saucepan over high heat, bring 2 c water and 1 T ranch salad dressing mix to a boil.

18 MINUTES BEFORE DINNER, stir 4 c No-Yolk noodles into the water. Return to a boil, then reduce heat to medium. Cover and simmer for 8 minutes, or until the pasta is tender.

10 MINUTES BEFORE DINNER, turn off the heat and stir in the roast beef. Cover and let set for 5 minutes to heat the roast beef.

9 MINUTES BEFORE DINNER, start the vegetable medley. In a medium microwavable bowl cook 1 bag frozen broccoli and 1 can drained sliced mushrooms for 9 minutes.

Cut the 2 slices of reduced-fat natural Swiss cheese in half diagonally and set aside.

5 MINUTES BEFORE DINNER, spread ¹/₄ c ranch salad dressing over the cooked pasta. Arrange the cheese slices in a flower petal design on top of the casserole. Sprinkle the top of the casserole with ¹/₂ t dried parsley. Cover and let the casserole sit for 3 to 4 minutes, or until the cheese is melted.

2 MINUTES BEFORE DINNER, put the cooked broccoli in a serving bowl and stir with 5 quartered Holland-style onions, 1 T butter, 1 T butter sprinkles, and 1 T bacon pieces. Cover with aluminum foil and place on the dinner table.

1 MINUTE BEFORE DINNER, place the casserole on a hot pad on the dinner table. Put salad plates on the dinner table.

*NOTE: When it comes to bottled onions there is a huge difference in taste between Holland-style whole onions and cocktail onions. Make sure you use the Holland-style onions for this recipe.

Supplies List

Timer
Medium bowl
Medium microwavable bowl
12-inch nonstick saucepan
   with lid
Serving bowl

Grocery List

PACKAGED

1 (12-ounce) bag No-Yolk
   noodles
5 Holland-style whole onions
1 (8-ounce) bottle fat-free
   French salad dressing
Fat-free ranch salad dressing
Ranch salad dressing mix
1 (7-ounce) can sliced
   mushrooms
30%-less-fat real bacon
   pieces
2 (12-ounce) cans roast beef
   with gravy

PRODUCE

1 large head romaine lettuce
1 red onion
1 medium tomato
1 medium cucumber

FROZEN

1 (16-ounce) bag frozen
   broccoli cuts

DAIRY

2 slices reduced–fat Swiss
   cheese
Light butter

Pantry List

Dried parsley
Imitation butter-flavored
   sprinkles

>>> Mediterranean Pork & Brown Rice Casserole

Spring Salad with Sweet & Tangy Salad Dressing • Greek-Inspired Bagel Crisps

This recipe will have you busy the entire thirty minutes, so you cannot have any distractions; but once you sit down to dinner you will see that it was thirty minutes well spent. Your family will agree, too.

MEDITERRANEAN PORK & BROWN RICE CASSEROLE

Yield: 7¹/₂ servings

(1 cup per serving)

Calories: 249 (16% fat); Total Fat: 4g; Cholesterol: 52mg; Carbohydrate: 26g; Dietary Fiber: 2g; Protein 25g; Sodium: 1010mg; Diabetic Exchanges: 1¹/₂ starch, 3 very lean meat

SPRING SALAD WITH SWEET & TANGY SALAD DRESSING

Yield: 6 servings

(1¹/₂ cup per serving)

Calories: 44 (19% fat); Total Fat: 1g; Cholesterol: 1mg; Carbohydrate: 7g; Dietary Fiber: 2g; Protein 2g; Sodium: 534mg; Diabetic Exchanges: 1¹/₂ vegetable

GREEK-INSPIRED BAGEL CRISPS

Yield: 6 servings

(2 bagel crisps per serving)

Calories: 125 (23% fat); Total Fat: 3g; Cholesterol: 0mg; Carbohydrate: 21g; Dietary Fiber: 2g; Protein 3g; Sodium: 259mg; Diabetic Exchanges: 1¹/₂ starch

MEDITERRANEAN PORK & BROWN RICE CASSEROLE

1¹/₂ pounds pork tenderloin, cut into bite-size pieces
2³/₄ cups chicken broth
¹/₄ cup tabbouleh (found in deli)
1¹/₄ cup fat-free Italian salad dressing

1¹/₂ cups whole grain instant brown rice
1 (14-ounce) artichokes, drained
¹/₂ cup fat-free feta cheese crumbles

SPRING SALAD WITH SWEET & TANGY SALAD DRESSING

³/₄ cup fat-free Italian salad dressing
1 teaspoon dried parsley
6 green olives, cut into thin slices
3 mild cherry peppers, cut into thin slices

2 thin slices red onion, separated rings
9 cups spring mix prewashed lettuce

GREEK-INSPIRED BAGEL CRISPS

12 bagel chips
24 sprays fat-free butter spray
1 teaspoon Italian seasoning

3 green olives, finely chopped
2 tablespoons fat-free feta cheese crumbles

Instructions

30 MINUTES BEFORE DINNER, start the casserole. Remove all of the visible fat from the $1^1/_2$ lb pork tenderloin and cut into bite-size pieces.

25 MINUTES BEFORE DINNER, in a 12-inch nonstick saucepan that has been generously sprayed with nonfat cooking spray, cook the pork over high heat until browned.

20 MINUTES BEFORE DINNER, once the pork is browned, add $2^3/_4$ c chicken broth, $^1/_4$ c tabbouleh, and $1^1/_4$ c Italian salad dressing. Bring to a boil.

17 MINUTES BEFORE DINNER, stir $1^1/_2$ c rice into the boiling broth. Return to a boil, then reduce the heat to medium. Cover and simmer for 12 minutes, or until the rice is tender.

15 MINUTES BEFORE DINNER, preheat the oven to 350 degrees. Start the salad dressing. In a large salad bowl, combine $^3/_4$ c Italian salad dressing, 1 t dried parsley, 6 thinly sliced green olives, and 3 thinly sliced cherry peppers. Cover and keep chilled in the refrigerator.

10 MINUTES BEFORE DINNER, make the bagel crisps. Arrange 12 bagel chips on a baking sheet. Spray each bagel chip with 2 sprays fat-free butter spray. Sprinkle the chips lightly with 1 t Italian seasoning, 3 finely chopped green olives, and 1 T feta cheese crumbles. Bake the bagel crisps in the oven at 350 degrees for 5 minutes.

5 MINUTES BEFORE DINNER, turn off the heat to the rice and stir in 1 can drained artichokes. Sprinkle $^1/_2$ c feta on top of casserole. Cover and let sit for 3 to 4 minutes on the warm burner.

3 MINUTES BEFORE DINNER, add 9 c prewashed spring mix salad greens and the red onion rings to the salad dressing in the large bowl. Toss until the greens are well coated with the dressing. Set the salad on the dinner table.

2 MINUTES BEFORE DINNER, remove the bagel crisps from the oven and place on a hot pad on the dinner table.

1 MINUTE BEFORE DINNER, place the casserole on a hot pad on the dinner table.

Supplies List

Timer
12-inch nonstick saucepan with lid
Large salad bowl
Baking sheet

Grocery List

PACKAGED

Whole grain instant brown rice
1 (14-ounce) can artichokes
Tabbouleh
1 bag bagel chips
1 (16-ounce) bottle fat-free Italian salad dressing
Green olives
3 mild cherry peppers

PRODUCE

1 red onion
9 cups prewashed spring mix lettuce

MEAT

$1^1/_2$ pounds pork tenderloin

DAIRY

$^1/_2$ cup plus 2 tablespoons fat-free feta cheese crumbles

Pantry List

$2^3/_4$ cups chicken broth
Dried parsley
Italian seasoning
Nonfat cooking spray
Fat-free butter spray

>>> Chicken Dijon Pasta Casserole

Cheesy Cheddar Broccoli

You will not believe how quick, easy, and delicious this meal is.

CHICKEN DIJON PASTA CASSEROLE

Yield: 6 servings (1 cup per serving)

Calories: 340 (6% fat); Total Fat: 2g; Cholesterol: 51mg; Carbohydrate: 40g; Dietary Fiber: 3g; Protein 32g; Sodium: 1211mg; Diabetic Exchanges: 2 1/2 starch, 4 very lean meat

CHEESY CHEDDAR BROCCOLI

Yield: 6 servings (3 3/4 cups per serving)

Calories: 87 (8% fat); Total Fat: 1g; Cholesterol: 8mg; Carbohydrate: 11g; Dietary Fiber: 5g; Protein 10g; Sodium: 571mg; Diabetic Exchanges: 2 vegetable, 1 very lean meat

CHICKEN DIJON PASTA CASSEROLE

- $1/2$ cup water
- $3/4$ cup chicken broth, drained from canned chicken
- $1 1/4$ cup fat-free honey Dijon salad dressing
- 4 cups No-Yolk noodles
- 2 (12-ounce) cans 98% fat-free chicken in water
- 1 cup shredded fat-free cheddar cheese

CHEESY CHEDDAR BROCCOLI

- 2 (16-ounce) bags frozen broccoli
- 2 tablespoons imitation butter-flavored sprinkles
- $1 1/2$ tablespoons reduced-fat Parmesan-style grated topping.
- $1/2$ teaspoon dried parsley
- 4 plus 3 slices fat-free cheddar cheese

Instructions

25 MINUTES BEFORE DINNER, start the broccoli. In a large microwavable bowl cover and cook 2 bags frozen broccoli in a carousel microwave on high for 6 minutes.

22 MINUTES BEFORE DINNER, start the casserole. Drain the cans of chicken, reserving the broth. Combine the reserved broth, $1/2$ c water, and $1^1/4$ c honey Dijon salad dressing in a 12-inch nonstick saucepan, and bring to a boil over high heat.

19 MINUTES BEFORE DINNER, stir the broccoli. Return to the microwave and cook for another 6 minutes.

17 MINUTES BEFORE DINNER, stir 4 c No-Yolk noodles into the boiling broth. Return to a low boil, then reduce the heat to medium. Cover and cook for 8 minutes.

13 MINUTES BEFORE DINNER, remove the broccoli from the microwave. Add 2 T butter sprinkles, $1^1/2$ T Parmesan topping, and $1/2$ t dried parsley, mixing well. Place 4 slices fat-free cheddar cheese on top of the broccoli, cover with waxed paper, and cook for 4 minutes in the microwave.

9 MINUTES BEFORE DINNER, turn off the heat to the pasta and stir in 2 cans chicken. Cover and let sit on the warm burner for 5 minutes.

7 MINUTES BEFORE DINNER, remove the broccoli from the microwave and stir the melted cheese into the broccoli. Add the remaining 3 slices cheddar cheese to the top of the broccoli and cover with a plate. The cheese will melt from the steam of the hot broccoli. Wrap the bowl with a dish towel to keep warm.

4 MINUTES BEFORE DINNER, sprinkle 1 c shredded cheddar cheese on top of the casserole. Spray the cheese with nonfat cooking spray. Cover and let sit for 3 minutes, or until the cheese is melted.

3 MINUTES BEFORE DINNER, remove the plate and place the broccoli on the dinner table. If you prefer your vegetables hotter, microwave for 1 to 2 more minutes. Place on a hot pad on the dinner table.

1 MINUTE BEFORE DINNER, place the casserole on a hot pad on the dinner table.

Supplies List

Timer
12-inch nonstick saucepan with lid
Large microwavable bowl

Grocery List

PACKAGED

1 (12-ounce) bag No-Yolk noodles
2 (12-ounce) cans 98% fat-free chicken
1 (16-ounce) bottle fat-free honey Dijon mustard salad dressing
Reduced-fat Parmesan-style grated topping

FROZEN

2 (16-ounce) bags frozen broccoli

DAIRY

1 cup shredded fat-free cheddar cheese
7 slices fat-free cheddar cheese

Pantry List

$3/4$ cup chicken broth
Dried parsley
Nonfat cooking spray
Imitation butter-flavored sprinkles

>>> Chicken & Broccoli Pasta Casserole

Excellent Spinach Salad

Because the spinach salad in this menu was so excellent, my assistant and I decided to call it just that, Excellent Spinach Salad. The toasted almonds, bacon, and raisins along with the lightly seasoned salad dressing are the perfect companion for the Chicken and Broccoli Casserole.

CHICKEN & BROCCOLI PASTA CASSEROLE
Yield: 6 servings
(1½ cups per serving)

Calories: 313 (10% fat); Total Fat: 3g; Cholesterol: 53mg; Carbohydrate: 32g; Dietary Fiber: 4g; Protein 35g; Sodium: 1255mg; Diabetic Exchanges: 2 starch, 1 vegetable, 4 very lean meat

EXCELLENT SPINACH SALAD
Yield: 6 servings (1 cup per serving)

Calories: 83 (24% fat); Total Fat: 2g; Cholesterol: 5mg; Carbohydrate: 14g; Dietary Fiber: 2g; Protein 4g; Sodium: 129mg; Diabetic Exchanges: 1 fruit, ½ lean meat

CHICKEN & BROCCOLI PASTA CASSEROLE

2¾ cups chicken broth
1 teaspoon rotisserie chicken seasoning
1 (10¾ ounce) can 98% fat-free cheese and broccoli soup
4 cups No-Yolk noodles
1 (16 ounce) bag frozen broccoli cuts
2 (12 ounce) cans 98% fat-free chicken in water, drained
1 cup shredded fat-free cheddar cheese

EXCELLENT SPINACH SALAD

3 tablespoons sliced almonds
2 tablespoons honey
1 tablespoon apple cider vinegar
1 (10-ounce) bag washed and ready-to-use fresh spinach
¼ cup raisins
3 tablespoons 30%-less-fat real bacon pieces

Instructions

22 MINUTES BEFORE DINNER, start the casserole. In a 12-inch nonstick saucepan over high heat, bring 2¾ c chicken broth, 1 t rotisserie chicken seasoning, and 1 can broccoli soup to a boil.

18 MINUTES BEFORE DINNER, preheat the oven to 500 degrees or broil.

17 MINUTES BEFORE DINNER, once the liquid is boiling, stir in 4 c No-Yolk noodles. Bring to a low boil again, then reduce the heat to medium. Cover and cook for 10 minutes, or until pasta is tender.

While the pasta is cooking, cut off one end of the bag of frozen broccoli cuts. Microwave the broccoli in the bag for 3 to 4 minutes, or until fully heated. Let the broccoli sit in the microwave until it is time to stir it into the pasta.

15 MINUTES BEFORE DINNER, start the salad. Put the 3 T sliced almonds on a baking sheet. Place on the top rack and broil for 1 minute, or until lightly browned. Let almonds cool on the baking sheet.

In a small microwavable bowl heat the 2 T honey and 1 T apple cider vinegar for 15 to 20 seconds, or until it comes to a boil. Stir until the honey is dissolved. Set aside. Remove the large stems from the spinach if needed and place the spinach in a large salad bowl. Using your hands, toss the spinach with the salad dressing, ¼ c raisins, 3 T bacon pieces, and the toasted almonds until the leaves are shiny and coated with the salad dressing. Place on the dinner table.

5 MINUTES BEFORE DINNER, turn off the heat to the pasta and stir in 2 cans drained chicken and the cooked broccoli. Sprinkle 1 c shredded cheddar cheese on top of the casserole. Spray the cheese with nonfat cooking spray. Cover and let sit on the warm burner for 3 to 4 minutes, or until the cheese is melted.

1 MINUTE BEFORE DINNER, place the casserole on a hot pad on the dinner table.

NOTE: Toasting the almonds enhances the flavor of the nut.

Supplies List

Timer
12-inch nonstick saucepan with lid
Baking sheet
Small microwavable bowl
Large salad bowl

Grocery List

PACKAGED

1 (12-ounce) bag No-Yolk noodles
1 (10¾-ounce) can 98% fat-free cheese and broccoli soup
2 (12-ounce) cans 98% fat-free chicken in water
30%-less-fat real crumbled bacon pieces
¼ cup raisins

PRODUCE

1 (10-ounce) bag prewashed fresh spinach

FROZEN

1 (16-ounce) bag frozen broccoli cuts

DAIRY

1 cup shredded fat-free cheddar

Pantry List

2¾ cups chicken broth
Honey
Apple cider vinegar
Sliced almonds
Nonfat cooking spray
Rotisserie chicken seasoning

>>> Southwestern Chicken Pasta Casserole

Tex-Mex Garden Salad

This entrée is so rich and creamy that it is hard to believe the creamy nacho cheese sauce that the pasta is covered in is low in fat and calories. The texture of the pasta is tender and every bite is as good as the last. The salad goes perfectly with this entrée and together they make a fantastic meal the entire family will love and most likely ask for over and over again!

SOUTHWESTERN CHICKEN PASTA CASSEROLE

Yield: 6 servings (1 cup per serving)

Calories: 307 (11% fat); Total Fat: 3g; Cholesterol: 53mg; Carbohydrate: 31g; Dietary Fiber: 2g; Protein 32g; Sodium: 1317mg; Diabetic Exchanges: 2 starch, $3^1/2$ very lean meat

TEX-MEX GARDEN SALAD

Yield: 6 servings ($1^1/2$ cup per serving)

Calories: 69 (0% fat); Total Fat: 0g; Cholesterol: 3mg; Carbohydrate: 11g; Dietary Fiber: 2g; Protein 5g; Sodium: 200mg; Diabetic Exchanges: 1 vegetable, $1/2$ other carbohydrate, $1/2$ very lean meat

SOUTHWESTERN CHICKEN PASTA CASSEROLE

$1^1/2$	cups chunky salsa	4	cups No-Yolk noodles
$1^1/4$	cups chicken broth	2	(12-ounce) cans 98% fat-free chicken, drained
1	plus $1/2$ teaspoon taco seasoning mix	1	cup shredded fat-free cheddar cheese
1	($10^3/4$ ounce) can 98% fat-free cream of celery soup		

TEX-MEX GARDEN SALAD

$1/4$	plus $1/4$ cup shredded fat-free cheddar cheese	1	large head iceberg lettuce
$1/4$	cup chunky salsa, chilled	18	grape tomatoes
$1/4$	cup fat-free sour cream	18	baked nacho cheese-flavored tortilla chips, crushed
1	teaspoon Splenda granular		

Instructions

22 MINUTES BEFORE DINNER, start the casserole. In a 12-inch nonstick saucepan over high heat, bring $1^1/_2$ c chunky salsa, $1^1/_4$ c chicken broth, 1 t taco seasoning mix, and 1 can cream of celery soup to a boil.

17 MINUTES BEFORE DINNER, once liquid is boiling stir in 4 c No-Yolk noodles. Return to a boil, then reduce the heat to medium-low. Cover and simmer for 10 minutes, or until the pasta is tender, stirring occasionally.

15 MINUTES BEFORE DINNER, make the salad. In a large bowl, stir together until well mixed $1/_4$ c shredded cheddar cheese, $1/_4$ c chilled chunky salsa, $1/_4$ c sour cream, and 1 t Splenda granular. Cover and keep refrigerated.

12 MINUTES BEFORE DINNER, stir the pasta.

10 MINUTES BEFORE DINNER, cut 1 large head iceberg lettuce into bite-size pieces to make about 9 c. Put the lettuce and 18 grape tomatoes in the large bowl on top of the salad dressing. Do not toss the salad yet.

7 MINUTES BEFORE DINNER, turn off the heat to the pasta and stir in 2 cans drained chicken.

Combine $1/_2$ t taco seasoning mix with 1 c shredded cheddar cheese and sprinkle on top of the casserole. Spray the cheese with nonfat cooking spray. Cover and let sit on the warm burner for 3 to 4 minutes, or until the cheese is melted.

3 MINUTES BEFORE DINNER, toss the salad with the salad dressing. Sprinkle the top of the salad with $1/_4$ c shredded cheddar cheese and 18 crushed tortilla chips. Place the salad on dinner table.

1 MINUTE BEFORE DINNER, place the casserole on a hot pad on the dinner table.

Supplies List

Timer
12-inch nonstick saucepan
   with lid
Large bowl

Grocery List

PACKAGED

1 (10-$^3/_4$-ounce) can 98%
   fat-free cream of celery
   soup
1 (12-ounce) bag No-Yolk
   noodles
2 (12-ounce) cans 98%
   fat-free chicken
Baked nacho cheese-flavored
   tortilla chips

PRODUCE

1 large head iceberg lettuce
18 grape tomatoes

DAIRY

$1^1/_2$ cups shredded fat-free
   cheddar cheese
$1/_4$ cup fat-free sour cream

SEASONINGS

Pantry List

1 (16-ounce) jar chunky salsa
$1^1/_4$ cups chicken broth
Nonfat cooking spray
Taco seasoning mix
Splenda granular

>>> Roadhouse Turkey Casserole

Mushroom, Onion & Asparagus Medley

Here's a yummy way to use leftover turkey from the holidays and disguise it as something totally different. Simply substitute $1^1/_4$ cups leftover turkey for the canned turkey in this recipe.

ROADHOUSE TURKEY CASSEROLE

Yield: 6 servings (1 cup per serving)

Calories: 337 (8% fat); Total Fat: 3g; Cholesterol: 67mg; Carbohydrate: 44g; Dietary Fiber: 1g; Protein 28g; Sodium: 878mg; Diabetic Exchanges: 2 starch, 1 other carbohydrate, 3 very lean meat

MUSHROOM, ONION & ASPARAGUS MEDLEY

Yield: 6 servings ($^1/_2$ cup per serving)

Calories: 41 (18% fat); Total Fat: 1g; Cholesterol: 0mg; Carbohydrate: 6g; Dietary Fiber: 2g; Protein 4g; Sodium: 562mg; Diabetic Exchanges: $1^1/_2$ vegetable

ROADHOUSE TURKEY CASSEROLE

3	cups water
1	cup barbeque sauce
$^1/_4$	cup 30%-less-fat real bacon pieces
4	cups No-Yolk noodles
1	($12^1/_2$-ounce) can turkey breast in water, drained
$^1/_4$	cup fat-free ranch salad dressing
1	cup fat-free cheddar cheese, shredded

MUSHROOM, ONION & ASPARAGUS MEDLEY

$^1/_4$	cup frozen chopped onion
2	($14^1/_2$-ounce) cans asparagus, drained
2	(4-ounce) can mushroom stems and pieces, drained
2	tablespoons imitation butter-flavored sprinkles
$^1/_2$	teaspoon garlic powder

Instructions

22 MINUTES BEFORE DINNER, start the casserole. In a 12-inch nonstick saucepan over high heat, bring 3 c water and 1 c barbeque sauce to a boil.

18 MINUTES BEFORE DINNER, stir 4 c No-Yolk noodles into the boiling liquid. Bring to a low boil again and then reduce the heat to medium. Cover and cook for 8 minutes, or until the pasta is tender.

8 MINUTES BEFORE DINNER, turn off the heat and stir 1 can drained turkey breast. Cover and let sit on the warm burner for 5 minutes to heat the turkey.

Start the vegetable medley. In a microwave-safe casserole dish, gently stir together until well mixed $1/4$ c frozen chopped onion, 2 cans drained asparagus, 2 cans drained mushroom stems and pieces, 2 T imitation butter-flavored sprinkles, and $1/2$ t garlic powder. Cover and cook on high in a microwave with a carousel for 2 to 3 minutes, or until heated through. Place dish on a hot pad on the dinner table.

5 MINUTES BEFORE DINNER, spread $1/4$ c fat-free ranch salad dressing over cooked pasta. Sprinkle with $1/4$ c real bacon pieces. Sprinkle the top of the casserole with $1/2$ cup shredded cheddar cheese. Spray the cheese with nonfat cooking spray. Cover and let the casserole sit on the warm burner for 3 to 4 minutes, or until the cheese is melted.

1 MINUTE BEFORE DINNER, place the casserole on a hot pad on the dinner table.

Supplies List

Timer
12-inch nonstick saucepan
    with lid
Microwave-safe casserole dish

Grocery List

PACKAGED

1 (12-ounce) bag No-Yolk
    noodles
1 ($12 1/2$-ounce) can turkey
    breast in water
1 (8-ounce) bottle barbeque
    sauce
Fat-free ranch salad dressing
$1/4$ cup 30%-less-fat real
    bacon pieces
2 (14-$1/2$-ounce) cans
    asparagus
2 (4-ounce) can mushroom
    stems and pieces

FROZEN

$1/4$ cup frozen chopped onion

DAIRY

1 cup shredded fat-free
    cheddar cheese

Pantry List

Garlic powder
Nonfat cooking spray
Imitation butter-flavored
    sprinkles

>>> Ranch-Style Chicken, Mushroom & Rice Casserole

Creamy Pear & Feta Tossed Salad

Here's an all-time favorite entrée made a lot simpler in one pan instead of the numerous pans the old recipe used. You'll also never miss all of the fat and calories the other recipe had. Once you've eaten this, most likely you'll never make the high-calorie version again. I think you'll also really like this original salad with its smooth and creamy homemade salad dressing blending both the sweet flavor of fresh pears and the slight saltiness of feta cheese.

RANCH-STYLE CHICKEN, MUSHROOM & RICE CASSEROLE

Yield: 6 servings

(1¼ cups per serving)

Calories: 303 (14% fat); Total Fat: 5g; Cholesterol: 54mg; Carbohydrate: 34g; Dietary Fiber: 2g; Protein 27g; Sodium: 1180mg; Diabetic Exchanges: 2 starch, 3 very lean meat

CREAMY PEAR & FETA TOSSED SALAD

Yield: 6 servings

(1½ cups per serving)

Calories: 48 (8% fat); Total Fat: 0g; Cholesterol: 2mg; Carbohydrate: 10g; Dietary Fiber: 2g; Protein 3g; Sodium: 193mg; Diabetic Exchanges: ½ fruit

RANCH-STYLE CHICKEN, MUSHROOM & RICE CASSEROLE

2	(12-ounce) cans chicken breast in water	8	ounces sliced fresh mushrooms
1	(14-ounce) can less-sodium chicken broth	1½	cups whole grain instant brown rice
¾	plus ¼ cup fat-free ranch salad dressing	2	slices reduced-fat natural Swiss cheese

CREAMY PEAR & FETA TOSSED SALAD

¼	cup fat-free feta cheese	1	tablespoon Splenda granular
1	teaspoon apple cider vinegar	1	fresh medium pear, chopped
¼	cup fat-free mayonnaise	1	large head iceberg lettuce
2	tablespoons fat-free sour cream		

Instructions

25 MINUTES BEFORE DINNER, start the casserole. Drain the liquid from 2 cans chicken breast in water into a 12-inch nonstick saucepan; set the chicken aside. Bring the liquid from the canned chicken, 1 can less-sodium chicken broth, $^3/_4$ c ranch salad dressing, and 8 oz sliced fresh mushrooms to a boil over high heat.

21 MINUTES BEFORE DINNER, stir $1^1/_2$ c rice into the boiling liquid. Return to a boil then reduce the heat to medium. Cover and cook for 12 minutes, or until the rice is tender.

While the rice is cooking, cut 2 slices of Swiss cheese into strips with a sharp knife.

18 MINUTES BEFORE DINNER, make the salad dressing. In a large salad bowl, stir together until well mixed $^1/_4$ c fat-free feta cheese, 1 t apple cider vinegar, $^1/_4$ c mayonnaise, 2 T sour cream, 1 T Splenda granular, and 1 chopped pear. Cover and refrigerate until dinner.

8 MINUTES BEFORE DINNER, turn off the heat to the rice and stir in the reserved canned chicken. Arrange the Swiss cheese on top of the casserole. Cover and let the casserole rest on the warm burner for 6 to 7 minutes.

5 MINUTES BEFORE DINNER, cut 1 head iceberg lettuce into bite-size pieces to make about 9 c. Put the lettuce into the large salad bowl with the salad dressing. Toss the salad and dressing together until all of the lettuce is covered in dressing. Place the salad on the dinner table.

1 MINUTE BEFORE DINNER, place the casserole on a hot pad on the dinner table.

Supplies List

Timer
Large salad bowl
12-inch nonstick saucepan
   with lid

Grocery List

PACKAGED

2 (12-ounce) cans chicken
   breast in water
Whole grain instant
   brown rice
1 (8-ounce) bottle fat-free
   ranch salad dressing

PRODUCE

8 ounces sliced fresh
   mushrooms
1 fresh medium pear
1 large head iceberg lettuce

DAIRY

Fat-free sour cream
3 slices reduced-fat Swiss
   cheese
Fat-free feta cheese

Pantry List

Fat-free mayonnaise
1 (14-ounce) can less-sodium
   chicken broth
Apple cider vinegar
Splenda granular

>>> Black & Blue Beef Pasta Casserole

Simple Spinach Salad with Honey Salad Dressing

If you like blue cheese, roast beef, and pasta, then you will like this creative dish combining these delicious flavors. This simple spinach salad is one of my all-time favorites because the light dressing compliments the spinach; it is not overpowering at all.

BLACK & BLUE BEEF PASTA CASSEROLE
Yield: 7 servings (1 cup per serving)

Calories: 189 (7% fat); Total Fat: 1g; Cholesterol: 23mg; Carbohydrate: 25g; Dietary Fiber: 2g; Protein 17g; Sodium: 831mg; Diabetic Exchanges: $1^1/_2$ starch, 1 vegetable, 2 very lean meat

SIMPLE SPINACH SALAD WITH HONEY SALAD DRESSING
Yield: 6 servings ($1^1/_2$ cups per serving)

Calories: 33 (0% fat); Total Fat: 0g; Cholesterol: 0mg; Carbohydrate: 8g; Dietary Fiber: 1g; Protein 1g; Sodium: 38mg; Diabetic Exchanges: $^1/_2$ other carbohydrate

BLACK & BLUE BEEF PASTA CASSEROLE

$3^1/_2$ cups beef broth	2 plus 1 tablespoons fat-free blue cheese crumbles
$^1/_2$ cup frozen onion, chopped	
1 cup thinly sliced fresh mushrooms	$^1/_4$ cup fat-free blue cheese salad dressing
4 cups No-Yolk noodles	
1 pound extra-lean deli-style sliced roast beef	

SIMPLE SPINACH SALAD WITH HONEY SALAD DRESSING

1 (10-ounce) bag washed and ready-to-use fresh spinach	2 tablespoons honey
	1 tablespoon apple cider vinegar

Instructions

22 MINUTES BEFORE DINNER, start the casserole. In a 12-inch nonstick saucepan over high heat, bring $3^1/_2$ c beef broth, $^1/_2$ c frozen chopped onion, and 1 c thinly sliced fresh mushrooms to a boil.

17 MINUTES BEFORE DINNER, once the liquid is boiling, stir in 4 c No-Yolk noodles. Return to a boil, then reduce the heat to medium-low. Cover and simmer for 10 minutes, or until the pasta is tender.

While the pasta is cooking, cut the 1 lb sliced roast beef into bite-size pieces. Set aside.

12 MINUTES BEFORE DINNER, make the salad. Remove any long stems from 1 bag fresh spinach and place the spinach in a large salad bowl. Set aside. To make the dressing, combine 2 T honey and 1 T apple cider vinegar in a small bowl and mix well.

6 MINUTES BEFORE DINNER, pour the dressing over the spinach. Toss until the spinach leaves are shiny and coated with salad dressing.

5 MINUTES BEFORE DINNER, turn off the heat to the pasta. Stir in the 1 lb sliced roast beef pieces and 2 T blue cheese crumbles. Spread $^1/_4$ c blue cheese salad dressing over the casserole. Sprinkle with 1 T blue cheese crumbles. Cover and let sit for 3 to 4 minutes.

2 MINUTES BEFORE DINNER, place the salad on the dinner table.

1 MINUTE BEFORE DINNER, place casserole on a hot pad on the dinner table.

Supplies List

Timer
12-inch nonstick saucepan with lid
Large salad bowl
Small bowl

Grocery List

PACKAGED
1 (12-ounce) bag No-Yolk noodles
Fat-free blue cheese salad dressing

PRODUCE
8 ounces sliced fresh mushrooms
1 (10-ounce) bag prewashed fresh spinach

MEAT
1 pound extra-lean deli-style sliced roast beef

FROZEN
$^1/_2$ cup frozen chopped onion

DAIRY
Fat-free blue cheese crumbles

Pantry List

Honey
Apple cider vinegar
$3^1/_2$ cups beef broth

>>> Antipasto Casserole

Vegetarian Sausage & Cheddar Broccoli

This zesty entrée is full of zip and will add pizzazz to any blah day. It is sure to awaken your taste buds.

ANTIPASTO CASSEROLE

Yield: 6 servings (1 cup per serving)

*Calories: 227 (18% fat); Total Fat: 4g;
Cholesterol: 29mg; Carbohydrate: 33g;
Dietary Fiber: 2g; Protein 12g;
Sodium: 1439mg; Diabetic Exchanges:
2 starch, 1 vegetable, 1 lean meat*

**VEGETARIAN SAUSAGE
& CHEDDAR BROCCOLI**

Yield: 6 servings ($^3/_4$ cup per serving)

*Calories: 125 (12% fat); Total Fat: 2g;
Cholesterol: 9mg; Carbohydrate: 14g;
Dietary Fiber: 5g; Protein 16g;
Sodium: 780mg; Diabetic Exchanges:
$1^1/_2$ vegetable, $^1/_2$ other carbohydrate,
2 very lean meat*

ANTIPASTO CASSEROLE

$2^3/_4$	cups water	10	green olives, sliced
$1^1/_4$	cup fat-free zesty Italian salad dressing	1	($14^1/_2$ ounce) can diced Italian-style tomatoes, drained
4	cups No-Yolk noodles	3	tablespoons reduced-fat Parmesan style grated topping
1	(4 ounce) package reduced-fat turkey pepperoni slices		

VEGETARIAN SAUSAGE & CHEDDAR BROCCOLI

2	(16-ounce) bags frozen broccoli	$^1/_2$	teaspoon dried parsley
2	tablespoons imitation butter-flavored sprinkles	1	plus $^1/_4$ cups vegetarian Italian sausage-flavored crumbles
$1^1/_2$	tablespoons reduced-fat Parmesan-style grated topping	7	plus 2 slices fat-free cheddar cheese

Instructions

25 MINUTES BEFORE DINNER, start the broccoli. Remove the tops off of the 2 bags frozen broccoli and cook in a carousel microwave on high for 6 minutes.

22 MINUTES BEFORE DINNER, start the casserole. In a 12-inch nonstick saucepan over high heat, bring $2^3/_4$ c water and $1^1/_4$ c Italian salad dressing to a boil.

19 MINUTES BEFORE DINNER, remove the 2 bags of broccoli from the microwave, shake them, and cook for another 6 minutes.

17 MINUTES BEFORE DINNER, once the liquid is boiling, stir in 4 c No-Yolk noodles. Bring to a low boil again, then reduce the heat to medium. Cover and simmer for 10 minutes, or until the pasta is tender.

16 MINUTES BEFORE DINNER, thinly slice the 10 green olives and set aside.

13 MINUTES BEFORE DINNER, remove the broccoli from the microwave and place in a large microwavable bowl. Add 2 T butter sprinkles, $1^1/_2$ T Parmesan topping, $^1/_2$ t dried parsley, and 1 c vegetarian Italian sausage-flavored crumbles, mixing well. Place 7 slices cheddar cheese on top of the broccoli. Cover with waxed paper and cook for 4 minutes.

7 MINUTES BEFORE DINNER, remove the broccoli from the microwave and stir. Cut the remaining 2 slices cheddar cheese diagonally and place on top of the broccoli.

5 MINUTES BEFORE DINNER, turn off the heat to the pasta and stir in 1 package turkey pepperoni slices, the sliced green olives, and 1 can drained diced Italian-style tomatoes. Sprinkle 3 T Parmesan topping over the casserole. Cover and let sit on the warm burner for 4 minutes.

3 MINUTES BEFORE DINNER, microwave $^1/_4$ c vegetarian Italian sausage-flavored crumbles for 30 seconds. Sprinkle the sausage on top of the cheddar cheese and microwave for 45 to 60 seconds, or until the cheese is slightly melted.

2 MINUTES BEFORE DINNER, remove the broccoli from the microwave and put on a hot pad on the dinner table.

1 MINUTE BEFORE DINNER, place casserole on a hot pad on the dinner table.

Supplies List

Timer
12-inch nonstick saucepan
  with lid
Large microwavable bowl

Grocery List

PACKAGED

1 (12-ounce) bag No-Yolk
  noodles
1 (16-ounce) bottle fat-free
  zesty Italian salad dressing
1 small jar green olives
1 ($14^1/_2$-ounce) can diced
  Italian style tomatoes
Reduced-fat grated
  Parmesan-style topping

FROZEN

2 (16-ounce) bags frozen
  broccoli
1 (12-ounce) bag vegetarian
  sausage-flavored
  crumbles

MEAT

1 (4-ounce) package
  reduced-fat turkey
  pepperoni slices

DAIRY

9 slices fat-free cheddar
  cheese slices

Pantry List

Dried parsley
Imitation butter-flavored
  sprinkles

>>> Cheesy Ham & Cheddar Pasta Casserole

Fresh Sliced Tomatoes with Honey French Salad Dressing • Seasoned Green Beans with Bacon & Onion

This super creamy and delicious homemade version of macaroni and cheese with ham is so simple to make that you may never make packaged macaroni and cheese again. Now you can afford to eat your favorite comfort food more often, guilt-free!

CHEESY HAM & CHEDDAR PASTA CASSEROLE

Yield: 8 servings (1$\frac{1}{3}$ cups per serving)

Calories: 387 (17% fat); Total Fat: 7g; Cholesterol: 37mg; Carbohydrate: 49g; Dietary Fiber: 2g; Protein 29g; Sodium: 764mg; Diabetic Exchanges: 3 starch, $\frac{1}{2}$ skim milk, 3 very lean meat

FRESH SLICED TOMATOES WITH HONEY FRENCH SALAD DRESSING

Yield: 6 servings ($\frac{1}{2}$ tomato and 1$\frac{1}{2}$ tablespoons dressing per serving)

Calories: 50 (0% fat); Total Fat: 0g; Cholesterol: 0mg; Carbohydrate: 12g; Dietary Fiber: 2g; Protein 1g; Sodium: 205mg; Diabetic Exchanges: 1 vegetable, $\frac{1}{2}$ other carbohydrate

SEASONED GREEN BEANS WITH BACON & ONION

Yield: 7 servings ($\frac{1}{2}$ cup per serving)

Calories: 31 (13% fat); Total Fat: 0g; Cholesterol: 3mg; Carbohydrate: 5g; Dietary Fiber: 2g; Protein 2g; Sodium: 636mg; Diabetic Exchanges: 1 vegetable

CHEESY HAM & CHEDDAR PASTA CASSEROLE

1	(16-ounce) box elbow pasta
1	(12-ounce) can evaporated skim milk
$\frac{1}{2}$	plus $\frac{1}{2}$ cup (4-ounces) shredded fat-free sharp cheddar cheese
1	(8 ounce) package shredded fat-free mild cheddar cheese
1	(8 ounce) package extra-lean ham, diced

FRESH SLICED TOMATOES WITH HONEY FRENCH SALAD DRESSING

3	large tomatoes
$\frac{1}{2}$	cup fat-free French salad dressing
1	teaspoon honey

SEASONED GREEN BEANS WITH BACON & ONION

2	(14$\frac{1}{2}$-ounce) cans French-style cut green beans, drained
2	teaspoons pimento
2	tablespoons chopped frozen onion
2	tablespoons 30%-less-fat real bacon pieces
2	tablespoons imitation butter-flavored sprinkles
$\frac{1}{2}$	teaspoon seasoned salt

Instructions

25 MINUTES BEFORE DINNER, prepare the tomatoes. In a small bowl, stir together $1/2$ c French salad dressing with 1 t honey. Slice the tomatoes and arrange on a large plate. Drizzle with the dressing. Cover and refrigerate until dinner time.

20 MINUTES BEFORE DINNER, start the casserole. Bring 4 quarts water in a large Dutch oven or soup pan over high heat to a rolling boil.

In a 12-inch nonstick saucepan over medium heat, combine 1 can evaporated skim milk, $1/2$ c of the shredded sharp cheddar cheese, and 1 package shredded mild cheddar cheese, stirring until the cheese is melted and creamy.

15 MINUTES BEFORE DINNER, add the elbow pasta to the boiling water and cook for 7 minutes, or until tender.

14 MINUTES BEFORE DINNER, start the green beans. In a microwave-safe casserole dish, combine 2 cans drained French-style cut green beans, 2 t pimento, 2 T chopped frozen onion, 2 T bacon pieces, 2 T butter sprinkles, and $1/2$ t seasoned salt. Set aside.

10 MINUTES BEFORE DINNER, stir the diced extra-lean ham into the cheese sauce.

8 MINUTES BEFORE DINNER, drain the cooked pasta. Stir the pasta into the ham and cheese sauce, continuing to stir until the pasta is covered with the cheese sauce.

5 MINUTES BEFORE DINNER, turn off the heat to the saucepan. Sprinkle the top of the casserole with the remaining $1/2$ c shredded sharp cheddar cheese. Cover and let the casserole sit on the warm burner until dinner is ready to be served.

3 MINUTES BEFORE DINNER, microwave the seasoned green beans for 2 minutes, or until hot.

1 MINUTE BEFORE DINNER, place the casserole and green beans on hot pads on the dinner table. Place the tomatoes on the dinner table.

Supplies List

Timer
Small bowl
Large plate
Dutch oven or large soup pan
12-inch nonstick saucepan
    with lid
Microwave-safe casserole dish

Grocery List

PACKAGED

1 (16-ounce) box elbow pasta
1 (12-ounce) can evaporated
    skim milk
2 (14-$1/2$-ounce) cans
    French-style cut green
    beans
1 (8-ounce) bottle fat-free
    French salad dressing
30%-less-fat real bacon pieces
Pimento

PRODUCE

3 large tomatoes

FROZEN

Frozen chopped onions

MEAT

1 (8-ounce) package
    extra-lean ham

DAIRY

1 (8-ounce) package shredded
    fat-free sharp cheddar
    cheese
1 (8-ounce) package shred-
    ded fat-free mild cheddar
    cheese

Pantry List

Honey
Seasoned salt
Imitation butter-flavored
    sprinkles

>>> Ham & Swiss Pasta Casserole

Oven-Steamed Asparagus Spears with Pimento • Marble Rye Bread

If you like Ham and Swiss cheese sandwiches, you will love this pasta casserole.

HAM & SWISS PASTA CASSEROLE
Yield: 6 servings
(1¹/₃ cups per serving)

*Calories: 360 (18% fat); Total Fat: 7g;
Cholesterol: 37mg; Carbohydrate: 47g;
Dietary Fiber: 2g; Protein 26g; Sodium:
990mg; Diabetic Exchanges: 3 starch,
¹/₂ skim milk, 2 very lean meat*

**OVEN-STEAMED ASPARAGUS SPEARS
WITH PIMENTO**
Yield: 6 servings
(³/₄ to 1 cup per serving)

*Calories: 28 (0% fat); Total Fat: 0g;
Cholesterol: 0mg; Carbohydrate: 6g;
Dietary Fiber: 2g; Protein 3g; Sodium:
235mg; Diabetic Exchanges:
1 vegetable*

HAM & SWISS PASTA CASSEROLE

8	ounces fresh mushrooms, sliced	1	(12-ounce) can evaporated skim milk
4	cups rigatoni pasta	1	(8-ounce) package diced ham
1	(6.67-ounce) package reduced-fat Swiss cheese slices	1	tablespoon cornstarch
		¹/₂	teaspoon dried parsley

OVEN-STEAMED ASPARAGUS SPEARS WITH PIMENTO

1	beef bouillon cube	2	teaspoons pimento
¹/₂	cup hot water	1	tablespoon imitation butter-flavored sprinkles
1¹/₂	pounds fresh asparagus spears		

Instructions

30 MINUTES BEFORE DINNER, preheat the oven to 400 degrees.

Start the casserole. Bring 4 quarts water in a large Dutch oven or soup pan over high heat to a rolling boil.

In a large 12-inch nonstick saucepan with a lid, cook the sliced mushrooms in 2 T of water over medium-high heat.

27 MINUTES BEFORE DINNER, prepare the asparagus. Dissolve 1 beef bouillon cube in $1/2$ c hot water.

Trim the tough ends off the asparagus and discard. Place the asparagus in a 9 x 13-inch baking dish. Pour the dissolved beef bouillon over the asparagus. Sprinkle 2 t pimento and 1 T imitation butter-flavored sprinkles over the asparagus. Cover with aluminum foil and bake for 20 to 27 minutes, depending on the thickness of the asparagus.

25 MINUTES BEFORE DINNER, add the pasta to the boiling water.

Set aside 3 slices of the Swiss cheese to use later. Cut the remaining 6 slices of cheese into bite-size pieces.

Drain the water from the mushrooms. Add 1 can evaporated skim milk and the bite-size pieces of cheese to the mushrooms in the skillet, stirring until the cheese is melted. (The cheese sauce may look thin and stringy but will thicken after it is covered and cooked). Add 1 package diced ham. Reduce the heat to low and continue stirring until the ham is coated with the cheese sauce.

14 MINUTES BEFORE DINNER, drain the cooked pasta and stir into the cheese and ham sauce.

8 MINUTES BEFORE DINNER, put the bread in a basket or serving bowl and place on the table.

5 MINUTES BEFORE DINNER, turn off the heat on the stove. Slice the remaining 3 slices Swiss cheese in half. Place the cheese on top of the casserole and cover with a lid. Let sit for 1 to 2 minutes, or until the cheese is melted.

3 MINUTES BEFORE DINNER, remove the asparagus from the oven and place on a hot pad on the dinner table.

1 MINUTE BEFORE DINNER, place ham and cheese pasta casserole on a hot pad on the dinner table.

Supplies List

Timer
Large Dutch oven or soup pan
12-inch nonstick saucepan
  with lid
9 x 13-inch baking dish

Grocery List

PACKAGED

1 (16-ounce) box rigatoni
  pasta
1 (12-ounce) can evaporated
  skim milk
Pimento

PRODUCE

8 ounces fresh mushrooms
1 1/2 pounds fresh asparagus
  spears

MEAT

1 (8-ounce) package
  diced ham

DAIRY

1 (6.67-ounce) package
  reduced-fat Swiss cheese
  slices

Pantry List

Dried parsley
1 beef bouillon cube
Cornstarch
Imitation butter-flavored
  sprinkles

>>> Chipotle Chicken Pasta

Sweet & Spicy Tossed Salad • Taco Biscuit Buttons

The flavors in this menu are on the bold side; therefore, it tends to be favored by those who like spicier foods.

CHIPOTLE CHICKEN PASTA

Yield: 7 servings (1 cup per serving)

Calories: 182 (8% fat); Total Fat: 2g; Cholesterol: 23mg; Carbohydrate: 26g; Dietary Fiber: 1g; Protein 15g; Sodium: 601mg; Diabetic Exchanges: 2 starch, 1 1/2 very lean meat

SWEET & SPICY TOSSED SALAD

Yield: 6 servings (1 1/2 cups per serving)

Calories: 48 (0% fat); Total Fat: 0g; Cholesterol: 3mg; Carbohydrate: 7g; Dietary Fiber: 2g; Protein 5g; Sodium: 385mg; Diabetic Exchanges: 1 1/2 vegetable, 1/2 very lean meat

TACO BISCUIT BUTTONS

Yield: 40 buttons (6 buttons per serving)

Calories: 82 (24% fat); Total Fat: 2g; Cholesterol: 0mg; Carbohydrate: 14g; Dietary Fiber: 0g; Protein 2g; Sodium: 309mg; Diabetic Exchanges: 1 starch

CHIPOTLE CHICKEN PASTA

3 1/2	cups rotini pasta	1	(13-ounce) can chicken breast, drained
1/2	cup frozen chopped onions	1	tablespoon Splenda granular
2	(8-ounce) cans tomato sauce	1	tablespoon reduced-fat Parmesan-style grated topping
1 3/4	tablespoons chipotle seasoning		

SWEET & SPICY TOSSED SALAD

1	(14 1/2-ounce) can petite-diced tomatoes with mild green chilies, chilled*	1/2	cup shredded fat-free cheddar cheese
1/4	cup fat-free sour cream	1	tablespoon Splenda granular
		1	large head iceberg lettuce

TACO BISCUIT BUTTONS

1	(7 1/2-ounce) can refrigerated buttermilk biscuits	1	teaspoon parsley flakes
1	teaspoon taco seasoning	1	teaspoon imitation butter-flavored sprinkles

Instructions

30 MINUTES BEFORE DINNER, start the pasta. In a 12-inch nonstick saucepan over high heat, bring 2 quarts water to a boil. Add 3 1/2 c rotini pasta and return to a boil. Cook the pasta for 8 minutes.

25 MINUTES BEFORE DINNER, prepare the salad. In a medium bowl, combine 1 can petite-diced tomatoes, $^1/_2$ c shredded cheddar cheese, $^1/_4$ c sour cream, and 1 T Splenda granular. Cover and refrigerate until dinner is ready to be served.

Cut 1 large head iceberg lettuce into bite-size pieces to make about 9 c. Place in a large salad bowl. Cover and refrigerate until dinner is ready to be served.

17 MINUTES BEFORE DINNER, drain the pasta and set aside.

Spray the 12-inch nonstick saucepan with nonfat cooking spray. Over medium-low heat, cook $^1/_2$ c frozen chopped onion. Sauté until tender, about 2 to 3 minutes.

While the onions are cooking, preheat the oven to 350 degrees.

15 MINUTES BEFORE DINNER, add 2 cans tomato sauce, $1^3/_4$ T chipotle seasoning, 1 can drained chicken breast, and 1 T Splenda granular to the sautéed onions, stirring until well mixed. Cook for about 5 minutes.

13 MINUTES BEFORE DINNER, prepare the biscuits. Generously coat a baking sheet with nonfat cooking spray. Set aside.

Cut each of the 10 biscuits into 4 pie-shaped pieces. Roll each piece into a ball and place on the prepared baking sheet. Spray each biscuit button with nonfat cooking spray and sprinkle with 1 t taco seasoning, 1 t parsley flakes, and 1 t butter sprinkles.

10 MINUTES BEFORE DINNER, place the prepared baking sheet in the oven and bake the Taco Biscuit Buttons for 8 minutes.

Turn off the stove and stir the pasta into the sauce. Sprinkle with 1 T Parmesan topping. Cover and let sit on the warm burner until dinner.

2 MINUTES BEFORE DINNER, remove the Taco Biscuit Buttons from the oven and place in a medium bowl on the dinner table.

1 MINUTE BEFORE DINNER, place the pasta on a hot pad on the dinner table. Toss the lettuce with the salad dressing until well coated. Place on the dinner table.

NOTE: *Prechill this ingredient by placing the can in the refrigerator as soon as you get home from the grocery store.*

Supplies List

Timer
12-inch nonstick saucepan
    with lid
2 medium bowls
Large salad bowl
Baking sheet

Grocery List

PACKAGED

1 (16-ounce) box rotini pasta
2 (8-ounce) cans tomato
    sauce
1 (13-ounce) can chicken
    breast in water
1 (14$^1/_2$-ounce) can
    petite-diced tomatoes
    with mild green chilies

PRODUCE

1 large head iceberg lettuce

FROZEN

$^1/_2$ cup frozen chopped
    onions

DAIRY

$^1/_2$ cup shredded fat-free
    cheddar cheese
$^1/_2$ cup fat-free sour cream
Reduced-fat Parmesan-style
    grated topping
1 (7$^1/_2$-ounce) can
    refrigerated buttermilk
    biscuits

Pantry List

Parsley flakes
Nonfat cooking spray
Splenda granular
Imitation butter-flavored
    sprinkles
Chipotle seasoning
Taco seasoning

>>> Mushroom & Swiss Chicken

Seasoned Button Potatoes • Dilly Cucumber & Tomato Salad • Rye Dinner Rolls

There's a synergy in this menu. These dishes taste better when served together than they do alone. But they are pretty darn good individually, too!

MUSHROOM & SWISS CHICKEN

Yield: 6 servings

(4 ounces per serving)

Calories: 167 (24% fat); Total Fat: 4g; Cholesterol: 73mg; Carbohydrate: 1g; Dietary Fiber: 0g; Protein 30g; Sodium: 106mg; Diabetic Exchanges: 4 very lean meat

DILLY CUCUMBER & TOMATO SALAD

Yield: 7 servings (1/2 cup per serving)

Calories: 38 (0% fat); Total Fat: 0g; Cholesterol: 1mg; Carbohydrate: 7g; Dietary Fiber: 1g; Protein 2g; Sodium: 101mg; Diabetic Exchanges: 1 1/2 vegetable

SEASONED BUTTON POTATOES

Yield: 6 servings

(2 to 3 potatoes per serving)

Calories: 85 (0% fat); Total Fat: 0g; Cholesterol: 0mg; Carbohydrate: 19g; Dietary Fiber: 3g; Protein 2g; Sodium: 471mg; Diabetic Exchanges: 1 1/2 starch

MUSHROOM & SWISS CHICKEN

3   (8-ounce) chicken breasts
1   tablespoon light butter
4   ounces sliced fresh mushrooms
Freshly ground black pepper
2   tablespoons water
3   slices natural reduced-fat deli-thin sliced Swiss cheese, cut in half

DILLY CUCUMBER & TOMATO SALAD

1   tablespoon dill pickle juice
1/4 cup fat-free sour cream
1/4 cup light Miracle Whip
1/2 teaspoon dried dill weed or 1 teaspoon fresh dill weed, plus more for garnish
1/2 teaspoon dried parsley
1   pint grape tomatoes*
1   medium cucumber, cut into thin slices

SEASONED BUTTON POTATOES

2   (15-ounce) cans whole white potatoes, drained
1   teaspoon garlic salt
1   teaspoon parsley flakes
1   teaspoon dried chopped chives
Fat-free butter spray

Instructions

25 MINUTES BEFORE DINNER, prepare the salad. In a medium mixing bowl, combine 1 t dill pickle juice, $^1/_4$ c sour cream, $^1/_4$ c Miracle Whip, $^1/_2$ t dried dill weed, and $^1/_2$ t dried parsley until well blended. Gently stir in 1 pint grape tomatoes and 1 medium, thinly sliced, cucumber, making sure the vegetables are well coated with dressing. If desired, sprinkle the salad very lightly with additional dill to garnish. Cover and refrigerate until ready to eat.

15 MINUTES BEFORE DINNER, start the chicken. Slice the 3 chicken breasts in half horizontally to make 6 (4-oz) servings. Set aside.

12 MINUTES BEFORE DINNER, over high heat melt 1 T butter in a 12-inch nonstick skillet. Add 4 oz fresh sliced mushrooms and sauté for 2 minutes, or until the mushrooms are tender.

Remove the mushrooms and place in a medium bowl. Cover and set aside.

Using the same skillet, cook the chicken breasts, covered, over high heat for 3 minutes, or until golden brown. Turn over the chicken pieces and sprinkle with freshly ground black pepper. Cover and continue cooking on high for another 2 to 3 minutes.

Add 2 T water to the skillet. Place 1 half-slice Swiss cheese on each chicken breast. Spoon the cooked mushrooms over the cheese. Reduce the heat to medium. Cover and cook for 2 more minutes, or until chicken is done and the cheese is melted. Once the chicken is fully cooked, turn off the heat and keep covered. Let sit on the warm burner until dinnertime.

5 MINUTES BEFORE DINNER, prepare the potatoes. Put 2 cans drained whole white potatoes in a medium microwavable bowl. Gently stir in 1 t garlic salt, 1 t parsley flakes, 1 t dried chopped chives, and 20 sprays butter spray. Cover with waxed paper and cook in a carousel microwave for 2 minutes, or until the potatoes are fully heated.

1 MINUTE BEFORE DINNER, place the potatoes and the chicken on individual hot pads on the dinner table, along with the salad and dinner rolls.

NOTE: Cherry tomatoes can be substituted; however the grape tomatoes tend to be sweeter.

Supplies List

Timer
2 medium mixing bowls
12-inch nonstick skillet
    with lid
Medium microwavable bowl

Grocery List

PACKAGED
2 (15-ounce) cans whole
    white potatoes

PRODUCE
1 pint grape tomatoes
1 medium cucumber
4 ounces fresh sliced
    mushrooms

POULTRY
3 (8-ounce) chicken breasts

DAIRY
$^1/_4$ cup fat-free sour cream
3 slices natural reduced-fat
    deli-thin sliced Swiss
    cheese
Light butter
Fat-free butter spray

Pantry List

Dried or fresh dill weed
Dried parsley flakes
Freshly ground black pepper
Garlic salt
Dried chopped chives
Light Miracle Whip
Dill pickle juice

>>> Beef & Mushroom Rice Casserole

Spinach Salad with French Bacon Salad Dressing • Fresh Strawberry Cream Salad

> Even the largest of appetites feels satisfied and content after this hearty meal.

BEEF & MUSHROOM RICE CASSEROLE

Yield: 7 servings (1 cup per serving)

Calories: 201 (19% fat); Total Fat: 4g; Cholesterol: 49mg; Carbohydrate: 18g; Dietary Fiber: 1g; Protein 23g; Sodium: 671mg; Diabetic Exchanges: 1 starch, 3 very lean meat

FRESH STRAWBERRY CREAM SALAD

Yield: 7 servings ($1/2$ cup per serving)

Calories: 107 (0% fat); Total Fat: 0g; Cholesterol: 6mg; Carbohydrate: 19g; Dietary Fiber: 2g; Protein 5g; Sodium: 170mg; Diabetic Exchanges: $1/2$ fruit, 1 other carbohydrate, 1 very lean meat

SPINACH SALAD WITH FRENCH BACON SALAD DRESSING

Yield: 6 servings (1 cup per serving)

Calories: 54 (11% fat); Total Fat: 1g; Cholesterol: 3mg; Carbohydrate: 10g; Dietary Fiber: 2g; Protein 3g; Sodium: 311mg; Diabetic Exchanges: 1 vegetable, $1/2$ other carbohydrate

BEEF & MUSHROOM RICE CASSEROLE

$2^1/2$ cups beef broth	2 (12-ounce) cans roast beef with gravy
$1/2$ cup frozen chopped onion	3 slices reduced-fat Swiss cheese
8 ounces sliced fresh mushrooms	
$1^1/2$ cups instant whole grain brown rice	

FRESH STRAWBERRY CREAM SALAD

1 (8-ounce) package fat-free cream cheese	$1/2$ teaspoon vanilla extract
1 $1/2$ pounds fresh strawberries	4 ounces fat-free whipped topping
1 cup Splenda granular	

SPINACH SALAD WITH FRENCH BACON SALAD DRESSING

1 (10-ounce) bag fresh baby spinach	2 tablespoons 30%-less-fat real bacon pieces
$1/2$ cup fat-free croutons	
$1/2$ cup fat-free French salad dressing	

Instructions

30 MINUTES BEFORE DINNER, start the strawberry cream salad. Soften 1 package cream cheese in a medium bowl. Set aside.

Remove the stems from $1^1/_2$ lb strawberries. Cut them into thin slices and put them into another medium bowl. Set aside.

22 MINUTES BEFORE DINNER, start the casserole. In a 12-inch nonstick saucepan over high heat, bring $2^1/_2$ c beef broth and $^1/_2$ c frozen chopped onion to a boil.

17 MINUTES BEFORE DINNER, once the liquid is boiling, stir in 8 oz sliced fresh mushrooms and $1^1/_2$ c rice. Return to a boil, then reduce the heat to medium. Cover and cook for 10 to 12 minutes, or until the rice is tender.

While the rice is cooking, cut 3 slices Swiss cheese into strips. Set aside.

12 MINUTES BEFORE DINNER, add 1 c Splenda granular, $^1/_2$ t vanilla extract, and 4 oz fat-free whipped topping to the softened cream cheese. Using an electric mixer on medium speed, beat until smooth and creamy. With a spatula, gently stir in the fresh sliced strawberries. Place the salad on the dinner table.

5 MINUTES BEFORE DINNER, turn off the heat to the rice and stir in 2 cans roast beef with gravy.

Sprinkle the thin slices of Swiss cheese on top of the rice casserole and then spray the cheese with nonfat cooking spray. Cover and let the casserole sit on the warm burner until dinner is ready to be served.

3 MINUTES BEFORE DINNER, prepare the spinach salad. If you desire dressing, combine the fresh baby spinach and $^1/_2$ c croutons in a large salad bowl. Toss with $^1/_2$ c French salad dressing. Sprinkle the top of the salad with 2 T bacon pieces. Place the salad on the dinner table.

1 MINUTE BEFORE DINNER, place the casserole on a hot pad on the dinner table.

NOTE: Save time by purchasing your mushrooms sliced in the produce department.

Supplies List

Timer
2 medium bowls
12-inch nonstick saucepan
    with lid
Electric mixer
Large salad bowl

Grocery List

PACKAGED

Whole grain instant
    brown rice
Fat-free croutons
1 (8-ounce) bottle fat-free
    French salad dressing
2 (12-ounce) cans roast beef
    with gravy
30% less-fat real bacon
    pieces

FROZEN

$^1/_2$ cup frozen chopped onion
8 ounces fat-free dessert
    whipped topping

PRODUCE

$1^1/_2$ pounds fresh strawberries
8 ounces fresh sliced
    mushrooms
1 (10-ounce) bag fresh baby
    spinach

DAIRY

1 (8-ounce) package fat-free
    cream cheese
3 slices reduced-fat Swiss
    cheese

Pantry List

Vanilla extract
$2^1/_2$ cups beef broth
Nonfat cooking spray
Splenda granular

HOME ON THE RANGE

>>> Southwestern Beef & Barley Soup

Cucumber Slices Stuffed with Smokey Bacon Cream Cheese • Fresh Baked Chipotle French Bread

This wonderful dinner is packed with savory flavors that compliment and enhance each course from beginning to end.

SOUTHWESTERN BEEF & BARLEY SOUP
Yield: 8 servings (1 cup per serving)

Calories: 179 (12% fat); Total Fat: 2g; Cholesterol: 24mg; Carbohydrate: 27g; Dietary Fiber: 3g; Protein 13g; Sodium: 851mg; Diabetic Exchanges: $1^1/2$ starch, 1 vegetable, $1^1/2$ very lean meat

CUCUMBER SLICES STUFFED WITH SMOKEY BACON CREAM CHEESE
Yield: 6 servings
(5 slices per serving)

Calories: 67 (64% fat); Total Fat: 5g; Cholesterol: 17mg; Carbohydrate: 2g; Dietary Fiber: 1g; Protein 4g; Sodium: 143mg; Diabetic Exchanges: $^1/2$ very lean meat, 1 fat

FRESH BAKED CHIPOTLE FRENCH BREAD
Yield: 6 servings
(1 slice per serving)

Calories: 125 (12% fat); Total Fat: 2g; Cholesterol: 0mg; Carbohydrate: 23g; Dietary Fiber: 1g; Protein 4g; Sodium: 325mg; Diabetic Exchanges: $1^1/2$ starch

SOUTHWESTERN BEEF & BARLEY SOUP

1 (12-ounce) can roast beef with gravy, broken into chunks	1 ($8^1/2$-ounce) can sweet corn, undrained
1 ($14^1/2$-ounce) can diced tomatoes with mild green chilies	1 cup quick pearl barley
	1 cup mild salsa
2 (14-ounce) cans fat-free, less-sodium beef broth	$1^1/2$ cups Bloody Mary mix

CUCUMBER SLICES STUFFED WITH SMOKEY BACON CREAM CHEESE

4 ounces $^1/3$-less-fat cream cheese	$^1/2$ teaspoon dried chopped chives
2 tablespoons 30%-less-fat real bacon pieces	$^1/2$ teaspoon Southwest chipotle seasoning
	2 large cucumbers

FRESH BAKED CHIPOTLE FRENCH BREAD

1 (11-ounce) can refrigerated French bread loaf	2 teaspoons Southwest chipotle seasoning
16 sprays nonfat butter spray	$^1/8$ teaspoon ground cinnamon

Instructions

30 MINUTES BEFORE DINNER, prepare the Frence bread. Preheat the oven to 350 degrees. Spray baking sheet with nonfat cooking spray. Lay the French bread dough on prepared baking sheet. Spray 16 sprays of nonfat butter spray on the dough. In a small bowl, mix 2 t Southwest chipotle seasoning and $1/8$ t ground cinnamon together. Sprinkle over the dough and then press into the dough with your hands. Place in the oven and set the timer for 23 minutes.

25 MINUTES BEFORE DINNER, start the soup. In a medium nonstick saucepan, put 1 can roast beef with gravy. Using a spoon, break up the pieces of beef. Add 1 can diced tomatoes, 2 cans beef broth, and 1 can undrained sweet corn. Cook over medium-high heat.

17 MINUTES BEFORE DINNER, once the soup comes to a boil, stir in $1/2$ c pearl barley. Reduce the heat to medium. Cover and let simmer for 12 minutes.

15 MINUTES BEFORE DINNER, prepare cucumber slices. In a medium bowl, combine 4 oz cream cheese, 2 T bacon pieces, $1/2$ t dried chopped chives, and $1/2$ t chipotle seasoning until well mixed. Set aside.

Cut off the ends of the cucumbers. Cut each cucumber in half lengthwise. Remove and discard the seeds.

Stuff each of 2 cucumber halves with $1/4$ c of the chipotle and bacon cream mixture. Stack one remaining cucumber half on top of each stuffed half. Using a very sharp knife, cut the stuffed cucumbers into $1/2$-inch-thick slices. Arrange the slices on a platter. Place the cucumbers on dinner table.

5 MINUTES BEFORE DINNER, remove the soup from the heat and let stand for 5 minutes.

3 MINUTES BEFORE DINNER, remove the French bread from the oven. If you like a crispier crust, let the bread bake a few minutes longer. Slice the bread into 6 slices and put in a basket on the dinner table.

1 MINUTE BEFORE DINNER, ladle the soup into 6 bowls and put each bowl on the table.

Supplies List

Timer
Baking sheet
Small bowl
Medium bowl
Medium nonstick saucepan
 with lid
Platter
Basket

Grocery List

PACKAGED

1 ($14^1/2$-ounce) can diced
 tomatoes with mild green
 chilies
1 ($8^1/2$-ounce) can sweet corn
1 cup mild salsa
Bloody Mary mix
 (non-alcoholic)
30%-less-fat real bacon
 pieces
1 (12-ounce) can roast beef
 with gravy
Quick pearl barley
Southwest chipotle seasoning

PRODUCE

2 large cucumbers

DAIRY

4 ounces $1/3$-less-fat cream
 cheese
1 (11-ounce) can refrigerated
 French bread loaf
Nonfat butter spray

Pantry List

Dried chopped chives
Nonfat butter spray
Ground cinnamon
1 (14-ounce) can fat-free,
 less-sodium beef broth
Nonfat cooking spray

>>> Chicken Barley Soup

Celery Stuffed with Creamy Blue Cheese • Onion & Chive Drop Biscuits

This soup is full of flavor. The celery stuffed with blue cheese and the onion and chive biscuits are a great accompaniment.

CHICKEN BARLEY SOUP
Yield: 6 servings (1 cup per serving)
Calories: 136 (10% fat); Total Fat: 1g; Cholesterol: 25mg; Carbohydrate: 15g; Dietary Fiber: 3g; Protein 14g; Sodium: 816mg; Diabetic Exchanges: $1^1/_2$ vegetable, $^1/_2$ starch, $1^1/_2$ very lean meat

CELERY STUFFED WITH CREAMY BLUE CHEESE
Yield: 6 servings ($2^1/_2$ ribs per serving)
Calories: 42 (21% fat); Total Fat: 1g; Cholesterol: 6mg; Carbohydrate: 4g; Dietary Fiber: 1g; Protein 4g; Sodium: 210mg; Diabetic Exchanges: 1 vegetable, $^1/_2$ very lean meat

ONION & CHIVE DROP BISCUITS
Yield: 6 servings (1 biscuit per serving)
Calories: 78 (15% fat); Total Fat: 1g; Cholesterol: 0mg; Carbohydrate: 15g; Dietary Fiber: 0g; Protein 2g; Sodium: 233mg; Diabetic Exchanges: 1 starch

CHICKEN BARLEY SOUP

1	($12^1/_2$-ounce) can chicken breast in water, undrained
$^1/_2$	cup finely chopped celery
1	($14^1/_2$-ounce) can stewed tomatoes with onion, celery, and green peppers
$1^1/_2$	tablespoons buffalo chicken wing sauce
2	(14-ounce) cans fat-free, less-sodium chicken broth
1	teaspoon Splenda granular
$^1/_2$	cup quick pearl barley

CELERY STUFFED WITH CREAMY BLUE CHEESE

6	celery ribs
4	ounces fat-free cream cheese, softened
2	tablespoons crumbled blue cheese
2	tablespoons fat-free blue cheese salad dressing

ONION & CHIVE DROP BISCUITS

1	cup low-fat baking mix
$^1/_4$	cup water
1	teaspoon dried chives
$^1/_2$	teaspoon onion powder
$^1/_4$	cup frozen chopped onion

Instructions

30 MINUTES BEFORE DINNER, prepare the biscuits. In a medium bowl, stir together 1 c baking mix, $^1/_4$ c water, 1 t chives, $^1/_2$ t onion powder, and $^1/_4$ c frozen chopped onion until well mixed.

Coat a baking sheet with nonfat cooking spray. Drop the dough by rounded tablespoonfuls onto the prepared baking sheet; set aside.

25 MINUTES BEFORE DINNER, start the soup. In a medium nonstick saucepan over medium-high heat, add 1 can chicken breast with the liquid. Break up the chicken with the back of a spoon. Add $^1/_2$ c celery, 1 can stewed tomatoes, $1^1/_2$ T buffalo chicken wing sauce, 2 cans chicken broth, and 1 t Splenda granular and mix well. Bring to a boil.

17 MINUTES BEFORE DINNER, once the soup comes to a boil, stir in $^1/_2$ c barley. Reduce the heat to medium. Cover and simmer for 12 minutes.

15 MINUTES BEFORE DINNER, preheat the oven to 400 degrees.

Prepare the celery. Remove and discard the ends of 6 celery ribs. Cut each rib in half.

In a small bowl, stir together 4 oz cream cheese, 2 T crumbled blue cheese, and 2 T blue cheese salad dressing until well mixed. With a butter knife, spread the blue cheese mixture onto the celery ribs. Arrange on a plate and place on the dinner table.

10 MINUTES BEFORE DINNER, bake the biscuits for 8 to 10 minutes.

5 MINUTES BEFORE DINNER, turn off the heat under the soup and let stand on the warm burner for 5 minutes.

2 MINUTES BEFORE DINNER, put biscuits on a serving dish and place on the dinner table. Ladle the soup in individual bowls and place on the dinner table.

Supplies List

Timer
Medium bowl
Baking sheet
Medium nonstick saucepan with lid
Small bowl
Serving dish

Grocery List

PACKAGED

1 (14$^1/_2$-ounce) can stewed tomatoes with onion, celery, and green peppers
1 (12$^1/_2$-ounce) can chicken breast in water
Buffalo chicken wing sauce
Fat-free blue cheese salad dressing
Quick-cook pearl barley

FROZEN

$^1/_4$ cup frozen chopped onion

PRODUCE

$^1/_2$ cup finely chopped celery
Celery

DAIRY

4 ounces fat-free cream cheese
Crumbled blue cheese

Pantry List

2 (14-ounce) cans fat-free, less-sodium chicken broth
Low-fat baking mix
Dried chives
Onion powder
Nonfat cooking spray
Splenda granular

>>> Smoked Sausage, Potatoes & Sauerkraut

Dill Corn Bread Drop Biscuits • Turnip Greens with Ham & Apple

Here's a yummy combination of southern home-style favorites combined for a meal made in less time than it took Granny to pick the greens from her garden.

SMOKED SAUSAGE, POTATOES & SAUERKRAUT

Yield: 8 servings (1 cup per serving)

Calories: 145 (0% fat); Total Fat: 0g; Cholesterol: 21mg; Carbohydrate: 27g; Dietary Fiber: 5g; Protein 10g; Sodium: 1471mg; Diabetic Exchanges: 1¹/₂ starch, 1 vegetable, 1 very lean meat

DILL CORN BREAD DROP BISCUITS

Yield: 12 servings (2 biscuits per serving)

Calories: 78 (18% fat); Total Fat: 2g; Cholesterol: 0mg; Carbohydrate: 14g; Dietary Fiber: 0g; Protein 2g; Sodium: 191mg; Diabetic Exchanges: 1 starch

TURNIP GREENS WITH HAM & APPLE

Yield: 6 servings (²/₃ cup per serving)

Calories: 72 (19% fat); Total Fat: 2g; Cholesterol: 10mg; Carbohydrate: 9g; Dietary Fiber: 4g; Protein 7g; Sodium: 799mg; Diabetic Exchanges: 2 vegetable, ¹/₂ lean meat

---

SMOKED SAUSAGE, POTATOES & SAUERKRAUT

1 (28-ounce) can sauerkraut	¹/₂ cup frozen chopped onion
1 medium gala apple, thinly sliced	2 (15-ounce) cans sliced white potatoes, drained
1 (14-ounce) package fat-free smoked sausage	2 teaspoons Splenda granular

DILL CORN BREAD DROP BISCUITS

1 (8¹/₂-ounce) box corn muffin mix	2 tablespoons water
2 egg whites	¹/₂ teaspoon dried dill, plus more for topping

TURNIP GREENS WITH HAM & APPLE

3 (14¹/₂-ounce) cans turnip greens with diced white turnips	4 ounces diced ham (¹/₂ cup, firmly packed)
1 teaspoon seasoned salt	1 Gala apple, finely chopped
³/₄ cup frozen chopped onion	

Instructions

30 MINUTES BEFORE DINNER, start making the biscuits. In a medium bowl mix together 1 box corn muffin mix, 2 egg whites, 2 T water, and $1/2$ t dried dill weed until well blended. Set aside.

25 MINUTES BEFORE DINNER, start the sausage. Put 1 can sauerkraut in a colander and rinse under cold running water for 1 minute. Press the sauerkraut between your hands to squeeze out as much water as possible. Set aside.

Cut 1 medium gala apple into thin slices, then cut the slices into quarters. Slice 1 package smoked sausage into $1/4$-inch-thick slices. In a 12-inch nonstick saucepan over medium heat, cook $1/2$ c frozen chopped onion, the quartered apple slices, and the smoked sausage slices until tender, about 3 to 4 minutes.

15 MINUTES BEFORE DINNER, preheat the oven to 400 degrees. Coat a non-stick baking sheet with cooking spray and set aside.

Add the sauerkraut, 2 cans drained sliced white potatoes, and 2 t Splenda granular to the apple mixture. Cover and cook for 14 minutes over medium-low heat.

13 MINUTES BEFORE DINNER, drop the biscuit dough by heaping table-spoonfuls onto the prepared baking sheet. Sprinkle the tops of the biscuits lightly with dried dill. Bake in the preheated oven on the middle rack for 8 minutes, or until golden brown.

10 MINUTES BEFORE DINNER, start the turnip greens. In a $2 1/2$-quart saucepan over medium-high heat, combine 3 cans turnip greens, 1 t seasoned salt, $3/4$ c frozen chopped onion, and 4 oz diced ham. While the turnip greens are cooking, finely chop 1 apple. Add to the saucepan. Cover, reduce heat to medium-low, and simmer until dinner is ready.

4 MINUTES BEFORE DINNER, remove the biscuits from the oven and place in a basket on the dinner table.

2 MINUTES BEFORE DINNER, put the turnip greens in a serving bowl and place on the dinner table.

1 MINUTE BEFORE DINNER, place the Smoked Sausage, Potatoes & Sauerkraut on a hot pad and put on the dinner table.

Supplies List

Timer
Medium bowl
12-inch nonstick saucepan
 with lid
Nonstick baking sheet
$2 1/2$ quart saucepan with lid
Basket

Grocery List

PACKAGED

1 (28-ounce) jar sauerkraut
2 (15-ounce) cans sliced
 white potatoes
3 ($14 1/2$-ounce) cans turnip
 greens with diced white
 turnips
1 ($8 1/2$-ounce) box corn
 muffin mix

PRODUCE

2 medium Gala apples

FROZEN

$1 1/4$ cup frozen chopped
 onion

MEAT

1 (14-ounce) package
 fat-free smoked sausage
4 ounces diced ham

DAIRY

2 eggs

Pantry List

Dried dill
Seasoned salt
Nonfat cooking spray
Splenda granular

>>> Grandma's Beef & Noodles

Easy as 1,2,3 Potatoes • Buttered Bean Medley

Back in the day, you would have to cook all day long to get a taste this good, but with this quick recipe no one but you will know the difference. My assistant, LuAnne Surgeson, created this quickie Beef and Noodles entrée, and I am sure you'll be glad she did.

GRANDMA'S BEEF & NOODLES
Yield: 6 servings (1 cup per serving)
Calories: 283 (18% fat); Total Fat: 5g; Cholesterol: 65mg; Carbohydrate: 26g; Dietary Fiber: 1g; Protein 30g; Sodium: 780mg; Diabetic Exchanges: 2 starch, 3 very lean meat

EASY AS 1, 2, 3 POTATOES
Yield: 6 servings (¹/₃ cup per serving)
Calories: 88 (0% fat); Total Fat: 0g; Cholesterol: 0mg; Carbohydrate: 21g; Dietary Fiber: 2g; Protein 2g; Sodium: 273mg; Diabetic Exchanges: 1¹/₂ starch

BUTTERED BEAN MEDLEY
Yield: 7 servings (¹/₂ cup per serving)
Calories: 35 (0% fat); Total Fat: 0g; Cholesterol: 0mg; Carbohydrate: 7g; Dietary Fiber: 2g; Protein 2g; Sodium: 677mg; Diabetic Exchanges: 1¹/₂ vegetable

GRANDMA'S BEEF & NOODLES

$2^3/4$ cups 99% fat-free beef broth
$1/2$ cup frozen chopped onion
4 cups No-Yolk noodles
2 (12-ounce) cans roast beef in gravy

EASY AS 1, 2, 3 POTATOES

4 cups frozen Southern-style hash browns
2 tablespoons imitation butter-flavored sprinkles
$1/4$ teaspoon seasoned salt
$1/8$ teaspoon ground black pepper

BUTTERED BEAN MEDLEY

2 ($14^1/4$-ounce) French-style green beans, undrained
1 ($14^1/2$-ounce) can cut waxed beans, undrained
1 tablespoon diced pimento
1 tablespoon dried minced onion
2 tablespoons imitation butter-flavored sprinkles

Instructions

25 MINUTES BEFORE DINNER, start the beef and noodles recipe. In a 12-inch nonstick saucepan, bring $2^3/_4$ c beef broth and $^1/_2$ c frozen chopped onion to a boil.

23 MINUTES BEFORE DINNER, start the potatoes. In a medium saucepan, bring 2 quarts of water for the potatoes to a boil.

22 MINUTES BEFORE DINNER, add 4 c No-Yolk noodles to the beef broth. Reduce the heat to medium. Cover and cook for 12 minutes.

13 MINUTES BEFORE DINNER, add 4 c frozen hash browns to the boiling water. Return to a boil.

10 MINUTES BEFORE DINNER, add 2 cans roast beef in gravy to the cooked pasta. Cover and reduce the heat to low. Cook for 5 more minutes to heat the beef.

8 MINUTES BEFORE DINNER, prepare the bean medley. In a medium microwavable bowl, combine 2 cans undrained French-style green beans, 1 can undrained cut waxed beans, 1 T diced pimento, and 1 T dried minced onion. Cover and cook for 3 minutes.

5 MINUTES BEFORE DINNER, stir the beans and cook, covered, for 2 minutes longer.

Turn off the burner under the beef and noodles and let stand, covered, on the warm burner until time for dinner.

4 MINUTES BEFORE DINNER, drain the hash browns and put them in a medium bowl. Add 2 T butter sprinkles, $^1/_4$ t seasoned salt, and $^1/_8$ t ground black pepper. Mix until well blended. Cover to keep warm.

2 MINUTES BEFORE DINNER, drain the Buttered Bean Medley. Put into a serving bowl and stir in 2 T of butter sprinkles. Place on the dinner table.

1 MINUTE BEFORE DINNER, put $^1/_3$ c of the potatoes on each dinner plate and top each serving with 1 c of Grandma's Beef and Noodles. Place each serving on the dinner table.

Supplies List

Timer
12-inch nonstick skillet
  with lid
Medium saucepan
Medium microwavable bowl
Medium bowl
Colander

Grocery List

PACKAGED
$2^3/_4$ cups 99% fat-free beef
  broth
1 (12-ounce) bag No-Yolk
  noodles
2 (12-ounce) cans roast beef
  in gravy
4 cups frozen Southern-style
  hash browns
2 ($14^1/_4$-ounce) can
  French-style green beans
1 ($14^1/_2$-ounce) can cut
  waxed beans
Diced pimento

FROZEN
$^1/_2$ cup frozen chopped onion

Pantry List

Seasoned salt
Ground black pepper
Dried minced onion
Imitation butter-flavored
  sprinkles

>>> Crabby Ham & Potato Au Gratin Chowder

Savvy Salad • Ham & Swiss Tomato Bread Crisps

Comfort food never had it this good! You'll find it hard to believe this out-of-this-world chowder is low fat, but I promise you it is! The Savvy Salad got its name from a savvy cook who used leftover green vegetables already in the refrigerator and didn't have to purchase other ingredients. Plus it's savvy to use green vegetables because they are a free caloric food and we can eat them to our heart's content, as long as we eat them with a fat-free, low-calorie salad dressing. If that's not savvy, I don't know what is.

CRABBY HAM & POTATO AU GRATIN CHOWDER

Yield: 6 servings (1 cup per serving)

Calories: 309 (9% fat); Total Fat: 3g; Cholesterol: 61mg; Carbohydrate: 39g; Dietary Fiber: 2g; Protein 32g; Sodium: 783mg; Diabetic Exchanges: 1¹/₂ starch, 1 skim milk, 3 very lean meat

SAVVY SALAD

Yield: 6 servings (1¹/₂ cups per serving)
(not including salad dressing)

Calories: 22 (0% fat); Total Fat: 0g; Cholesterol: 0mg; Carbohydrate: 4g; Dietary Fiber: 3g; Protein 2g; Sodium: 25mg; Diabetic Exchanges: 1 vegetable

HAM & SWISS TOMATO BREAD CRISPS

Yield: 6 servings (1 slice per serving)

Calories: 124 (24% fat); Total Fat: 3g; Cholesterol: 10mg; Carbohydrate: 16g; Dietary Fiber: 1g; Protein: 8g; Sodium: 298mg; Diabetic Exchanges: 1 starch, 1 lean meat

CRABBY HAM & POTATO AU GRATIN CHOWDER

3	tablespoons water	
3	cups frozen Potatoes O'Brien *	
1¹/₄	cup diced cooked ham	
2³/₄	cup fat-free half-and-half	
1	cup shredded fat-free cheddar cheese	

¹/₄ cup reduced-fat Parmesan-style grated topping
1 (16-ounce) package fat-free imitation crabmeat

SAVVY SALAD

9 cups chopped lettuce
2 cups fresh green vegetables, such as celery, broccoli, green bell pepper, green onion, green beans

³/₄ cups fat-free low-calorie salad dressing

HAM & SWISS TOMATO BREAD CRISPS

6 (¹/₃-inch-thick) slices French bread
3 slices reduced-fat natural Swiss cheese

6 tablespoons cooked ham, diced
12 grape tomatoes, sliced
2 tablespoons chopped green onion tops

Instructions

30 MINUTES BEFORE DINNER, start the chowder. In a 12-inch nonstick saucepan combine 3 T water, 3 c frozen Potatoes O'Brien, and 1 $1/4$ c diced cooked ham. Cook, covered, for 10 minutes over medium-high heat, stirring occasionally.

25 MINUTES BEFORE DINNER, while the potatoes are cooking, assemble the salad. Place in a large salad bowl 9 c lettuce and 2 c fresh green vegetables. Cover and store in the refrigerator until dinner is ready.

20 MINUTES BEFORE DINNER, reduce the heat under the potatoes to medium low and stir in $2^{3}/4$ c half-and-half, 1 c shredded cheddar cheese, and $1/4$ c Parmesan topping. Stir constantly until the cheese is melted and the chowder becomes thick.

14 MINUTES BEFORE DINNER, stir 1 package crabmeat into the chowder. Stir until well mixed. Turn off the heat to the chowder. Cover and let stand on the warm burner for 10 minutes. The chowder will thicken as it cools.

12 MINUTES BEFORE DINNER, preheat the oven to 350 degrees.

10 MINUTES BEFORE DINNER, prepare the bread crisps. Spray both sides of 6 slices of French bread generously with butter-flavored cooking spray and place on a baking sheet.

Cut 3 slices Swiss cheese into very thin pieces. Sprinkle over the bread slices. Spray the cheese with cooking spray. Top the bread slices with 6 T diced cooked ham, 12 sliced grape tomatoes, and 6 t chopped green onion tops.

6 MINUTES BEFORE DINNER, bake the bread crisps for 5 to 6 minutes, or until the bottom of the bread is crispy and golden brown.

3 MINUTES BEFORE DINNER, place the salad and your favorite fat-free low-calorie salad dressing on the dinner table.

2 MINUTES BEFORE DINNER, ladle 1 c chowder into 6 serving bowls and place on dinner table.

1 MINUTE BEFORE DINNER, put the bread crisps on a hot pad on the table.

*NOTE: Potatoes O'Brien are a type of hash brown with diced potatoes, onions, and peppers.

Supplies List

Timer
12-inch nonstick covered saucepan with lid
Baking sheet
Large salad bowl

Grocery List

PACKAGED

French bread
1 (8-ounce) bottle of your favorite low-calorie salad dressing

PRODUCE

2 cups fresh green vegetables, such as celery, broccoli, green bell pepper, green onion, fresh green beans
12 grape tomatoes
1 bunch green onions
9 cups chopped lettuce

FROZEN

3 cups frozen Potatoes O'Brien

MEAT/SEAFOOD

1 (16-ounce) package fat-free imitation crab
$1^{1}/4$ cup plus 6 tablespoons diced cooked ham

DAIRY

$2^{3}/4$ cup fat-free half-and-half
1 cup shredded fat-free cheddar cheese
3 slices reduced-fat Swiss cheese
$1/4$ cup reduced-fat Parmesan-style grated topping

Pantry List

Fat-free butter-flavored cooking spray

>>> Chipped Beef Gravy over Toast Points

Broccoli Slaw

I cannot believe how thick, rich, and creamy this hearty gravy is, and the best thing is that it is low in calories. Make sure you dissolve the cornstarch in the half-and-half before you turn on the heat to avoid lumps. The fabulous idea of including bacon in our broccoli slaw belongs to my helpful assistant, LuAnne Surgeson. This is the first time I have ever incorporated bacon into my homemade slaw dressing and I love the taste. I think you will, too.

CHIPPED BEEF GRAVY OVER TOAST POINTS
Yield: 6 servings (1 cup gravy and 1½ slices toast per serving)
Calories: 308 (12% fat); Total Fat: 4g; Cholesterol: 40mg; Carbohydrate: 51g; Dietary Fiber: 6g; Protein 25g; Sodium: 1410mg; Diabetic Exchanges: 2½ starch, 1 skim milk, 1½ very lean meat

BROCCOLI SLAW
Yield: 6 servings (½ cup per serving)
Calories: 65 (44% fat); Total Fat: 3g; Cholesterol: 7mg; Carbohydrate: 7g; Dietary Fiber: 2g; Protein 2g; Sodium: 270mg; Diabetic Exchanges: 1½ vegetable, ½ fat

CHIPPED BEEF GRAVY OVER TOAST POINTS

½	cup cornstarch	2	(6-ounce) packages chipped beef
3½	cups fat-free half-and-half, chilled	¼	teaspoon ground black pepper
2	tablespoons imitation butter-flavored sprinkles	10	slices light bread, toasted
1	(8½-ounce) can sweet peas, undrained		

BROCCOLI SLAW

⅓	cup fat-free mayonnaise	1	tablespoon 30%-less-fat real bacon pieces
⅓	cup light Miracle Whip	1	(12-ounce) bag broccoli coleslaw
1	tablespoon apple cider vinegar		
1	tablespoon Splenda granular		

Instructions

30 MINUTES BEFORE DINNER, prepare the slaw. In a medium mixing bowl, combine $^1/_3$ c mayonnaise, $^1/_3$ c Miracle Whip, 1 T apple cider vinegar, 1 T Splenda granular, and 1 T bacon pieces; stir until well mixed. (There may be a few lumps in the dressing that will break down when the broccoli coleslaw is added.)

Stir in 1 bag broccoli coleslaw until the coleslaw is completely coated with dressing. Cover and keep chilled in the refrigerator until dinner is ready.

25 MINUTES BEFORE DINNER, start the gravy. In a 12-inch nonstick saucepan, whisk $^1/_2$ c cornstarch into $3^1/_2$ c half-and-half until dissolved. Once the cornstarch is completely dissolved, place the saucepan over medium heat. Whisk in 2 T butter sprinkles. Continue stirring until the gravy thickens, about 5 to 10 minutes.

15 MINUTES BEFORE DINNER, pour the liquid from the can of peas into the gravy and continue stirring frequently.

Cut 2 packages chipped beef into bite-size pieces by stacking the pieces so you have to make fewer cuts.

10 MINUTES BEFORE DINNER, stir the chipped beef and $^1/_4$ t ground black pepper into the gravy. Reduce the heat to low. Cover and stir occasionally.

8 MINUTES BEFORE DINNER, start toasting the bread.

5 MINUTES BEFORE DINNER, slice each piece of toast diagonally into quarters, to make triangular-shaped toast points. Place 6 toast points on each dinner plate.

1 MINUTE BEFORE DINNER, place the slaw on the dinner table. Spoon 1 c chipped beef gravy over the 6 toast points. Place each serving on the dinner table.

NOTE: *I used Light Five Grain Fiber for Life by Aunt Millie's, which has 80 calories and 5 grams of fiber for 2 slices. To save time, toast the bread in batches throughout the preparation of the menu so that all ten pieces are ready when you need them.*

Supplies List

Timer
Medium mixing bowl
Toaster oven
12-inch nonstick pan with lid

Grocery List

PACKAGED
1 (8-$^1/_2$-ounce) can sweet peas
Light bread
Splenda granular
30%-less-fat real bacon pieces

PRODUCE
1 (12-ounce) bag broccoli coleslaw

MEAT
2 (6-ounce) packages chipped beef

DAIRY
1 pint fat-free half-and-half

Pantry List

Apple cider vinegar
Ground black pepper
Cornstarch
Fat-free mayonnaise
Imitation butter-flavored sprinkles
Light Miracle Whip

>>> Smoked Sausage & Sauerkraut

Potato Biscuits • Spiced Peaches & Cream Salad

This menu fulfills the requirements of hearty appetites such as those of lumberjacks and tradesmen, but is also light enough for those watching their waistline. If this menu had its own commercial it would say, "Hearty enough for a man, but low enough in calories for a woman." The flavors of each recipe in this menu complement and enhance each other. When eaten together, the recipes are better than when eaten alone, even though each of these is good individually as well!

SMOKED SAUSAGE & SAUERKRAUT

Yield: 6 servings (1 cup per serving)

Calories: 122 (14% fat); Total Fat: 2g; Cholesterol: 23mg; Carbohydrate: 16g; Dietary Fiber: 6g; Protein 8g; Sodium: 1670mg; Diabetic Exchanges: $^1/_2$ starch, $1^1/_2$ vegetable, 1 very lean meat

1	(14-ounce) package lean smoked sausage
1	(32-ounce) jar sauerkraut
1	medium Gala apple
$^1/_2$	cup frozen chopped onion
2	teaspoons Splenda granular

CHUNKY POTATO BISCUITS

Yield: 6 servings (2 biscuits per serving)

Calories: 119 (4% fat); Total Fat: 1g; Cholesterol: 0mg; Carbohydrate: 25g; Dietary Fiber: 4g; Protein 5g; Sodium: 280mg; Diabetic Exchanges: $1^1/_2$ starch

1	(15 ounce) can potatoes
2	egg whites
1	cup whole wheat flour
3	tablespoons Splenda granular
$^1/_2$	teaspoon baking soda

SPICED PEACHES & CREAM SALAD

Yield: 6 servings ($^1/_2$ cup per serving)

Calories: 121 (6% fat); Total Fat: 1g; Cholesterol: 0mg; Carbohydrate: 27g; Dietary Fiber: 1g; Protein 0g; Sodium: 17mg; Diabetic Exchanges: 2 fruit

$^1/_2$	cup fat-free dessert whipped topping, thawed
$^1/_4$	teaspoon vanilla extract
$^1/_4$	teaspoon ground allspice
2	tablespoons Splenda Brown Sugar Blend
3	(15-ounce) cans peach slices in juice, chilled, drained
1	tablespoon finely chopped walnuts

Instructions

30 MINUTES BEFORE DINNER, preheat the oven to 350 degrees.
Prepare the biscuits. Drain the liquid from 1 can potatoes, reserving $^1/_4$ c.

27 MINUTES BEFORE DINNER, in a medium bowl, mash the potatoes and stir in the reserved $^1/_4$ c potato liquid. Stir 2 egg whites, 1 c flour, 3 T Splenda granular, and $^1/_2$ t baking soda into the mashed potatoes. Spray a nonstick baking sheet with nonfat cooking spray. Drop the biscuit dough by rounded tablespoonfuls onto the prepared baking sheet. Set aside.

20 MINUTES BEFORE DINNER, start the sausage. Slice 1 package lean smoked sausage into $^1/_4$-inch slices. Drain 1 jar sauerkraut in a colander and rinse under cold running water in the sink for 1 minute. Press the sauerkraut between your hands to squeeze out as much of the water as possible. Set aside.
Slice 1 medium apple into thin slices, less than a $^1/_4$-inch thick. In a 12-inch nonstick saucepan over medium heat cook $^1/_2$ c onion, the sliced apple, and the smoked sausage until tender, about 3 minutes. Stir the squeeze-dried sauerkraut into the apples and onion. Cover and cook for 3 minutes. Reduce the heat to medium low and cook, covered, for 16 minutes.

16 MINUTES BEFORE DINNER, bake the biscuits in the preheated oven for 14 minutes, or until the bottoms are golden brown and a toothpick comes out clean when inserted in the center of the biscuits.

8 MINUTES BEFORE DINNER, make the salad. In a medium bowl, combine $^1/_2$ c whipped topping, $^1/_4$ t vanilla extract, $^1/_4$ t ground allspice, and 2 T Splenda Brown Sugar Blend. Gently stir 3 cans drained chilled peach slices into the cream mixture. Sprinkle the top of the salad with 1 T finely chopped walnuts. Place the Spiced Peaches & Cream Salad on the dinner table.

2 MINUTES BEFORE DINNER, remove the biscuits from the oven and let cool on the baking sheet for 2 minutes.

1 MINUTE BEFORE DINNER, place the sausage & sauerkraut on a hot pad on the dinner table. Put the biscuits in a basket and put on the dinner table.

NOTE: These unique biscuits taste best after they have cooled 2 to 3 minutes on the baking sheet with a little butter served on the side. I do not recommend baking them ahead of time, reheating them later, or eating them cold.

Supplies List

Timer
Nonstick baking sheet
12-inch nonstick saucepan
with lid
2 medium bowls
Basket

Grocery List

PACKAGED

1 (15-ounce) can potatoes
3 (15-ounce) cans peach
slices in juice
1 (32-ounce) jar sauerkraut

PRODUCE

1 medium Gala apple

FROZEN

Fat-free dessert whipped
topping
$^1/_2$ cup frozen chopped onion

MEAT

1 (14-ounce) package lean
smoked sausage

Pantry List

Whole wheat flour
Ground allspice
Finely chopped walnuts
Vanilla extract
Baking soda
Eggs
Splenda granular
Splenda Brown Sugar Blend

>>> Creamed Chicken

Country Green Beans • Biscuits

This southern home-style favorite is every bit as good as Grandma use to make, but our easy version takes only a fraction of the time and has a lot less calories, too (even though it doesn't tastes like it).

CREAMED CHICKEN
Yield: 6 (³/₄-cup) servings

Calories: 219 (4% fat); Total Fat: 1g; Cholesterol: 26mg; Carbohydrate: 33g; Dietary Fiber: 1g; Protein 22g; Sodium: 777mg; Diabetic Exchanges: 1 starch, 1 skim milk, 1 vegetable, 1¹/₂ very lean meat

COUNTRY GREEN BEANS
Yield: 7 (¹/₂-cup) servings

Calories: 29 (13% fat); Total Fat: 0g; Cholesterol: 3mg; Carbohydrate: 4g; Dietary Fiber: 2g; Protein 2g; Sodium: 399mg; Diabetic Exchanges: 1 vegetable

CREAMED CHICKEN

3¹/₂ cups fat-free half-and-half

2¹/₂ tablespoons imitation butter-flavored sprinkles

¹/₂ cup cornstarch

1 (13-ounce) can chicken breast, drained

1 (8¹/₂-ounce) can sweet peas and carrots, drained

¹/₄ teaspoon ground black pepper

¹/₄ teaspoon seasoned salt

COUNTRY GREEN BEANS

2 tablespoons 30%-less-fat bacon pieces

¹/₂ cup frozen chopped onion

2 (14-ounce) cans whole green beans, drained

1 teaspoon imitation butter-flavored sprinkles

1¹/₂ teaspoons pimento

Nonfat cooking spray

Instructions

20 MINUTES BEFORE DINNER, start the creamed chicken. In a 12-inch non-stick saucepan over medium heat, combine $3^1/2$ c half-and-half, $2^1/2$ T butter sprinkles, and $^1/2$ c cornstarch. Be sure the cornstarch is completely dissolved before turning on the heat. Bring to a low boil for 5 minutes, stirring continuously while the sauce thickens.

13 MINUTES BEFORE DINNER, reduce the heat to low. Stir in 1 can drained chicken breast, 1 can drained sweet peas and carrots, $^1/4$ t ground black pepper, and $^1/4$ t seasoned salt until well mixed.

12 MINUTES BEFORE DINNER, preheat the oven to 450 degrees.

10 MINUTES BEFORE DINNER, prepare the biscuits. Place the biscuits on a baking sheet that has been coated with nonfat cooking spray. Bake for 8 minutes.

7 MINUTES BEFORE DINNER, make the green beans. Coat a 12-inch nonstick skillet with cooking spray. Add 2 T bacon pieces and $^1/2$ c frozen chopped onion. Sauté over medium heat for 2 minutes, or until the onion becomes tender.

5 MINUTES BEFORE DINNER, stir 2 cans drained green beans, 1 t butter sprinkles, and $1^1/2$ t pimento into the onion mixture. Reduce the heat to low and cook until the green beans are heated through, about 3 minutes.

2 MINUTES BEFORE DINNER, remove the green beans from pan and put in a medium bowl. Place on the dinner table.

1 MINUTE BEFORE DINNER, remove the biscuits from oven. Put on a plate and place on the dinner table. Place the creamed chicken on the dinner table.

*****NOTE:** *Pillsbury brand of biscuits has only 150 calories and less than 1 gram of fat per serving.*

Supplies List

Timer
12-inch nonstick saucepan with lid
12-inch nonstick skillet
Baking sheet
Medium bowl

Grocery List

PACKAGED

1 ($8^1/2$-ounce) can sweet peas and carrots
1 (13-ounce) can chicken breast
2 (14-ounce) can whole green beans
30%-less-fat bacon pieces
Pimento

FROZEN

$^1/2$ cup frozen chopped onions

DAIRY

1 pint fat-free half-and-half
Can of refrigerated buttermilk biscuits*

Pantry List

Fat-free cooking spray
Cornstarch
Ground black pepper
Seasoned salt
Imitation butter-flavored sprinkles

>>> Frittata Olé with Chili

Green Chili Salsa Salad • Fat-Free Sour Cream, Lettuce, and Chopped Onion

The combination of all the flavors in this menu will make your mouth happy.

FRITTATA OLÉ WITH CHILI
Yield: 6 servings
($3^1/_2$ -inch-wedge per serving)
Calories: 178 (9% fat); Total Fat: 2g;
Cholesterol: 10mg; Carbohydrate: 20g;
Dietary Fiber: 3g; Protein 19g;
Sodium: 706mg; Diabetic Exchanges:
$1^1/_2$ starch, 2 very lean meat

GREEN CHILI SALSA SALAD
Yield: 6 servings
($1^1/_2$ cup per serving)
Calories: 47 (0% fat); Total Fat: 0g;
Cholesterol: 3mg; Carbohydrate: 8g;
Dietary Fiber: 2g; Protein 4g; Sodium:
354mg; Diabetic Exchanges:
$1^1/_2$ vegetable

FRITTATA OLÉ WITH CHILI

6 corn tortillas
1 (16-ounce) carton pasteurized egg substitute
1 (15-ounce) can 99% fat-free chili with beans
1 cup shredded fat-free cheddar cheese
Nonfat cooking spray

GREEN CHILI SALSA SALAD

1 (14-$1/_2$-ounce) can diced tomatoes with green chilies, chilled and drained
$1/_3$ cup fat-free sour cream
$1/_3$ cup shredded fat-free cheddar cheese
1 tablespoon Splenda granular
1 (16-ounce) bag romaine lettuce, torn into pieces

Instructions

30 MINUTES BEFORE DINNER, start to make the salad. Drain 1 can diced tomatoes.

In a small bowl, add $^1/_3$ c sour cream, $^1/_3$ c shredded cheddar cheese, and 1 T Splenda granular, mixing until well blended. Add the canned tomatoes and mix together. Cover and place in the refrigerator until time for dinner.

25 MINUTES BEFORE DINNER, place 1 bag romaine lettuce in a large salad bowl. Cover and place in the refrigerator until time for dinner.

20 MINUTES BEFORE DINNER, coat a nonstick 12-inch skillet with cooking spray and preheat over medium heat.

Make the Frittata Olé. Cut or tear 6 corn tortillas in 1-inch pieces. Add the corn tortillas pieces to the skillet and cook, turning often, until the tortillas are brown and hot, about 3 minutes.

17 MINUTES BEFORE DINNER, add 1 carton egg substitute to the tortillas. Cook like an omelet, lifting the tortilla pieces so the egg substitute can run under them.

7 MINUTES BEFORE DINNER, place 1 can chili in a small microwavable bowl and heat in the microwave until hot, about 3 minutes.

4 MINUTES BEFORE DINNER, turn off the heat to the stove and pour the hot chili over the frittata.

Sprinkle 1 c shredded cheddar cheese over the top of the chili. Spray the cheese with nonfat cooking spray. Cover and let stand on the hot burner to melt the cheese.

2 MINUTES BEFORE DINNER, pour the salad dressing into the large salad bowl and toss until the romaine lettuce is well coated. Place on the dinner table.

1 MINUTE BEFORE DINNER, cut the Frittata Olé into 6 pie-shaped pieces, place on a platter, and set on the dinner table.

NOTE: This Frittata Olé is good served with nonfat sour cream, lettuce, and chopped onion.

Supplies List

Timer
Small microwavable bowl
Small bowl
Large salad bowl
Nonstick 12-inch skillet

Grocery List

PACKAGED

1 (15-ounce) can 99% fat-free chili with beans
1 (14½-ounce) can diced tomatoes with green chilies
6 corn tortillas
Splenda granular

PRODUCE

1 (16-ounce) bag romaine lettuce

DAIRY

1 (16-ounce) carton pasteurized egg substitute
1⅓ cup shredded fat-free cheddar cheese
⅓ cup fat-free sour cream

Pantry List

Nonfat cooking spray

>>> Home on the Range Chicken Tenders

Corny Barbequed Bean Salad • Buckshot Coleslaw

> This menu is a fun way to get children to eat things they normally wouldn't. Children will enjoy eating like cowboys and cowgirls for this one, using pie tins for plates and red bandana handkerchiefs for napkins. Use a red and white gingham tablecloth for extra flair.

HOME ON THE RANGE CHICKEN TENDERS

Yield: 6 servings
(4 ounces per serving)
Calories: 182 (13% fat); Total Fat: 3g; Cholesterol: 66mg; Carbohydrate: 12g; Dietary Fiber: 1g; Protein 28g; Sodium: 234mg; Diabetic Exchanges: 1 starch, 3 very lean meat

CORNY BARBEQUED BEAN SALAD

Yield: 6 servings ($^1/_2$ cup per serving)
Calories: 162 (7% fat); Total Fat: 1 g; Cholesterol: 0mg; Carbohydrate: 32g; Dietary Fiber: 5g; Protein 6g; Sodium: 486mg; Diabetic Exchanges: 2 starch

BUCKSHOT COLESLAW

Yield: 8 servings ($^2/_3$ cup per serving)
Calories: 57 (37% fat); Total Fat: 2g; Cholesterol: 4mg; Carbohydrate: 8g; Dietary Fiber: 2g; Protein 1g; Sodium: 262mg; Diabetic Exchanges: $^1/_2$ other carbohydrate, $^1/_2$ fat

HOME ON THE RANGE CHICKEN TENDERS

$^1/_2$ cup reduced-fat baking mix
$^1/_2$ cup oat bran
2   tablespoons chipotle seasoning
$^1/_2$ teaspoon rotisserie chicken seasoning
$1^1/_2$ pounds chicken tenders (about 13 tenders)

CORNY BARBEQUED BEAN SALAD

1   ($15^1/_4$-ounce) can whole kernel sweet corn, chilled and drained*
1   ($15^1/_2$-ounce) can dark red kidney beans, chilled and drained*
$^1/_3$ cup honey barbeque sauce, chilled*
1   tablespoon sweet pickle relish

BUCKSHOT COLESLAW

$^3/_4$ cup fat-free mayonnaise
$^1/_4$ cup light Miracle Whip
2   tablespoons red wine vinegar
$1^1/_2$ teaspoons poppy seeds
$^1/_4$ teaspoon pepper
3   tablespoons Splenda granular
1   (16-ounce) bag shredded coleslaw

Instructions

30 MINUTES BEFORE DINNER, make the salad. In a medium bowl, combine 1 can chilled and drained whole kernel sweet corn, 1 can chilled and drained dark red kidney beans, $^1/_3$ c chilled honey barbeque sauce, and 1 T sweet pickle relish until well mixed. Cover and refrigerate until dinner is ready to be served.

25 MINUTES BEFORE DINNER, prepare the coleslaw. In a medium bowl, mix together $^3/_4$ c mayonnaise, $^1/_4$ c Miracle Whip, 2 T red wine vinegar, $1^1/_2$ t poppy seeds, $^1/_4$ t pepper, and 3 T Splenda granular until well blended.

Add 1 bag shredded coleslaw to the dressing and mix until the coleslaw is well coated. Cover and put in the refrigerator to chill.

15 MINUTES BEFORE DINNER, heavily coat a 12-inch nonstick skillet with cooking spray; set aside.

Make the chicken tenders. In a 1-gallon zip-top bag, combine the $^1/_2$ c baking mix, $^1/_2$ c oat bran, 2 T chipotle seasoning, and $^1/_2$ t rotisserie chicken seasoning. Seal the bag tightly and shake to mix the ingredients. Add the chicken tenders to the zip-top bag and toss to coat. Once the chicken tenders are covered, spray each side of the chicken tenders with nonfat cooking spray and place in the prepared skillet. Cook over medium-high heat for 3 to 4 minutes. Turn over the tenders and continue cooking an additional 3 to 4 minutes, or until chicken is cooked through.

1 MINUTE BEFORE DINNER, place the chicken tenders on a serving plate and place on the dinner table. Place the bean salad and the coleslaw on the table.

*NOTE: Save time by putting these ingredients in the refrigerator as soon as you get home from the grocery store so they are chilled when you are ready to assemble this recipe.

Supplies List

Timer
2 medium bowls
12-inch nonstick skillet
1-gallon zip-top bag
Serving plate

Grocery List

PACKAGED

1 ($15^1/_4$-ounce) can whole kernel sweet corn
1 ($15^1/_2$-ounce) can dark red kidney beans
Oat bran
Honey barbeque sauce
1 (16-ounce) bag shredded coleslaw
Chipotle seasoning

POULTRY

$1^1/_2$ pounds chicken tenders

Pantry List

Nonfat cooking spray
Reduced-fat baking mix
Red wine vinegar
Poppy seeds
Ground black pepper
Splenda granular
Sweet pickle relish
Fat-free mayonnaise
Light Miracle Whip
Rotisserie chicken seasoning

>>> Quicker Than Granny's Home-Style Chicken

Country Parmesan Potatoes • Garlic Green Beans

This is a quick and easy way to make a homemade meal like your grandma use to make. All the flavor without all the fuss and hard work. Full credit goes to LuAnne Surgeson of Delta, Ohio, for this menu. Thank you very much, Luanne. It is a yummy one!

QUICKER THAN GRANNY'S
HOME-STYLE CHICKEN
Yield: 6 servings
(4 ounces per serving)

Calories: 170 (9% fat); Total Fat: 2g; Cholesterol: 66mg; Carbohydrate: 9g; Dietary Fiber: 0g; Protein 28g; Sodium: 567mg; Diabetic Exchanges: 1/2 starch, 3 very lean meat

COUNTRY PARMESAN POTATOES
Yield: 6 servings (1/2 cup per serving)

Calories: 109 (0% fat); Total Fat: 0g; Cholesterol: 1mg; Carbohydrate: 25g; Dietary Fiber: 3g; Protein 3g; Sodium: 244mg; Diabetic Exchanges: 1 1/2 starch

GARLIC GREEN BEANS
Yield: 6 servings (5 cups per serving)

Calories: 54 (0% fat); Total Fat: 0g; Cholesterol: 0mg; Carbohydrate: 11g; Dietary Fiber: 4g; Protein 2g; Sodium: 353mg; Diabetic Exchanges: 2 vegetable

QUICKER THAN GRANNY'S HOME-STYLE CHICKEN

- 1/2 cup Italian-style bread crumbs
- 2 tablespoons ranch salad dressing mix
- 6 (4-ounce) boneless skinless chicken breasts

COUNTRY PARMESAN POTATOES

- 4 cups O'Brien frozen potatoes*
- 1/2 cup frozen chopped onion
- 2 teaspoons ranch salad dressing mix
- 2 teaspoons reduced-fat Parmesan-style grated topping
- 3 teaspoons imitation butter-flavored sprinkles
- 1/4 teaspoon ground black pepper

GARLIC GREEN BEANS

- 2 (16-ounce) bags frozen French-style green beans
- 2 tablespoons imitation butter-flavored sprinkles
- 2 teaspoons garlic powder

Instructions

30 MINUTES BEFORE DINNER, start the potatoes by bringing 2 quarts water in a medium saucepan to a boil over high heat.

27 MINUTES BEFORE DINNER, prepare the chicken. While the water is coming to a boil, in a shallow dish combine $^1/_2$ c bread crumbs and 2 T ranch salad dressing mix until well mixed.

24 MINUTES BEFORE DINNER, heavily coat a 12-inch nonstick skillet with cooking spray. Put over medium heat.

Generously coat both sides of each boneless skinless chicken breast with cooking spray. Dredge each chicken breast, one at a time, in the bread crumb mixture, coating each side well.

21 MINUTES BEFORE DINNER, place the chicken breasts in the preheated 12-inch skillet. Cook for 5 minutes.

Once the water for the potatoes is boiling add 4 c frozen potatoes and $^1/_2$ c frozen onion. Cook for 12 minutes.

20 MINUTES BEFORE DINNER, make the green beans. Cut the tops off of the 2 bags frozen French-style green beans and cook on high in the microwave for 10 minutes.

16 MINUTES BEFORE DINNER, turn over the chicken breasts and cook for another 5 minutes. Reduce heat to low, cover, and cook for 10 minutes.

10 MINUTES BEFORE DINNER, remove the green beans from the microwave and place in a large microwave-safe bowl. Cover and cook 6 minutes.

8 MINUTES BEFORE DINNER, drain the potatoes. Place the potatoes in a medium bowl. Add 2 t ranch salad dressing mix, 2 t Parmesan topping, 3 t butter sprinkles, and $^1/_4$ t ground black pepper until well mixed. Cover to keep warm. Place the potatoes on the dinner table.

3 MINUTES BEFORE DINNER, remove the green beans from the microwave and mix in 2 T butter sprinkles and 2 t garlic powder. Stir until well mixed. Place the beans on the dinner table.

1 MINUTE BEFORE DINNER, place the chicken on a serving platter and place on the dinner table.

Supplies List

Timer
Medium saucepan
2 Medium bowls
12-inch nonstick skillet
    with lid
Large microwavable bowl
Serving Platter
Colander

Grocery List

FROZEN

4 cups frozen O'Brien
    Potatoes
$^1/_2$ cup frozen chopped onion
2 (16-ounce) bags frozen
    French-style green beans

POULTRY

6 (4-ounce) boneless skinless
    chicken breasts

DAIRY

Reduced-fat Parmesan-style
    grated topping

Pantry List

Nonfat butter flavored
    cooking spray
Italian-style bread crumbs
Imitation butter-flavored
    sprinkles
Ground black pepper
Garlic powder
Ranch salad dressing mix

>>> Hot Ham & Swiss Chicken Sandwiches

Really Dilly Tossed Salad • Baby Carrot Sticks

> I combined ordinary ingredients to create an extraordinary sandwich and salad that your family will most likely ask for again and again. Lucky for us, this menu is simple to make.

HOT HAM & SWISS CHICKEN SANDWICHES
Yield: 6 sandwiches
(1 sandwich per serving)
Calories: 177 (28% fat); Total Fat: 6g; Cholesterol: 15mg; Carbohydrate: 23g; Dietary Fiber: 3g; Protein 11g; Sodium: 408mg; Diabetic Exchanges: 1½ starch, 1 lean meat

REALLY DILLY TOSSED SALAD
Yield: 6 servings
(1½ cup per serving)
Calories: 31 (0% fat); Total Fat: 0g; Cholesterol: 3mg; Carbohydrate: 5g; Dietary Fiber: 1g; Protein 3g; Sodium: 106mg; Diabetic Exchanges: 1 vegetable

HOT HAM & SWISS CHICKEN SANDWICHES

1	tablespoon light butter
4	ounces sliced fresh mushrooms
3	(8-ounce) chicken breasts, halved
3	slices deli-thin reduced-fat Swiss cheese, cut in half
2	tablespoons water
3	slices thin-sliced deli ham
6	rye hamburger buns or hamburger-size rye rolls, cut in half horizontally

Optional garnishes: tomato slices, honey mustard, and lettuce

REALLY DILLY TOSSED SALAD

¼	cup dill pickle juice, chilled
¼	dill pickle spear, cut into tiny pieces
¼	teaspoon dried dill weed
¼	cup fat-free sour cream
2	teaspoons Splenda granular
¼	cup fat-free ricotta cheese
1	large head iceberg lettuce

Instructions

30 MINUTES BEFORE DINNER, prepare the salad. In a medium bowl, combine ¼ c dill pickle juice, chopped dill pickle spear, ¼ t dried dill weed, ¼ c sour cream, 2 t Splenda granular, and ¼ c ricotta cheese. Cover and refrigerate until dinner is almost ready.

Cut 1 large head iceberg lettuce into bite-size pieces to make about 9 c. Place the lettuce in a large bowl. Cover and refrigerate.

25 MINUTES BEFORE DINNER, start the sandwiches. Cut the 3 chicken breasts in half horizontally to make 6 servings; set aside. In a 12-inch nonstick skillet, sauté 1 T butter and 4 ounces sliced mushrooms over medium heat for 2 minutes, or until the mushrooms are tender. Place the mushrooms in a small bowl. Cover and set aside. In the same 12-inch nonstick skillet over high heat, cook the chicken breast halves, covered, for 3 to 4 minutes, or until golden brown. Turn over the chicken. Cover and continue cooking on high another 3 to 4 minutes.

12 MINUTES BEFORE DINNER, add 2 T water to the skillet. Place $^1/_2$ cheese slice on each chicken breast. Spoon the cooked mushrooms on top of each slice of cheese. Reduce the heat to medium. Cover and cook 2 minutes longer, or until the chicken is completely white on the inside.

10 MINUTES BEFORE DINNER, remove the chicken from the pan. Cover to keep warm and set aside. Preheat the oven to 450 degrees or broil.

8 MINUTES BEFORE DINNER, coat the bottom halves of 6 rye hamburger buns with butter-flavored nonfat cooking spray and place on a baking sheet. Broil for 2 to 4 minutes, or until toasted.
Cook 3 slices deli ham in the chicken drippings for 1 to 2 minutes, just long enough to heat the ham. Remove the toasted bun halves from the oven and set aside.

4 MINUTES BEFORE DINNER, coat the top halves of the buns with cooking spray and place on a baking sheet. Broil for 2 to 4 minutes, or until toasted.
While top halves of the buns are toasting, place 1 slice of ham on each bottom half of the buns. Top with 1 smothered chicken breast. Place the toasted top halves of the buns on top of the chicken breasts. Put each sandwich on a plate and place on dinner table.

2 MINUTES BEFORE DINNER, place fresh baby carrots in a serving bowl and put on the dinner table.

1 MINUTE BEFORE DINNER, toss the salad dressing with the iceberg lettuce until well mixed. Place the salad on dinner table.

Supplies List
Timer
Serving bowl
Medium bowl
Large bowl
12-inch nonstick skillet
    with lid
Baking sheet

Grocery List
PACKAGED
6 rye hamburger buns or
    hamburger-size rye rolls
Dill pickle spears

PRODUCE
4 ounces fresh sliced mush-
    rooms
1 large head iceberg lettuce
1½ lbs baby carrots

MEAT
3 slices thin-sliced deli ham
3 (8-ounce) chicken breasts

DAIRY
Light butter
3 slices reduced-fat deli-thin
    Swiss cheese
¼ cup fat-free sour cream
¾ cup fat-free ricotta cheese

Pantry List
Dried dill weed
Splenda granular
Dill pickle juice
Butter-flavored cooking spray

>>> Home-Style Pork Chops with Apple Dressing

Savory Peach Chutney Gravy ● Gala Apple Tossed Salad

You are gong to be so blessed by the wonderful flavor combination of this menu! It received huge reviews from everyone. The guys especially liked it, which surprised me because of the fruit being in it. One guy ate three servings and asked if there was more!

HOME-STYLE PORK CHOPS WITH APPLE DRESSING

Yield: 6 servings (4 ounces pork chops & $^2/_3$ cup dressing per serving)

Calories: 293 (30% fat); Total Fat: 10g; Cholesterol: 63mg; Carbohydrate: 14g; Dietary Fiber: 4g; Protein 37g; Sodium: 849mg; Diabetic Exchanges: 1 starch, $4^1/_2$ lean meat

SAVORY PEACH CHUTNEY GRAVY

Yield: 6 servings ($^1/_4$ cup per serving)

Calories: 59 (42% fat); Total Fat: 3g; Cholesterol: 10mg; Carbohydrate: 8g; Dietary Fiber: 0g; Protein 1g; Sodium: 563mg; Diabetic Exchanges: $^1/_2$ fruit, $^1/_2$ fat

GALA APPLE TOSSED SALAD

Yield: 6 ($1^1/_2$ -cup) servings

Calories: 75 (14% fat); Total Fat: 1g; Cholesterol: 0mg; Carbohydrate: 12g; Dietary Fiber: 1g; Protein 1g; Sodium: 259mg; Diabetic Exchanges: 1 vegetable, $^1/_2$ other carbohydrate

HOME-STYLE PORK CHOPS WITH APPLE DRESSING

$^1/_2$	cup water
3	slices light rye bread with seeds
$^1/_2$	Gala apple, finely chopped ($^3/_4$ cup)
$^1/_3$	cup frozen chopped onion
1	(12-ounce) package vegetarian sausage-style crumbles
$^1/_8$	teaspoon ground sage
6	(4-ounce) boneless pork loin chops, trimmed*

SAVORY PEACH CHUTNEY GRAVY

1	(12-ounce) jar pork gravy
1	($8^1/_4$ -ounce) can light peaches, drained
$^1/_4$	teaspoon pumpkin pie spice
1	teaspoon seasoned salt

GALA APPLE TOSSED SALAD

$^3/_4$	cup fat-free Miracle Whip
1	tablespoon apple cider vinegar
$1^1/_2$	tablespoons Splenda Brown Sugar Blend
$^1/_2$	Gala apple, finely chopped ($^3/_4$ cup)
$^1/_2$	teaspoon Splenda granular
1	head iceberg lettuce
1	tablespoon walnuts, finely chopped

Instructions

30 MINUTES BEFORE DINNER, make the salad. In a large salad bowl combine $^3/_4$ c Miracle Whip, 1 T apple cider vinegar, $1^1/_2$ T Splenda Brown Sugar Blend, $^3/_4$ cup chopped Gala apple, and $^1/_2$ t Splenda granular until well mixed.

Remove and discard the core of the iceberg lettuce. Cut into bite-size pieces to make about 9 c and place on top of the salad dressing in the large bowl. Do not toss. Cover and refrigerate until time for dinner.

20 MINUTES BEFORE DINNER, make the apple dressing. In a medium saucepan over high heat, bring $^1/_2$ c water to a boil.

Toast 3 pieces light rye bread. Cut the toasted rye bread into small bite-size pieces; set aside.

17 MINUTES BEFORE DINNER, add to the boiling water $^3/_4$ cup chopped apple, $^1/_3$ c frozen chopped onion, 1 package vegetarian sausage-flavored crumbles, and $^1/_8$ t ground sage. Return to a boil. Add the bite-size pieces of light rye bread to the sausage. Turn off the heat and cover. Let stand on the hot burner for 10 minutes.

16 MINUTES BEFORE DINNER, coat a 12-inch nonstick skillet with cooking spray. Over high heat, cook the 6 pork chops for about 3 minutes. Turn the pork and cook for another 3 minutes, or until done. The meat will be fully cooked when it is cut at the thickest part and it is completely white.

6 MINUTES BEFORE DINNER, remove the pork from the pan and place on a plate. Cover with foil and a dish towel to keep warm.

Add 2 T water to the pork drippings. Over low heat, using a spatula, loosen the drippings from the pan. Stir in 1 jar pork gravy, 1 can drained light peaches, $^1/_4$ t pumpkin pie spice, and 1 t seasoned salt until well mixed. Continue cooking for 2 to 3 minutes, or until the gravy comes to a low boil.

4 MINUTES BEFORE DINNER, toss the salad until the lettuce is well coated. Place on the dinner table.

3 MINUTES BEFORE DINNER, on each dinner plate spoon $^2/_3$ c of the apple dressing. Place 1 pork chop at an angle over half the dressing. Drizzle $^1/_4$ c gravy over the pork chop and dressing. Place the plates on the dinner table.

NOTE: To trim pork chops, cut away the visible fat on the outside of the chop.

Supplies List

Timer
Large salad bowl
Medium saucepan with lid
12-inch nonstick skillet

Grocery List

PACKAGED
Light Rye bread with seeds
1 (12-ounce) jar pork gravy
1 (8$^1/_4$-ounce) can light peaches

PRODUCE
1 Gala apple
1 head iceberg lettuce

FROZEN
$^1/_3$ cup frozen chopped onion
1 (12-ounce) package vegetarian sausage-style crumbles

MEAT
6 (4-ounce) boneless pork loin chops

Pantry List

Seasoned salt
Ground sage
Apple cider vinegar
Walnuts
Splenda Brown Sugar Blend
Splenda granular
Fat-free Miracle Whip
Pumpkin pie spice

>>> Rotisserie Chicken Tenders

Cheddar & Chive Buttermilk Biscuits • Creamy Vegetable Medley

If you like the seasoning of rotisserie chicken, you will especially like the flavor of these chicken tenders.

ROTISSERIE CHICKEN TENDERS
Yield: 6 servings
(4 ounces per serving)

Calories: 179 (10% fat); Total Fat: 2g; Cholesterol: 67mg; Carbohydrate: 13g; Dietary Fiber: 1g; Protein 29g; Sodium: 436mg; Diabetic Exchanges: 1 starch, 3 very lean meat

CHEDDAR & CHIVE BUTTERMILK BISCUITS
Yield: 10 servings
(1 biscuit per serving)

Calories: 60 (26% fat); Total Fat: 2g; Cholesterol: 1mg; Carbohydrate: 9g; Dietary Fiber: 0g; Protein 2g; Sodium: 206mg; Diabetic Exchanges: $^1/_2$ starch, $^1/_2$ fat

CREAMY VEGETABLE MEDLEY
Yield: 6 servings (1 cups per serving)

Calories: 84 (0% fat); Total Fat: 0g; Cholesterol: 0mg; Carbohydrate: 17g; Dietary Fiber: 4g; Protein 6g; Sodium: 296mg; Diabetic Exchanges: 2 vegetable, $^1/_2$ skim milk

ROTISSERIE CHICKEN TENDERS

1 cup low-fat buttermilk	$^1/_2$ cup corn flake crumbs
$^1/_2$ teaspoon lemon pepper	1 tablespoon rotisserie chicken seasoning
$1^1/_2$ pounds chicken tenders	
$^1/_2$ cup oat bran	1 teaspoon parsley flakes

CHEDDAR & CHIVE BUTTERMILK BISCUITS

$^1/_2$ tablespoon light butter, melted	$^1/_4$ cup shredded fat-free cheddar cheese
1 plus $^1/_2$ teaspoons dried chives	1 ($7^1/_2$-ounce) can biscuits

CREAMY VEGETABLE MEDLEY

2 (16-ounce) bags frozen California blend vegetables	$^1/_4$ teaspoon celery salt
	1 tablespoon imitation butter-flavored sprinkles
1 cup fat-free half-and-half	
$^1/_2$ teaspoon garlic salt	2 tablespoons cornstarch

Instructions

30 MINUTES BEFORE DINNER, preheat the oven to 450 degrees. Coat a baking sheet with nonfat cooking spray; set aside.

Prepare chicken tenders. In a medium bowl, combine 1 c low-fat buttermilk and $^1/_2$ t lemon pepper. Add $1^1/_2$ lb chicken tenders to the bowl; set aside.

In a plastic zip-top bag, combine $^1/_2$ c oat bran, $^1/_2$ c corn flake crumbs, 1 T rotisserie chicken seasoning, and 1 t parsley flakes.

Add the chicken tenders a few pieces at a time to the crumb mixture. Place on the prepared baking sheet. Coat the chicken tenders with cooking spray.

20 MINUTES BEFORE DINNER, place the chicken tenders on the bottom rack in the preheated oven for 15 to 20 minutes, or until chicken is tender and white when cut in the center.

18 MINUTES BEFORE DINNER, prepare the biscuits. In a small bowl, heat $1/2$ T butter in the microwave for 15 seconds, or until melted. Stir in 1 t of the dried chives; set aside.

Coat another baking sheet with nonfat cooking spray and set aside.

15 MINUTES BEFORE DINNER, separate 1 can biscuits at the perforations and place the biscuits on the prepared baking sheet. Brush the melted butter and chive mixture over each biscuit. Sprinkle the remaining $1/2$ t dried chives over the biscuits. Sprinkle $1/4$ c shredded cheddar cheese evenly over each biscuit. Spray the cheese with cooking spray. Place the biscuits on the middle rack of the oven and bake for 10 minutes.

13 MINUTES BEFORE DINNER, start preparing the vegetable medley. Put 2 bags frozen California blend vegetables in a large microwavable bowl. Cover with waxed paper and microwave for 8 to 10 minutes, or until the vegetables are tender and hot.

11 MINUTES BEFORE DINNER, make the cream sauce for the vegetables. Coat a medium saucepan with nonfat cooking spray.

In the prepared saucepan, whisk together 1 c half-and-half, $1/2$ t garlic salt, $1/4$ t celery salt, 1 T butter sprinkles, and 2 T cornstarch until smooth and there are no lumps.

Place the saucepan over medium heat and cook until the sauce is thick and creamy, stirring frequently.

3 MINUTES BEFORE DINNER, remove the biscuits from the oven and place in a serving bowl on the table until dinnertime.

2 MINUTES BEFORE DINNER, remove the vegetables from the microwave. Stir in the cream sauce, coating all the vegetables. Transfer to a serving bowl and place on the dinner table.

1 MINUTE BEFORE DINNER, remove the chicken tenders from the oven, place on a serving platter, and place on the dinner table.

Supplies List

Timer
Baking sheets
Small bowl
Medium bowl
Large microwavable bowl
Medium saucepan
Plastic zip-top bag

Grocery List

PACKAGED
Oat bran
Corn flakes

FROZEN
2 (16-ounce) bags frozen California blend vegetables

POULTRY
$1/2$ pounds chicken tenders

DAIRY
1 cup low-fat buttermilk
Light butter
$1/4$ cup shredded fat-free cheddar cheese
1 cup fat-free half-and-half
1 ($7^{1}/_{2}$-ounce) can refrigerated biscuits

Pantry List

Parsley flakes
Garlic salt
Celery salt
Cornstarch
Dried chives
Lemon pepper
Nonfat cooking spray
Imitation butter-flavored sprinkles
Rotisserie chicken seasoning

>>> Beefy Enchilada Nachos

Vegetarian Taco Salad

This menu is a terrific combination of spicy and cool, crunchy and creamy, and above all delicious and satisfying. The timeline for this menu will keep you hopping the entire time, so make sure your ingredients are ready! These nachos would be fantastic for a party. Just make sure you do not assemble them until everyone is ready to eat, otherwise the crispy tortilla chips will become soggy from the refried beans.

BEEFY ENCHILADA NACHOS
Yield: 6 servings
(7 nachos per serving)

Calories: 464 (11% fat); Total Fat: 5g; Cholesterol: 54mg; Carbohydrate: 61g; Dietary Fiber: 10g; Protein 41g; Sodium: 1690mg; Diabetic Exchanges: 4 starch, 4^1/$_2$ very lean meat

VEGETARIAN TACO SALAD
Yield: 6 servings
(1^1/$_2$ cup per serving)

Calories: 126 (8% fat); Total Fat: 1g; Cholesterol: 3mg; Carbohydrate: 22g; Dietary Fiber: 3g; Protein 8g; Sodium: 567mg; Diabetic Exchanges: 1^1/$_2$ vegetable, 1 other carbohydrate, 1 very lean meat

BEEFY ENCHILADA NACHOS

1	pound extra-lean ground beef
1	(19-ounce) can mild enchilada sauce
42	restaurant-style fat-free tortilla chips
2	(16-ounce) cans fat-free refried beans
1	cup chopped onion
2	cups shredded fat-free cheddar cheese
^{3}/$_4$	cup plus 2 teaspoons fat-free sour cream

VEGETARIAN TACO SALAD

9	cups shredded iceberg lettuce
1	cup shredded fat-free cheddar cheese
1^1/$_2$	cups cherry tomatoes
^{1}/$_2$	cup chopped onion
^{1}/$_4$	cup black olives
^{3}/$_4$	cups fat-free French salad dressing
^{1}/$_2$	cup crushed restaurant-style fat-free tortilla chips

Instructions

30 MINUTES BEFORE DINNER, start the nachos. In a 12-inch nonstick saucepan over high heat, cook 1 lb ground beef until brown, stirring to crumble.

Reduce the heat to medium and stir in 1 can mild enchilada sauce.

25 MINUTES BEFORE DINNER, arrange 42 tortilla chips onto 2 jelly-roll pans. Put 1 rounded teaspoonful fat-free refried beans on top of each tortilla chip.

20 MINUTES BEFORE DINNER, stir the meat and enchilada sauce. Reduce the heat to medium-low and simmer.

17 MINUTES BEFORE DINNER, assemble the taco salad. Place 9 c shredded iceberg lettuce into a large salad bowl. In this order, top the salad with 1 c shredded cheddar cheese, $1\frac{1}{2}$ cups cherry tomatoes, $\frac{1}{2}$ c chopped onion, and $\frac{1}{4}$ c black olives. Cover the salad and refrigerate until dinner is ready to be served.

11 MINUTES BEFORE DINNER, preheat the oven to 450 degrees.

10 MINUTES BEFORE DINNER, spoon $1\frac{1}{2}$ t of the beef enchilada sauce over the beans on each chip. Sprinkle 2 c shredded cheddar cheese evenly over the nachos. Spray the cheddar cheese with cooking spray. Sprinkle 1 c chopped fresh onion evenly over the cheese.

5 MINUTES BEFORE DINNER, place the jelly-roll pans in the preheated oven and bake for 2 minutes, or until the cheese is lightly melted. Watch carefully so they do not burn.

3 MINUTES BEFORE DINNER, remove the jelly-roll pans of nachos from the oven.

2 MINUTES BEFORE DINNER, top each chip with 1 t sour cream. Place the jelly-roll pans of Beefy Enchilada Nachos on hot pads on the dinner table.

1 MINUTE BEFORE DINNER, place $\frac{3}{4}$ cup French salad dressing and the taco salad from the refrigerator on the dinner table so dinner guests can dress their own salad. Sprinkle the top of the salad with $\frac{1}{2}$ c crushed tortilla chips.

Supplies List

Timer
12-inch saucepan
Jelly-roll pans
Large salad bowl

Grocery List

PACKAGED

1 (19-ounce) can mild
  enchilada sauce
2 (16-ounce) cans fat-free
  refried beans
1 bag restaurant-style
  fat-free tortilla chips
1 (8-ounce) bottle fat-free
  French salad dressing
1 small can black olives

PRODUCE

$1\frac{1}{2}$ cup chopped onion
9 cups shredded iceberg
  lettuce
$1\frac{1}{2}$ cups cherry tomatoes

MEAT

1 pound extra-lean ground
  beef

DAIRY

2 (8-ounce) bags shredded
  fat-free cheddar cheese
1 (8-ounce) container
  fat-free sour cream

Pantry List

Nonfat cooking spray

>>> Hot Roast Beef with Dumplings

Southern-Style Mixed Greens

You won't believe that, as easy as this dish is to make, you can get such a Southern down-home taste just like mom use to make in a fraction of the time.

HOT ROAST BEEF
Yield: 6 servings
(8 cups per serving)
Calories: 163 (21% fat); Total Fat: 4g; Cholesterol: 49mg; Carbohydrate: 9g; Dietary Fiber: 0g; Protein 22g; Sodium: 1386mg; Diabetic Exchanges: 1/2 starch, 3 lean meat

DUMPLINGS
Yield: 6 servings (2 dumplings per serving)
Calories: 116 (15% fat); Total Fat: 2g; Cholesterol: 0mg; Carbohydrate: 22g; Dietary Fiber: 1g; Protein 2g; Sodium: 350mg; Diabetic Exchanges: 1 1/2 starch

SOUTHERN-STYLE MIXED GREENS
Yield: 7 servings
(1/2 cups per serving)
Calories: 48 (0% fat); Total Fat: 0g; Cholesterol: 3mg; Carbohydrate: 5g; Dietary Fiber: 3g; Protein 4g; Sodium: 852mg; Diabetic Exchanges: 1 vegetable

HOT ROAST BEEF

2 (10 1/2-ounce) cans beef gravy
1/4 teaspoon thyme
1 1/2 pounds deli-style lean roast beef, sliced thin

DUMPLINGS

1 1/2 cups reduced-fat baking mix
1 teaspoon dried chives
1/2 cup plus 1 tablespoon water
1/2 cup frozen chopped onion

SOUTHERN-STYLE MIXED GREENS

3 (14-1/2-ounce) cans mixed greens (turnip and mustard), drained
3 tablespoons imitation butter-flavored sprinkles
2 tablespoons 30%-less-fat real bacon pieces
3/4 teaspoon seasoned salt
3/4 teaspoon Splenda granular

Instructions

25 MINUTES BEFORE DINNER, start making the roast beef. In a 12-inch non-stick saucepan over medium heat, bring 2 cans beef gravy and $1/4$ t thyme to a low boil.

Cut $1^1/_2$ pounds sliced roast beef into bite-size pieces and add to the gravy.

17 MINUTES BEFORE DINNER, start the dumplings. In a medium bowl, mix together $1^1/_2$ c baking mix, 1 t chives, and $1/2$ c plus 1 T water until a dough is formed. Stir in $1/2$ c frozen chopped onion.

12 MINUTES BEFORE DINNER, drop 12 heaping tablespoons of dough into the gravy. Cover the saucepan and cook for 10 minutes.

8 MINUTES BEFORE DINNER, prepare mixed greens. Drain 3 cans mixed greens and place in a medium microwavable bowl. Add 3 T butter sprinkles, 2 T bacon pieces, $3/4$ t seasoned salt, and $3/4$ t Splenda granular. Place in the microwave and cook for 3 to 4 minutes, or until hot.

2 MINUTES BEFORE DINNER, put the roast beef with dumplings into a serving bowl and put on a hot pad on the dinner table.

1 MINUTE BEFORE DINNER, remove the mixed greens from the microwave and place on the table.

Supplies List

Timer
12-inch nonstick saucepan with lid
Medium bowl
Medium microwavable bowl

Grocery List

PACKAGED

2 ($10^1/_2$-ounce) cans beef gravy
Canned mixed greens (turnip and mustard)
30%-less-fat real bacon pieces

FROZEN

$1/2$ cup frozen chopped onion

MEAT

$1^1/_2$ pounds deli-style lean roast beef, sliced thin

Pantry List

Thyme
Chives
Seasoned salt
Imitation butter-flavored sprinkles
Splenda granular
$1^1/_2$ cups reduced-fat baking mix

>>> Turkey Roll-Ups with Cranberry Stuffing & Savory Turkey Gravy

Fruity Coleslaw

Tastes like Thanksgiving without all the fuss and mess.

**TURKEY ROLL-UPS
WITH CRANBERRY STUFFING**
**Yield: 6 servings (4 ounces turkey
and $^1/_2$ cup stuffing per serving)**
*Calories: 201 (9% fat); Total Fat: 2g;
Cholesterol: 40mg; Carbohydrate: 18g;
Dietary Fiber: 3g; Protein 27g;
Sodium: 1251mg; Diabetic Exchanges:
1 starch, 3 very lean meat*

SAVORY TURKEY GRAVY
Yield: 6 servings ($^1/_4$ cup per serving)
*Calories: 22 (0% fat); Total Fat: 0g;
Cholesterol: 4mg; Carbohydrate: 4g;
Dietary Fiber: 0g; Protein 1g; Sodium:
280mg; Diabetic Exchanges: $^1/_2$ starch*

FRUITY COLESLAW
Yield: 6 servings (1 cup per serving)
*Calories: 108 (0% fat); Total Fat: 0g;
Cholesterol: 0mg; Carbohydrate: 22g;
Dietary Fiber: 2g; Protein 1g; Sodium:
276mg; Diabetic Exchanges:
1 fruit, $1^1/_2$ vegetable*

TURKEY ROLL-UPS WITH CRANBERRY STUFFING

1	small celery rib	$^1/_3$	cup frozen chopped onion
3	slices light rye bread, toasted	$1^1/_2$	pounds mesquite turkey
$^1/_2$	cup water		($12^1/_4$-inch-thick slices)
$^1/_2$	cup dried cranberries		
$^1/_2$	cup vegetarian sausage-flavored crumbles		

SAVORY TURKEY GRAVY

1	($10^1/_2$-ounce) jar turkey gravy	1	teaspoon dried chives
$^1/_4$	teaspoon rubbed sage		

FRUITY COLESLAW

$^3/_4$	cup fat-free Miracle Whip	1	celery rib
1	tablespoon apple cider vinegar	$^1/_3$	cup raisins
2	tablespoons Splenda Brown Sugar Blend	1	(12-ounce) bag preshredded coleslaw mix
1	medium Gala apple		

Instructions

30 MINUTES BEFORE DINNER, start the cranberry stuffing. Finely chop 1 small celery rib. Toast 3 slices light rye bread in the toaster. In a medium saucepan over high heat, bring $1/2$ c water to a boil. Cut the rye toast into small bite-size pieces.

25 MINUTES BEFORE DINNER, add to the boiling water $1/2$ c dried cranberries, $1/2$ c vegetarian sausage-flavored crumbles, $1/3$ c frozen chopped onion, and $1/3$ c celery. Return to a boil for 2 minutes.

23 MINUTES BEFORE DINNER, stir the rye toast pieces into the boiling stuffing. Turn off the heat, cover, and let set on the hot burner for 5 minutes.

22 MINUTES BEFORE DINNER, place the $1^1/2$ lb mesquite turkey on a microwave-safe plate and heat in the microwave for 1 to 2 minutes, or until the turkey is hot.

20 MINUTES BEFORE DINNER, preheat the oven to 200 degrees.

In a small microwave-safe bowl, combine 1 jar turkey gravy, $1/4$ t rubbed sage, and 1 t dried chives. Heat in the microwave for about 1 minute.

18 MINUTES BEFORE DINNER, prepare the turkey roll-ups. Place 2 T cranberry stuffing on top of 1 mesquite turkey slice. Roll the turkey into a log and place in a 9 x 13-inch casserole dish. Repeat for all 12 slices of the turkey. Pour the hot gravy over the turkey roll-ups. Cover and place in the oven until time for dinner.

13 MINUTES BEFORE DINNER, make the coleslaw. In a medium bowl, mix together: $3/4$ c Miracle Whip, 1 T apple cider vinegar, and 2 T Splenda Brown Sugar Blend until well blended. Set aside.

10 MINUTES BEFORE DINNER, finely chop the 1 apple and 1 celery rib. Add to the salad dressing. Stir in the raisins and 1 bag preshredded coleslaw mix. Stir until the coleslaw is well coated with the dressing. Place on the dinner table.

2 MINUTES BEFORE DINNER, turn off the oven and put the hot turkey roll-ups on a hot pad on the dinner table.

Supplies List

Timer
Toaster
Medium saucepan with lid
Small bowl
Medium bowl
9 x 13-inch casserole dish

Grocery List

PACKAGED
Light Rye bread
1 ($10^1/2$-ounce) jar turkey gravy
Dried cranberries
Raisins

PRODUCE
Celery
1 medium Gala apple
1 (12-ounce) bag shredded coleslaw mix

FROZEN
$1/3$ cup frozen chopped onions
$1/2$ cup vegetarian sausage-flavored crumbles

POULTRY
$1^1/2$ pounds mesquite turkey

Pantry List

Rubbed sage
Dried chives
Apple cider vinegar
Splenda Brown Sugar Blend
Fat-free Miracle Whip

>>> Turkey Gravy with Chive Dumplings

Very Peary Tossed Salad

You won't find a better combination of food to melt in your mouth than this menu.

**TURKEY GRAVY
WITH CHIVE DUMPLINGS**
Yield: 6 servings
($1^1/_3$ cup per serving)
Calories: 373 (25% fat); Total Fat: 10g; Cholesterol: 95mg; Carbohydrate: 35g; Dietary Fiber: 0g; Protein 34g; Sodium: 1866mg; Diabetic Exchanges: $2^1/_2$ starch, 4 lean meat

VERY PEARY TOSSED SALAD
Yield: 6 servings
($1^1/_2$ cups per serving)
Calories: 105 (9% fat); Total Fat: 1g; Cholesterol: 0mg; Carbohydrate: 21g; Dietary Fiber: 3g; Protein 1g; Sodium: 260mg; Diabetic Exchanges: $1^1/_2$ fruit

TURKEY GRAVY WITH CHIVE DUMPLINGS

4	($10^1/_2$-ounce) cans fat-free turkey gravy	$1/_2$	teaspoon ground sage
2	($12^1/_2$-ounce) cans 98% fat-free turkey breast in water, drained	$1^1/_2$	cups reduced-fat baking mix
		1	teaspoon dried chives
		$1/_2$	cup plus 1 tablespoon water

VERY PEARY TOSSED SALAD

$3/_4$	cup fat-free Miracle Whip, chilled	1	large head iceberg lettuce (about 9 cups chopped)
1	tablespoon apple cider vinegar	1	tablespoon walnuts, finely chopped
$2^1/_2$	tablespoons Splenda granular		
$1/_4$	cup raisins		
2	medium pears, finely chopped ($1^3/_4$ cups)		

Instructions

20 MINUTES BEFORE DINNER, start making the turkey gravy. In a 12-inch nonstick saucepan, over medium heat bring 4 cans turkey gravy, 2 cans drained turkey breast, and $1/2$ t sage to a boil.

15 MINUTES BEFORE DINNER, start making the dumplings. In a medium bowl, combine $1^1/_2$ c baking mix, 1 t dried chives, and $1/2$ c plus 1 T water, mixing well until a dough is formed.

12 MINUTES BEFORE DINNER, drop the dough by heaping tablespoonfuls into the boiling gravy. Cover and cook at a low boil for 10 minutes.

7 MINUTES BEFORE DINNER, start making the tossed salad. In a large salad bowl, stir together until well mixed $3/4$ c Miracle Whip, 1 T apple cider vinegar, $2^1/_2$ T Splenda granular, $1/4$ c raisins, and 2 finely chopped pears.

Remove and discard the core of 1 head iceberg lettuce. Cut the lettuce into bite-size pieces and place on top of the salad dressing in the large salad bowl. Toss the salad and salad dressing together until the lettuce is well coated with the salad dressing.

Sprinkle the top of the salad with 1 T walnuts. Place the salad on the dinner table.

1 MINUTE BEFORE DINNER, put the gravy with dumplings in a serving bowl, put on a hot pad, and place on the dinner table.

Supplies List

Timer
12-inch nonstick skillet
    with lid
Medium bowl
Large salad bowl

Grocery List

PACKAGED

4 ($10^1/_2$-ounce) cans fat-free
    turkey gravy
2 ($12^1/_2$-ounce) cans 98%
    fat-free turkey breast in
    water

PRODUCE

2 medium pears
1 large head iceberg lettuce

Pantry List

1 cup walnuts
Ground sage
Dried chives
Apple cider vinegar
Fat-free Miracle Whip
Splenda granular
$1^1/_2$ cups reduced-fat
    baking mix
Raisins

>>> Southwestern Frittata

Cool & Zesty Tossed Salad • Fat-Free Sour Cream, Lettuce, and Chopped Onion

The combination of the Southwestern-flavored eggs and the bacon will have you smiling. This frittata is good served with nonfat sour cream, lettuce, and chopped onion.

SOUTHWESTERN FRITTATA
Yield: 6 servings
(1 wedge per serving)
Calories: 132 (14% fat); Total Fat: 2g; Cholesterol: 13mg; Carbohydrate: 11g; Dietary Fiber: 1g; Protein 17g; Sodium: 542mg; Diabetic Exchanges: 1/2 starch, 2 very lean meat

COOL & ZESTY TOSSED SALAD
Yield: 6 servings
(1 1/2 cups per serving)
Calories: 53 (0% fat); Total Fat: 0g; Cholesterol: 3mg; Carbohydrate: 9g; Dietary Fiber: 2g; Protein 5g; Sodium: 367mg; Diabetic Exchanges: 2 vegetable

SOUTHWESTERN FRITTATA

6   corn tortillas
1   (15-ounce) Southwestern liquid egg substitute
6   tablespoons 30%-less-fat real bacon pieces
1   cup fat-free shredded cheddar
Salt and pepper to taste

COOL & ZESTY TOSSED SALAD

1   (14 1/2-ounce) can diced tomatoes with green chilies, chilled and drained
1/3   cup fat-free sour cream
1/4   cup fat-free half-and-half
1/3   cup shredded fat-free cheddar cheese
1   tablespoon Splenda granular
1   teaspoon dried parsley flakes
1   large head iceberg lettuce (about 9 cups chopped)

Instructions

30 MINUTES BEFORE DINNER, start making the tossed salad. Drain 1 can diced tomatoes with green chilies.

In a large bowl, add $^1/_3$ c sour cream, $^1/_4$ c half-and-half, $^1/_3$ c shredded cheddar cheese, 1 T Splenda granular, and 1 t dried parsley flakes, mixing until well blended. Stir in the drained diced tomatoes.

25 MINUTES BEFORE DINNER, remove and discard core from 1 head iceberg lettuce. Cut the lettuce into bite-size pieces and place in the large bowl on top of the salad dressing but do not mix together or salad will get soggy. Cover and place the salad in the refrigerator until time for dinner.

20 MINUTES BEFORE DINNER, prepare the frittata. Spray a nonstick 12-inch skillet with nonfat cooking spray. Preheat the skillet over medium heat. Cut or tear 6 corn tortillas into 1-inch pieces. Add the corn tortilla pieces to the skillet and cook, turning often, until the tortillas are brown and hot, about 3 minutes.

17 MINUTES BEFORE DINNER, add 1 carton Southwestern liquid egg substitute to the skillet with the cooked tortillas and cook like an omelet, lifting the tortilla pieces so the egg substitute can run under them.

7 MINUTES BEFORE DINNER, turn off the heat and sprinkle 6 T bacon pieces over the frittata. Sprinkle 1 c shredded fat-free cheddar cheese over the top of the bacon. Spray the cheese with cooking spray. Cover and let sit on the hot burner to melt the cheese.

4 MINUTES BEFORE DINNER, toss the iceberg lettuce with the salad dressing until the salad is well coated. Place on the dinner table.

2 MINUTES BEFORE DINNER, cut the frittata into 6-pie-shaped pieces. Place on a platter and set on the dinner table.

NOTE: To remove the core from a head of iceberg lettuce hold the lettuce with both hands with the core facing down. Firmly hit the core of the head of lettuce on the counter. This will allow you to easily remove the core.

Supplies List

Timer
Large bowl
Nonstick 12-inch skillet
   with lid
Platter

Grocery List

PACKAGED
6 corn tortillas
1 (14$^1/_2$-ounce) can diced
   tomatoes with green
   chilies
6 tablespoons 30%-less-fat
   real bacon pieces

PRODUCE
1 large head iceberg lettuce

DAIRY
1 (15-ounce) Southwestern
   liquid egg substitute
1 $^1/_3$ cup fat free shredded
   cheddar cheese
$^1/_3$ cup fat-free sour cream
$^1/_4$ cup fat-free half-and-half

Pantry List

Salt and pepper
Dried parsley flakes
Splenda granular

>>> Beans-R-Boss Chili with Corn Dog Dumplings

Corn Dog Dumplings • Assorted Bell Pepper Tray with Blue Cheese Dip

This would be super for a tailgate party! It's just like having your favorite corn dog on top of a hearty bowl of chili.

BEANS-R-BOSS CHILI
Yield: 6 servings (1 cup per serving)

Calories: 166 (6% fat); Total Fat: 1g; Cholesterol: 0mg; Carbohydrate: 31g; Dietary Fiber: 9g; Protein 8g; Sodium: 1241mg; Diabetic Exchanges: 1 1/2 starch, 2 vegetable

CORN DOG DUMPLINGS
Yield: 6 servings (2 dumplings per serving)

Calories: 180 (16% fat); Total Fat: 3g; Cholesterol: 10mg; Carbohydrate: 30g; Dietary Fiber: 1g; Protein 8g; Sodium: 707mg; Diabetic Exchanges: 2 starch, 1/2 very lean meat

ASSORTED BELL PEPPER TRAY WITH BLUE CHEESE DIP
Yield: 6 (1/2-bell pepper and 1 1/2-tablespoons dressing) servings

Calories 42 (0% fat); Total Fat: 0g; Cholesterol: 1mg; Carbohydrate: 10g; Dietary Fiber: 2g; Protein 1g; Sodium: 184mg; Diabetic Exchanges: 1 vegetable, 1/2 other carbohydrate

BEANS-R-BOSS CHILI
- 1 (30-ounce) can chili beans
- 2 (14 1/2-ounce) cans zesty chili-style diced tomatoes
- 1 teaspoon Splenda Brown Sugar Blend

CORN DOG DUMPLINGS
- 4 fat-free hot dogs, sliced thin
- 1 (8 1/2-ounce) box corn muffin mix
- 2 egg whites
- 1/3 cup water

ASSORTED BELL PEPPER TRAY WITH BLUE CHEESE DIP
- 1 large green bell pepper
- 1 large red bell pepper
- 1 large yellow bell pepper
- 1/2 cup fat-free blue cheese salad dressing

Instructions

30 MINUTES BEFORE DINNER, start making the chili. In a 12-inch nonstick saucepan over medium-high heat, bring 1 can chili beans, 2 cans zesty chili-style diced tomatoes, and 1 t Splenda Brown Sugar Blend to a low boil.

27 MINUTES BEFORE DINNER, start making the dumplings. Thinly slice 4 hot dogs; set aside.

In a medium bowl, make the dumpling batter. Combine 1 box corn muffin mix, 2 egg whites, and $1/3$ c water; and mix until well blended. Stir in the sliced hot dogs.

20 MINUTES BEFORE DINNER, add the dumpling batter by heaping table-spoonfuls to the low-boiling chili. Reduce the heat to medium-low and cook, covered, for 19 minutes.

15 MINUTES BEFORE DINNER, make the pepper tray. Slice 1 large green bell pepper, 1 large red bell pepper and 1 large yellow bell pepper into strips and arrange on a plate around a small bowl filled with $1/2$ c blue cheese salad dressing to use as a dip. Place on the dinner table.

1 MINUTE BEFORE DINNER, turn the heat off under the chili and transfer to a hot pad on the dinner table.

Supplies List

Timer
12-inch nonstick saucepan
　　with lid
Small bowl
Medium bowl
Serving plate

Grocery List

PACKAGED

1 (30-ounce) can chili beans
2 (14$1/2$-ounce) cans zesty
　　chili style diced tomatoes
1 (8$1/2$-ounce) box corn
　　muffin mix
1 (8-ounce) bottle fat-free
　　blue cheese salad dressing

PRODUCE

1 large green bell pepper
1 large red bell pepper
1 large yellow bell pepper

MEAT

4 fat-free hot dogs

Pantry List

2 eggs
Splenda Brown Sugar Blend

>>> Sloppy Joe's Pepper Medley

Johnnycake • Fresh Garden Greens with Boot-Legger Dressing

Gramps says one day Jonhhy's cake batter spilled all over Sloppy Joe's pepper medley just before Grammie was ready to cook them. Money being tight as it was, Grammie cooked it anyway. All the folks liked it so much, now it's a family favorite.

SLOPPY JOE'S PEPPER MEDLEY
Yield: 6 servings

Calories: 105 (0% fat); Total Fat: 0g; Cholesterol: 0mg; Carbohydrate: 12g; Dietary Fiber: 4g; Protein 13g; Sodium: 606mg; Diabetic Exchanges: 1 other carbohydrate, 2 very lean meat

JOHNNYCAKE
Yield: 6 servings (1 wedge per serving)

Calories: 179 (27% fat); Total Fat: 5g; Cholesterol: 16mg; Carbohydrate: 29g; Dietary Fiber: 1g; Protein 4g; Sodium: 305mg; Diabetic Exchanges: 2 starch

FRESH GARDEN GREENS WITH BOOT-LEGGER DRESSING
Yield: 6 servings (1 2/3 cups per serving)

Calories: 102 (7% fat); Total Fat: 1g; Cholesterol: 2mg; Carbohydrate: 22g; Dietary Fiber: 3g; Protein 3g; Sodium: 628mg; Diabetic Exchanges: 1 1/2 vegetable, 1 other carbohydrate

SLOPPY JOE'S PEPPER MEDLEY

1   (12-ounce) bag vegetarian meatless crumbles*
1/2 cup frozen pepper medley
1   (14 1/2-ounce) jar fat-free Not-So-Sloppy Sloppy Joe Sauce

JOHNNYCAKE

1   (8 1/2-ounce) box corn muffin mix
2   egg whites
2/3 cup water

FRESH GARDEN GREENS WITH BOOT-LEGGER DRESSING

2   (11-ounce) packages spring mix salad greens
1   (15 1/4-ounce) can beets, drained, diced, and chilled
3   tablespoons low-fat blue cheese crumbles
1   cup fat-free red wine vinaigrette, chilled
1   teaspoon Splenda granular

Instructions

30 MINUTES BEFORE DINNER, start making the pepper medley. In a 12-inch nonstick saucepan over medium-high heat, bring 1 bag vegetarian meatless crumbles, $1/2$ c frozen pepper medley, and 1 jar sloppy joe sauce to a low boil.

26 MINUTES BEFORE DINNER, make the johnnycake batter. In a medium bowl, mix together 1 box corn muffin mix, 2 egg whites, and $2/3$ c water until well blended.

24 MINUTES BEFORE DINNER, stir the sloppy joe mixture and reduce the heat to medium low.

22 MINUTES BEFORE DINNER, pour the johnnycake batter over the Sloppy Joe's Pepper Medley. Cover and cook for 20 minutes.

19 MINUTES BEFORE DINNER, assemble the greens by putting 2 packages spring mix salad greens in a large glass salad bowl. Arrange 1 can drained, diced beets on top. Sprinkle 3 T blue cheese crumbles on top. Cover and keep chilled in the refrigerator until dinner is ready.

10 MINUTES BEFORE DINNER, make the dressing. In a small bowl, stir together 1 c red wine vinaigrette and 1 t Splenda until well blended. Cover and keep chilled in the refrigerator.

3 MINUTES BEFORE DINNER, turn off the heat under the Sloppy Joe's Pepper Medley. Cut into 6 pie-shaped pieces. Place on a hot pad and put on the dinner table.

1 MINUTE BEFORE DINNER, drizzle the salad dressing over the salad and put it on the dinner table. Place the greens on the dinner table.

__NOTE:__ One pound of ground beef may be substituted for the vegetarian crumbles if you prefer.

Supplies List

Timer
12-inch nonstick saucepan
    with lid
Medium bowl
2 small bowls
Large glass salad bowl

Grocery List

PACKAGED

1 ($14^1/2$-ounce) jar fat-free
    Not-So-Sloppy Sloppy Joe
    Sauce
1 ($15^1/4$-ounce) can beets
1 ($8^1/2$-ounce) box corn
    muffin mix
1 (8-ounce) bottle fat-free
    red wine vinaigrette salad
    dressing
Splenda granular

PRODUCE

2 (11-ounce) packages spring
    mix salad greens

FROZEN

$1/2$ cup frozen pepper medley
1 (12-ounce) bag vegetarian
    meatless crumbles

DAIRY

Low-fat blue cheese crumbles

Pantry List

2 eggs

>>> Swiss-Stuffed Kielbasa & Rye Sandwiches

Mushroom & Broccoli Medley • Harvest Spiced Apple Salad

This meal is full of robust flavor and is exceptionally tasty in the fall when fresh apples are in season.

SWISS-STUFFED KIELBASA & RYE SANDWICHES
Yield: 6 servings
(1 sandwich per serving)
Calories: 176 (17% fat); Total Fat: 3g; Cholesterol: 25mg; Carbohydrate: 22g; Dietary Fiber: 1g; Protein 13g; Sodium: 897mg; Diabetic Exchanges: 1 1/2 starch, 1 1/2 very lean meat

MUSHROOM & BROCCOLI MEDLEY
Yield: 6 servings (1 cup per serving)
Calories: 81 (0% fat); Total Fat: 0g; Cholesterol: 2mg; Carbohydrate: 11g; Dietary Fiber: 4g; Protein 8g; Sodium: 619mg; Diabetic Exchanges: 2 vegetable, 1/2 very lean meat

HARVEST SPICED APPLE SALAD
Yield: 6 servings (2/3 cup per serving)
Calories: 131 (13% fat); Total Fat: 2g; Cholesterol: 0mg; Carbohydrate: 27g; Dietary Fiber: 3g; Protein 1g; Sodium: 12mg; Diabetic Exchanges: 1 fruit, 1 other carbohydrate, 1/2 fat

SWISS-STUFFED KIELBASA & RYE SANDWICHES

1	(14-ounce) package lean turkey kielbasa	1 1/2	slices fat-free Swiss cheese singles
1/2	cup water	6	slices Jewish rye bread
6	teaspoons Dijon mustard		

MUSHROOM & BROCCOLI MEDLEY

1	tablespoon bottled minced garlic	1/4	cup imitation butter-flavored sprinkles
1	teaspoon seasoned salt	1/2	cup shredded fat-free mild cheddar cheese
2	(16-ounce) packages frozen broccoli florets		
1	(8-ounce) package sliced fresh button mushrooms		

HARVEST SPICED APPLE SALAD

4	Gala apples	1	teaspoon ground cinnamon
1 1/2	cups fat-free dessert whipped topping, thawed	1/4	teaspoon pumpkin pie spice
2	tablespoons Splenda Brown Sugar Blend	3	tablespoons raisins
		1	plus 1 tablespoons finely chopped walnuts

Instructions

30 MINUTES BEFORE DINNER, start the broccoli. In a large saucepan over high heat, combine 1 T minced garlic, 1 t seasoned salt, and 4 c of hot water. Add 2 packages broccoli florets and 1 package button mushrooms. Cover and cook on high for 10 minutes. Turn off the heat when the water is boiling. Let the vegetables remain in the hot pan.

26 MINUTES BEFORE DINNER, start making the apple salad. Core and cut into small pieces 4 apples.

15 MINUTES BEFORE DINNER, start making the dressing for the apple salad. In a medium bowl combine $1^1/_2$ c whipped topping, 2 T Splenda Brown Sugar Blend, 1 t ground cinnamon, $^1/_4$ t pumpkin pie spice, 3 T raisins, and 1 T of the walnuts. Stir in the apples and coat with the dressing. Sprinkle the remaining 1 T walnuts on top of the salad. Place the salad on the table until time for dinner.

7 MINUTES BEFORE DINNER, preheat a 12-inch nonstick skillet over high heat. Start making the sandwiches. Slice 1 package lean turkey kielbasa into 6 links. Slice the links in half lengthwise, cutting to, but not through, the other side.

5 MINUTES BEFORE DINNER, put the kielbasa links, cut side down, into the preheated skillet.

4 MINUTES BEFORE DINNER, drain the broccoli and mushrooms. Place in a serving bowl and stir in $^1/_4$ c imitation butter-flavored sprinkles until well mixed. Sprinkle $^1/_2$ cheddar cheese over the broccoli mixture and cover. Put the broccoli on the dinner table.

3 MINUTES BEFORE DINNER, reduce the heat under the skillet with the kielbasa to low. Add $^1/_2$ c water to the skillet. Let the water evaporate for 1 minute, then carefully spread 1 t Dijon mustard on each sausage link. Cut $1^1/_2$ slices Swiss cheese singles into 4 strips. Place 1 strip of cheese on one half of each kielbasa link. Top with the other half of the kielbasa link. Cover the skillet and continue cooking on low.

1 MINUTE BEFORE DINNER, microwave 6 slices Jewish rye bread for 30 seconds, or until heated. Assemble the sandwiches by placing 1 cheese stuffed kielbasa in the center of each slice of Jewish rye bread and place on serving plate. Put the sandwiches on the dinner table.

Supplies List

Timer
Large saucepan with lid
Medium bowl
12 inch nonstick skillet
  with lid
Serving bowl
Serving plate

Grocery List

PACKAGED
Jewish rye bread
Raisins

PRODUCE
4 Gala apples
1 (8-ounce) package sliced
  button mushrooms

FROZEN
2 (16-ounce) packages frozen
  broccoli florets
1 (12-ounce) container
  fat-free dessert whipped
  topping

MEAT
1 (14-ounce) package lean
  turkey kielbasa

DAIRY
$^1/_2$ cup shredded fat-free mild
  cheddar cheese
Fat-free Swiss cheese singles

Pantry List

Walnuts
Dijon mustard
Minced garlic
Seasoned salt
Ground cinnamon
Splenda Brown Sugar Blend
Imitation butter-flavored
  sprinkles
Pumpkin pie spice

>>> Sweet Potato Soup with Whole Wheat Corn Bread Dumplings

Whole Wheat Corn Bread Dumplings • Southern-Style Turnip Greens with Diced White Turnips

This creamy Sweet Potato Soup with salty ham topped with hearty corn bread is a flavorful combination of Southern holiday favorites my family really loves.

SWEET POTATO SOUP

Yield: 6 servings (1 cup per serving)

Calories: 184 (11% fat); Total Fat: 2g; Cholesterol: 20mg; Carbohydrate: 31g; Dietary Fiber: 2g; Protein 9g; Sodium: 856mg; Diabetic Exchanges: 2 starch, 1 very lean meat

WHOLE WHEAT CORN BREAD DUMPLINGS

Yield: 6 servings (2 dumplings per serving)

Calories: 186 (16% fat); Total Fat: 3g; Cholesterol: 0mg; Carbohydrate: 35g; Dietary Fiber: 2g; Protein 5g; Sodium: 383mg; Diabetic Exchanges: 2 1/2 starch

SOUTHERN-STYLE TURNIP GREENS WITH DICED WHITE TURNIPS

Yield: 7 servings (1/2 cup per serving)

Calories: 53 (22% fat); Total Fat: 1g; Cholesterol: 9mg; Carbohydrate: 5g; Dietary Fiber: 3g; Protein 6g; Sodium: 800mg; Diabetic Exchanges: 1 vegetable, 1/2 very lean meat

SWEET POTATO SOUP

2	(15-ounce) cans sweet potatoes in light syrup, undrained
1	(14-ounce) can fat-free chicken broth
3	tablespoons imitation butter-flavored sprinkles
2	tablespoons cornstarch
1/8	teaspoon ground black pepper
1	(8-ounce) package lean cooked ham, diced

WHOLE WHEAT CORN BREAD DUMPLINGS

1	(8 1/2-ounce) box corn muffin mix
2	egg whites
2/3	cup water
1	teaspoon Splenda granular
1/4	cup plus 3 tablespoons whole wheat flour

SOUTHERN-STYLE TURNIP GREENS WITH DICED WHITE TURNIPS

3	(14 1/2-ounce) cans turnip greens with diced white turnips, drained
1	teaspoon liquid smoke
1	teaspoon Splenda granular
1 1/2	tablespoons imitation butter-flavored sprinkles
1/4	cup frozen chopped onion
4	ounces lean ham, diced (1/2 cup firmly packed)

Instructions

20 MINUTES BEFORE DINNER, start making the soup. Using a potato masher, in a 12-inch nonstick saucepan, mash 2 cans sweet potatoes with the light syrup. Heat the saucepan over medium heat. Add to the saucepan 1 can chicken broth, 3 T butter sprinkles, 2 T cornstarch, $1/8$ t ground black pepper, and 1 package ham. Bring to a low boil, stirring constantly until the cornstarch dissolves.

15 MINUTES BEFORE DINNER, make the corn bread batter. In a medium bowl, combine 1 box corn muffin mix, 2 egg whites, $2/3$ c water, 1 t Splenda granular, and $1/4$ c plus 3 T whole wheat flour. The batter will be thin and runny.

12 MINUTES BEFORE DINNER, gently drop the corn bread batter by rounded tablespoonfuls into the boiling soup. Cover and cook for 10 minutes.

8 MINUTES BEFORE DINNER, make the turnip greens. Combine 3 cans drained turnip greens in a medium microwavable bowl. Add 1 t liquid smoke, 1 t Splenda granular, $1^{1}/2$ T butter sprinkles, $1/4$ c chopped onion, and 4 oz diced ham. Stir together until well mixed. Cover with waxed paper and microwave for 4 minutes, or until fully heated.

2 MINUTES BEFORE DINNER, place the soup in a serving bowl on a hot pad, and place on the dinner table.

1 MINUTE BEFORE DINNER, place the turnip greens on a hot pad on the dinner table.

NOTE: *It is important to stir the cornstarch until it dissolves with the other ingredients before all of the ingredients get warm; otherwise the cornstarch could become lumpy.*

Supplies List

Timer
12-inch nonstick saucepan
 with lid
Potato masher
Medium bowl
Medium microwavable bowl

Grocery List

PACKAGED

2 (15-ounce) cans sweet
 potatoes in light syrup
1 (14-ounce) can fat-free
 chicken broth
1 ($8^{1}/2$-ounce) box corn
 muffin mix
3 ($14^{1}/2$-ounce) cans turnip
 greens with diced white
 turnips
Liquid smoke

FROZEN

$1/4$ cup frozen chopped onions

MEATS

12 ounces packaged lean
 cooked ham

DAIRY

2 eggs

Pantry List

Whole wheat flour
Ground black pepper
Imitation butter-flavored
 sprinkles
Cornstarch
Splenda granular

>>> Cream of Greens Soup

Bell Pepper Vegetable Tray with French Dip • Rye Kaiser Bread Bowls (optional)

If you love cream of spinach soup you will love this!

CREAM OF GREENS SOUP

Yield: 6 servings (1 cup per serving)

*Calories: 195 (19% fat); Total Fat: 4g;
Cholesterol: 32mg; Carbohydrate: 23g;
Dietary Fiber: 5g; Protein 20g;
Sodium: 1895mg; Diabetic Exchanges:
1 starch, 1 vegetable, 2½ lean meat*

BELL PEPPER VEGETABLE TRAY
WITH FRENCH DIP
Yield: 6 servings

*Calories 51 (0% fat); Total Fat: 0g;
Cholesterol: 0mg; Carbohydrate: 12g;
Dietary Fiber: 2g; Protein 1g; Sodium:
202mg; Diabetic Exchanges:
1 vegetable, ½ other carbohydrate*

CREAM OF GREENS SOUP

1	Gala apple, finely chopped (1½ cups)
½	cup frozen chopped onion
12	ounces 98%-fat-free diced ham
3	(14½-ounce) cans turnip greens with diced white turnips, drained
1	teaspoon seasoned salt
1	(10¾-ounce) can 98% fat-free broccoli cheese soup
1½	cups fat-free half-and-half
6	large rye Kaiser rolls (optional)

BELL PEPPER VEGETABLE TRAY WITH FRENCH DIP

½	cup fat-free French salad dressing
1	yellow bell pepper
1	orange bell pepper
1	red bell pepper

Instructions

30 MINUTES BEFORE DINNER, prepare the bread bowls if desired. Using a sharp serrated knife, cut $1/2$ inch off the top of 6 rye Kaiser rolls, reserving the top. Hollow out the bread, leaving a $1/2$-inch-thick shell. Place each bread bowl and the reserved lid on a dinner plate.

20 MINUTES BEFORE DINNER, make the vegetable tray and French dip. Put $1/2$ c French salad dressing in a small bowl and place in the center of a serving platter. Slice 1 yellow bell pepper, 1 orange bell pepper, and 1 red bell pepper into strips and place on the serving platter. Cover and refrigerate until time for dinner.

12 MINUTES BEFORE DINNER, start making the Cream of Greens Soup. Heat the chopped apple in the microwave for 1 minute.

Combine $1/2$ c frozen chopped onion and 12 oz diced ham in a 12-inch non-stick saucepan and cook over medium-low heat for 1 to 2 minutes, or until the onion is tender.

Add the apple, 3 cans drained turnip greens with diced white turnips, and 1 t seasoned salt to the saucepan. Reduce the heat to low and simmer for 3 to 4 minutes. Stir in 1 can broccoli cheese soup and $1^{1}/2$ c half-and-half. Bring to a low boil, stirring constantly, about 4 to 5 minutes.

1 MINUTE BEFORE DINNER, ladle the soup into the prepared bread bowls and place on the dinner table along with the bell pepper strips and French salad dressing.

NOTE: A good place to cut back (if you are counting your calories) is to not eat the hollowed part of your bread bowl. If you do have the rolls, add 125 calories (13% fat), 2g total fat, 23 carbohydrates, 1g dietary fiber, 4g protein, 233mg sodium, and $1^{1}/2$ starch.

Supplies List

Timer
Small bowl
Serving platter
12-inch nonstick saucepan
    with lid

Grocery List

PACKAGED

6 large Rye Kaiser rolls
3 ($14^{1}/2$-ounce) cans turnip
    greens with diced white
    turnips
1 ($10^{3}/4$-ounce) can
    98% fat-free Broccoli
    Cheese soup
Fat-free French salad dressing

PRODUCE

1 Gala apple
1 yellow bell pepper
1 orange bell pepper
1 red bell pepper

FROZEN

$1/2$ cup frozen chopped onion

MEAT

12 ounces 98% fat-free
    diced ham

DAIRY

$1^{1}/2$ cups fat-free
    half-and-half

Pantry List

Seasoned salt

>>> Chili Dog Chili with Whole Wheat Corn Bread Dumplings

Whole Wheat Corn Bread Dumplings • Cool & Creamy Zesty Vegetable Dip with Celery Sticks

Here's a terrific tailgate party menu that's inexpensive, hearty, and perfect for fall.

CHILI DOG CHILI

Yield: 7 servings (1 cup per serving)

*Calories: 124 (0% fat); Total Fat: 0g;
Cholesterol: 17mg; Carbohydrate: 19g;
Dietary Fiber: 5g; Protein 11g;
Sodium: 1395mg; Diabetic Exchanges:
1 starch, 1 vegetable, 1 very lean meat*

WHOLE WHEAT CORN BREAD DUMPLINGS

**Yield: 6 servings
(2 dumplings per serving)**

*Calories: 165 (17% fat); Total Fat: 3g;
Cholesterol: 0mg; Carbohydrate: 31g;
Dietary Fiber: 1g; Protein 4g; Sodium:
383mg; Diabetic Exchanges: 2 starch*

COOL & CREAMY ZESTY VEGETABLE DIP WITH CELERY STICKS

**Yield: 6 servings (6 celery sticks
& 1 tablespoon dip per serving)**

*Calories: 21 (0% fat); Total Fat: 0g;
Cholesterol: 1mg; Carbohydrate: 5g;
Dietary Fiber: 1g; Protein 1g; Sodium:
190mg; Diabetic Exchanges:
1 vegetable*

CHILI DOG CHILI

2   (14 1/2-ounce) cans diced chili-style tomatoes
1   (15-ounce) can spicy chili beans with seasoning
1   teaspoon Splenda granular
1   (14-ounce) package fat-free hot dogs, cut into 1/4-inch pieces

WHOLE WHEAT CORN BREAD DUMPLINGS

1   (8 1/2-ounce) box corn muffin mix
2   egg whites
1/3 cup water
2   tablespoons whole wheat flour

COOL & CREAMY ZESTY VEGETABLE DIP WITH CELERY STICKS

6   large celery ribs
1/4 cup chili sauce, chilled*
1   teaspoon Splenda granular
2   tablespoons fat-free sour cream

Instructions

20 MINUTES BEFORE DINNER, start the chili. In a 12-inch nonstick saucepan over medium heat, combine 2 cans diced chili-style tomatoes, 1 can spicy chili beans, 1 t Splenda granular, and 1 package hot dogs. Bring to a low boil.

15 MINUTES BEFORE DINNER, start the dumpling batter. In a medium bowl, stir together 1 box corn muffin mix, 2 egg whites, $^1/_3$ c water, and 2 T flour until well mixed.

13 MINUTES BEFORE DINNER, carefully drop the dumpling batter by rounded tablespoonfuls into the low boiling chili. Cover and cook at a low boil for 10 minutes.

10 MINUTES BEFORE DINNER, start the dip and celery sticks. Cut 6 celery ribs in half lengthwise and then into 3-inch long sticks. Set aside.

In a small bowl, stir together until well mixed $^1/_4$ c chili sauce, 1 t Splenda granular, and 2 T sour cream. Place the celery sticks around the dip on a serving plate and place on the dinner table.

3 MINUTES BEFORE DINNER, put the chili in a serving bowl on a hot pad and place on the dinner table.

*NOTE: Have the chili sauce ready to use and prechilled by storing in the refrigerator.

Supplies List

Timer
12-inch nonstick saucepan
   with lid
Medium bowl
Small bowl

Grocery List

PACKAGED
2 (14½-ounce) cans diced
   chili-style tomatoes
1 (15-ounce) can spicy chili
   beans with seasoning
Chili sauce
1 (8½-ounce) box corn
   muffin mix

PRODUCE
1 large bunch celery

MEAT
1 (14-ounce) package
   fat-free hotdogs

DAIRY
Fat-free sour cream
2 eggs

Pantry List

Whole wheat flour
Splenda granular

>>> Not-Too-Sour Sauerkraut with Corn Dog Dumplings

Whole Wheat Corn Dog Dumplings • Fresh Salad with Homemade Creamy Dill Dressing

Oh man! This is such a great flavor combination I'm surprised someone else didn't think of it first. The sauerkraut isn't sour and it goes super with the corn dog! If you like sauerkraut on hot dogs and you like corn dogs, you'll really like this winning meal that would be super for a World Series Baseball Game Party! The portions of the corn dog dumplings are large, so beware, this is filling!

NOT-TOO-SOUR SAUERKRAUT

Yield: 6 servings (½ cup per serving)

Calories: 49 (20% fat); Total Fat: 1g; Cholesterol: 3mg; Carbohydrate: 9g; Dietary Fiber: 6g; Protein 0g; Sodium: 1126mg; Diabetic Exchanges: 2 vegetable

1	(32-ounce) jar sauerkraut	1	tablespoon light butter
1	medium Gala apple, thinly sliced	½	cup frozen chopped onion
		2	teaspoons Splenda granular

WHOLE WHEAT CORN DOG DUMPLINGS

Yield: 6 servings (2 dumplings per serving)

Calories: 211 (14% fat); Total Fat: 3g; Cholesterol: 20mg; Carbohydrate: 33g; Dietary Fiber: 1g; Protein: 12g; Sodium: 1031mg; Diabetic Exchanges: 2 starch, 1 very lean meat

1	(14-ounce) package fat-free hot dogs, sliced very thin	2	egg whites
1	(8½-ounce) box corn muffin mix	¼	cup water
		2	tablespoons whole wheat flour

FRESH SALAD WITH HOMEMADE CREAMY DILL DRESSING

Yield: 7 servings (½ cup per serving)

Calories: 34 (0% fat); Total Fat: 0g; Cholesterol: 1mg; Carbohydrate: 6g; Dietary Fiber: 1g; Protein: 1g; Sodium: 83mg; Diabetic Exchanges: 1 vegetable

¼	cup fat-free sour cream	½	medium onion, sliced and separated into rings (½ cup)
¼	cup fat-free Miracle Whip	1	cup grape tomatoes
½	teaspoon dried dill weed		
1	teaspoon Splenda granular		
1	large cucumber, peeled and sliced		

Instructions

30 MINUTES BEFORE DINNER, slice 1 package hot dogs into $1/4$-inch slices. Set aside.

27 MINUTES BEFORE DINNER, make the dumpling batter. In a medium bowl stir together 1 box corn muffin mix, 2 egg whites, $1/4$ c water, and 2 T flour. Stir until well mixed. The batter will be stiff and sticky. Stir in the sliced hot dogs. Set aside.

22 MINUTES BEFORE DINNER, prepare the sauerkraut. Drain 1 jar sauerkraut in a colander and rinse under cold running water in the sink for 1 minute. Press the sauerkraut between your hands to squeeze out as much of the water as possible. Set aside.

Slice 1 medium apple into slices less than a $1/4$-inch thick.

In a 12-inch nonstick saucepan over medium heat melt 1 T butter. Cook $1/2$ c frozen chopped onion and the sliced apple until tender, about 2 to 3 minutes.

Stir the sauerkraut into the apples and onions. Cover and cook for 2 to 3 minutes.

12 MINUTES BEFORE DINNER, drop the dumpling batter by heaping table-spoonfuls into the sauerkraut. Reduce the heat to medium low. Cover and cook for 10 minutes.

10 MINUTES BEFORE DINNER, prepare the salad and dressing. In a medium bowl stir together $1/4$ c sour cream, $1/4$ c Miracle Whip, $1/2$ t dried dill weed, and 1 t Splenda granular until well blended. Add 1 peeled and sliced cucumber, onion slices , and 1 c grape tomatoes to the salad dressing. Mix until the vegetables are well coated with the salad dressing. Place the salad on the dinner table.

1 MINUTE BEFORE DINNER, put the Not-Too-Sour-Sauerkraut with Corn Dog Dumplings in a serving bowl and put it on a hot pad on the dinner table.

Supplies List

Timer
2 medium bowls
12-inch nonstick saucepan
   with lid

Grocery List

PACKAGED
1 (32-ounce) jar sauerkraut
1 ($8^{1}/_{2}$-ounce) box corn
   muffin mix

PRODUCE
1 medium Gala apple
1 large cucumber
1 cup grape tomatoes
1 medium onion

FROZEN
$1/2$ cup frozen chopped onion

MEAT
1 (14-ounce) package
   fat-free hot dogs

DAIRY
Light butter
$1/4$ cup fat-free sour cream
2 eggs

Pantry List

Whole wheat flour
Dried dill weed
Splenda granular
Fat-free Miracle Whip

>>> Rotini with Home-Style Chicken Breasts & Mushroom Gravy

Harvest Turnip Greens with Diced White Turnips

This is one of those comfort food meals that's hard to believe is so low in calories.

HOME-STYLE CHICKEN BREASTS
Yield: 6 servings (4 ounces per serving)

Calories: 143 (10% fat); Total Fat: 2g; Cholesterol: 66mg; Carbohydrate: 4g; Dietary Fiber: 0g; Protein 27g; Sodium: 145mg; Diabetic Exchanges: $1/2$ starch, 3 very lean meat

ROTINI
Yield: 8 servings ($1/2$ cup per serving)

Calories: 78 (0% fat); Total Fat: 0g; Cholesterol: 7mg; Carbohydrate: 15g; Dietary Fiber: 0g; Protein 4g; Sodium: 522mg; Diabetic Exchanges: 1 starch

WORLD'S EASIEST MUSHROOM GRAVY
Yield: 6 servings ($1/3$ cup per serving)

Calories: 19 (0% fat); Total Fat: 0g; Cholesterol: 5mg; Carbohydrate: 4g; Dietary Fiber: 0g; Protein 1g; Sodium: 375mg; Diabetic Exchanges: Free

HARVEST TURNIP GREENS WITH DICED WHITE TURNIPS
Yield: 8 servings ($1/2$ cup per serving)

Calories: 33 (0% fat); Total Fat: 0g; Cholesterol: 0mg; Carbohydrate: 7g; Dietary Fiber: 3g; Protein 2g; Sodium: 618mg; Diabetic Exchanges: $1 1/2$ vegetable

HOME-STYLE CHICKEN BREASTS

6   (4-ounce) boneless skinless chicken breasts

$1/4$ cup Italian-style bread crumbs

ROTINI

1   (14-ounce) can fat-free chicken broth

2   (12-ounce) cans fat-free chicken gravy

2   cups rotini

$1/2$ teaspoon garlic powder

WORLD'S EASIEST MUSHROOM GRAVY

1   (12-ounce) can fat-free chicken gravy

2   (4-ounce) cans mushroom slices, drained

Dash ground pepper

HARVEST TURNIP GREENS WITH DICED WHITE TURNIPS

1   Gala apple, finely chopped ($1 1/2$ cups)

3   ($14 1/2$-ounce) cans turnip greens with diced white turnips, drained

1   teaspoon seasoned salt

$1/2$ cup frozen chopped onion

Instructions

30 MINUTES BEFORE DINNER, coat a 12-inch nonstick saucepan with cooking spray and set aside.

Start the chicken breasts. Put the $1/4$ c bread crumbs in a freezer bag and set aside.

Rinse the chicken breasts and pat dry. Place in the bag of bread crumbs; shake well to coat the chicken. Heat the prepared skillet over medium-high heat. Add the chicken to the pan. Cook for 10 minutes, or until the chicken is done, turning occasionally.

20 MINUTES BEFORE DINNER, remove the chicken from the skillet and place on a platter. Cover with aluminum foil to keep warm and set aside.

Prepare the rotini. Add to the same saucepan 1 can chicken broth, 2 cans chicken gravy, and $1/2$ t garlic powder. Mix well and bring to a low boil over medium-high heat.

18 MINUTES BEFORE DINNER, reduce the heat to medium and add 2 c rotini. Cover and cook for 10 minutes, stirring occasionally.

15 MINUTES BEFORE DINNER, start making the turnip greens. Cook chopped apple in a medium microwave-safe bowl for 1 minute. Stir 3 cans drained turnip greens, 1 t seasoned salt, and $1/2$ c frozen chopped onion into the cooked apple. Cover with waxed paper and cook in the microwave an additional 3 minutes, or until fully heated.

8 MINUTES BEFORE DINNER, add the chicken to the skillet with the rotini. Reduce the heat to low, cover, and cook for 5 minutes, or until the chicken is warm.

6 MINUTES BEFORE DINNER, make the gravy by stirring together in a microwave-safe medium bowl 1 can fat-free chicken gravy, 2 cans drained mushroom slices, and dash of ground pepper. Stir until well mixed and microwave for 1 minute, or until fully heated. Pour the cooked gravy over the chicken and rotini.

3 MINUTES BEFORE DINNER, place the skillet on a hot pad and put on the dinner table.

2 MINUTES BEFORE DINNER, microwave the turnip greens for 1 more minute. Place on the dinner table with a hot pad underneath it.

Supplies List

Timer
12-inch nonstick saucepan with lid
Platter
2 medium microwave-safe bowls

Grocery List

PACKAGED

Italian-style bread crumbs
1 (14-ounce) can fat-free chicken broth
3 (12-ounce) cans fat-free chicken gravy
2 cups rotini pasta
2 (4-ounce) cans mushroom slices
3 (14$1/2$-ounce) cans turnip greens with diced white turnips

PRODUCE

1 Gala apple

FROZEN

$1/2$ cup frozen chopped onion

POULTRY

6 (4-ounce) boneless skinless chicken breasts

Pantry List

Garlic powder
Ground pepper
Seasoned salt
Nonfat cooking spray

>>> Creamy Northern Bean Soup with Dumplings

Ham & Cheese Corn Bread Dumplings • Tomato & Mozzarella Salad

No one will ever miss any of the fat. Granny wishes she could have made it so good and still have it be so good for you, too! All my family could say was, "This is good! This is really good!"

CREAMY NORTHERN BEAN SOUP

Yield: 6 servings (1 cup per serving)

Calories: 142 (25% fat); Total Fat: 4g; Cholesterol: 14mg; Carbohydrate: 18g; Dietary Fiber: 5g; Protein 9g; Sodium: 1105mg; Diabetic Exchanges: 1 starch, 1 lean meat

HAM & CHEESE CORN BREAD DUMPLINGS

Yield: 6 servings (2 dumplings per serving)

Calories: 199 (19% fat); Total Fat: 4g; Cholesterol: 12mg; Carbohydrate: 30g; Dietary Fiber: 1g; Protein 11g; Sodium: 703mg; Diabetic Exchanges: 2 starch, 1 lean meat

TOMATO & MOZZARELLA SALAD

Yield: 6 servings ($^1/_2$ cup per serving)

Calories: 62 (0% fat); Total Fat: 0g; Cholesterol: 3mg; Carbohydrate: 13g; Dietary Fiber: 1g; Protein 3g; Sodium: 382mg; Diabetic Exchanges: 1 vegetable, $^1/_2$ other carbohydrate

CREAMY NORTHERN BEAN SOUP

1   ($15^1/_2$-ounce) can great Northern beans, undrained
$^1/_2$ cup frozen onion, chopped
$^1/_4$ teaspoon dried dill weed
2   ($10^3/_4$-ounce) cans 98%-fat-free cream of celery soup
4   ounces lean cooked ham, diced
2   cups water

HAM & CHEESE CORN BREAD DUMPLINGS

1   ($8^1/_2$-ounce) box corn muffin mix
2   egg whites
$^1/_3$ cup water
$^1/_2$ cup shredded fat-free cheddar cheese
4   ounces lean cooked ham, diced

TOMATO & MOZZARELLA SALAD

3   cups grape tomatoes, chilled
$^1/_2$ cup chili sauce, chilled
2   teaspoons Splenda granular
$^1/_4$ cup fat-free sour cream
$^1/_4$ cup fat-free shredded mozzarella cheese
$^1/_4$ teaspoon dried parsley

Instructions

30 MINUTES BEFORE DINNER, start making the soup. Mash 1 can great Northern beans with a potato masher in a 12-inch nonstick saucepan until half the beans are smashed.

Turn the heat to medium and stir in $1/2$ c frozen chopped onion, $1/4$ t dried dill weed, 2 cans cream of celery soup, 4 ounces lean cooked diced ham, and 2 c water. Continue stirring until well mixed.

25 MINUTES BEFORE DINNER, start making the dumplings. In a medium bowl, combine 1 box corn muffin mix, 2 egg whites, and $1/3$ c water. Mix until well blended. Stir in $1/2$ c shredded cheddar cheese and 4 ounces lean cooked diced ham

20 MINUTES BEFORE DINNER, carefully drop the dumpling batter by heaping tablespoonfuls into the low-boiling soup. Cover and reduce the heat to medium low. Cook for 15 minutes.

15 MINUTES BEFORE DINNER, make the salad. In a medium bowl, stir together $1/2$ c chilled chili sauce, 2 t Splenda granular, and $1/4$ c sour cream until well blended. Add $1/4$ c mozzarella cheese and 3 c grape tomatoes and gently stir until the tomatoes and cheese are coated well with the dressing. Cover and keep chilled in the refrigerator until dinner is ready.

5 MINUTES BEFORE DINNER, turn off the heat under the soup and let stand for a few minutes. The soup will thicken as it cools.

1 MINUTE BEFORE DINNER, place the soup and dumplings on a hot pad on the dinner table. Place the salad on the dinner table.

NOTE: Have ingredients prechilled by storing them in the refrigerator as soon as you unload groceries.

Supplies List

Timer
12-inch nonstick saucepan
    with lid
2 medium bowls
Potato masher or back of a
    pancake turner

Grocery List

PACKAGED

1 ($15\frac{1}{2}$-ounce) can great
    Northern beans
1 (8-ounce) bottle chili
    sauce
2 ($10\frac{3}{4}$-ounce) cans 98%-
    fat-free cream of celery
    soup
1 ($8\frac{1}{2}$-ounce) box corn
    muffin mix

PRODUCE

3 cups grape tomatoes

FROZEN

$1/2$ cup frozen chopped onion

MEAT

8 ounces lean cooked ham

DAIRY

$1/2$ cup shredded fat-free
    cheddar cheese
$1/4$ cup shredded fat-free
    mozzarella cheese
2 eggs
$1/4$ cup fat-free sour cream

Pantry List

Dried dill weed
Dried parsley
Splenda granular

>>> Mandarin & Oriental Vegetable Chicken Dinner

Whole Grain Brown Rice • Fortune Cookies

Not a stir fry, yet every bit as tasty and good! The combined flavors of this meal are light, refreshing, and satisfying. Even people who don't like brown rice will be impressed with how tender and moist this rice dish is.

MANDARIN & ORIENTAL VEGETABLE CHICKEN DINNER
Yield: 7¹/₂ servings
(1 cup per serving)
Calories: 183 (13% fat); Total Fat: 3g; Cholesterol: 46mg; Carbohydrate: 15g; Dietary Fiber: 3g; Protein 23g; Sodium: 876mg; Diabetic Exchanges: ¹/₂ fruit, 1¹/₂ vegetable, 3 very lean meat

WHOLE GRAIN BROWN RICE
Yield: 9 servings
(¹/₂ cup per serving)
Calories: 69 (7% fat); Total Fat: 1g; Cholesterol: 0mg; Carbohydrate: 14g; Dietary Fiber: 1g; Protein 2g; Sodium: 64mg; Diabetic Exchanges: 1 starch

MANDARIN & ORIENTAL VEGETABLE CHICKEN DINNER

- 1 (15-ounce) can mandarin oranges
- 1 tablespoon blue cheese crumbles
- 3 tablespoon 30%-less-fat real bacon pieces
- ³/₄ cup fat-free zesty Italian salad dressing
- 3 teaspoons Splenda granular
- 2 (14-ounce) packages frozen oriental stir-fry vegetables*
- 2 (13-ounce) cans 98%-fat-free white chicken in water, drained

WHOLE GRAIN BROWN RICE

- Juice from mandarin oranges
- Water
- ¹/₂ cup frozen chopped onion
- 1 tablespoon imitation butter-flavored sprinkles
- 1¹/₂ cups whole grain instant brown rice

Instructions

25 MINUTES BEFORE DINNER, pour the juice from the 1 can mandarin oranges into a large measuring cup, reserving the oranges. Set aside.

Pour $^1/_4$ c of the mandarin orange juice into a medium microwave-safe bowl. Set aside. Add enough water to the mandarin orange juice in the measuring cup to measure $2^1/_2$ c liquid. Pour liquid into a 1-quart nonstick saucepan.

21 MINUTES BEFORE DINNER, prepare the rice. Heat the 1-quart saucepan with the juice and water mixture over high heat. Add $^1/_2$ c frozen chopped onion and 1 T butter sprinkles and bring to a boil. Once the liquid is boiling add $1^1/_2$ c rice. Reduce the heat to medium low. Cover and let simmer for 12 minutes.

17 MINUTES BEFORE DINNER, start making the chicken dinner. Add 1 T blue cheese crumbles, 3 T bacon pieces, $^3/_4$ c zesty Italian salad dressing, and 3 teaspoons Splenda granular to the $^1/_4$ c reserved mandarin orange juice in the medium microwave-safe bowl. Stir in 2 packages frozen oriental stir-fry vegetables until the vegetables are well coated. Cover with waxed paper and cook in the microwave on high for 4 minutes.

10 MINUTES BEFORE DINNER, put fortune cookies on a plate on the dinner table.

8 MINUTES BEFORE DINNER, stir the vegetables in the microwave. Cover and cook on high for another 4 minutes.

7 MINUTES BEFORE DINNER, turn off the heat to the rice. Let stand until dinner is ready.

4 MINUTES BEFORE DINNER, add the reserved mandarin oranges and 2 cans of drained white chicken into the stir-fry vegetables. Shred the chicken with your fingers. Gently stir. Cover again and cook for another 2 to 3 minutes, or until the chicken is fully heated.

1 MINUTE BEFORE DINNER, place the rice in a serving bowl on the table. Place the chicken dinner on a hot pad on the dinner table.

NOTE: *The brand of stir-fry vegetables that we used contained broccoli, sugar snap peas, green beans, carrots, celery, water chestnuts, onions, and red peppers.*

Supplies List

Timer
Medium microwave-safe bowl
1-quart nonstick saucepan with lid

Grocery List

PACKAGED

1 (15-ounce) can mandarin oranges
30%-less-fat real bacon pieces
Fat-free zesty Italian salad dressing
Fortune cookies
Whole grain instant brown rice

FROZEN

2 (14-ounce) packages frozen oriental stir-fry vegetables*
$^1/_2$ cup frozen chopped onion

POULTRY

2 (13-ounce) cans 98% fat-free white chicken in water

DAIRY

Blue cheese crumbles

Pantry List

Splenda granular
Imitation butter-flavored sprinkles

>>> Beef & Oriental Vegetables Dinner

Whole Grain Mandarin Orange Brown Rice ● Fortune Cookies

This meal is very filling and loaded with nutrition.

BEEF & ORIENTAL
VEGETABLES DINNER
Yield: 6 servings (1 cup per serving)
*Calories: 166 (12% fat); Total Fat: 2g;
Cholesterol: 57mg; Carbohydrate: 15g;
Dietary Fiber: 3g; Protein 24g;
Sodium: 770mg; Diabetic Exchanges:
3 vegetable, 3 very lean meat*

WHOLE GRAIN MANDARIN ORANGE
BROWN RICE
Yield: 6 servings
(about 1 cup per serving)
*Calories: 114 (6% fat); Total Fat: 1g;
Cholesterol: 0mg; Carbohydrate: 24g;
Dietary Fiber: 2g; Protein 2g; Sodium:
99mg; Diabetic Exchanges:
1 starch, 1/2 fruit*

BEEF & ORIENTAL VEGETABLES DINNER

1/4 cup light red wine vinaigrette
3 teaspoons Splenda granular
2 (14-ounce) packages frozen oriental stir-fry vegetables
2 (13-ounce) cans roast beef with gravy, drained

WHOLE GRAIN MANDARIN ORANGE BROWN RICE

1 (15-ounce) can mandarin oranges, undrained
Water
2 tablespoons dried chives
1 tablespoon imitation butter-flavored sprinkles
1 1/2 cups whole grain instant brown rice

Philly Cheese Steak Macaroni Casserole, Fresh Strawberry Spinach Salad with Sweet Bacon & Blue Cheese Vinaigrette, and Dinner Rolls, *pages 39–41*

Turkey Roll-Ups with Cranberry Stuffing, Savory Turkey Gravy, and Fruity Coleslaw, *pages 120–121*

Savory Pork Tenderloin with Grilled Red Onion, Garlic & Bacon Smashed Potatoes, and Tossed Salad with Bold & Hearty Salad Dressing, *pages 178–179*

Sweet & Succulent Shrimp Kebabs,
Sunshine Vegetable Medley, and New Horizon Rice, *pages 188–189*

Instructions

27 MINUTES BEFORE DINNER, drain the juice from 1 can mandarin oranges into a 4-cup measuring cup. Set the oranges aside.

Add enough water to the mandarin orange juice to equal $2^1/_2$ c liquid. Pour into a 1-quart saucepan.

24 MINUTES BEFORE DINNER, start making the rice. Heat the saucepan over high heat. Add 2 T dried chives and 1 T butter sprinkles and bring to a boil.

20 MINUTES BEFORE DINNER, once the liquid is boiling, add $1^1/_2$ c rice. Reduce the heat to medium low. Cover and simmer for 14 minutes.

19 MINUTES BEFORE DINNER, start making the vegetables. In a microwave-safe bowl, combine $^1/_4$ c red wine vinaigrette, 3 t Splenda granular, and 2 packages frozen oriental vegetables. Cover with waxed paper and microwave on high for 8 minutes.

10 MINUTES BEFORE DINNER, stir the vegetables. Cover and cook on high 4 minutes longer.

8 MINUTES BEFORE DINNER, arrange the fortune cookies on a plate and set on the dinner table.

6 MINUTES BEFORE DINNER, turn off the heat to the rice. Stir in the reserved mandarin oranges and cover. Keep the rice on the burner until dinner is ready.

5 MINUTES BEFORE DINNER, add 2 cans drained roast beef into the cooked vegetables. Shred the beef with your fingers. Gently stir the ingredients together. Cover and cook 2 to 3 minutes, or until fully heated.

2 MINUTES BEFORE DINNER, spoon the rice into a serving bowl and place on the table.

1 MINUTE BEFORE DINNER, place the vegetables on a hot pad on the dinner table.

Supplies List

Timer
1-quart saucepan with lid
Microwave-safe bowl
Serving bowl

Grocery List

PACKAGED

1 (15-ounce) can mandarin oranges
Whole grain instant brown rice
2 (13-ounce) cans roast beef with gravy
Light red wine vinaigrette
Fortune cookies

FROZEN

2 (14-ounce) packages frozen oriental stir-fry vegetables

Pantry List

Dried chives
Splenda granular
Imitation butter-flavored sprinkles

>>> Buffalo Chicken Chili

Bacon & Onion Spinach Salad • Whole Wheat Saltine Crackers

If you like bean soup and chicken wings, then you will like this sure-fire winning meal! The salad dressing is so light that it enhances the flavors of the ingredients rather than overpowering them, like some salad dressings do. Because of this, it is very important that the fresh onion is sweet, otherwise the onion could overpower the salad.

BUFFALO CHICKEN CHILI

Yield: 9 servings (¹/₂ cup per serving)

Calories: 210 (9% fat); Total Fat: 2g; Cholesterol: 33mg; Carbohydrate: 22g; Dietary Fiber: 8g; Protein 23g; Sodium: 948mg; Diabetic Exchanges: 1¹/₂ starch, 2¹/₂ very lean meat

BACON & ONION SPINACH SALAD

Yield: 6 servings (1 cup per serving)

Calories: 47 (16% fat); Total Fat: 1g; Cholesterol: 5mg; Carbohydrate: 8g; Dietary Fiber: 1g; Protein 3g; Sodium: 128mg; Diabetic Exchanges: ¹/₂ other carbohydrate

BUFFALO CHICKEN CHILI

3	tablespoons bottled buffalo chicken wing sauce*	¹/₂	cup frozen chopped onion
1	(48-ounce) jar deluxe great Northern beans	1¹/₂	teaspoons chili powder
2	(13-ounce) cans chicken breast, undrained	1	cup vegetable juice

BACON & ONION SPINACH SALAD

2	tablespoons honey	2	plus 1 tablespoons 30%-less-fat real crumbled bacon pieces
1	tablespoon apple cider vinegar		
1	(10-ounce) package washed and ready-to-use fresh spinach	2	thin slices Vidalia onion, separated into rings

Instructions

30 MINUTES BEFORE DINNER, start the chili. In a large nonstick Dutch oven over medium-high heat, combine 3 T wing sauce, 1 jar great Northern beans, 2 cans undrained chicken breast, $1/2$ c frozen chopped onion, $1^1/_2$ t chili powder, and 1 c vegetable juice until well mixed. Bring to a low boil.

22 MINUTES BEFORE DINNER, cover and reduce the heat to medium low and simmer for 20 minutes.

20 MINUTES BEFORE DINNER, start the salad. In a small microwavable bowl, heat the 2 T honey and 1 T apple cider vinegar for 15 to 20 seconds, or until boiling. Stir until the honey is dissolved. Set aside.

Remove any large stems from 1 package fresh spinach and place in a large salad bowl. Using your hands, toss the spinach with the salad dressing and 2 T of the bacon pieces until the spinach is coated with the salad dressing. Sprinkle the remaining 1 T bacon pieces over the salad, and place the 2 thin slices of Vidalia onion on top. Cover and refrigerate until time for dinner.

4 MINUTES BEFORE DINNER, place whole wheat saltine crackers in a bowl and put on the dinner table.

2 MINUTES BEFORE DINNER, remove the salad from the refrigerator and place on the dinner table.

1 MINUTE BEFORE DINNER, place the chili on a hot pad on the dinner table.

NOTE: Buffalo chicken wing sauce is found in the barbeque aisle and is loaded with Cajun seasonings.

Supplies List

Timer
Dutch oven with lid
Small microwavable bowl
Salad bowl

Grocery List

PACKAGED
1 (48-ounce) jar deluxe great Northern beans
Buffalo chicken wing sauce
8 ounces vegetable juice
30%-less-fat real crumbled bacon pieces
Whole wheat saltines

PRODUCE
1 Vidalia onion
1 (10-ounce) package fresh spinach

FROZEN
$1/2$ cup frozen chopped onion

POULTRY
2 (10-ounce) cans chicken breast in water

Pantry List

Honey
Chili powder
Apple cider vinegar

>>> Chicken in the Clouds Chowder

Citrus Salad

This thick and hearty chowder is a combination of chicken and dumplings, and cream of chicken soup mixed together. It's hearty like dumplings and creamy like soup. "This was the first recipe I taught my grandchildren when they were so small that they had to stand on a chair to help," said my assistant, Brenda Crosser.

CHICKEN IN THE CLOUDS CHOWDER
Yield: 11 servings
(1 cup per serving)

Calories: 218 (15% fat); Total Fat: 3g; Cholesterol: 27mg; Carbohydrate: 26g; Dietary Fiber: 2g; Protein 19g; Sodium: 996mg; Diabetic Exchanges: 1^1/$_2$ starch, 1 vegetable, 2 very lean meat

CITRUS SALAD
Yield: 6 servings
(1^1/$_2$ cup per serving)

Calories: 57 (0% fat); Total Fat: 0g; Cholesterol: 0mg; Carbohydrate: 13g; Dietary Fiber: 3g; Protein 2g; Sodium: 14mg; Diabetic Exchanges: 1 fruit

CHICKEN IN THE CLOUDS CHOWDER

4   (14-ounce) cans fat-free low-sodium chicken broth
1   teaspoon rotisserie chicken seasoning
3   cups low-fat baking mix
6   egg whites or ^{3}/$_4$ cup liquid egg substitute

2   (12^1/$_2$-ounce) cans 98%-fat-free chicken breast in water, undrained
1   (8^1/$_2$-ounce) can sweet peas and carrots

CITRUS SALAD

1   (15-ounce) can mandarin oranges in light juice, drained
1   (15-ounce) can ruby red grapefruit in light juice, drained

1   large head romaine lettuce (9 cups chopped)
^{1}/$_4$ cup light red wine vinaigrette

Instructions

30 MINUTES BEFORE DINNER, start the chowder. In a large Dutch oven, bring 4 cans chicken broth and 1 t rotisserie chicken seasoning to a boil, covered, over high heat.

27 MINUTES BEFORE DINNER, in a medium mixing bowl combine 3 c baking mix with 6 egg whites.

18 MINUTES BEFORE DINNER, using your fingers, drop pieces of the dough into the boiling broth. Stir vigorously with a whisk to separate the dough into tiny pieces. Reduce the heat to medium low and simmer, covered.

16 MINUTES BEFORE DINNER, using your hands shred the 2 cans chicken breast. Briskly whisk the shredded chicken and liquid into the simmering chowder.

14 MINUTES BEFORE DINNER, begin making the citrus salad. Drain 1 can mandarin oranges and 1 can ruby red grapefruit. Set the fruit aside.

10 MINUTES BEFORE DINNER, cut 1 large head romaine lettuce into bite-size pieces and place in a large salad bowl. Add the mandarin oranges and grapefruit.

7 MINUTES BEFORE DINNER, briskly whisk the chowder to separate any large pieces of dough. Reduce the heat to low.

Toss the citrus salad with $1/4$ c light red wine vinaigrette. Place the salad on the dinner table.

2 MINUTES BEFORE DINNER, briskly whisk the soup to break up any remaining large pieces. Stir in 1 can sweet peas and carrots.

1 MINUTE BEFORE DINNER, put a ladle in the chowder and place the chowder on a hot pad on the table.

Supplies List

Timer
Dutch oven or soup pan
  with lid
Medium mixing bowl

Grocery List

PACKAGED

2 ($12\frac{1}{2}$-ounce) cans 98%
  fat-free chicken breast in
  water
1 ($8\frac{1}{2}$-ounce) can sweet
  peas and carrots
1 (15-ounce) can mandarin
  oranges in light juice
1 (15-ounce) can ruby red
  grapefruit in light juice
Light red wine vinaigrette

PRODUCE

1 large head romaine lettuce

Pantry List

$1/2$ dozen eggs or $3/4$ cup
  liquid egg substitute
4 (14-ounce) cans fat-free
  less-sodium chicken broth
Rotisserie chicken seasoning
3 cups low-fat baking mix

>>> Hickory Smoked Chicken & Bean Chowder

Cucumber & Red Bell Pepper Salad • Bacon & Tomato Cheddar Bread Crisps

Savory flavor abounds in this unique chowder. The key is to make sure you use your favorite brand of hickory smoked barbeque sauce. Even though this chowder makes thirteen servings, after serving this to a family of six I only had one serving left because so many people ate seconds. I especially like the leftover chowder reheated the next day for lunch because the flavor of the seasonings marinates into the beans and becomes more intense.

HICKORY SMOKED CHICKEN & BEAN CHOWDER

Yield: 13 servings (1 cup per serving)

Calories: 221 (6% fat); Total Fat: 1g; Cholesterol: 24mg; Carbohydrate: 32g; Dietary Fiber: 6g; Protein 17g; Sodium: 987mg; Diabetic Exchanges: 1 starch, 1 other carbohydrate, 2 very lean meat

CUCUMBER & RED BELL PEPPER SALAD

Yield: 6 servings (1 cup per serving)

Calories: 51 (11% fat); Total Fat: 1g; Cholesterol: 1mg; Carbohydrate: 10g; Dietary Fiber: 2g; Protein 2g; Sodium: 576mg; Diabetic Exchanges: 2 vegetable

BACON & TOMATO CHEDDAR BREAD CRISPS

Yield: 6 servings (1 slice per serving)

Calories: 111 (12% fat); Total Fat: 1g; Cholesterol: 6mg; Carbohydrate: 16g; Dietary Fiber: 1g; Protein 8g; Sodium: 377mg; Diabetic Exchanges: 1 starch, 1 very lean meat

HICKORY SMOKED CHICKEN & BEAN CHOWDER

1	(18-ounce) bottle hickory smoked barbeque sauce	1	($14^1/_2$-ounce) can diced tomatoes, undrained
1	(48-ounce) jar deluxe great Northern beans	$1/_2$	cup frozen chopped onion
2	(13-ounce) cans 98%-fat-free chicken breast in water	$1/_4$	cup chopped green bell pepper

CUCUMBER & RED BELL PEPPER SALAD

2	large cucumbers, chilled and thinly sliced (about 4 cups)	1	cup fat-free Italian salad dressing, chilled
1	large red bell pepper, chilled and sliced (about $1^1/_2$ cups)	$1/_4$	teaspoon ground black pepper
$1/_2$	medium onion, chilled and thinly sliced (about $1/_2$ cup)		

BACON & TOMATO CHEDDAR BREAD CRISPS

6	($1/_3$-inch-thick) slices French bread	6	teaspoons 30%-less-fat real bacon pieces
$3/_4$	cup shredded fat-free cheddar cheese	12	grape tomatoes, sliced thin

Instructions

30 MINUTES BEFORE DINNER, make the chowder. In a large Dutch oven combine 1 bottle hickory smoke barbeque sauce, 1 jar deluxe great Northern beans, 2 cans chicken breast, 1 can diced tomatoes with juice, $^1/_2$ c frozen chopped onion, and $^1/_4$ c frozen chopped green bell pepper over medium-high heat. Bring to a low boil.

25 MINUTES BEFORE DINNER, stir the chowder. Reduce the heat to medium low. Cover and simmer for about 20 minutes, stirring occasionally.

23 MINUTES BEFORE DINNER, make the salad. Slice 2 large cucumbers into thin slices to make 4 c. Cut 1 large red bell pepper into slices to make $1^1/_2$ c. Thinly slice $^1/_2$ medium onion to make $^1/_2$ c. Put the sliced vegetables into a large plastic zip-top bag. Add $^1/_2$ c Italian salad dressing and $^1/_4$ t ground black pepper. Seal the bag and shake gently to coat the vegetables with the dressing. Place in the refrigerator to keep chilled.

11 MINUTES BEFORE DINNER, start making the bread crisps. Preheat the oven to 425 degrees. Coat both sides of 6 ($^1/_3$-inch-thick) slices French bread generously with butter-flavored cooking spray. Arrange the bread slices on a baking sheet and sprinkle evenly with $^3/_4$ c shredded cheddar cheese. Spray the cheese with butter-flavored cooking spray. Sprinkle 1 t bacon pieces over and place 2 sliced grape tomatoes on each of the 6 slices of bread.

6 MINUTES BEFORE DINNER, bake bread crisps for five minutes, or until the bottom of bread is crispy and golden brown.

4 MINUTES BEFORE DINNER, put the salad into a medium serving bowl and place on the dinner table.

3 MINUTES BEFORE DINNER, ladle the chowder into 6 serving bowls and place on the dinner table.

1 MINUTE BEFORE DINNER, place the bread crisps on a hot pad on the dinner table.

NOTE: As soon as you get home from the grocery store, put the cucumbers, bell peppers, onion, and salad dressing in the refrigerator to prechill them.

Supplies List

Timer
Dutch oven or soup pan
 with lid
Medium serving bowl
Baking sheet
1 gallon zip-top bag

Grocery List

PACKAGED

1 (48-ounce) jar deluxe great
 Northern beans
1 (14$^1/_2$-ounce) can diced
 tomatoes
French bread
1 (18-ounce) bottle hickory
 smoke barbeque sauce
1 (8-ounce) bottle fat-free
 Italian salad dressing
2 tablespoons 30%-less-fat
 real bacon crumbles

PRODUCE

2 large cucumbers
1 large red bell pepper
1 medium onion
$^1/_4$ cup chopped green bell
 pepper
12 grape tomatoes

FROZEN

$^1/_2$ cup frozen chopped onion

POULTRY

2 (13-ounce) cans
 98%-fat-free chicken
 breast in water

DAIRY

$^3/_4$ cup shredded fat-free
 Cheddar cheese

Pantry List

Ground black pepper
Fat-free butter-flavored
 cooking spray

>>> Spinach, Barley & Italian Sausage Soup

Bacon Swiss Bread Crisps

This hearty comfort soup is a complete meal in itself, loaded with lots of healthy carbohydrates, protein, and vegetables. It is perfect served on a chilly or gloomy day. Eating it makes me feel all cozy inside.

SPINACH, BARLEY
& ITALIAN SAUSAGE SOUP
Yield: 13 servings
(1 cup per serving)
Calories: 147 (29% fat); Total Fat: 5g;
Cholesterol: 36mg; Carbohydrate: 15g;
Dietary Fiber: 3g; Protein 11g; Sodium:
594mg; Diabetic Exchanges:
1 starch, 1 lean meat

BACON SWISS BREAD CRISPS
Yield: 6 servings (1 slice per serving)
Calories: 111 (12% fat); Total Fat: 1g;
Cholesterol: 6mg; Carbohydrate: 16g;
Dietary Fiber: 1g; Protein 8g; Sodium:
377mg; Diabetic Exchanges:
1 starch, 1 very lean meat

SPINACH, BARLEY & ITALIAN SAUSAGE SOUP

1 ($19^1/_2$-ounce) package sweet Italian Turkey Sausage, sliced into $^1/_4$-inch slices
1 (48-ounce) can beef broth
2 cups water

1 (10-ounce) can diced tomatoes with green chilies, undrained
$1^1/_2$ cups quick barley
2 (10-ounce) packages frozen chopped spinach

BACON SWISS BREAD CRISPS

6 ($^1/_3$-inch-thick) slices French bread
6 slices fat-free Swiss cheese

6 teaspoons 30% less-fat real bacon pieces
12 grape tomatoes, sliced thin

Instructions

30 MINUTES BEFORE DINNER, start the soup. Slice 1 package sweet Italian turkey sausage into $1/4$-inch slices.

27 MINUTES BEFORE DINNER, in a large nonstick soup pan brown the sliced Italian sausage over high heat until fully cooked, stirring occasionally.

23 MINUTES BEFORE DINNER, add 1 can beef broth, 2 c water, 1 can diced tomatoes with green chilies and juice, and $1^1/2$ c quick cooking barley and bring to a boil.

18 MINUTES BEFORE DINNER, reduce the heat to low and cook for 10 minutes.

15 MINUTES BEFORE DINNER, start making the bread crisps. Preheat the oven to 425 degrees. Coat both sides of 6 ($1/3$-inch-thick) slices French bread generously with fat-free butter-flavored cooking spray. Arrange the bread slices on a baking sheet and place 1 slice fat-free Swiss cheese on each slice of bread. Spray the cheese with fat-free butter-flavored cooking spray. Sprinkle 1 t bacon pieces over and put 2 sliced grape tomatoes on each of the 6 slices of bread. Set aside.

8 MINUTES BEFORE DINNER, stir 2 packages frozen chopped spinach into the soup. Increase the heat to high and cook another 5 minutes, or until the soup is heated through.

6 MINUTES BEFORE DINNER, bake bread crisps for five minutes, or until the bottom of bread is crispy and golden brown.

3 MINUTES BEFORE DINNER, ladle the soup into individual serving bowls and place on the dinner table.

1 MINUTE BEFORE DINNER, place the bread crisps on a hot pad on the dinner table

NOTE: *The sausage is easiest to slice when it is partially frozen, so put in the freezer until you are ready to make the soup.*

Supplies List

Timer
Large nonstick soup pan
Baking Sheet

Grocery List

PACKAGED

1 (10-ounce) can diced tomatoes with green chilies
Quick barley
French bread
30%-less-fat real bacon pieces

PRODUCE

12 grape tomatoes

FROZEN

2 (10-ounce) packages frozen chopped spinach

MEAT

1 ($19^1/2$-ounce) package sweet Italian Turkey Sausage

DAIRY

6 slices fat-free Swiss cheese slices

Pantry List

1 (48-ounce) can beef broth
Fat-free butter-flavored cooking spray

>>> Garlic Fettuccini with Kielbasa Alfredo Sauce

Wedged Salads • Creamy Feta Salad Dressing

This unique entrée received huge reviews even from the younger children who thought they didn't like spinach!

GARLIC FETTUCCINI
Yield: 6 servings (1 cup per serving)

Calories: 211 (4% fat); Total Fat: 1g; Cholesterol: 0mg; Carbohydrate: 43g; Dietary Fiber: 1g; Protein 7g; Sodium: 84mg; Diabetic Exchanges: 3 starch

KIELBASA ALFREDO SAUCE
Yield: 7 servings ($^1/_2$ cup per serving)

Calories 150 (16% fat); Total Fat: 3g; Cholesterol: 26mg; Carbohydrate: 20g; Dietary Fiber: 0g; Protein 13g; Sodium: 715mg; Diabetic Exchanges: $^1/_2$ skim milk, 1 starch, 1 very lean meat

WEDGED SALADS
Yield: 6 servings (1 wedge per serving)

Calories: 23 (0% fat); Total Fat: 0g; Cholesterol: 0mg; Carbohydrate: 5g; Dietary Fiber: 2g; Protein 1g; Sodium: 14mg; Diabetic Exchanges: 1 vegetable

CREAMY FETA SALAD DRESSING
Yield: 6 servings (2$^1/_2$ tablespoons per serving)

Calories 38 (0% fat); Total Fat: 0g; Cholesterol: 2mg; Carbohydrate: 7g; Dietary Fiber: 1g; Protein 2g; Sodium: 186mg; Diabetic Exchanges: $^1/_2$ starch

GARLIC FETTUCCINI

12	ounces fettuccini pasta, uncooked
1	teaspoon garlic salt
1	tablespoon minced garlic (jar is fine)

Reduced-fat Parmesan-style grated topping

KIELBASA ALFREDO SAUCE

1	pint fat-free half-and-half
2	tablespoons flour
1	tablespoon imitation butter-flavored sprinkles
$^1/_3$	cup reduced-fat Parmesan-style grated topping

1	(14-ounce) package 80% less fat lean turkey kielbasa, sliced thin
1	cup finely chopped fresh spinach with stems removed

WEDGED SALADS

1	large head Iceberg lettuce, cut into 6 wedges

1	large tomato, chopped (1 cup)

CREAMY FETA SALAD DRESSING

$^1/_4$	cup fat-free feta cheese
3	tablespoons tabbouleh*
$^1/_2$	tablespoon red wine vinegar

$^1/_4$	cup fat-free mayonnaise
2	tablespoons fat-free sour cream
2$^1/_2$	teaspoons Splenda granular

Instructions

30 MINUTES BEFORE DINNER, bring 4 qt water to a boil in a Dutch oven.

29 MINUTES BEFORE DINNER, start salads. Chop 1 large tomato for the salad and set aside.

27 MINUTES BEFORE DINNER, start preparing the ingredients for the Alfredo sauce. Thinly slice 1 package lean turkey kielbasa; set aside.

23 MINUTES BEFORE DINNER, make the dressing. In a small bowl, combine $^1/_4$ c feta cheese, 3 T tabbouleh, $^1/_2$ T red wine vinegar, $^1/_4$ c mayonnaise, 2 T sour cream, and $2^1/_2$ t Splenda granular until well mixed. Cover and refrigerate until time for dinner.

20 MINUTES BEFORE DINNER, prepare pasta. Add 12 oz uncooked Fettuccini, 1 t garlic salt, and 1 T minced garlic to the boiling water. Return to a boil and cook for 12 minutes, or until the pasta is tender.

18 MINUTES BEFORE DINNER, make the salads by removing the core from 1 large head iceberg lettuce. Cut the head of lettuce into 6 wedges. Put each wedge of lettuce on an individual salad plate and set aside.

15 MINUTES BEFORE DINNER, while the pasta is cooking, start the Alfredo sauce.

Pour 1 pt half-and-half into a 12-inch nonstick saucepan. Whisk in 2 T flour and continue whisking until dissolved. Only after the flour is dissolved turn on the heat to medium. Whisk in 1 T imitation butter-flavored sprinkles and $^1/_3$ c Parmesan topping. Cook for 5 minutes, or until thick, stirring frequently.

10 MINUTES BEFORE DINNER, once the sauce is thick, stir in the thinly sliced turkey kielbasa. Reduce the heat to low and continue cooking to heat the kielbasa, stirring frequently.

6 MINUTES BEFORE DINNER, drain the cooked pasta.

4 MINUTES BEFORE DINNER, turn off the heat under the Alfredo sauce. Stir in 1 c fresh spinach.

CONTINUED ON NEXT PAGE >>>

Supplies List

Timer
Small bowl
12-inch nonstick saucepan
    with lid
Dutch oven
Colander

Grocery List

PACKAGED
12 ounces fettuccini pasta
Tabbouleh

PRODUCE
1 large head iceberg lettuce
1 large tomato
1 cup fresh spinach

MEAT
1 (14-ounce) package 80%
    less fat lean turkey
    kielbasa

DAIRY
Fat-free feta cheese
Fat-free sour cream
1 pint fat-free half-and-half
$^1/_3$ cup reduced-fat
    Parmesan-style grated
    topping

Pantry List

Red wine vinegar
Fat-free mayonnaise
Flour
Garlic salt
Minced garlic
Splenda granular
Imitation butter-flavored
    sprinkles

>>> Garlic Fettuccini with
Kielbasa Alfredo Sauce
CONTINUED FROM PREVIOUS PAGE

3 MINUTES BEFORE DINNER, spoon $2^1/_2$ T dressing on each wedge of lettuce. Divide and sprinkle the chopped tomato over each salad, then place on the dinner table.

2 MINUTES BEFORE DINNER, place 1 c fettuccini on each dinner plate. Spoon $^1/_2$ c Alfredo sauce over the fettucini and place on the dinner table.

*NOTE: Tabbouleh is a salad of bulgur wheat mixed with fresh parsley, garlic, and tomatoes and is found in the deli department.

GREAT GRILLING

>>> Grilled Teriyaki Chicken Sandwiches

Homemade Creamy Coleslaw • Watermelon Wedges

This is one of my all-time favorite sandwiches. For those of you who have had to stay away from creamy coleslaw because they are so high in fat and calories, you are going to love this homemade slaw recipe.

GRILLED TERIYAKI
CHICKEN SANDWICHES
Yield: 6 servings
(1 sandwich per serving)
Calories: 316 (10% fat); Total Fat: 3g; Cholesterol: 66mg; Carbohydrate: 39g; Dietary Fiber: 2g; Protein 31g; Sodium: 691mg; Diabetic Exchanges: 1 1/2 starch, 1 fruit, 3 very lean meat

HOMEMADE CREAMY COLESLAW
Yield: 6 servings (2/3 cup per serving)
Calories: 88 (39% fat); Total Fat: 4g; Cholesterol: 13mg; Carbohydrate: 10g; Dietary Fiber: 2g; Protein 3g; Sodium: 470mg; Diabetic Exchanges: 1 vegetable, 1/2 other carbohydrate, 1 fat

GRILLED TERIYAKI CHICKEN SANDWICHES

3	(8-ounce) chicken breasts	6	tablespoons Teriyaki Baste & Glaze
6	home-style honey wheat hamburger buns	1/4	cup chopped green onion tops
6	canned pineapple slices		

HOMEMADE CREAMY COLESLAW

3/4	cup fat-free mayonnaise	1/4	cup 30%-less-fat real bacon pieces
1/4	cup light Miracle Whip		
1	tablespoon apple cider vinegar	1	(16-ounce) package preshredded coleslaw
2	tablespoon Splenda granular		

Instructions

25 MINUTES BEFORE DINNER, make the coleslaw. In a medium bowl, stir together $^3/_4$ c fat-free mayonnaise, $^1/_4$ c light Miracle Whip, 1 T apple cider vinegar, 2 T Splenda granular, and $^1/_4$ c bacon pieces. Add 1 package coleslaw and mix until the coleslaw is well coated. Cover and refrigerate until time for dinner.

20 MINUTES BEFORE DINNER, start the sandwiches. Coat a gas grill with nonfat cooking spray and preheat to high.

Slice a watermelon into 1-inch wedges. Cover and place in the refrigerator until dinner.

15 MINUTES BEFORE DINNER, slice the 3 chicken breasts in half horizontally into 6 (4-oz) servings; set aside

Reduce the grill heat to medium and place the chicken on the grill. Brush $^1/_2$ T Teriyaki Baste & Glaze over each chicken breast. Arrange 6 pineapple slices on the grill. Close the lid and cook for 3 to 4 minutes. Turn over the chicken and pineapple. Brush $^1/_2$ T Teriyaki Baste & Glaze over each chicken breast. Sprinkle the chicken with $^1/_4$ cup green onion tops. Spray the cut sides of 6 home-style honey hamburger buns with nonfat cooking spray and place cut side down on the grill. Close the lid and cook for another 2 to 3 minutes. Check to see if the buns are toasted. Continue cooking until the chicken is white in the center.

Assemble the sandwiches by placing 1 grilled chicken breast on the bottom half of each hamburger bun. Top each with 1 grilled pineapple slice and the top half of the hamburger bun. Place the sandwiches on a serving platter and put on the dinner table.

1 MINUTE BEFORE DINNER, place the watermelon wedges and coleslaw on the dinner table.

NOTE: Because we are working with open flames and the temperature of the heat varies, it is important to periodically check the food on the grill to make sure it is not burning. Once you start grilling, these sandwiches come together quickly, so have all ingredients at the grill before you start cooking.

Supplies List

Timer
Medium bowl
Serving platter
Outdoor gas grill

Grocery List

PACKAGED

6 home-style honey wheat hamburger buns
1 (20-ounce) can pineapple slices
Teriyaki Baste & Glaze
¼ cup 30%-less-fat real bacon pieces

PRODUCE

Watermelon
1 (16-ounce) package pre-shredded coleslaw
1 bunch green onions

POULTRY

3 (8-ounce) chicken breasts

Pantry List

Apple cider vinegar
Nonfat cooking spray
Fat-free mayonnaise
Splenda granular
Light Miracle Whip

>>> Grilled Hawaiian Pork Steaks

Paradise Rice • Island Tossed Salad

> The tropical flavors of the Hawaiian Islands inspired this menu. The flavor combinations of the meal had me longing to go back to Hawaii. This meal goes well with your favorite fruity drink.

GRILLED HAWAIIAN PORK STEAKS

Yield: 6 steaks (4 ounce per serving)

Calories: 215 (28% fat); Total Fat: 6g; Cholesterol: 65mg; Carbohydrate: 14g; Dietary Fiber: 0g; Protein 24g; Sodium: 457mg; Diabetic Exchanges: 1 fruit, 3 lean meat

PARADISE RICE

Yield: 7 servings (1/2 cup per serving)

Calories: 175 (7% fat); Total Fat: 1g; Cholesterol: 0mg; Carbohydrate: 36g; Dietary Fiber: 2g; Protein 4g; Sodium: 99mg; Diabetic Exchanges: 2 starch, 1/2 fruit

ISLAND TOSSED SALAD

Yield: 6 servings

(1 1/3 cups per serving)

Calories: 89 (0% fat); Total Fat: 0g; Cholesterol: 3mg; Carbohydrate: 19g; Dietary Fiber: 2g; Protein 2g; Sodium: 31mg; Diabetic Exchanges: 1 fruit, 1 vegetable

GRILLED HAWAIIAN PORK STEAKS

6 (4-ounce) boneless pork loin steaks
6 canned pineapple slices
6 tablespoons Teriyaki Baste & Glaze

PARADISE RICE

1 cup pineapple juice from salad ingredients
1 cup mandarin orange juice from salad ingredients
3/4 cup water
1 tablespoon light soy sauce
1/4 cup frozen chopped onion
1/2 teaspoon ground allspice
3 cups instant whole-grain brown rice

ISLAND TOSSED SALAD

1 (20-ounce) can crushed pineapple in juice
1 (15-ounce) mandarin oranges in juice
1/2 cup fat-free sour cream
1 teaspoon apple cider vinegar
1 tablespoon Splenda Brown Sugar Blend
1 large head iceberg lettuce (about 9 cups chopped)

Instructions

30 MINUTES BEFORE DINNER, drain 1 can crushed pineapple, reserving 1 c of juice. Set aside the crushed pineapple. Pour the reserved juice into a medium nonstick saucepan. Drain 1 can mandarin oranges, reserving $3/4$ c of juice. Set aside the mandarin oranges. Add the reserved mandarin orange juice to the pineapple juice. Set the saucepan aside.

Begin to prepare the tossed salad by putting the reserved crushed pineapple in a large salad bowl. Add $1/2$ c sour cream, 1 t apple cider vinegar, and 1 T Splenda Brown Sugar Blend and mix well.

Cut the lettuce into bite-size pieces and add to the large salad bowl with the salad dressing ingredients. Set aside $1/4$ c of mandarin oranges. Add the remaining mandarin oranges to the salad and gently toss until the salad is completely coated with the dressing.

Arrange the reserved $1/4$ c mandarin oranges on top of the salad. Cover and keep in the refrigerator until dinner is ready.

18 MINUTES BEFORE DINNER, prepare the rice. Heat the pineapple and mandarin orange juices over high heat. Add $3/4$ c water, 1 T light soy sauce, $1/4$ c frozen chopped onion, and $1/2$ t ground allspice and bring to a boil. Stir in 3 c instant whole-grain brown rice and return to a boil. Reduce the heat to medium-low. Simmer, covered, for 5 minutes.

13 MINUTES BEFORE DINNER, preheat a gas grill to high.

11 MINUTES BEFORE DINNER, turn off the heat to rice. Remove from the heat and stir to fluff the rice. Cover and let stand until dinner.

Start the steaks. Reduce the grill heat to medium and place the pork steaks on the grill. Brush $1/2$ T Teriyaki Baste & Glaze on top of each pork steak. Arrange 6 slices pineapple on the grill. Close the lid and cook for 3 to 4 minutes. Turn over the pork steaks and the pineapple. Brush $1/2$ T Teriyaki Baste & Glaze on top of each pork steak. Grill another 3 to 4 minutes, or until the pork is done.

1 MINUTE BEFORE DINNER, place the salad on the dinner table. Place the rice in a serving bowl and the pork on a serving plate. Place on the dinner table.

Supplies List

Timer
Medium nonstick saucepan with lid
Large salad bowl
Serving Plate
Outdoow gas grill

Grocery List

PACKAGED

1 (20-ounce) can pineapple slices
Teriyaki Baste & Glaze
1 (20-ounce) can crushed pineapple in juice
1 (15-ounce) can mandarin oranges in juice
Instant whole-grain brown rice

PRODUCE

1 large head iceberg lettuce

FROZEN

$1/4$ cup frozen chopped onion

MEAT

6 (4-ounce) boneless pork loin steaks

DAIRY

$1/2$ cup fat-free sour cream

Pantry List

Ground allspice
Light soy sauce
Apple cider vinegar
Splenda Brown Sugar Blend

>>> Southwest Chipotle Steak Dinner

Chipotle Cream Dinner Rolls • Leafy Green Salad with Homemade French Chipotle Salad Dressing

Southwestern chipotle seasoning is the secret ingredient I use in every one of these recipes, but don't worry, every recipe tastes different. I think you'll be impressed with the creative way I have used the seasoning to add zest to an otherwise traditional salad dressing. My family didn't miss having any other starch or carbohydrate with this meal because the rolls are so large and filling.

SOUTHWEST CHIPOTLE STEAK DINNER
Yield: 6 servings
(4 ounces per serving)
Calories: 169 (30% fat); Total Fat: 5g; Cholesterol: 54mg; Carbohydrate: 0g; Dietary Fiber: 0g; Protein 28g; Sodium: 539mg; Diabetic Exchanges: 4 lean meat

CHIPOTLE CREAM DINNER ROLLS
Yield: 6 servings (1 roll per serving)
Calories: 184 (19% fat); Total Fat: 4g; Cholesterol: 4mg; Carbohydrate: 30g; Dietary Fiber: 1g; Protein 6g; Sodium: 545mg; Diabetic Exchanges: 2 starch, $^1/_2$ fat

LEAFY GREEN SALAD WITH HOMEMADE FRENCH CHIPOTLE SALAD DRESSING
Yield: 6 servings
($1^1/_2$ cups per serving)
Calories: 71 (0% fat); Total Fat: 0g; Cholesterol: 2mg; Carbohydrate: 12g; Dietary Fiber: 2g; Protein 4g; Sodium: 389mg; Diabetic Exchanges: 1 vegetable, $^1/_2$ other carbohydrate

SOUTHWEST CHIPOTLE STEAK DINNER

2 pounds boneless top sirloin steak, trimmed
1 tablespoon garlic salt
1 tablespoon Southwest chipotle seasoning

CHIPOTLE CREAM DINNER ROLLS

1 tablespoon Southwest chipotle seasoning
2 tablespoons light Miracle Whip
$^1/_4$ cup fat-free sour cream
2 tablespoons fat-free French salad dressing
1 (11 ounce) can refrigerated low-fat breadsticks
$^1/_4$ cup shredded fat-free mozzarella cheese

LEAFY GREEN SALAD WITH HOMEMADE FRENCH CHIPOTLE SALAD DRESSING

2 small heads green leaf lettuce
$^1/_2$ cup mild salsa
1 tablespoon Southwest chipotle seasoning
$^1/_2$ cup fat-free French salad dressing
$^1/_2$ cup shredded fat-free mild cheddar cheese
1 large red bell pepper

Instructions

30 MINUTES BEFORE DINNER, preheat the oven to 375 degrees and preheat a gas grill to high.

28 MINUTES BEFORE DINNER, start the rolls. Spray a baking sheet with non-fat cooking spray, set aside. Prepare the Chipotle Cream. In a medium bowl, combine 1 T Southwest chipotle seasoning, 2 T Miracle Whip, $^1/_4$ c sour cream, and 2 T French salad dressing until well mixed; set aside.

25 MINUTES BEFORE DINNER, separate 1 can refrigerated low-fat breadstick dough at the perforated marks. Place the 6 spirals face-up on the prepared baking sheet. (Two bread sticks are in each spiral.) Spread 2 t of the Chipotle Cream over each roll. Set aside the remaining Chipotle Cream to use on the steaks. Sprinkle each roll with $^1/_4$ cup cheese and spray the cheese with non-fat cooking spray; set aside.

20 MINUTES BEFORE DINNER, make the salad. Remove and discard the cores of 2 small heads of lettuce. Arrange the lettuce leaves on a large serving platter facing the same direction.

18 MINUTES BEFORE DINNER, prepare the salad dressing. In a medium bowl, combine the $^1/_2$ c mild salsa, 1 T Southwest chipotle seasoning, and $^1/_2$ c French salad dressing until well blended. Pour the salad dressing down the center of the lettuce leaves. Sprinkle $^1/_2$ cup shredded cheese over the entire salad. Cut 1 large red bell pepper into strips. Arrange the red bell pepper strips on the salad. Place the salad in the refrigerator until dinner is ready.

15 MINUTES BEFORE DINNER, prepare the steaks. Remove all the visible fat from the steak. Slice the steak into six smaller steaks. Sprinkle the steaks evenly with 1 T garlic salt and 1 T Southwest chipotle seasoning. Pierce the steaks with a fork to tenderize the meat and incorporate the seasonings into the steak.

13 MINUTES BEFORE DINNER, bake the dinner rolls in the preheated oven for 12 minutes.

Place the steaks at a 45-degree angle on the preheated grill. Press the steaks firmly with tongs to create grill marks into the meat. Close the lid of grill and cook the steaks over high heat for 2 to 3 minutes.

CONTINUED ON NEXT PAGE >>>

Supplies List

Timer
Baking sheet
2 medium bowls
Large platter
Serving plate
Large plate
Outdoor gas grill

Grocery List

PACKAGED

$^1/_2$ cup mild salsa
1 (8-ounce) bottle fat-free French salad dressing

PRODUCE

2 small heads green leaf lettuce
1 large red bell pepper

MEAT

2 pounds boneless top sirloin steak

DAIRY

$^1/_2$ cup fat-free sour cream
$^1/_2$ cup shredded fat-free mild cheddar cheese
$^1/_4$ cup shredded fat-free mozzarella cheese
1 (11-ounce) can refrigerated low-fat breadsticks

SEASONINGS

Southwest chipotle seasoning

Pantry List

Nonfat cooking spray
Garlic salt
Light Miracle Whip

10 MINUTES BEFORE DINNER, rotate the steaks 45 degrees to create diamond-shaped grill marks. Press the steaks firmly with the tongs to sear the grill marks into the meat. Cover and cook the steaks for another 2 to 3 minutes.

7 MINUTES BEFORE DINNER, turn over the steaks and place the steaks at a 45-degree angle on the grill. Press the steaks firmly with the tongs to create grill marks into the meat. Close lid of grill and cook the steaks over high heat for 2 to 3 minutes. Rotate the steaks 45 degrees to create diamond-shaped grill marks. Press the steaks firmly with the tongs to sear the grill marks into the meat. Cover and cook the steaks for another 2 to 3 minutes.

5 MINUTES BEFORE DINNER, place the salad on table.

3 MINUTES BEFORE DINNER, remove the steaks from the grill and place on a serving plate. Put a little dab of the leftover cream spread on each steak and place the plate on the table.

1 MINUTE BEFORE DINNER, place the dinner rolls on a large plate.

>>> Pork Steaks with Sweet & Sassy Chilled Pear Salsa

Tangy Tossed Salad • Sweet & Sassy Chilled Pear Salsa • Southwestern Corny Brown Rice

The saddest part of this meal is when it is over.

PORK STEAKS
Yield: 6 servings
(4 ounces per serving)
*Calories: 160 (38% fat); Total Fat: 6g;
Cholesterol: 65mg; Carbohydrate: 0g;
Dietary Fiber: 0g; Protein 24g; Sodium;
301mg; Diabetic Exchanges; 3 lean meat*

TANGY TOSSED SALAD
Yield: 6 servings
(1¹/₂ cups per serving)
*Calories: 66 (0% fat); Total Fat: 0g;
Cholesterol. 0mg; Carbohydrate: 13g;
Dietary Fiber: 2g; Protein 1g; Sodium:
267mg; Diabetic Exchanges:
¹/₂ fruit, 1 vegetable*

SWEET & SASSY CHILLED PEAR SALSA
Yield: 6 servings (¹/₃ cup per serving)
*Calories: 41 (0% fat); Total Fat: 0g;
Cholesterol: 0mg; Carbohydrate: 10g;
Dietary Fiber: 1g; Protein 0g; Sodium:
174mg; Diabetic Exchanges: ¹/₂ fruit*

SOUTHWESTERN CORNY BROWN RICE
Yield: 6 servings (¹/₂ cup per serving)
*Calories: 108 (4% fat); Total Fat: 1g;
Cholesterol: 0mg; Carbohydrate: 23g;
Dietary Fiber: 2g; Protein 3g; Sodium:
509mg; Diabetic Exchanges: 1¹/₂ starch*

PORK STEAKS

6	(4-ounce) boneless pork loin steaks, trimmed*	1	teaspoon seasoned salt

TANGY TOSSED SALAD

³/₄	cup fat-free Miracle Whip, chilled	¹/₂	cup chopped celery
1	tablespoon apple cider vinegar	1	large pear, finely chopped
2¹/₂	tablespoons Splenda granular	1	large head Iceberg lettuce (about 9 cups chopped)

SWEET & SASSY CHILLED PEAR SALSA

1¹/₂	cups finely chopped pears, chilled	²/₃	cup mild salsa, chilled
2	tablespoons Splenda granular	2	tablespoons fat-free Italian salad dressing, chilled

SOUTHWESTERN CORNY BROWN RICE

¹/₂	cup frozen 3-Pepper & Onion Blend	1	(8-ounce) can tomato sauce
1	cup instant whole-grain brown rice, uncooked	1	(11-ounce) can Mexicorn

CONTINUED ON NEXT PAGE >>>

Supplies List

Timer
Large salad bowl
Medium bowl
Medium microwave-safe bowl
Large serving plate
Outdoor gas grill

Grocery List

PACKAGED
Instant whole-grain brown
  rice
1 (8-ounce) can tomato
  sauce
1 (11-ounce) can Mexicorn
Fat-free Italian salad dressing
$^2/_3$ cup mild salsa

FROZEN
$^1/_2$ cup frozen 3-Pepper Onion
  Blend
Produce
$^1/_2$ cup chopped celery
1 large had iceberg lettuce
2 large pears

MEAT
6 (4-ounce) boneless pork
  loin steaks

Pantry List

Seasoned salt
Nonfat cooking spray
Apple cider vinegar
Splenda granular
$^3/_4$ cup fat-free Miracle Whip

Instructions

30 MINUTES BEFORE DINNER, start making the salad. In a large salad bowl, combine $^3/_4$ c Miracle Whip, 1 T apple cider vinegar, $2^1/_2$ T Splenda granular, $^1/_2$ c celery, and the chopped pear.

Remove and discard the core of the iceberg lettuce. Cut the lettuce into bite-size pieces and place on top of the salad dressing in the large salad bowl. *Do not stir the dressing with the lettuce at this time, as the salad will become soggy.* Cover and store in the refrigerator to keep chilled until dinnertime.

25 MINUTES BEFORE DINNER, start making the salsa. In a medium bowl, combine $1^1/_2$ c chopped pears, 2 T Splenda granular, $^2/_3$ c chilled mild salsa, and 2 T chilled Italian salad dressing. Cover and refrigerate until dinner is ready.

20 MINUTES BEFORE DINNER, coat a gas grill with cooking spray. Preheat the grill on high.

19 MINUTES BEFORE DINNER, start making the brown rice. Chop $^1/_2$ c frozen 3-Pepper & Onion Blend vegetable mixture. Combine the chopped 3-Pepper & Onion Blend with 1 c brown rice, 1 can tomato sauce, and 1 can Mexicorn in a medium microwave-safe bowl. Cover with waxed paper and microwave on high for 10 minutes.

15 MINUTES BEFORE DINNER, remove all the visible fat from the pork steaks. Begin grilling the pork steaks. Place the pork steaks at a 45-degree angle on the preheated grill. Press the pork steaks firmly with tongs to create grill marks into the meat. Sprinkle 1 t seasoned salt evenly over the pork steaks. Close the lid of the grill and cook over high heat for 2 or 3 minutes.

8 MINUTES BEFORE DINNER, rotate the pork steaks 45 degrees to create diamond-shaped grill marks. Press the pork steaks firmly with the tongs to help sear the grill marks into the meat. Cover and grill for another 2 minutes.

6 MINUTES BEFORE DINNER, remove the brown rice from the microwave and stir to fluff the rice. Cover with a dish towel and place on a hot pad on the dinner table.

5 MINUTES BEFORE DINNER, turn over the pork steaks and place the steaks at a 45-degree angle on the grill. Press the steaks firmly with the tongs to help sear the grill marks into the meat. Close the grill lid and cook the steaks over high heat for 2 minutes. The pork is done when completely white in the center.

3 MINUTES BEFORE DINNER, remove the salad from the refrigerator and toss with the dressing. Place the salad on the dinner table.

2 MINUTES BEFORE DINNER, remove the pork steaks from the grill and place on a large serving plate. Spoon $1/3$ c of salsa on top of each grilled pork steak.

1 MINUTE BEFORE DINNER, remove the towel from the bowl of brown rice and stir with a fork to fluff.

NOTE: *To trim, simply cut off and discard the fat on the outside of the meat. If you use an indoor electric grill there is no need to turn the meat as both the top and bottom sides cook simultaneously.*

>>> Grilled Pepperoni & Cheesy Chicken

Grande Italian Pinwheel Dinner Rolls • Fresh Mushroom & Baby Spinach Salad with
Sweet Italian Salad Dressing

> This chicken is fabulous reheated in the microwave for leftovers that you might want to consider doubling the recipe simply so you will have leftovers.

GRILLED PEPPERONI & CHEESY CHICKEN
Yield: 6 servings
(4 ounces per serving)
Calories: 170 (13% fat); Total Fat: 2g;
Cholesterol: 76mg; Carbohydrate: 2g;
Dietary Fiber: 1g; Protein 33g;
Sodium: 423mg; Diabetic Exchanges:
4 1/2 very lean meat

GRANDE ITALIAN PINWHEEL
DINNER ROLLS
Yield: 6 servings (1 roll per serving)
Calories: 158 (17% fat); Total Fat: 3g;
Cholesterol: 1mg; Carbohydrate: 26g;
Dietary Fiber: 1g; Protein 6g; Sodium:
496mg; Diabetic Exchanges: 2 starch

FRESH MUSHROOM & BABY SPINACH
SALAD WITH SWEET ITALIAN
SALAD DRESSING
Yield: 6 servings
(1 1/2 cups per serving)
Calories: 46 (11% fat); Total Fat: 1g;
Cholesterol: 1mg; Carbohydrate: 8g;
Dietary Fiber: 2g; Protein 3g; Sodium:
442mg; Diabetic Exchanges:
1 1/2 vegetable

GRILLED PEPPERONI & CHEESY CHICKEN

6	(4-ounce) boneless skinless chicken breasts	3/4	cup shredded fat-free mozzarella cheese
1/2	teaspoon Italian seasoning	18	slices 70% less-fat turkey pepperoni
1/2	teaspoon garlic powder		
6	tablespoons pizza sauce		

GRANDE ITALIAN PINWHEEL DINNER ROLLS

1	teaspoon Italian seasoning	1	(11-ounce) can refrigerated low-fat breadsticks
1/8	teaspoon garlic salt	1/4	cup fat-free mozzarella cheese
3	tablespoons pizza sauce		

FRESH MUSHROOM & BABY SPINACH SALAD
WITH SWEET ITALIAN SALAD DRESSING

2/3	cup fat-free Italian salad dressing	2	(6-ounce) packages fresh baby spinach
1	tablespoon Splenda granular	1/2	cup zesty Italian croutons
8	ounces sliced fresh mushrooms		

Instructions

30 MINUTES BEFORE DINNER, preheat the oven to 375 degrees. Coat a gas grill with nonfat cooking spray and preheat to high. Spray a baking sheet with nonfat cooking spray; set aside.

28 MINUTES BEFORE DINNER, start making the rolls. Separate 1 can breadstick dough at the perforated marks. Place the 6 spirals face-up on the prepared baking sheet. (Two bread sticks are in each spiral.) Sprinkle the spirals with the 1 t Italian seasoning and $1/8$ t garlic salt. Turn over the dough and spread $1/2$ T pizza sauce over each spiral. Evenly sprinkle $1/4$ c mozzarella cheese over spiral. Spray the cheese with nonfat cooking spray; set aside.

20 MINUTES BEFORE DINNER, start making the pizzas. Place 6 boneless skinless chicken breasts on the preheated grill. Sprinkle $1/2$ t Italian seasoning and $1/2$ t garlic powder over the chicken. Press down firmly on the the chicken breasts to create grill marks. Reduce the heat of the grill to medium. Close the lid and cook over medium heat for 10 more minutes.

13 MINUTES BEFORE DINNER, bake the dinner rolls on the middle rack of the preheated oven for 12 minutes.

10 MINUTES BEFORE DINNER, turn over the chicken breasts and press the chicken breasts firmly with the tongs to make grill marks into the chicken. Spread 1 T pizza sauce over each chicken breast. Evenly sprinkle each chicken breast with $3/4$ c mozzarella cheese. Spray with cooking spray. Place 3 slices of the turkey pepperoni on each piece of chicken. Close grill lid and cook the chicken another 2 or 3 minutes, or until white in the center. Place on a serving platter and cover to keep warm. Place on the dinner table.

5 MINUTES BEFORE DINNER, start making the salad. In the bottom of a large salad bowl, combine $2/3$ c Italian salad dressing, and 1 T Splenda granular until well mixed. Add 8 ounces sliced mushrooms, 2 packages baby spinach, and $1/2$ c croutons. Toss with the salad dressing until well combined.
   Place the salad on the dinner table.

1 MINUTE BEFORE DINNER, place the dinner rolls on a large plate.

Supplies List

Timer
Baking sheet
Serving platter
Large salad bowl
Large plate
Outdoor gas grill

Grocery List

PRODUCE
8 ounces sliced fresh
   mushrooms
2 (6-ounce) packages baby
   spinach

PACKAGED
9 tablespoons pizza sauce
Zesty Italian croutons
1 (8-ounce) bottle fat-free
   Italian salad dressing

POULTRY/MEAT
6 (4-ounce) boneless skinless
   chicken breasts
18 slices 70% less-fat turkey
   pepperoni

DAIRY
1 cup shredded fat-free
   mozzarella cheese
1 (11-ounce) can refrigerated
   low-fat breadsticks

Pantry List

Italian seasoning
Garlic salt
Garlic powder
Nonfat cooking spray
Splenda granular

>>> Tex-Mex Dinner

Cattleman Corn & Potatoes ● Southwest Chipotle Tossed Salad

Here's a favorite meal men especially go crazy over. It must be a meat thing.

TEX-MEX DINNER
Yield: 6 servings
(4 ounces per serving)
Calories: 161 (39% fat); Total Fat: 7g;
Cholesterol: 45mg; Carbohydrate: 1g;
Dietary Fiber: 0g; Protein 23g;
Sodium: 460mg; Diabetic Exchanges:
3 lean meat

CATTLEMAN CORN & POTATOES
Yield: 6 servings ($^1/_2$ cup per serving)
Calories: 132 (0% fat); Total Fat: 0g;
Cholesterol: 0mg; Carbohydrate: 30g;
Dietary Fiber: 4g; Protein 4g; Sodium:
895mg; Diabetic Exchanges: 2 starch

SOUTHWEST CHIPOTLE TOSSED SALAD
Yield: 9 servings
($1^1/_2$ cups per serving)
Calories: 79 (0% fat); Total Fat: 0g;
Cholesterol: 3mg; Carbohydrate: 15g;
Dietary Fiber: 3g; Protein 4g; Sodium:
324mg; Diabetic Exchanges:
1 vegetable, $^1/_2$ other carbohydrate

TEX-MEX DINNER

$2^1/_2$	pounds flank steak, trimmed
3	teaspoons taco seasoning mix
3	teaspoons steak seasoning

CATTLEMAN CORN & POTATOES

$^1/_2$	cup chunky salsa
2	(11-ounce) cans Mexicorn,* drained
1	(15-ounce) can sliced white potatoes, drained
1	tablespoon imitation butter-flavored sprinkles

SOUTHWEST CHIPOTLE TOSSED SALAD

9	cups precut and washed iceberg lettuce
$^1/_2$	cup black beans
1	pint grape tomatoes
$^3/_4$	cup fat-free French salad dressing
$^1/_3$	cup fat-free sour cream
1	teaspoon Southwest chipotle seasoning
$^1/_2$	cup shredded fat-free cheddar cheese

Instructions

30 MINUTES BEFORE DINNER, start preparing the steak. Remove all of the visible fat from the steak. In a small bowl, make the rub for the steak by stirring together 3 t taco seasoning mix and 3 t steak seasoning. With your hands, rub the Tex-Mex rub evenly on both sides of the steak. Pierce the steak 30 to 40 times with a fork on both sides of the steak. Set aside.

20 MINUTES BEFORE DINNER, start preparing the corn and potatoes. Combine $^1/_2$ c salsa, 2 cans Mexicorn, 1 can white potatoes, and 1 T butter sprinkles in a microwavable bowl. Stir until well mixed. Cover and set aside. (Preheat the indoor grill now if you want your steak cooked medium well.)

16 MINUTES BEFORE DINNER, preheat an indoor electric grill. (Spray the indoor grill and cook the steaks now if you want them cooked medium well. See 10 minutes before for more instructions.)

15 MINUTES BEFORE DINNER, start making the tossed salad. In a large bowl combine 9 c lettuce, $^1/_2$ c black beans, and 1 pint grape tomatoes. Put salad in the refrigerator to keep chilled.

In a small bowl, combine $^3/_4$ c French salad dressing, $^1/_3$ c sour cream, and 1 t Southwest chipotle seasoning until well mixed. Put the salad dressing in the refrigerator to keep chilled.

10 MINUTES BEFORE DINNER, spray the upper and lower grilling surfaces of the indoor electric grill with nonfat cooking spray. Place the steak at a 45-degree angle on the preheated grill. Close the lid firmly, pressing down to help sear grill marks into the meat. Cook the steak for 2 to 3 minutes. Rotate the steak 45 degrees to create diamond-shaped grill marks. Close the electric grill lid firmly to help sear the grill marks into the meat. Cook the steak for another 2 to 3 minutes. Transfer to a cutting board.

4 MINUTES BEFORE DINNER, microwave the corn and potatoes. Cover and cook for 3 minutes until fully heated.

3 MINUTES BEFORE DINNER, drizzle the salad with the salad dressing. Sprinkle the top of the salad with $^1/_2$ c cheddar cheese. Place the salad on the dinner table.

2 MINUTES BEFORE DINNER, slice the steak against the grain at a 45-degree angle into $^1/_4$-inch-thick slices. Place the steak pieces on a platter and place the platter on the dinner table.

1 MINUTE BEFORE DINNER, stir the corn and potatoes. Put the bowl on a hot pad on the dinner table.

*NOTE: Mexicorn is sweet corn with red bell pepper pieces in it.

Supplies List

Timer
Small bowls
Large bowl
Microwavable bowl
Indoor electric grill
Serving platter

Grocery List

PACKAGED
$^1/_2$ cup chunky salsa
2 (11-ounce) cans Mexicorn*
1 (15-ounce) can sliced white potatoes
$^1/_2$ cup black beans
Fat-free French salad dressing
Southwest chipotle seasoning

PRODUCE
1 pint grape tomatoes
9 cups precut and washed iceberg lettuce

MEAT
$2^1/_2$ pounds flank steak

DAIRY
$^1/_3$ cup fat-free sour cream
$^1/_2$ cup shredded fat-free cheddar cheese

Pantry List

Imitation butter-flavored sprinkles
Nonfat cooking spray
Taco seasoning
Steak seasonings

>>> Loose Tex-Mex Pork Kebabs

Southwestern Spicy Rice

If you like Mexican foods, then you are sure to like this Mexican-inspired menu full of robust flavor!

LOOSE TEX-MEX PORK KEBABS

Yield: 8 servings

(4 ounces meat, ⅛ onion and ½ bell pepper per serving)

Calories: 161 (23% fat); Total Fat: 4g; Cholesterol: 63mg; Carbohydrate: 7g; Dietary Fiber: 2g; Protein 24g; Sodium: 311mg; Diabetic Exchanges: 3 lean meat, 1½ vegetable

SOUTHWESTERN SPICY RICE

Yield: 9 servings (½ cup per serving)

Calories: 103 (6% fat); Total Fat: 1g; Cholesterol: 0mg; Carbohydrate: 21g; Dietary Fiber: 1g; Protein 2g; Sodium: 355mg; Diabetic Exchanges: 1½ starch

LOOSE TEX-MEX PORK KEBABS

2 large red bell peppers
2 large green bell peppers
1 large onion
2 pounds boneless pork medallions or tenderloin

3 teaspoons taco seasoning
1 teaspoon light salt
1 teaspoon Southwest chipotle seasoning

SOUTHWESTERN SPICY RICE

1 (8½-ounce) can no-salt-added whole kernel sweet corn, drained
1 (11½-ounce) vegetable juice

2½ cups mild salsa
1½ cups uncooked instant whole-grain brown rice

Instructions

30 MINUTES BEFORE DINNER, start making the rice. In a 12-inch nonstick saucepan over medium-high heat, bring 1 can drained whole kernel sweet corn, 1 can vegetable juice, and 2½ c mild salsa to a boil.

27 MINUTES BEFORE DINNER, add 1½ c rice to the boiling liquid in the saucepan and return to a boil.

24 MINUTES BEFORE DINNER, reduce the heat of the rice to medium low. Cover and cook for 12 minutes.

22 MINUTES BEFORE DINNER, preheat the electric indoor grill. Start making the pork kebabs. Cut 2 red bell peppers, 2 green bell peppers and 1 onion into 1-inch pieces and set aside. Separate the layers of the onion.

17 MINUTES BEFORE DINNER, cut 2 lb boneless pork medallions into 1-inch pieces; set aside.

14 MINUTES BEFORE DINNER, spray the upper and lower grilling surfaces of the electric grill with nonfat cooking spray. Place the pork pieces in a single layer on the prepared grill. Sprinkle the meat with 3 t taco seasoning mix, 1 t light salt, and 1 t chipotle seasoning. Close the grill lid and cook the pork for 3 to 4 minutes, or until no longer pink.

12 MINUTES BEFORE DINNER, stir the rice. Cover, turn off the heat, and let stand on the warm burner until dinner is ready.

9 MINUTES BEFORE DINNER, remove the meat from the grill and place in a large bowl. Cover to keep warm. The pork will continue to cook as it rests.

8 MINUTES BEFORE DINNER, spray the grilling surfaces again with nonfat cooking spray. Do not wipe off any seasoning that may be remaining from the pork. Place half the bell pepper pieces and half the onion pieces on the grill. Spray the vegetables with nonfat cooking spray. Close the lid and cook for 3 minutes.

5 MINUTES BEFORE DINNER, remove the cooked vegetables from the grill and place in the bowl with the pork. Cover to keep warm.

Spray the grill again with nonfat cooking spray. Place the remaining bell pepper pieces and the remaining onion pieces on the grill. Spray the vegetables with nonfat cooking spray. Close the lid and cook for 3 minutes.

3 MINUTES BEFORE DINNER, place the rice on a large serving platter or in a 9 x 13-inch baking dish.

2 MINUTES BEFORE DINNER, remove the remaining vegetables from the grill and put them in the bowl with the cooked pork and vegetables. Stir the grilled pork and vegetables together.

1 MINUTE BEFORE DINNER, assemble the pork kebabs and rice by spooning the pork and vegetables down the center of the rice. Place on the dinner table.

Supplies List

Timer
12-inch nonstick saucepan
     with lid
Large bowl
Large serving platter or
     9 x 13-inch baking dish
Indoor electric grill

Grocery List

PACKAGED

1 (8½-ounce) can no-salt-
     added whole kernel sweet
     corn
1 (11½-ounce) vegetable
     juice
2½ cups mild salsa
Instant whole-grain
     brown rice
Southwest chipotle seasoning

PRODUCE

2 large red bell peppers
2 large green bell peppers
1 large onion

MEAT

2 pounds boneless pork
     medallions

Pantry List

Nonfat cooking spray
Light salt
Taco seasoning

>>> Barbequed Mini Meatloaves

Creamy Spiced Apricot Salad • Green Jean Beans

This is one of those "feel good meals" that you could eat over and over again.

BARBEQUED MINI MEATLOAVES
Yield: 9 servings
(1 mini meatloaf per serving)
Calories: 188 (25% fat); Total Fat: 5g;
Cholesterol: 37mg; Carbohydrate: 16g;
Dietary Fiber: 1g; Protein 19g;
Sodium: 446mg; Diabetic Exchanges:
1 starch, 2 1/2 lean meat

CREAMY SPICED APRICOT SALAD
Yield: 6 servings (1/2 cup per serving)
Calories: 112 (7% fat); Total Fat: 1g;
Cholesterol: 2mg; Carbohydrate: 24g;
Dietary Fiber: 3g; Protein 3g; Sodium:
57mg; Diabetic Exchanges: 1 1/2 fruit

GREEN JEAN BEANS
Yield: 7 servings (1/2 cup per serving)
Calories: 43 (0% fat); Total Fat: 0g;
Cholesterol: 3mg; Carbohydrate: 8g;
Dietary Fiber: 2g; Protein 2g; Sodium:
186mg; Diabetic Exchanges:
1 1/2 vegetable

BARBEQUED MINI MEATLOAVES

1	medium Gala apple
1	cup quick-cooking oats
1/2	cup frozen chopped onion
1	cup shredded fat-free cheddar cheese
1	teaspoon seasoned salt
1 1/4	pounds lean ground beef
9	tablespoons honey barbeque sauce

CREAMY SPICED APRICOT SALAD

2	ounces fat-free cream cheese, softened
1/4	teaspoon vanilla extract
1/8	teaspoon ground cloves
2	tablespoons Splenda granular
1/2	cup fat-free dessert whipped topping, thawed
3	(15-ounce) cans apricots in juice, chilled
1	tablespoon finely chopped walnuts

GREEN JEAN BEANS

2	reserved apricot halves
2 1/4	cup apricot juice
1/4	cup diced cooked ham
1/4	cup fat-free zesty Italian salad dressing
1/2	teaspoon Splenda granular
1	(16-ounce) bag frozen French-style green beans

Instructions

30 MINUTES BEFORE DINNER, coat the grill with cooking spray and preheat on high. Start making the mini meatloaves. Finely chop 1 medium apple, set aside. In a large bowl, using your hands combine 1 c oats, $^1/_2$ c frozen chopped onion, 1 c cheddar cheese, the chopped apple, 1 t seasoned salt, and $1^1/_4$ lb lean ground beef until well mixed. Measure $^1/_2$ c meat mixture and shape into 9 mini meatloaves. Set aside.

23 MINUTES BEFORE DINNER, make the salad. In a medium bowl using an electric mixer, beat together 2 oz softened cream cheese, $^1/_4$ t vanilla extract, $^1/_8$ t ground gloves, and 2 T Splenda granular until smooth and creamy. Using a spatula, fold in $^1/_2$ c whipped topping.

Drain 3 cans apricots, reserving $^1/_4$ c apricot juice and set aside. Reserve 2 apricot halves. Fold in the remaining apricots to the cream cheese mixture. Sprinkle the top of the salad with 1 T chopped walnuts. Cover and keep chilled in the refrigerator until ready for dinner.

17 MINUTES BEFORE DINNER, start making the green beans. Chop the reserved 2 apricot halves. In a 12-inch nonstick saucepan over medium heat, combine the reserved $^1/_4$ c apricot juice, the chopped apricot, $^1/_4$ c ham, $^1/_4$ c Italian salad dressing, and $^1/_2$ t Splenda granular.

15 MINUTES BEFORE DINNER, place the mini meatloaves on the preheated grill. Grill over medium-high heat for 6 to 8 minutes with the lid closed.

Continue making the green beans. Add 1 bag frozen green beans to the saucepan and bring to a boil. Reduce heat to low and cook, covered, for 10 minutes.

7 to 8 MINUTES BEFORE DINNER, turn over the mini meatloaves. Spread 1 T barbeque sauce over each mini meatloaf. Continue grilling with the grill lid closed for another 6 to 7 minutes, or until the mini meatloaves are no longer pink in the center. Put mini meatloaves on a large platter.

2 to 3 MINUTES BEFORE DINNER, turn off the heat under the green beans and let stand on the hot burner until time for dinner.

1 MINUTE BEFORE DINNER, place the green beans in a serving bowl and place on the dinner table. Place the salad and the mini meatloaves on the table.

NOTE: Save time by storing the can of apricots in the refrigerator as soon as you get home from the grocery store.

Supplies List

Timer
Large bowl
Medium bowl
Electric mixer
12-inch nonstick saucepan
with lid
Large platter
Serving bowl
Outdoor gas grill

Grocery List

PACKAGED

3 (15-ounce) cans apricots in juice
Fat-free zesty Italian salad dressing
Honey barbeque sauce

PRODUCE

1 medium Gala apple

FROZEN

$^1/_2$ cup frozen chopped onions
1 (16-ounce) bag frozen French-style green beans
$^1/_2$ cup fat-free dessert whipped topping

MEAT

$1^1/_4$ pounds lean ground beef
$^1/_4$ cup diced cooked ham

DAIRY

1 cup shredded fat-free cheddar cheese
2 ounces fat-free cream cheese

Pantry List

Finely chopped walnuts
Vanilla extract
Nonfat cooking spray
Quick-cooking oats
Seasoned salt
Ground cloves
Splenda granular

>>> Savory Pork Tenderloin with Grilled Red Onion

Tossed Salad with Bold & Hearty Salad Dressing • Garlic & Bacon Smashed Potatoes

Steak sauce is the secret ingredient that I use in the salad dressing. It adds the bold and hearty flavor people think we spent a lot of time creating. The slight crispness of the red onion enhances these aromatic and juicy boneless pork chops. The smashed potatoes are a masterpiece to what is traditionally thought of as "off-limits and high-fat" comfort food. Now, thanks to this melt-in-your-mouth recipe, they are enjoyable to all who are watching their health.

SAVORY PORK TENDERLOIN WITH GRILLED RED ONION

Yield: 6 servings (3 ounces per serving)

Calories: 95 (23% fat); Total Fat: 2g; Cholesterol: 41mg; Carbohydrate: 1g; Dietary Fiber: 0g; Protein 16g; Sodium: 248mg; Diabetic Exchanges: 2 1/2 very lean meat

TOSSED SALAD WITH BOLD & HEARTY SALAD DRESSING

Yield: 6 servings (1 1/2 cups per serving)

Calories: 55 (0% fat); Total Fat: 0g; Cholesterol: 2mg; Carbohydrate: 9g; Dietary Fiber: 2g; Protein 5g; Sodium: 480mg; Diabetic Exchanges: 2 vegetable

GARLIC & BACON SMASHED POTATOES

Yield: 9 servings (1/2 cup per serving)

Calories: 92 (20% fat); Total Fat: 2g; Cholesterol: 9mg; Carbohydrate: 15g; Dietary Fiber: 1g; Protein 4g; Sodium: 479mg; Diabetic Exchanges: 1 starch

SAVORY PORK TENDERLOIN WITH GRILLED RED ONION

6   (3-ounce) top loin boneless pork chops
9   teaspoons steak sauce
2   (1/4-inch-thick) slices red onion, halved and separated

TOSSED SALAD WITH BOLD & HEARTY SALAD DRESSING

1/2   cup fat-free Italian salad dressing
2   tablespoons steak sauce
1   (16-ounce) bag iceberg garden salad mix
1   cup grape tomatoes
1/2   cup shredded fat-free cheddar cheese
1/2   cup fat-free croutons

GARLIC & BACON SMASHED POTATOES

3   medium russet potatoes (4 cups cubed)
1   tablespoon garlic salt
8   cups water
1   tablespoon minced garlic
1/4   cup imitation butter-flavored sprinkles
2   tablespoons light butter
1/2   cup fat-free half and half
1/4   cup plus 2 teaspoons 30%-less-fat real bacon pieces

Instructions

30 MINUTES BEFORE DINNER, start the potatoes. Cut the 3 potatoes into 1-inch cubes. In Dutch oven, put 1 T garlic salt in 8 c water. Add the potatoes. Bring to a boil.

23 MINUTES BEFORE DINNER, start the salad. In the bottom of a large salad bowl, stir together $1/2$ c Italian salad dressing and 2 T steak sauce until well blended. Add 1 package garden salad mix, 1 cup grape tomatoes, and $1/2$ c cheddar cheese to the large salad bowl. *Do not toss the salad with the salad dressing.* Cover and put in the refrigerator to keep chilled.

18 MINUTES BEFORE DINNER, turn off the boiled potatoes. Cover and let sit on the hot burner.
  Preheat the indoor electric grill.
  Prepare the pork. Cut 2 ($1/4$-inch-thick) slices red onion in half. Separate into rings. Set aside.

11 MINUTES BEFORE DINNER, spray the upper and lower grilling surfaces of the indoor electric grill with cooking spray. Place 6 pork top loin boneless chops on the preheated grill. Close the lid firmly, pressing down to help sear grill marks into the meat. Cook for 2 minutes.

9 MINUTES BEFORE DINNER, spread $1^{1}/2$ t steak sauce on each pork chop. Place the onion slices on top of the pork chops and close the lid firmly. Cook for 2 more minutes.

7 MINUTES BEFORE DINNER, remove the pork chops from the electric grill and sprinkle evenly with $1/2$ t dried parsley. Put the pork chops on a serving plate. Cover and let rest 5 minutes. Place the pork chops on the dinner table.

6 MINUTES BEFORE DINNER, toss the salad with the salad dressing* and top with $1/2$ c croutons. Place the tossed salad on the dinner table.

4 MINUTES BEFORE DINNER, drain the potatoes. Add 1 tablespoon minced garlic, $1/4$ cup butter sprinkles, 2 tablespoons light butter, $1/2$ c half and half, and $1/4$ c bacon pieces. Mix well with a wooden spoon.

1 MINUTE BEFORE DINNER, put the potatoes in a serving bowl. Sprinkle the top of the potatoes with 2 t bacon pieces. Place on the dinner table.

Supplies List

Timer
Dutch oven
Large salad bowl
Indoor electric grill
Serving plate
Serving bowl

Grocery List

PACKAGED

Fat-free croutons
1 (8-ounce) bottle fat-free
  Italian salad dressing
$1/4$ cup plus 2 teaspoons
  30%-less-fat real bacon
  pieces

PRODUCE

1 (16-ounce) bag iceberg
  garden salad mix
1 cup grape tomatoes
3 medium russet potatoes
1 red onion

MEAT

6 (3-ounce) top loin boneless
  pork chops

DAIRY

$1/2$ cup shredded fat-free
  cheddar cheese
Light butter
$1/2$ cup fat-free half and half

Pantry List

Garlic salt
Minced garlic
Nonfat cooking spray
Steak sauce
Imitation butter-flavored
  sprinkles

>>> Sweet & Savory Boneless Smoked Pork Chops

Citrus Green Beans • Cheesy Hot Potatoes

This is a wonderful menu combining flavors of slightly hot, slightly sweet, and citrus.

SWEET & SAVORY BONELESS SMOKED PORK CHOPS
Yield: 6 servings
(4 ounces per serving)
Calories: 178 (28% fat); Total Fat: 5g; Cholesterol: 61mg; Carbohydrate: 12g; Dietary Fiber: 0g; Protein 20g; Sodium: 1330mg; Diabetic Exchanges: 1 other carbohydrate, 3 lean meat

CITRUS GREEN BEANS
Yield: 6 servings
(1/2 cup per serving)
Calories: 57 (0% fat); Total Fat: 0g; Cholesterol: 2mg; Carbohydrate: 13g; Dietary Fiber: 3g; Protein 2g; Sodium: 423mg; Diabetic Exchanges: 1/2 fruit, 1 vegetable

CHEESY HOT POTATOES
Yield: 6 servings
(1/2 cup per serving)
Calories: 99 (0% fat); Total Fat: 0g; Cholesterol: 2mg; Carbohydrate: 18g; Dietary Fiber: 3g; Protein 4g; Sodium: 588mg; Diabetic Exchanges: 1 starch

SWEET & SAVORY BONELESS SMOKED PORK CHOPS

6 (4-ounce) boneless smoked pork chops
1/4 teaspoon ground allspice
1/4 cup honey
1 tablespoon canned diced jalapeño chile

CITRUS GREEN BEANS

2 (14 1/2-ounce) cans cut green beans, drained
1 (10 1/2-ounce) can light mandarin oranges, drained
1 tablespoon 30%-less-fat real bacon pieces
1 teaspoon liquid smoke

CHEESY HOT POTATOES

1 (4-ounce) can diced jalapeño chiles, drained
4 cups frozen Potatoes O'Brien*
2 tablespoons imitation butter-flavored sprinkles
1/2 cup shredded fat-free cheddar cheese

Instructions

25 MINUTES BEFORE DINNER, start the green beans. In a $2^1/_2$-quart non-stick saucepan, add—in this order—2 cans drained cut green beans, 1 can mandarin oranges, 1 T bacon pieces, and 1 t liquid smoke. Cover and cook over low heat until time for dinner. *Do not stir the green beans.*

20 MINUTES BEFORE DINNER, start the potatoes. Drain 1 can diced jalapeño chiles. Set aside 1 T jalapeño in a small bowl to use in the pork chops. Put the remaining diced jalapeños in a 12-inch nonstick skillet with $1^1/_2$ inches of water and 4 cups frozen Potatoes O'Brien. Bring to a boil over high heat.

14 MINUTES BEFORE DINNER, preheat the electric indoor grill. Start making the pork chops. Finely chop the reserved 1 T jalapeño and stir it in a small bowl with $^1/_4$ c honey.

9 MINUTES BEFORE DINNER, spray the upper and lower grilling surfaces of the indoor electric grill with nonfat cooking spray. Place the boneless smoked pork chops on the preheated grill. Brush each pork chop with 1 t of the honey-jalapeno mixture. Once each pork chop is covered with the mixture, pour any remaining mixture over the pork chops. Close the lid and cook for 2 minutes.

6 MINUTES BEFORE DINNER, lightly sprinkle the pork chops with $^1/_4$ tea-spoon ground allspice. Close the lid and cook for 1 minute longer.

5 MINUTES BEFORE DINNER, place the pork chops on a plate. Cover with aluminum foil to keep warm and place on the dinner table.

4 MINUTES BEFORE DINNER, drain the potatoes and place in a bowl. Stir in 2 T butter-flavored sprinkles until well mixed. Spray the potatoes with butter-flavored cooking spray. Sprinkle with $^1/_2$ c cheddar cheese. Spray the cheese with nonfat butter-flavored cooking spray. Cover with a plate to melt the cheese. Place the potatoes on the dinner table.

1 MINUTE BEFORE DINNER, drain the green beans. Place in a bowl and put them on the dinner table.

*****NOTE:** *Potatoes O'Brien are diced potatoes with onion and green and red bell peppers.*

Supplies List

Timer
$2^1/_2$-quart nonstick saucepan with lid
Small bowl
Indoor electric grill
Colander
Serving plate

Grocery List

PACKAGED
2 ($14^1/_2$-ounce) can cut green beans
1 (4-ounce) can diced jalapeño chiles
1 ($10^1/_2$-ounce) can light mandarin oranges
30%-less-fat real bacon pieces
Liquid smoke

MEAT
6 (4-ounce) boneless smoked pork chops

FROZEN
4 cups Potatoes O'Brien

DAIRY
$^1/_2$ cup shredded fat-free cheddar cheese

Pantry List

Ground allspice
Nonfat cooking spray
Honey
Imitation butter-flavored sprinkles

>>> Mild & Light Mahi-Mahi

Creamy Blueberry & Pineapple Salad • Romaine, Tomato & Feta Salad • Creamy Tabbouleh
Salad Dressing • Seasoned French Bread Crisps

If you are not a big fish fan but you want to eat more fish for health reasons, then try this recipe. It
doesn't have a strong fish flavor at all. It's mild and light.

MILD & LIGHT MAHI-MAHI
Yield: 6 servings (4 ounces per serving)

*Calories: 98 (8% fat); Total Fat: 1g;
Cholesterol: 83mg; Carbohydrate: 0g;
Dietary Fiber: 0g; Protein 21g; Sodium:
228mg; Diabetic Exchanges: 3 very lean meat*

CREAMY BLUEBERRY & PINEAPPLE SALAD
Yield: 6 servings ($1/2$ cup per serving)

*Calories: 100 (9% fat); Total Fat: 1g;
Cholesterol: 3mg; Carbohydrate: 18g;
Dietary Fiber: 1g; Protein 3g; Sodium:
106mg; Diabetic Exchanges:
1 fruit, $1/2$ very lean meat*

ROMAINE, TOMATO & FETA SALAD WITH CREAMY TABBOULEH SALAD DRESSING
Yield: 6 servings ($1^1/2$ cups per serving)

*Calories: 63 (10% fat); Total Fat: 1g;
Cholesterol: 2mg; Carbohydrate: 12g;
Dietary Fiber: 3g; Protein 4g; Sodium:
205mg; Diabetic Exchanges:
$1/2$ starch, 1 vegetable*

SEASONED FRENCH BREAD CRISPS
Yield: 6 servings (1 piece per serving)

*Calories: 57 (9% fat); Total Fat: 1g;
Cholesterol: 0mg; Carbohydrate: 10g;
Dietary Fiber: 1g; Protein 3g; Sodium:
190mg; Diabetic Exchanges: $1/2$ starch*

MILD & LIGHT MAHI-MAHI

3	($1/2$ pound) mahi-mahi fillets	1	large fresh lemon
$3/4$	teaspoon Old Bay seasoning	18	sprays fat-free butter spray
$1^1/2$	teaspoons imitation butter-flavored sprinkles		Dried parsley

CREAMY BLUEBERRY & PINEAPPLE SALAD

4	ounces fat-free cream cheese, softened	2	tablespoons Splenda granular
$1/2$	teaspoon vanilla extract	1	(20-ounce) can pineapple tidbits, drained
1	cup fat-free dessert whipped topping, thawed	1	cup fresh blueberries
		1	tablespoon finely chopped walnuts

ROMAINE, TOMATO & FETA SALAD

$3/4$	cup grape tomatoes	9	cups prewashed and cut romaine lettuce (about 1 large head)
$1/4$	cup fat-free feta cheese		
$1/3$	cup fat-free croutons		

CREAMY TABBOULEH SALAD DRESSING

3	tablespoons tabbouleh	2	tablespoons fat-free sour cream
$1/2$	tablespoon red wine vinegar	2	tablespoons green onions, chopped
$1/4$	cup fat-free mayonnaise	$2^1/2$	teaspoons Splenda granular

SEASONED FRENCH BREAD CRISPS

$1/2$	loaf French bread	3	tablespoon fat-free feta cheese crumbles
1	teaspoon Italian seasoning		

Instructions

30 MINUTES BEFORE DINNER, start the fruit dessert salad. In a medium bowl using an electric mixer, beat 4 oz softened cream cheese, $^1/_2$ t vanilla extract, 1 c whipped topping, and 2 T Splenda granular until smooth and creamy. Set aside.

Fold in 1 can drained pineapple tidbits and 1 c blueberries to the cream cheese mixture and stir until the fruit is covered. Sprinkle the top of the salad with 1 T walnuts. Cover and chill in the refrigerator until ready for dinner.

23 MINUTES BEFORE DINNER, make the salad dressing by combining 2 T green onions, 3 T tabbouleh, $^1/_2$ T red wine vinegar, $^1/_4$ c mayonnaise, 2 T sour cream, and $2^1/_2$ T Splenda granular in a large bowl until well blended.

19 MINUTES BEFORE DINNER, make the salad. Place 9 c lettuce, the tomatoes, and $^1/_4$ c feta cheese in the large bowl on top of the salad dressing. *Do not toss the salad with the dressing.* Cover and put in the refrigerator to keep chilled until dinner.

16 MINUTES BEFORE DINNER, start making the bread crisps by slicing the bread at a 45-degree angle into thin $^1/_3$-inch slices. Generously spray both sides of each of the bread slices with nonfat butter-flavored cooking spray and place on a baking sheet. Evenly sprinkle the 6 slices of bread with 1 t Italian seasoning and 3 T feta cheese crumbles. Set aside.

14 MINUTES BEFORE DINNER, preheat an indoor electric grill.

10 MINUTES BEFORE DINNER, preheat the oven to 350 degrees.

9 MINUTES BEFORE DINNER, cook the fish. Spray the upper and lower grilling surfaces of the indoor electric grill with butter-flavored cooking spray. Place the mahi-mahi fillets at a 45-degree angle on the preheated grill. Close the lid firmly, pressing down to help sear grill marks into the fish. Cook the fish for 2 to 3 minutes.

While fish is cooking, prepare the other ingredients for the fish. In a small bowl, combine $^3/_4$ t Old Bay Seasoning and $1^1/_2$ t butter sprinkles. Set aside. Cut 1 fresh lemon into 6 ($^1/_4$ to $^1/_2$-inch thick) slices. Set aside.

7 MINUTES BEFORE DINNER, bake the bread crisps in the preheated oven for 5 minutes, or until lightly golden and crispy.

CONTINUED ON NEXT PAGE >>>

Supplies List

Timer
Medium bowl
Electric mixer
Large bowl
Baking sheet
Indoor electric grill
2 serving plates

Grocery List

PACKAGED
1 (20-ounce) can pineapple tidbits
Fat-free croutons
Tabbouleh
$^1/_2$ loaf French bread

PRODUCE
1 cup fresh blueberries
9 cups pre-cut romaine lettuce
$^3/_4$ cup grape tomatoes
1 bunch green onions
1 large lemon

FISH
3 ($^1/_2$ pound) mahi-mahi fillets

DAIRY
1 cup fat-free dessert whipped topping
Fat-free sour cream
4 ounces fat-free cream cheese
Fat-free feta cheese crumbles

Pantry List

Finely chopped walnuts
Red wine vinegar
Nonfat butter-flavored cooking spray
Vanilla extract
Dried parsley
Italian seasoning
Old Bay seasoning
Imitation butter-flavored sprinkles
Fat-free mayonnaise
Splenda granular

6 MINUTES BEFORE DINNER, rotate the fish 45 degrees to create diamond-shaped grill marks.

Sprinkle the top of the fish with the prepared seasoning mixture. Place 2 lemon slices on each piece of fish. Close the electric grill lid firmly to help sear the grill marks into the fish and lemon slices. Cook the fish for 2 to 3 minutes, or until the center of the fish flakes easily with a fork.

4 MINUTES BEFORE DINNER, toss the salad with the salad dressing until the lettuce is well coated with salad dressing. Sprinkle $1/3$ c croutons over the salad. Place the prepared salad on the dinner table.

2 MINUTES BEFORE DINNER, remove the fish from the grill and place on a serving plate. Cut each of the fillets in half. Place 1 grilled lemon slice on each fillet. Lift the lemon slices slightly and spray each fillet with 6 sprays of fat-free butter spray and lay the lemon slices back down on the fish. Lightly sprinkle the grilled fish with dried parsley.

Remove the bread crisps from the oven.

1 MINUTE BEFORE DINNER, place the bread crisps on a serving plate and put on the dinner table, along with the mahi-mahi and the Creamy Blueberry & Pineapple Salad.

NOTE: Using frozen fish is fine, but allow for a minute or two more of cooking time.

>>> Ham with Fried Cabbage

Fried Cabbage • Cheesy Ranch Biscuits • Spiced Applesauce

A potato side dish is not needed with the carbohydrates and calories of the biscuits and applesauce in this menu. However, if you want a potato, put one in the microwave before you start this meal.

GRILLED HAM STEAKS
Yield: 6 servings
(4 ounces per serving)
Calories: 143 (23% fat); Total Fat: 3g; Cholesterol: 33mg; Carbohydrate: 7g; Dietary Fiber: 1g; Protein 19g; Sodium: 1427mg; Diabetic Exchanges: ¹/₂ fruit, 3 very lean meat

FRIED CABBAGE
Yield: 6 servings (¹/₂ cup per serving)
Calories: 33 (0% fat); Total Fat: 0g; Cholesterol: 0mg; Carbohydrate: 5g; Dietary Fiber: 2g; Protein 1g; Sodium: 194mg; Diabetic Exchanges: 1 vegetable

CHEESY RANCH BISCUITS
Yield: 10 servings
(1 biscuit per serving)
Calories: 56 (24% fat); Total Fat: 2g; Cholesterol: 0mg; Carbohydrate: 9g; Dietary Fiber: 0g; Protein 2g; Sodium: 189mg; Diabetic Exchanges: ¹/₂ starch

SPICED APPLESAUCE
Yield: 6 servings (¹/₂ cup per serving)
Calories: 93 (0% fat); Total Fat: 0g; Cholesterol: 0mg; Carbohydrate: 22g; Dietary Fiber: 1g; Protein 0g; Sodium: 3mg; Diabetic Exchanges: 1¹/₂ fruit

GRILLED HAM STEAKS

6	(4-ounce) 96% fat-free ham steaks	1	large Gala apple
		3	maraschino cherries

FRIED CABBAGE

1	(16-ounce) bag coleslaw mix*	¹/₂	teaspoon garlic salt
¹/₂	plus ¹/₂ cup apple cider		
1	tablespoon imitation butter-flavored sprinkles		

CHEESY RANCH BISCUITS

¹/₂	teaspoon light ranch salad dressing	2	tablespoons shredded fat-free cheddar cheese
1	(7¹/₂-ounce) can refrigerated buttermilk biscuits	1	teaspoon dried chopped chives

SPICED APPLESAUCE

3	cups unsweetened applesauce	¹/₂	teaspoon ground allspice
4	tablespoons Splenda Brown Sugar Blend		

CONTINUED ON NEXT PAGE >>>

Supplies List

Timer
12-inch nonstick skillet
   with lid
Nonstick baking sheet
Medium bowl
Electric grill
Platter

Grocery List

PACKAGED
3 maraschino cherries
Apple cider
Light ranch salad dressing
Splenda Brown Sugar Blend
3 cups unsweetened
   applesauce

PRODUCE
1 large Gala apple
1 (16-ounce) bag coleslaw
   mix

MEAT
6 (4-ounce) 96% fat-free
   ham steaks

DAIRY
Shredded fat-free cheddar
   cheese
1 (7$^1/_2$-ounce) can refrigerated
   buttermilk biscuits

Pantry List

Nonfat cooking spray
Dried chopped chives
Ground allspice
Garlic salt
Imitation butter-flavored
   sprinkles

Instructions

30 MINUTES BEFORE DINNER, start the cabbage. In a 12-inch nonstick skillet sprayed with nonfat cooking spray over medium heat combine 1 bag coleslaw mix and $^1/_2$ c apple cider to the skillet. Cover and cook 10 minutes, stirring occasionally.

25 MINUTES BEFORE DINNER, preheat the oven to 450 degrees.
Stir the fried cabbage.
Spray a nonstick baking sheet with nonfat cooking spray and set aside.
Prepare the biscuits. Spread $^1/_2$ t light ranch salad dressing on top of each biscuit. Evenly sprinkle 2 T shredded fat-free cheddar cheese over the tops of the biscuits. Spray the cheese with nonfat cooking spray. Sprinkle 1 t dried chopped chives over the top of the biscuits and set aside.

20 MINUTES BEFORE DINNER, make the applesauce. In a medium bowl, combine 3 c unsweetened applesauce, 4 T Splenda Brown Sugar Blend, and $^1/_2$ t ground allspice until well blended. Cover and refrigerate until time for dinner.
Stir $^1/_2$ c apple cider, 1 T butter-flavored sprinkles, and $^1/_2$ t garlic salt into the fried cabbage. Cook, uncovered, 4 to 5 minutes stirring occasionally.

18 MINUTES BEFORE DINNER, preheat the electric grill.
Stir the cabbage again.

15 MINUTES BEFORE DINNER, turn off the heat under the cabbage. Stir, cover and let stand on the warm burner until dinner time.

11 MINUTES BEFORE DINNER, bake the prepared biscuits for 8 minutes, or until golden brown.

10 MINUTES BEFORE DINNER, prepare the ham. Slice 1 Gala apple horizontally into 6 ($^1/_4$-inch-thick) slices. Remove the seeds from the centers of each slice. Slice the 3 maraschino cherries in half.

8 MINUTES BEFORE DINNER, spray the hot grill with nonstick cooking spray. Place 4 ham steaks on the preheated electric grill. Top each with an apple slice. Place $^1/_2$ of a maraschino cherry in the center of each apple slice. Close the lid and cook for 3 minutes.

5 MINUTES BEFORE DINNER, remove the 4 ham steaks from the grill and stack on a platter. Cover to keep warm.

4 MINUTES BEFORE DINNER, place the remaining 2 ham steaks on the grill. Top each with an apple slice. Place $1/2$ of a maraschino cherry in the center of each apple slice. Close the lid and cook for 3 minutes.

3 MINUTES BEFORE DINNER, remove the biscuits from the oven.

2 MINUTES BEFORE DINNER, place the cabbage on a hot pad and place on the dinner table. Place the applesauce on the dinner table along with the biscuits. (If desired, put biscuits in a basket or serving plate first.)

1 MINUTE BEFORE DINNER, remove the remaining ham steaks from the grill and place on the platter with the other ham steaks. Place on the dinner table.

NOTE: *Coleslaw mix is easily found in the produce section of grocery stores. It has only shredded green cabbage and carrots in it. (No red cabbage.)*

>>> Sweet & Succulent Shrimp Kebabs

New Horizon Rice • Sunshine Vegetable Medley

You may never want to eat high-fat fried shrimp again. These shrimp are so flavorful that you are going to want them for dinner every night. The rice is full of flavor and the vegetables are naturally sweetened from steaming in apple cider.

SWEET & SUCCULENT SHRIMP KEBABS
Yield: 6 servings
(2 kebabs per serving)

Calories: 150 (9% fat); Total Fat: 1g; Cholesterol: 224mg; Carbohydrate: 9g; Dietary Fiber: 1g; Protein 25g; Sodium: 554mg; Diabetic Exchanges: ¹/₂ other carbohydrate, 4 very lean meat

NEW HORIZON RICE
Yield: 6 servings
(¹/₂ cup per serving)

Calories: 83 (8% fat); Total Fat: 1g; Cholesterol: 0mg; Carbohydrate: 18g; Dietary Fiber: 2g; Protein 2g; Sodium: 194mg; Diabetic Exchanges: 1 starch

SUNSHINE VEGETABLE MEDLEY
Yield: 6 servings
(³/₄ cup per serving)

Calories: 56 (0% fat); Total Fat: 0g; Cholesterol: 0mg; Carbohydrate: 12g; Dietary Fiber: 3g; Protein: 3g; Sodium: 214mg; Diabetic Exchanges: 2¹/₂ vegetable

SWEET & SUCCULENT SHRIMP KEBABS

12	wooden skewers
1	(2-pound) bag frozen 31-40 count, tail-on shrimp, thawed, peeled, and deveined
1¹/₂	teaspoons Old Bay seasoning
¹/₂	cup cocktail sauce
2	tablespoons honey

NEW HORIZON RICE

¹/₂	cup cocktail sauce
¹/₂	cup plus 2 tablespoons water
1	cup plus 2 tablespoons whole-grain instant brown rice
1	cup frozen 3-Pepper & Onion Blend
¹/₂	teaspoon Old Bay seasoning

SUNSHINE VEGETABLE MEDLEY

1	(l-pound, 8-ounce) package frozen California blend vegetables
1	cup apple cider or apple juice
1	(16-ounce) package frozen 3-Pepper & Onion Blend
2	tablespoons imitation butter-flavored sprinkles

Instructions

30 MINUTES BEFORE DINNER, start the rice. In a medium saucepan over high heat, bring to a boil ¹/₂ c cocktail sauce, ¹/₂ c plus 2 T water, and 1 c plus 2 T rice.

26 MINUTES BEFORE DINNER, chop 1 c of the vegetable blend into small pieces. Set the remaining frozen vegetables aside.

23 MINUTES BEFORE DINNER, add the chopped vegetables to the rice and return to a boil. Stir $^1/_2$ t Old Bay seasoning into the rice. Reduce heat to low. Cover and cook for 10 minutes.

19 MINUTES BEFORE DINNER, prepare the vegetable medley. In a 2-quart saucepan combine 1 package frozen California blend, the reserved bag of the vegetable blend, and 1 c apple cider. Cover and cook over high.

15 MINUTES BEFORE DINNER, preheat the electric grill to preheat.

Start preparing the shrimp kebabs. Thread 5 peeled and deveined shrimp onto each skewer. If needed, run the shrimp under cold water to partially thaw.

12 MINUTES BEFORE DINNER, stir and turn off the rice. Keep covered and let the rice stand on the warm burner until time for dinner.

Stir the vegetables. Cover and continue cooking on high.

8 MINUTES BEFORE DINNER, spray the upper and lower grilling surfaces of the indoor electric grill generously with butter-flavored cooking spray. Lay the shrimp kebabs on the grill. Sprinkle $1^1/_2$ t Old Bay seasoning on the shrimp. Close lid and cook for 2 minutes. The skewers will stick out of the grill, but make sure the shrimp are inside the grill.

6 MINUTES BEFORE DINNER, stir together $^1/_2$ c cocktail sauce and 2 T honey until well mixed. Using a pastry brush, spread the cocktail and honey mixture on both sides of the shrimp. Close the lid and continue cooking for 4 minutes longer.

2 MINUTES BEFORE DINNER, turn off the vegetable medley. Drain and place in a serving bowl. Stir in 2 T butter-flavored sprinkles. Put on the dinner table.

Spoon the rice onto the center of a large serving platter.

Place the shrimp kebabs on top of the rice and put on the dinner table. (If desired, use the pastry brush to remove sauce from the grill and spread onto the shrimp.)

Supplies List

Timer
Serving bowl
Medium saucepan with lid
Large serving platter
2-quart saucepan with lid
Pastry brush
12 wooden kebab skewers
Indoor electric grill
Colander

Grocery List

PACKAGED
Whole-grain instant
    brown rice
1 (8-ounce) jar cocktail
    sauce
Apple cider or juice

FROZEN
1 (1-pound, 8-ounce) pack-
    age frozen California
    blend vegetables
1 (16-ounce) package plus
    1 cup frozen 3-Pepper &
    Onion Blend
1 (2-pound) bag frozen
    tail-on shrimp (31-40
    count)

Pantry List

Nonfat butter-flavored
    cooking spray
Honey
Old Bay seasoning
Imitation butter-flavored
    sprinkles

>>> Honey Dijon Salmon

Herbed Rice Pilaf • Cheesy Turnip Green Casserole

Here's a menu fit for a king. This grilled savory salmon tastes like a specialty entrée that could be served at any fine restaurant. Even people who think they do not like turnip greens will like this turnip green casserole with its smooth creamy base. The rice is anything but boring and completes this mouth-watering meal nicely.

HONEY DIJON SALMON

$1^1/2$	pounds partially frozen salmon fillets	3	tablespoons Dijon mustard
		2	tablespoons honey

HERBED RICE PILAF

1	(14-ounce) can 99%-fat-free chicken broth	$1^1/2$	cups instant whole-grain brown rice
$3/4$	cup fat-free zesty Italian salad dressing	$1^1/2$	teaspoons Italian seasoning

CHEESY TURNIP GREEN CASSEROLE

1	Gala apple	8	ounces diced lean ham
3	($14^1/2$-ounce) can turnip greens with diced white turnips, drained	1	($10^3/4$-ounce) can 98% fat-free broccoli cheese soup
1	teaspoon seasoned salt	1	tablespoon reduced-fat Parmesan-style grated topping
$3/4$	cup frozen chopped onion		

HONEY DIJON SALMON

Yield: 6 servings

(4 ounces per serving)

Calories: 175 (25% fat); Total Fat: 5g; Cholesterol: 65mg; Carbohydrate: 7g; Dietary Fiber: 0g; Protein 25g; Sodium: 237mg; Diabetic Exchanges: 1/2 other carbohydrate, 3 lean meat

HERBED RICE PILAF

Yield: 8 servings

(1/2 cup per serving)

Calories: 83 (9% fat); Total Fat: 1g; Cholesterol: 1mg; Carbohydrate: 16g; Dietary Fiber: 1g; Protein 2g; Sodium: 404mg; Diabetic Exchanges: 1 starch

CHEESY TURNIP GREEN CASSEROLE

Yield: 9 servings (1/2 cup per serving)

Calories: 89 (23% fat); Total Fat: 2g; Cholesterol: 16mg; Carbohydrate: 10g; Dietary Fiber: 3g; Protein 8g; Sodium: 1085mg; Diabetic Exchanges: 1 vegetable, 1/2 starch, 1 very lean meat

Instructions

25 MINUTES BEFORE DINNER, start the rice. In a medium nonstick saucepan over medium-high heat, combine 1 can chicken broth, $^3/_4$ c Italian salad dressing, $1^1/_2$ c rice, and $^1/_2$ T Italian seasoning. Bring to a boil.

23 MINUTES BEFORE DINNER, start the casserole. Finely chop 1 apple to make about $1^1/_2$ cups.

22 MINUTES BEFORE DINNER, microwave the chopped apple in an 8 x 8-inch glass baking dish for 1 minute. Add 3 cans turnip greens with turnips, 1 t seasoned salt, $^3/_4$ c frozen onion, ham, and 1 can broccoli cheese soup. Mix well and microwave for 3 to 4 minutes, or until hot.

18 MINUTES BEFORE DINNER, reduce the heat under rice to medium low. Cook, covered, at a low boil for 15 minutes.

17 MINUTES BEFORE DINNER, remove the casserole from the microwave. Sprinkle with 1 T Parmesan topping. Cover and set aside.

15 MINUTES BEFORE DINNER, preheat the electric grill.

9 MINUTES BEFORE DINNER, prepare the salmon. Spray both the upper and lower grilling surfaces of the preheated electric grill with nonfat butter-flavored cooking spray. Place the $1^1/_2$ lb partially frozen salmon fillet on the hot grill. Close the lid and cook for 4 minutes. While the fish is grilling, in a small bowl combine 3 T Dijon mustard and 2 T honey. Set aside.

6 MINUTES BEFORE DINNER, turn off the heat under the rice. Stir, cover, and let stand on the warm burner until time for dinner.

5 MINUTES BEFORE DINNER, rotate the salmon fillet to create diamond-shaped grill marks. Close the lid and continuing cooking for 2 more minutes, or until the fish flakes easily with a fork.

3 MINUTES BEFORE DINNER, remove the salmon fillet from the grill and place on a platter. Drizzle the grilled fish with the honey Dijon glaze. Let the fish rest 1 to 2 minutes before slicing to heat the glaze.

Microwave the casserole for 1 to 2 minutes to reheat.

1 MINUTE BEFORE DINNER, place the casserole and rice pilaf on the dinner table on hot pads. Cut the fish into 6 (4-oz) servings and put on the table.

Supplies List

Timer
Small bowl
Medium nonstick saucepan
  with lid
8 x 8-inch glass baking dish
Electric Grill

Grocery List

PACKAGED
Instant whole-grain
  brown rice
3 ($14^1/_2$-ounce) can turnip
  greens with diced white
  turnips
1 ($10^3/_4$-ounce) can 98%
  fat-free broccoli cheese
  soup
1 (14-ounce) can
  99%-fat-free chicken broth
Reduced-fat Parmesan-style
  grated topping
1 (8-ounce) bottle fat-free
  zesty Italian salad dressing

PRODUCE
1 Gala apple

FROZEN
$^3/_4$ cup frozen chopped onion

MEAT
8 ounces diced lean ham

FISH
$1^1/_2$ pounds frozen salmon
  fillet

Pantry List

99%-fat-free chicken broth
Dijon mustard
Honey
Italian seasoning
Seasoned salt
Nonfat butter-flavored
  cooking spray

>>> Maple Glazed Salmon

Teriyaki Oriental Vegetables • Seasoned Rice

This delicious maple glazed salmon is so easy and inexpensive to make at home that I can't imagine ordering it at a fine restaurant any more. The package of stir-fry vegetables includes broccoli, sugar snap peas, green beans, carrots, celery, water chestnuts, onions, and red peppers. The teriyaki vegetables and seasoned rice are the perfect accompaniment for a well-rounded, balanced menu that is absolutely delicious.

MAPLE GLAZED SALMON
Yield: 6 servings
(4 ounces per serving)
Calories: 148 (27% fat); Total Fat: 4g; Cholesterol: 65mg; Carbohydrate: 3g; Dietary Fiber: 0g; Protein 25g; Sodium: 153mg; Diabetic Exchanges: 3 lean meat

TERIYAKI ORIENTAL VEGETABLES
Yield: 6 servings
(^{2}/$_3$ cup per serving)
Calories: 86 (0% fat); Total Fat: 0g; Cholesterol: 0mg; Carbohydrate: 20g; Dietary Fiber: 3g; Protein 4g; Sodium: 397mg; Diabetic Exchanges: ^{1}/$_2$ fruit, 2 vegetables

SEASONED RICE
Yield: 6 servings
(^{1}/$_2$ cup per serving)
Calories: 67 (8% fat); Total Fat: 1g; Cholesterol: 0mg; Carbohydrate: 13g; Dietary Fiber: 1g; Protein 2g; Sodium: 165mg; Diabetic Exchanges: 1 starch

MAPLE GLAZED SALMON

1^1/$_2$	pounds salmon fillet, partially frozen
2	tablespoons sugar-free maple syrup
^{1}/$_4$	teaspoon allspice
^{1}/$_4$	teaspoon light salt
^{1}/$_2$	teaspoon toasted sesame seeds

TERIYAKI ORIENTAL VEGETABLES

2	(14-ounce) bags frozen stir-fry vegetables
^{1}/$_4$	cup Teriyaki Baste & Glaze
1	(8-ounce) can crushed pineapple in juice, drained
1	tablespoon Splenda Brown Sugar Blend
1	tablespoon light soy sauce

SEASONED RICE

1	(14-ounce) can 99% fat-free beef broth
1	cup plus 2 tablespoons instant whole-grain brown rice
^{1}/$_2$	teaspoon liquid smoke
^{1}/$_2$	teaspoon Old Bay seasoning
1	teaspoon dried chopped chives

Instructions

30 MINUTES BEFORE DINNER, prepare the vegetables. In a 12-inch nonstick skillet, stir together 2 bags stir-fry vegetables and $^1/_4$ c Teriyaki Baste & Glaze; cover and cook for 10 minutes over medium heat.

25 MINUTES BEFORE DINNER, start the rice. In a medium nonstick saucepan over high heat, combine 1 can beef broth, 1 c plus 2 T rice, $^1/_2$ t liquid smoke, $^1/_2$ t Old Bay seasoning, and 1 t chives and bring to a boil.

20 MINUTES BEFORE DINNER, stir the vegetables. Cover and continue cooking over medium heat.

19 MINUTES BEFORE DINNER, reduce the heat under rice to low. Cover and cook at a low boil for 10 minutes.

Preheat the indoor electric grill.

16 MINUTES BEFORE DINNER, add 1 can crushed pineapple, 1 T Splenda Brown Sugar Blend, and 1 T light soy sauce to the stir-fry vegetables. Stir until well mixed. Cover and continue cooking.

9 MINUTES BEFORE DINNER, spray the upper and lower grilling surfaces of the electric grill generously with nonfat butter-flavored cooking spray.

Prepare the salmon. Place a $1^1/_2$ lb partially frozen salmon fillet on the grill. Close the lid.

Turn off the heat under the rice and stir. Covered and let stand on the warm burner until dinner is ready.

7 MINUTES BEFORE DINNER, stir the vegetables. Continue cooking, uncovered, to let some of the liquid evaporate.

4 MINUTES BEFORE DINNER, rotate the salmon fillet 45 degrees to create diamond-shaped grill marks. Close the lid and continue cooking. In a small bowl, combine 2 T maple syrup, $^1/_4$ t allspice, $^1/_4$ t salt, and $^1/_2$ t toasted sesame seeds.

2 MINUTES BEFORE DINNER, remove the salmon from the grill and place on a large serving platter. Drizzle the maple glaze over the salmon fillet. As the fish rests, it will heat the maple glaze. Cut the salmon fillet into 6 (4-oz) servings. Spoon the rice on the large serving platter next to the grilled salmon. Place the vegetables on the other side of the salmon. Place the platter on the dinner table.

Supplies List

Timer
12-inch nonstick skillet with lid
Small bowl
Medium nonstick saucepan with lid
Large serving platter
Indoor electric grill

Grocery List

PACKAGED

1 (8-ounce) can crushed pineapple in juice
Instant whole-grain brown rice
Teriyaki Baste & Glaze (check the barbeque aisle)
Splenda Brown Sugar Blend
Liquid smoke

FROZEN

2 (14-ounce) bags frozen stir-fry vegetables

FISH

$1^1/_2$ pounds salmon fillet

Pantry List

1 14-ounce) can 99% fat-free beef broth
Light soy sauce
Old Bay seasoning
Dried chopped chives
Sugar-free maple syrup
Allspice
Light salt
Toasted sesame seeds
Nonfat butter flavored cooking spray

>>> Grilled Chicken Cordon Bleu

Herbed California Blend Vegetables • Hot Italian Potato Salad

This is a low-fat, fast, and simple way to make Chicken Cordon Bleu. It's so tasty that none of us even missed the fat. The vegetable side dishes are a great accompaniment for a well-balanced, low-calorie meal that is satisfying to the last bite.

GRILLED CHICKEN CORDON BLEU
Yield: 6 servings
(4 ounces per serving)

Calories: 191 (23% fat); Total Fat: 5g; Cholesterol: 84mg; Carbohydrate: 1g; Dietary Fiber: 0g; Protein 35g; Sodium: 392mg; Diabetic Exchanges: 5 very lean meat

HERBED CALIFORNIA BLEND VEGETABLES
Yield: 6 servings
(3/4 cup per serving)

Calories: 41 (0% fat); Total Fat: 0g; Cholesterol: 0mg; Carbohydrate: 8g; Dietary Fiber: 3g; Protein 3g; Sodium: 304mg; Diabetic Exchanges: 1 1/2 vegetable

HOT ITALIAN POTATO SALAD
Yield: 6 servings (3/4 cup per serving)

Calories: 107 (0% fat); Total Fat: 0g; Cholesterol: 1mg; Carbohydrate: 23g; Dietary Fiber: 4g; Protein 2g; Sodium: 305mg; Diabetic Exchanges: 1 1/2 starch

GRILLED CHICKEN CORDON BLEU

6   (4-ounce) boneless, skinless chicken breasts

3   slices reduced-fat Swiss cheese

12   slices extra-lean smoked ham, sliced thin (1/3 pound)

HERBED CALIFORNIA BLEND VEGETABLES

1   (24-ounce) package frozen California blend vegetables

1/2   cup water

1   tablespoon Italian seasoning

3   tablespoons imitation butter-flavored sprinkles

HOT ITALIAN POTATO SALAD

1   (16-ounce) package frozen 3-Pepper & Onion Blend

4   cups frozen Potatoes O'Brien

1/2   cup fat-free zesty Italian salad dressing

Instructions

30 MINUTES BEFORE DINNER, start the vegetables. In a 2-quart nonstick saucepan, combine 1 package frozen California blend vegetables, $1/2$ c water, and 1 T Italian seasoning. Cover and cook over medium heat for 30 minutes, stirring occasionally.

26 MINUTES BEFORE DINNER, start the potato salad. In a 12-inch nonstick skillet over medium heat, combine 1 package frozen pepper and onion blend, 4 c frozen Potatoes O'Brien, and $1/2$ c Italian salad dressing. Cover and cook for 20 minutes, stirring occasionally.

15 MINUTES BEFORE DINNER, preheat the indoor electric grill.
  Cut the 3 slices Swiss cheese in half and set aside.

10 MINUTES BEFORE DINNER, generously spray the upper and lower grilling surfaces of the electric grill with nonfat cooking spray.

9 MINUTES BEFORE DINNER, prepare the chicken. Place the 6 boneless, skinless chicken breasts on the preheated electric grill. Close the lid and cook for 4 minutes.

6 MINUTES BEFORE DINNER, turn off the heat under the potatoes. Cover and let stand on the burner.

5 MINUTES BEFORE DINNER, rotate the chicken 45 degrees to create diamond-shaped grill marks. Place 1 half-slice of cheese on top of each chicken breast. Top each with 2 slices of ham. Close the lid and cook for 1 more minute.

3 MINUTES BEFORE DINNER, remove the chicken from the grill and place on a platter.

2 MINUTES BEFORE DINNER, place the potato salad in a serving bowl and place on the dinner table.

1 MINUTE BEFORE DINNER, drain the vegetables. Place in a serving bowl. Stir in 3 T butter sprinkles. Place on the dinner table.

Supplies List

Timer
2-quart nonstick saucepan with lid
12-inch nonstick skillet with lid
Serving bowls
Platter
Colander
Indoor electric grill

Grocery List

PACKAGED
1 (8-ounce) bottle fat-free zesty Italian salad dressing

FROZEN
1 (24-ounce) package California blend vegetables
1 (16-ounce) package 3-Pepper & Onion Blend
1 (2-lb) bag Potatoes O'Brien

POULTRY
6 (4-ounce) boneless, skinless chicken breasts

MEAT
12 slices (1 lb) extra-lean smoked ham

DAIRY
3 slices reduced-fat Swiss cheese

Pantry List

Italian seasoning
Imitation butter-flavored sprinkles
Nonfat cooking spray

>>> Buffalo Chicken Pieces

Chunky Celery Salad • Bacon & Tomato American Bread Crisps

The entrée and salad are low enough in calories so that the serving size for the bread crisps is two rather than just one. I purposely created the Chicken Buffalo Pieces to be mild so children will like them as well. However, if your family likes things spicy, then by all means kick it up a notch by cutting back on the honey and increasing the buffalo hot wing sauce. Serve the buffalo hot wing sauce on the side.

BUFFALO CHICKEN PIECES
Yield: 6 servings
(5 ounces per serving)

Calories: 211 (9% fat); Total Fat: 2g; Cholesterol: 88mg; Carbohydrate: 12g; Dietary Fiber: 0g; Protein 35g; Sodium: 241mg; Diabetic Exchanges: 1 other carbohydrate, 5 very lean meat

CHUNKY CELERY SALAD
Yield: 5 servings
(³/₄ cup per serving)

Calories: 60 (61% fat); Total Fat: 4g; Cholesterol: 4mg; Carbohydrate: 4g; Dietary Fiber: 1g; Protein 2g; Sodium: 330mg; Diabetic Exchanges: 1 vegetable, 1 fat

BACON & TOMATO AMERICAN BREAD CRISPS
Yield: 6 servings
(2 slices per serving)

Calories: 222 (12% fat); Total Fat: 3g; Cholesterol: 12mg; Carbohydrate: 31g; Dietary Fiber: 2g; Protein 16g; Sodium: 753mg; Diabetic Exchanges: 2 starch, 1¹/₂ very lean meat

BUFFALO CHICKEN PIECES

2 tablespoons buffalo chicken wing sauce

$1/4$ cup honey

2 pounds chicken breasts, cut into 1-inch pieces

CHUNKY CELERY SALAD

1 large bunch celery

$1/4$ cup reduced-fat mayonnaise

$1/4$ cup fat–free feta cheese crumbles

$1/2$ teaspoon ranch salad dressing mix

$2^1/2$ tablespoons skim milk

BACON & TOMATO AMERICAN BREAD CRISPS

12 ($1/3$-inch-thick) slices French bread

12 slices fat-free American cheese

12 teaspoons 30%-less-fat real bacon pieces

24 grape tomatoes, sliced thin

Instructions

30 MINUTES BEFORE DINNER, prepare the chicken. Cut 2 lb boneless, skinless chicken breasts into 1-inch pieces, removing all the fat. Combine 2 T buffalo chicken wing sauce and $^1/_4$ c honey into one-gallon zip-top bag; seal. Mix together by squeezing the bag. Add the chicken pieces into the bag and mix well. Set aside until ready to cook.

24 MINUTES BEFORE DINNER, start the salad. Remove the ends from 1 large celery heart. Cut the ribs into 1-inch pieces.

In a medium bowl, stir together $^1/_4$ c mayonnaise, $^1/_4$ c feta cheese crumbles, $^1/_2$ t ranch salad dressing mix, and $2^1/_2$ T milk. Using the back of a spoon, crumble the feta cheese into small pieces.

Stir the celery pieces into the dressing. Cover and put in the refrigerator until ready for dinner.

16 MINUTES BEFORE DINNER, preheat the oven to 425 degrees. Start making the bread crisps. Coat both sides of 12 slices French bread generously with butter-flavored cooking spray. Arrange the bread slices on a baking sheet. Place 1 slice of American cheese on each slice of bread. Generously spray the cheese with butter-flavored cooking spray. Sprinkle 1 t bacon pieces and 2 sliced grape tomatoes over each slice of bread.

10 MINUTES BEFORE DINNER, preheat the indoor electric grill.

6 MINUTES BEFORE DINNER, bake the bread crisps in the oven for 5 minutes, or until the bottom of bread is crispy and golden brown.

5 MINUTES BEFORE DINNER, spray the upper and lower grilling surfaces of the indoor electric grill with nonfat cooking spray. Arrange the chicken pieces in one layer on the hot grill. Close the lid and cook for 3 minutes.

3 MINUTES BEFORE DINNER, place the celery salad on the dinner table.

2 MINUTES BEFORE DINNER, check the chicken for doneness. Close the lid and continue cooking for 1 minute longer.

1 MINUTE BEFORE DINNER, place the chicken in a large serving bowl and put on the dinner table. If desired, serve with wing sauce on the side. Remove the bread crisps from the oven and place on a hot pad on the dinner table.

Supplies List

Timer
1-gallon zip-top bags
Medium bowl
Baking sheet
Large serving bowl
Indoor electric grill

Grocery List

PACKAGED
4 tablespoons 30%-less-fat real bacon pieces
French bread

PRODUCE
1 large bunch celery
1 pint grape tomatoes

POULTRY
2 pounds chicken breasts

DAIRY
Fat-free feta cheese crumbles
Skim milk
12 slices fat-free American cheese slices

SEASONINGS
Buffalo chicken wing sauce
Ranch salad dressing mix

Pantry List

Fat-free butter-flavored cooking spray
Honey
Reduced-fat mayonnaise

>>> Hickory Smoked Sausage with Cheddar Cheese

Grilled Red Skin Taters • Brown Sugar & Cinnamon Apple Salad

The potatoes are grilled in this menu and that is why this menu is in the grilling chapter. I had never prepared red skin potatoes this way before and my dinner guests and family thought they were very good, as did I! This menu definitely keeps you on your toes without a moment to spare, so make sure you have all of your ingredients and supplies ready. The meal will be worth your concentrated effort!

HICKORY SMOKED SAUSAGE WITH CHEDDAR CHEESE

Yield: 6 servings

(3½ ounces per serving)

Calories: 253 (13% fat); Total Fat: 3g; Cholesterol: 50mg; Carbohydrate: 29g; Dietary Fiber: 0g; Protein 22g; Sodium: 1677mg; Diabetic Exchanges: 1 starch, 1 other carbohydrate, 3 very lean meat

GRILLED RED SKIN TATERS

Yield: 6 servings

(½-cup per serving)

Calories: 110 (0% fat); Total Fat: 0g; Cholesterol: 0mg; Carbohydrate: 24g; Dietary Fiber: 3g; Protein 3g; Sodium: 307mg; Diabetic Exchanges: 1½ starch

BROWN SUGAR & CINNAMON APPLE SALAD

Yield: 6 servings (⅔ cup per serving)

Calories: 107 (9% fat); Total Fat: 1g; Cholesterol: 0mg; Carbohydrate: 23g; Dietary Fiber: 3g; Protein 0g; Sodium: 11mg; Diabetic Exchanges: 1 fruit, ½ other carbohydrate

HICKORY SMOKED SAUSAGE WITH CHEDDAR CHEESE

2	(14-ounce) packages lean smoked turkey sausage	1	cup shredded fat-free cheddar cheese
¾	cup honey hickory smoked barbeque sauce		

GRILLED RED SKIN TATERS

6	medium red skin potatoes	1½	teaspoons imitation butter-flavored sprinkles
1	teaspoon seasoned salt		

BROWN SUGAR & CINNAMON APPLE SALAD

4	Gala apples	1½	cup fat-free dessert whipped topping
2	tablespoon Splenda Brown Sugar Blend	1	teaspoon ground cinnamon
		1	tablespoon finely chopped pecans

Instructions

30 MINUTES BEFORE DINNER, cut 6 potatoes into ¼-inch-thick slices. Preheat the indoor electric grill.

26 MINUTES BEFORE DINNER, core 4 apples and cut them into small pieces.

20 MINUTES BEFORE DINNER, grill the potatoes. Spray the indoor electric grill with cooking spray. Place half the sliced potatoes in a single layer on the grill. Spray the potatoes, close the lid, and grill for 9 minutes.

16 MINUTES BEFORE DINNER, preheat the oven to 250 degrees. Prepare the salad. In a medium bowl mix together $1^1/2$ c whipped topping, 2 T Splenda Brown Sugar Blend, and 1 t ground cinnamon. Stir in the apples until well coated. Sprinkle with 1 T finely chopped pecans. Place on the table until time for dinner.

10 MINUTES BEFORE DINNER, remove the cooked potato slices from the grill and place on a baking sheet in the oven to keep warm.

9 MINUTES BEFORE DINNER, spray the electric grill again with cooking spray. Arrange the remaining potato slices in a single layer on the grill and spray with butter-flavored cooking spray. Close the lid and cook.

8 MINUTES BEFORE DINNER, prepare the sausage. Preheat two 12-inch nonstick skillets over high heat. Slice the 2 packages lean smoked turkey sausage into 6 links. Slice the links in half lengthwise, cutting to, but not through, the other side. Place the sausage links cut side down in the preheated skillets. Cover and cook for $1^1/2$ to 2 minutes. Reduce the heat to medium and add $1/4$ c water to each skillet. Turn over the sausage links.

3 MINUTES BEFORE DINNER, spread 1 T honey hickory smoked barbeque sauce over each sausage link.

2 MINUTES BEFORE DINNER, evenly sprinkle 1 c shredded cheddar cheese over the sausage links. Spray the cheese with nonfat cooking spray. Cover and turn off the burners and let stand on the stove to melt the cheese.

1 MINUTE BEFORE DINNER, remove the potatoes from the oven. Arrange the potatoes from the electric grill on the baking sheet. Sprinkle 1 t seasoned salt and $1^1/2$ t imitation butter-flavored sprinkles over the potatoes. Set on a hot pad on the dinner table. Place the sausage links on a platter and put on the dinner table.

Supplies List

Timer
2 (12-inch) nonstick skillets
   with lids
Indoor electric grill
Baking sheet
Platter

Grocery List

PACKAGED

Imitation butter-flavored
   sprinkles
Splenda Brown Sugar Blend
$3/4$ cup honey hickory smoked
   barbeque sauce

PRODUCE

6 medium red skin potatoes
4 Gala apples

FROZEN

$1^1/2$ cup dessert fat-free
   whipped topping

MEAT

2 (14-ounce) packages lean
   smoked turkey sausage

DAIRY

1 cup shredded fat-free
   cheddar cheese

Pantry List

Seasoned salt
Ground cinnamon
Finely chopped pecans
Nonfat butter-flavored
   cooking spray

>>> Coconut Chicken

Asian-Inspired Rice • Sweet & Sour Oriental Vegetables

The Coconut Chicken and Asian Inspired Rice remind me of flavors you would eat in Middle Eastern countries.

COCONUT CHICKEN
Yield: 6 servings
(4 ounces per serving)
Calories: 165 (16% fat); Total Fat: 3g;
Cholesterol: 77mg; Carbohydrate: 2g;
Dietary Fiber: 0g; Protein 31g;
Sodium: 94mg; Diabetic Exchanges:
4 very lean meat

ASIAN-INSPIRED RICE
Yield: 6 servings (½ cup per serving)
Calories: 69 (9% fat); Total Fat: 1g;
Cholesterol: 0mg; Carbohydrate: 13g;
Dietary Fiber: 1g; Protein 2g; Sodium:
172mg; Diabetic Exchanges: 1 starch

SWEET & SOUR ORIENTAL VEGETABLES
Yield: 6 servings (⅔ cup per serving)
Calories: 76 (0% fat); Total Fat: 0g;
Cholesterol: 0mg; Carbohydrate: 18g;
Dietary Fiber: 3g; Protein 3g; Sodium:
30mg; Diabetic Exchanges:
½ fruit, 2 vegetable

COCONUT CHICKEN

$1^3/_4$ pounds boneless, skinless chicken breast, cut into chunks all fat removed

1 cup piña colada mix
3 tablespoons shredded coconut

ASIAN-INSPIRED RICE

1 (14-ounce) can 99% fat-free chicken broth
1 cup plus 2 tablespoons whole-grain instant brown rice

$^3/_4$ teaspoon pumpkin pie spice
$^1/_4$ teaspoon seasoned salt

SWEET & SOUR ORIENTAL VEGETABLES

$^1/_4$ cup sweet and sour sauce
1 (8-ounce) can crushed pineapple in juice

2 (14-ounce) packages frozen stir-fry vegetables

Instructions

30 MINUTES BEFORE DINNER, start the rice. In a 1-quart nonstick saucepan over high heat, combine 1 can chicken broth, 1 c plus 2 T rice, $^3/_4$ t pumpkin pie spice, and $^1/_4$ t seasoned salt and bring to a boil.

25 MINUTES BEFORE DINNER, reduce the heat to medium low under the rice. Cover and simmer for 10 minutes.

24 MINUTES BEFORE DINNER, start the vegetables. In a 12-inch nonstick saucepan over medium-high heat, combine $^1/_4$ c sweet & sour sauce, 1 can crushed pineapple with juice, and 2 packages frozen stir-fry vegetables. Bring to a low boil and simmer for 4 to 5 minutes.

19 MINUTES BEFORE DINNER, stir the vegetables. Cover and turn off the heat. Let stand on the warm burner until dinner.

18 MINUTES BEFORE DINNER, start preparing the chicken. Trim the visible fat from 2 lb boneless, skinless chicken breasts. Cut the chicken breasts into $1^1/_2$ to 2-inch pieces. Place the chicken pieces in a 1-gallon zip-top bag with $^1/_2$ c piña colada mix. Seal the bag and lay flat, making sure the chicken is covered with the piña colada mix. Marinate the chicken in the refrigerator for 15 minutes.

15 MINUTES BEFORE DINNER, turn off the heat to the rice. Preheat the indoor electric grill.

5 MINUTES BEFORE DINNER, generously spray the upper and lower grilling surfaces of the indoor electric grill with nonfat cooking spray. Place the chicken pieces in a single layer on the hot grill. Close the lid firmly and cook for 3 minutes.

3 MINUTES BEFORE DINNER, spoon the rice down the center of a large serving platter. Spoon the vegetables around the rice.

2 MINUTES BEFORE DINNER, sprinkle 3 T shredded coconut over the chicken. Close the lid and cook for 1 minute longer.

1 MINUTE BEFORE DINNER, spoon the chicken on top of the rice. Sprinkle any leftover coconut from the grill over the chicken. Sprinkle the chicken lightly with $^1/_4$ t light salt. Place on the dinner table.

Supplies List

Timer
1-quart nonstick saucepan with lid
12-inch nonstick skillet with lid
1-gallon zip-top bag
Large serving platter
Indoor electric grill

Grocery List

PACKAGED

Piña colada mix (nonalcoholic)
Shredded coconut
Whole-grain instant brown rice
1 (8-ounce) can crushed pineapple in juice
Sweet and sour sauce

FROZEN

2 (14-ounce) packages frozen stir-fry vegetables

POULTRY

$1^3/_4$ pounds boneless, skinless chicken breast

Pantry List

Seasoned salt
1 (14-ounce) can 99% fat-free chicken broth
Pumpkin pie spice
Nonfat cooking spray

>>> Honey Dijon Pork Medallions

Mashed Sweet Potatoes • Asparagus Spears with Mushrooms

Everybody went crazy over these creamy Mashed Sweet Potatoes, and the pork was so succulent with the warm honey Dijon cream sauce. Each bite of the asparagus was as tender as the last.

HONEY DIJON PORK MEDALLIONS

Yield: 6 servings (4 ounces pork and

1½ tablespoons sauce per serving)

Calories: 188 (20% fat); Total Fat: 4g; Cholesterol: 63mg; Carbohydrate: 13g; Dietary Fiber: 1g; Protein 23g; Sodium: 306mg; Diabetic Exchanges: 1 other carbohydrate, 3 lean meat

MASHED SWEET POTATOES

Yield: 9 servings

(½ cup per serving)

Calories: 162 (12% fat); Total Fat: 2g; Cholesterol: 5mg; Carbohydrate: 33g; Dietary Fiber: 4g; Protein 2g; Sodium: 315mg; Diabetic Exchanges: 2 starch

ASPARAGUS SPEARS WITH MUSHROOMS

Yield: 6 servings

(6 ounces per serving)

Calories: 42 (0% fat); Total Fat: 0g; Cholesterol: 0mg; Carbohydrate: 8g; Dietary Fiber: 3g; Protein 4g; Sodium: 148mg; Diabetic Exchanges: 1½ vegetable

HONEY DIJON PORK MEDALLIONS

1¾	pounds pork tenderloin	2	tablespoons honey
½	cup fat-free honey Dijon salad dressing	2	teaspoons Dijon mustard

MASHED SWEET POTATOES

3	tablespoons Splenda granular	⅓	cup Splenda Brown Sugar Blend
2	large sweet potatoes	½	teaspoon steak seasoning
3	tablespoons imitation butter-flavored sprinkles	1	teaspoon ground cinnamon
		3	tablespoons light salted butter

ASPARAGUS SPEARS WITH MUSHROOMS

2½	teaspoons concentrated lemon juice	4	ounces fresh sliced mushrooms
1½	tablespoons Splenda granular	1	tablespoon imitation butter-flavored sprinkles
2½	pounds fresh asparagus spears*	½	teaspoon steak seasoning

Instructions

30 MINUTES BEFORE DINNER, start the water for the sweet potatoes. Add 4 c water and 3 T Splenda granular to a 4½-quart saucepan. Place over high heat. Peel 2 large sweet potatoes and cut into 1-inch pieces. Add the sweet potato pieces to the boiling water. Return to a boil and let it boil for 2 to 3 minutes.

22 MINUTES BEFORE DINNER, start the asparagus. Trim the asparagus spears.

19 MINUTES BEFORE DINNER, turn off the sweet potatoes. Cover and let stand on the hot burner.

Combine 1 c water, $2^1/_2$ t lemon juice, and $1^1/_2$ T Splenda granular into a 12-inch nonstick saucepan. Place over high heat. Place the asparagus in the saucepan and cover. Cook for 8 minutes.

15 MINUTES BEFORE DINNER, preheat the indoor electric grill.

Trim the fat from the pork tenderloin and cut into 12 (1-inch-thick) medallions.

10 MINUTES BEFORE DINNER, turn off the heat under the asparagus. Add 4 oz sliced mushrooms on top of the asparagus. Cover and let the asparagus and mushrooms sit on the hot burner.

8 MINUTES BEFORE DINNER, spray upper and lower grilling surfaces with nonfat cooking spray. Place the pork medallions on preheated grill and close the lid to cook.

In a small microwave-safe bowl, stir together $^1/_2$ c honey Dijon salad dressing, 2 T honey, and 2 t Dijon mustard. Heat in the microwave for 1 minute.

6 MINUTES BEFORE DINNER, drain the sweet potatoes and put them in a $2^1/_2$-quart mixing bowl. Add 3 T butter sprinkles, $^1/_3$ c Splenda Brown Sugar Blend, $^1/_2$ t steak seasoning, 1 t cinnamon, and 3 T butter. Mix with an electric mixer until smooth and creamy. Cover and place on the dinner table.

2 MINUTES BEFORE DINNER, drain the asparagus spears using the lid of the pan to hold the vegetables in place. Gently slide the asparagus spears and mushrooms into a 9 x 13-inch baking dish, keeping the mushrooms on top of the asparagus. Sprinkle 1 T butter sprinkles and $^1/_2$ t steak seasoning on top. Place on the dinner table.

1 MINUTE BEFORE DINNER, remove the pork medallions from the grill and place them on a serving plate. Pour the warm Honey Dijon Sauce over the medallions and place on the table.

NOTE: *The more slender the asparagus the more tender they will be. Avoid purchasing thick ribs of asparagus.*

Supplies List

Timer
$4^1/_2$-quart saucepan with lid
12-inch nonstick skillet with lid
$2^1/_2$-quart mixing bowl
9 x 13-inch baking dish
Small bowl
Indoor Electric Grill
Electric mixer
Serving plate
Colander

Grocery List

PACKAGED

$^1/_2$ cup fat-free honey Dijon salad dressing
Concentrated lemon juice

PRODUCE

2 large sweet potatoes
$2^1/_2$ pounds fresh asparagus spears
4 ounces fresh sliced mushrooms

MEAT

$1^3/_4$ pounds pork tenderloin

DAIRY

3 tablespoons light salted butter

Pantry List

Dijon mustard
Honey
Ground cinnamon
Splenda granular
Imitation butter-flavored sprinkles
Splenda Brown Sugar Blend
Steak seasoning
Nonfat cooking spray

>>> Loose Hawaiian-Style Pork Kebabs

Teriyaki Rice • Hawaiian-Style Tomato, Onion & Cucumber Salad

For added fun, set the table in a Hawaiian theme and set a lei at each place setting. Play Hawaiian music and have guests wear Hawaiian clothing.

Loose Hawaiian-Style Pork Kebabs

Yield: 6 servings (4 ounces pork, $^1/_3$ onion, $^1/_2$ pineapple slice, $1^1/_3$ tablespoons Teriyaki sauce per serving)

Calories: 204 (18% fat); Total Fat: 4g; Cholesterol: 63mg; Carbohydrate: 17g; Dietary Fiber: 1g; Protein 24g; Sodium: 587mg; Diabetic Exchanges: $1^1/_2$ vegetable, $^1/_2$ other carbohydrate, 3 lean meat

Teriyaki Rice

Yield: 6 servings ($^1/_2$ cup per serving)

Calories: 89 (6% fat); Total Fat: 1g; Cholesterol: 0mg; Carbohydrate: 19g; Dietary Fiber: 1g; Protein 2g; Sodium: 209mg; Diabetic Exchanges: 1 starch, $^1/_2$ fruit

Hawaiian-Style Tomato, Onion & Cucumber Salad

Yield: 6 servings ($^2/_3$ cup per serving)

Calories: 61 (8% fat); Total Fat: 1g; Cholesterol: 12mg; Carbohydrate: 10g; Dietary Fiber: 1g; Protein 4g; Sodium: 306mg; Diabetic Exchanges: 2 vegetable

LOOSE HAWAIIAN-STYLE PORK KEBABS

$1^1/_2$	pounds boneless pork tenderloin	1	($1^1/_2$-inch-thick) fresh pineapple slice
$^1/_4$	plus $^1/_4$ cup Teriyaki Baste & Glaze	2	large mild white onions

TERIYAKI RICE

1	cup water	1	cup plus 2 tablespoons whole-grain instant brown rice
1	(8-ounce) can crushed pineapple in juice	2	teaspoons Splenda granular
2	tablespoons light soy sauce		

HAWAIIAN-STYLE TOMATO, ONION & CUCUMBER SALAD

1	medium cucumber	1	cup imitation crabmeat, flaked
1	cup grape tomatoes	$^1/_2$	cup fat-free zesty Italian dressing
1	small white onion, sliced into thin slivers		

Instructions

30 MINUTES BEFORE DINNER, preheat the oven to 250 degrees. Preheat the electric grill.

29 MINUTES BEFORE DINNER, start the rice. In a $2^1/2$-quart saucepan over medium-high heat, combine 1 c water, 1 can crushed pineapple with juice, 2 T soy sauce, and 1 c plus 2 T rice. Bring to a boil.

25 MINUTES BEFORE DINNER, reduce the heat to low. Cover and simmer for 10 minutes.
Cut $1^1/2$ lb boneless pork tenderloin into 1 to 2-inch thick pieces

20 MINUTES BEFORE DINNER, put the pork pieces into a 1-gallon zip-top bag. Add $^1/4$ c of the Teriyaki Baste & Glaze, coat the pork with sauce, and set aside.

19 MINUTES BEFORE DINNER, slice the $1^1/2$-thick slice of fresh pineapple into 3 ($^1/2$-inch) slices horizontally. Stack the 3 slices and, using a serrated knife, cut into 8 wedges. If desired, remove the core of the pineapple but leave the skin.

15 MINUTES BEFORE DINNER, turn off the rice. Stir in 2 t Splenda granular. Cover and let stand on the warm burner.
Cut 2 mild white onions into eighths by cutting each onion in half horizontally, removing the core, then cutting each half in quarters. Separate the layers

13 MINUTES BEFORE DINNER, generously spray the upper and lower grilling surfaces of the electric grill with nonfat cooking spray. Arrange the pineapple wedges in a single layer on the grill. Close the lid and cook.

12 MINUTES BEFORE DINNER, start the salad. Thinly slice 1 cucumber and then quarter the slices. Place the cucumber in a salad bowl with 1 cup grape tomatoes, 1 small onion sliced into thin slivers, 1 c crabmeat, and $^1/2$ c zesty Italian dressing. Stir until well mixed and place the salad on the dinner table.

Supplies List

Timer
$2^1/2$-quart saucepan with lid
1-gallon zip-top bag
Electric Indoor Grill
Jelly-roll pan
Large platter

Grocery List

PACKAGED
1 (8-ounce) can crushed pineapple in juice
Whole-grain instant brown rice
$^1/2$ cup teriyaki Baste & Glaze
Light soy sauce
$^1/2$ cup fat-free zesty Italian dressing

PRODUCE
1 fresh pineapple
2 large mild white onions
1 small white onion
1 medium cucumber
1 cup grape tomatoes

MEAT
$1^1/2$ pounds boneless pork tenderloin

SEAFOOD
1 (8-ounce) package imitation crabmeat salad style chunks

Pantry List

Splenda granular

CONTINUED ON NEXT PAGE >>>

>>> Loose Hawaiian-Style
Pork Kebabs
CONTINUED FROM PREVIOUS PAGE

7 MINUTES BEFORE DINNER, remove the pineapple wedges from the electric grill. Put on a on a jelly-roll pan and place in the preheated oven.

6 MINUTES BEFORE DINNER, grill the onion slices. Spray the onions with cooking spray. Close the lid, pressing down firmly and cook for 2 minutes.

4 MINUTES BEFORE DINNER, add the grilled onions to the jelly-roll pan. Return the pan to the oven.

3 MINUTES BEFORE DINNER, arrange the pork pieces on the grill in a single layer. Close the lid, pressing down firmly to sear the meat. Cook for 2 minutes.

2 MINUTES BEFORE DINNER, spoon the rice down the center of a large platter.

1 MINUTE BEFORE DINNER, remove the pineapple and onion from the oven. Place the grilled pork on the jelly-roll pan. Add the remaining $1/4$ c Teriyaki Baste & Glaze. Toss the ingredients to coat. Pour the grilled pork, pineapple, and onions over the rice. Place on the dinner table.

>>> Steak Tips with Onions & Gravy

Loaded Smashed Potatoes • Buttered Broccoli & Mushrooms

Save yourself lots of time and money by preparing this specialty steak house menu at home. It is every bit as good as any fine steak house and, with cleanup included, you'll still be finished with dinner sooner than if you had to drive and wait at a restaurant.

STEAK TIPS WITH ONIONS & GRAVY
Yield: 6 servings
(³/₄ cup per serving)
Calories: 182 (23% fat); Total Fat: 5g; Cholesterol: 46mg; Carbohydrate: 8g; Dietary Fiber: 1g; Protein 26g; Sodium: 352mg; Diabetic Exchanges: 1¹/₂ vegetable, 3 lean meat

LOADED SMASHED POTATOES
Yield: 9 servings
(¹/₂ cup per serving)
Calories: 75 (0% fat); Total Fat: 0g; Cholesterol: 3mg; Carbohydrate: 12g; Dietary Fiber: 1g; Protein 6g; Sodium: 496mg; Diabetic Exchanges: 1 starch, ¹/₂ very lean meat

BUTTERED BROCCOLI & MUSHROOMS
Yield: 6 servings (1 cup per serving)
Calories: 59 (8% fat); Total Fat: 1g; Cholesterol: 0mg; Carbohydrate: 11g; Dietary Fiber: 5g; Protein 6g; Sodium: 424mg; Diabetic Exchanges: 2 vegetable

STEAK TIPS WITH ONIONS & GRAVY

1	(12-ounce) jar fat-free beef gravy	1¹/₂	pounds sirloin steak
¹/₂	tablespoon Worcestershire sauce	2	medium to large sweet white onions
1¹/₂	teaspoon bottled minced garlic	¹/₄	teaspoon ground black pepper

LOADED SMASHED POTATOES

1	tablespoon seasoned salt	³/₄	cup fat-free half-and-half
6	medium red potatoes*	4	teaspoons 30%-less-fat real bacon pieces
4	tablespoons fat-free cream cheese	¹/₂	cup shredded fat-free cheddar cheese
3	tablespoons imitation butter-flavored sprinkles		

BUTTERED BROCCOLI & MUSHROOMS

1	(14-ounce) can 99% fat-free beef broth	1	(8-ounce) package sliced fresh mushrooms
2	(16-ounce) packages frozen broccoli cuts	¹/₄	cup imitation butter-flavored sprinkles

CONTINUED ON NEXT PAGE >>>

Supplies List

Timer
4¹/₂-quart nonstick saucepan
   with lid
12-inch nonstick saucepan
   with lid
2¹/₂-quart oven safe
   casserole dish
2¹/₂-quart mixing bowl
Electric mixer
Large serving bowl
Indoor electric grill
Colander

Grocery List

PACKAGED
1 (14-ounce) can
   99% fat-free beef broth
1 (12-ounce) jar fat-free
   beef gravy
30%-less-fat real bacon pieces

PRODUCE
1 (8-ounce) package sliced
   fresh mushrooms
6 medium red potatoes
2 medium to large sweet
   white onions

FROZEN
2 (16-ounce) packages frozen
   broccoli cuts

MEAT
1¹/₂ pounds sirloin steak

DAIRY
Fat-free cream cheese
³/₄ cup fat-free half-and-half
¹/₂ cup shredded fat-free
   cheddar cheese

Pantry List on page 209

Instructions

30 MINUTES BEFORE DINNER, start the water for the potatoes. Put 4 c water into a 4¹/₂-quart nonstick saucepan. Add 1 T seasoned salt to the water and bring the water to a boil over high heat.

Cut 6 medium red potatoes into 1-inch pieces.

25 MINUTES BEFORE DINNER, add the potato pieces to the boiling salt water, making sure that the potatoes are covered with the water. Cook for 4 minutes.

24 MINUTES BEFORE DINNER, start the broccoli. Combine 1 can beef broth and 2 packages frozen broccoli cuts in a 12-inch nonstick saucepan. Cover and cook over high heat.

21 MINUTES BEFORE DINNER, turn off the heat under the potatoes. Cover and let the potatoes sit on the hot burner.

20 MINUTES BEFORE DINNER, preheat the indoor electric grill.

Preheat the oven to 350 degrees.

Prepare the steak tips. Coat a 2¹/₂-quart baking dish with nonfat cooking spray. Combine 1 can beef gravy, ¹/₂ T Worcestershire sauce, and 1¹/₂ t minced garlic and stir until well mixed. Place in the oven.

16 MINUTES BEFORE DINNER, trim the fat from 1¹/₂ lb sirloin steak. Cut the steak into 1 to 2-inch pieces; set aside.

14 MINUTES BEFORE DINNER, cut 2 medium to large sweet white onions into eighths by cutting each onion in half horizontally, removing the core, then cutting each half into quarters. Separate the layers of the onion.

11 MINUTES BEFORE DINNER, spray the upper and lower grilling surfaces of the preheated electric grill with nonfat cooking spray. Place the onions in a single layer on the grill. Spray the onions generously with nonfat cooking spray. Close the lid and cook for 6 minutes.

9 MINUTES BEFORE DINNER, turn off the heat to the broccoli. Place 1 package sliced fresh mushrooms on top of the broccoli. Cover and let sit on the warm burner.

8 MINUTES BEFORE DINNER, start the smashed potatoes. Drain the potatoes and place into a $2^1/_2$-quart mixing bowl. Using an electric mixer, beat the potatoes, 4 T cream cheese, 3 T butter sprinkles, $^3/_4$ c half-and-half, 4 t bacon pieces, and $^1/_2$ c cheddar cheese until creamy.

5 MINUTES BEFORE DINNER, remove the gravy from the oven. Remove the onions from the grill and stir into the gravy.

4 MINUTES BEFORE DINNER, arrange the sirloin steak pieces on the grill in a single layer. Close the lid and cook.

3 MINUTES BEFORE DINNER, if needed, continue making the smashed potatoes, and then place them on the dinner table.

2 MINUTES BEFORE DINNER, drain the broccoli and mushrooms and spoon into a large serving bowl. Stir with $^1/_4$ c butter sprinkles, and place on the dinner table.

1 MINUTE BEFORE DINNER, remove the meat from the grill and stir into the gravy and onions. Add $^1/_4$ t ground black pepper and continue stirring until the steak is covered in onions and gravy. Place on the dinner table.

__NOTE:__ A medium red potato is about the size of a woman's tightly clenched fist.

Pantry List

Seasoned salt
Worcestershire sauce
Ground black pepper
Nonfat cooking spray
Imitation butter-flavored
    sprinkles
Minced garlic

>>> London Broil with Mushroom Gravy

Seasoned Potatoes • Bacon & Cheddar Broccoli

This menu's presentation is impressive and every bit as tasty and satisfying. Meat and potato lovers especially like this hearty meal.

LONDON BROIL

Yield: 6 servings (4 ounces per serving)

Calories: 141 (24% fat); Total Fat: 4g; Cholesterol: 64mg; Carbohydrate: 0g; Dietary Fiber: 0g; Protein 26g; Sodium: 32mg; Diabetic Exchanges: 3 lean meat

MUSHROOM GRAVY

Yield: 6 servings (1/2 cup per serving)

Calories: 37 (0% fat); Total Fat: 0g; Cholesterol: 0mg; Carbohydrate: 7g; Dietary Fiber: 0g; Protein 3g; Sodium: 575mg; Diabetic Exchanges: 1/2 other carbohydrate

SEASONED POTATOES

Yield: 10 servings (1/2 cup per serving)

Calories: 87 (0% fat); Total Fat: 0g; Cholesterol: 0mg; Carbohydrate: 20g; Dietary Fiber: 3g; Protein 2g; Sodium: 143mg; Diabetic Exchanges: 1 1/2 starch

BACON & CHEDDAR BROCCOLI

Yield: 6 servings (3/4 cup per serving)

Calories: 76 (9% fat); Total Fat: 1g; Cholesterol: 8mg; Carbohydrate: 9g; Dietary Fiber: 5g; Protein 10g; Sodium: 366mg; Diabetic Exchanges: 2 vegetable, 1 very lean meat

LONDON BROIL

1 3/4 pounds beef top round (London broil), about 1-inch thick

MUSHROOM GRAVY

1	(8-ounce) package sliced mushrooms	1/8	teaspoon ground thyme
2	(12-ounce) jar fat-free savory beef gravy	1/4	teaspoon Worcestershire sauce

SEASONED POTATOES

5	medium russet potatoes, unpeeled (about 7 cups chopped)	1	medium sweet onion
		2	teaspoons steak seasoning

BACON & CHEDDAR BROCCOLI

2	(16-ounce) bags frozen broccoli cuts	5	plus 1 slices fat-free sharp cheddar cheese
1 1/2	tablespoons plus		
1/2	teaspoon 30%-less-fat real crumbled bacon pieces		

Canadian Top Sirloin, Buttered Bi-Colored Sweet Corn on the Cob, Seasoned Button Mushrooms, and Kiwi Lemonade, *pages 228–229*

Salmon Florentine, Maple Sweet Potatoes, and Always Tender Asparagus Spears, *pages 242–243*

Dill-icious Tilapia with Shrimp, Asparagus & Portobello Mushroom Medley, and Raspberry Pecan Salad with Cranberries, *pages 244–245*

Fettuccini Alfredo, Garlic-Buttered Broccoli, and Italian Herb Bread Twists, *pages 282–283*

Instructions

30 MINUTES BEFORE DINNER, put 2 bags frozen broccoli cuts into a 2-quart microwave-safe dish. Cover with waxed paper and cook for 6 minutes.

28 MINUTES BEFORE DINNER, start the potatoes. Put 4 c water into a Dutch oven and place over high heat. Cut 5 medium russet potatoes into slices about $1/4$ inch thick.

23 MINUTES BEFORE DINNER, put the potatoes into the boiling water and cover.

22 MINUTES BEFORE DINNER, thinly slice 1 medium sweet onion and place on top of the potatoes, cover and cook for 3 minutes.

21 MINUTES BEFORE DINNER, stir the broccoli and cook for 6 more minutes.

19 MINUTES BEFORE DINNER, turn off the burner under the potatoes and onion and let sit on the warm burner.
Preheat the indoor electric grill.

18 MINUTES BEFORE DINNER, start the mushroom gravy. Coat a 12-inch nonstick saucepan with nonfat butter-flavored cooking spray. Add 1 package sliced mushrooms. Cover and cook over medium heat.

17 MINUTES BEFORE DINNER, trim the fat from $1\,3/4$ lb beef top round.

14 MINUTES BEFORE DINNER, stir the broccoli. Cover and cook for another 6 minutes.

13 MINUTES BEFORE DINNER, generously spray the upper and lower grilling surfaces of the electric grill with nonfat cooking spray. Place the meat on the grill. Close the lid and cook for 5 minutes.

11 MINUTES BEFORE DINNER, increase the heat under the mushrooms to high and stir in 2 jars beef gravy and $1/8$ t thyme. Cook for 2 minutes.

9 MINUTES BEFORE DINNER, reduce the heat to medium under the gravy and cover.

CONTINUED ON NEXT PAGE >>>

Supplies List

Timer
2-quart microwave casserole dish
12-inch nonstick saucepan with lid
2 large serving platters
Dutch oven with lid
Indoor electric grill
Colander

Grocery List

PACKAGED
2 (12-ounce) jars fat-free savory beef gravy
30%-less-fat real crumbled bacon pieces

PRODUCE
5 medium russet potatoes
1 medium sweet onion
1 (8-ounce) package sliced mushrooms

FROZEN
2 (16-ounce) bags frozen broccoli cuts

MEAT
$1^3/4$ pounds beef top round

DAIRY
6 slices fat-free sharp cheddar cheese

Pantry List

Ground thyme
Worcestershire sauce
Steak seasoning

>>> London Broil
with Mushroom Gravy
CONTINUED FROM PREVIOUS PAGE

8 MINUTES BEFORE DINNER, rotate the steak 45 degrees to create diamond-shaped grill marks. Close the lid and continue for 5 more minutes.

7 MINUTES BEFORE DINNER, drain the potatoes and onion. Return to the Dutch oven and place on the warm burner.

5 MINUTES BEFORE DINNER, gently stir 2 t steak seasoning into the potatoes, being careful not to break the potatoes.

Stir 5 slices cheddar cheese and $1^1/_2$ T bacon pieces into the broccoli. Cover and cook for 3 minutes.

3 MINUTES BEFORE DINNER, remove the London broil from the grill. Turn off the mushroom gravy and let sit on the hot burner. Slice the steak against the grain into $^1/_4$-inch-thick slices.

2 MINUTES BEFORE DINNER, arrange the steak on a large serving platter. Place the seasoned potatoes around the meat. Stir $^1/_4$ t Worcestershire sauce into the gravy. Pour the mushroom gravy along the center of the steak. Place on the dinner table.

1 MINUTE BEFORE DINNER, stir the broccoli. Cut 1 slice cheddar cheese in half diagonally and place on top of the broccoli. Sprinkle with $^1/_2$ t bacon pieces and place on the dinner table.

>>> Sirloin Steak Topped with Garlic-Butter Crab

Savory Sweet Potatoes ● Ham & Swiss Broccoli

Men will enjoy this hearty dinner that is low enough in calories for women to enjoy guilt free.

SIRLOIN STEAK TOPPED WITH GARLIC-BUTTER CRAB

Yield: 6 servings (4 ounces steak and 2 ounces crabmeat per serving)

Calories: 216 (27% fat); Total Fat: 6g; Cholesterol: 92mg; Carbohydrate: 1g; Dietary Fiber: 0g; Protein 37g; Sodium: 361mg; Diabetic Exchanges: 5 lean meat

SAVORY SWEET POTATOES

Yield: 11 servings (1/2 cup per serving)

Calories: 91 (0% fat); Total Fat: 0g; Cholesterol: 0mg; Carbohydrate: 21g; Dietary Fiber: 3g; Protein 2g; Sodium: 298mg; Diabetic Exchanges: 1 1/2 starch

HAM & SWISS BROCCOLI

Yield: 6 servings (3/4 cup per serving)

Calories: 110 (10% fat); Total Fat: 1g; Cholesterol: 14mg; Carbohydrate: 12g; Dietary Fiber: 5g; Protein 14g; Sodium: 740mg; Diabetic Exchanges: 1 vegetable, 1/2 other carbohydrate, 1 1/2 very lean meat

SIRLOIN STEAK TOPPED WITH GARLIC-BUTTER CRAB

1 1/2 pounds beef sirloin steak (1-inch thick)

3/4 pounds imitation crabmeat (about 2 cups)

1 tablespoon light butter

1/2 teaspoon garlic salt

1/2 teaspoon dried parsley

SAVORY SWEET POTATOES

2 large sweet potatoes (about 8 cups chopped)

1/2 cup steak sauce

1 tablespoon imitation butter-flavored sprinkles

1/2 teaspoon steak seasoning

HAM & SWISS BROCCOLI

2 (16-ounce) bags frozen broccoli cuts

2 tablespoons imitation butter-flavored sprinkles

1 1/2 tablespoons reduced-fat Parmesan-style grated topping

1/2 teaspoon dried parsley

1/4 cup plus 2 tablespoons cooked lean diced ham

7 plus 2 slices fat-free Swiss cheese

Supplies List

Timer
Large microwavable bowl
Medium serving bowl
Dutch oven with lid
Indoor electric grill
Serving plate
Colander

Grocery List

PACKAGED
$1/2$ cup steak sauce
Reduced-fat Parmesan-style
    grated topping

PRODUCE
2 large sweet potatoes

FROZEN
2 (16-ounce) bags frozen
    broccoli cuts

MEAT/SEAFOOD
$1/3$ cup cooked lean diced
    ham
$1^1/2$ pounds beef sirloin steak
$3/4$ pounds imitation crabmeat

DAIRY
Light butter
9 slices fat-free Swiss cheese

Pantry List

Dried parsley
Garlic salt
Dried parsley
Imitation butter-flavored
    sprinkles
Steak seasoning

Instructions

30 MINUTES BEFORE DINNER, start the potatoes. Put 4 c water in a Dutch oven and place over high heat. Chop 2 large sweet potatoes into $1/2$-inch pieces.

25 MINUTES BEFORE DINNER, start the broccoli. Cut the tops off 2 packages frozen broccoli cuts. Cook the broccoli in a carousel microwave on high for 6 minutes.

24 MINUTES BEFORE DINNER, place the sweet potatoes into the boiling water and return to a boil for 2 minutes.

22 MINUTES BEFORE DINNER, turn off the boiling water to the sweet potatoes and cover. Let sit on the warm burner.

20 MINUTES BEFORE DINNER, trim all visible fat from $1^1/2$ lb sirloin steak and cut into 6 (4-ounce) steaks. Set aside.

17 MINUTES BEFORE DINNER, remove the 2 bags of broccoli from the microwave and shake to mix the vegetables. Cook for another 6 minutes.

16 MINUTES BEFORE DINNER, preheat the indoor electric grill.

Place 1 package imitation crabmeat in a medium microwave-safe bowl. Top with 1 T butter, $1/2$ t garlic salt, and $1/2$ t dried parsley. Do not stir. Set aside.

13 MINUTES BEFORE DINNER, remove the broccoli from the microwave and place in a large microwavable bowl. Add 2 T butter-flavored sprinkles, $1^1/2$ T Parmesan, $1/2$ t dried parsley, and $1/4$ c of the lean diced ham, mixing well. Cut 7 slices of the Swiss cheese into small pieces. Stir into the broccoli until well mixed. Cover with waxed paper and cook for 4 minutes.

8 MINUTES BEFORE DINNER, put the steaks on the preheated grill.

7 MINUTES BEFORE DINNER, drain the sweet potatoes and place in a medium serving bowl. Add $1/2$ c steak sauce, 1 T butter sprinkles, and $1/2$ t steak seasoning to the potatoes. Gently stir, trying not to break up the potatoes. Cover and place on a hot pad on the dinner table.

5 MINUTES BEFORE DINNER, remove the broccoli from the microwave and stir. Cut the remaining 2 slices Swiss cheese diagonally into 4 triangles and place on top of the broccoli in a pretty design. Sprinkle the remaining 2 T diced ham on top of the Swiss cheese. Cover and microwave the broccoli for 45 seconds to 1 minute, or until the cheese is slightly melted.

4 MINUTES BEFORE DINNER, rotate the steaks 45 degrees to create diamond-shaped grill marks. Close the lid, pressing down to help sear grill marks into the meat. Cook for 3 mintues.

3 MINUTES BEFORE DINNER, remove the broccoli from the microwave and put on a hot pad on the dinner table.

Cover and put the crabmeat in the microwave. Cook for 2 minutes, or until fully heated.

1 MINUTE BEFORE DINNER, remove the steaks from the grill and place on a serving plate. Remove the crabmeat from the microwave. Spoon the crabmeat on top of the steaks. Place on the dinner table.

>>> Loose Steak Kebabs

Cheesy California Vegetable Medley • Herbed Rice Pilaf

Not only is this menu good with beef, it is also tasty when chicken or pork tenderloin are substituted.

LOOSE STEAK KEBABS
Yield: 6 servings
(4 ounces sirloin, ¹/₂ bell pepper,
and ¹/₆ onion per serving)
Calories: 180 (24% fat); Total Fat: 5g;
Cholesterol: 46mg; Carbohydrate: 8g;
Dietary Fiber: 2g; Protein 25g;
Sodium: 481mg; Diabetic Exchanges:
1¹/₂ vegetable, 3 lean meat

CHEESY CALIFORNIA
VEGETABLE MEDLEY
Yield: 6 servings (1 cup per serving)
Calories: 80 (0% fat); Total Fat: 0g;
Cholesterol: 2mg; Carbohydrate: 13g;
Dietary Fiber: 4g; Protein 8g; Sodium:
584mg; Diabetic Exchanges:
2¹/₂ vegetable, ¹/₂ very lean meat

HERBED RICE PILAF
Yield: 8 servings (¹/₂ cup per serving)
Calories: 83 (9% fat); Total Fat: 1g;
Cholesterol: 1mg; Carbohydrate: 16g;
Dietary Fiber: 1g; Protein 2g; Sodium:
404mg; Diabetic Exchanges: 1 starch

LOOSE STEAK KEBABS

1³/₄	pounds beef sirloin
¹/₃	cup plus 3 tablespoons steak sauce
1	tablespoon red wine vinegar
1	green bell pepper
1	red bell pepper
1	yellow bell pepper
1	medium white onion
1	teaspoon steak seasoning

CHEESY CALIFORNIA VEGETABLE MEDLEY

1	tablespoon bottled minced garlic
1	teaspoon seasoned salt
2	(16-ounce) packages frozen California blend vegetables
1	(8-ounce) package fresh sliced mushrooms
¹/₄	cup imitation butter-flavored sprinkles
¹/₂	cup shredded fat-free mild cheddar cheese

HERBED RICE PILAF

1	(14-ounce) can 99% fat-free chicken broth
³/₄	cup fat-free zesty Italian salad dressing
1¹/₂	cups instant whole-grain brown rice
¹/₂	tablespoon Italian seasoning

Instructions

30 MINUTES BEFORE DINNER, preheat the oven to 250 degrees.

29 MINUTES BEFORE DINNER, start the vegetable medley. Combine 4 c water, 1 T minced garlic, and 1 t seasoned salt into a large nonstick Dutch oven. Turn the heat on high and add 2 packages frozen California blend vegetables. Cover and cook on high for about 10 minutes. Once the water comes to a full rolling boil and steam is lifting the lid, turn off the heat and let the vegetables sit in the Dutch oven.

25 MINUTES BEFORE DINNER, start the rice. In a medium nonstick saucepan, combine 1 can chicken broth, $3/4$ c Italian salad dressing, $1^1/_2$ c rice, and $^1/_2$ T Italian seasoning over high heat. Bring to a boil.

22 MINUTES BEFORE DINNER, remove visible fat from $1^3/_4$ lb sirloin. Cut the sirloin into $1^1/_2$ to 2-inch pieces. Place the pieces in a 1-gallon zip-top bag with $^1/_3$ c steak sauce and 1 T red wine vinegar, coating the meat with sauce.

18 MINUTES BEFORE DINNER, reduce the heat under the rice to medium. Cover and cook at a low boil for 15 minutes.

17 MINUTES BEFORE DINNER, preheat the indoor electric grill.

16 MINUTES BEFORE DINNER, cut 1 green bell pepper, 1 red bell pepper, 1 yellow bell pepper, and 1 white onion into 1 to 2-inch pieces. Set aside.

11 MINUTES BEFORE DINNER, spray both grilling surfaces of the preheated indoor electric grill generously with butter-flavored cooking spray.

Place the pieces of bell peppers and onion on the prepared grill in a single layer. Spray the vegetables generously with butter-flavored cooking spray. Close the lid and cook for 4 minutes.

7 MINUTES BEFORE DINNER, transfer the vegetables to a jelly roll pan. They will be crispy and tender. Place in the oven at 250 degrees to keep warm.

Supplies List

Timer
1-gallon zip-top bag
2-quart casserole dish with lid
Medium nonstick saucepan
Large serving platter or a
    9 x 13-inch casserole dish
Indoor electric grill
Colander

Grocery List

PACKAGED
Whole-grain brown rice
1 (8-ounce) bottle fat-free
    zesty Italian salad
    dressing

PRODUCE
1 green bell pepper
1 red bell pepper
1 yellow bell pepper
1 medium white onion
1 (8-ounce) package fresh
    sliced mushrooms

FROZEN
2 (16-ounce) packages
    frozen California Blend
    vegetables

MEAT
$1^3/_4$ pounds beef sirloin

DAIRY
$^1/_2$ cup shredded fat-free mild
    cheddar cheese

Pantry List on page 218

CONTINUED ON NEXT PAGE >>>

>>> Loose Steak Kebabs
CONTINUED FROM PREVIOUS PAGE

Pantry List

Seasoned salt
Nonfat butter-flavored
    cooking spray
Italian seasoning
Minced garlic
Red wine vinegar
1 (14-ounce) can
    99% fat-free chicken
    broth
Imitation butter-flavored
    sprinkles
Steak sauce
Steak seasoning

6 MINUTES BEFORE DINNER, turn off the heat under the rice and stir. Let sit on the warm burner.

5 MINUTES BEFORE DINNER, place the meat on the grill in a single layer. Close the lid and cook.

4 MINUTES BEFORE DINNER, drain the vegetables. Place in a 2-quart casserole dish with a lid. Stir in $1/4$ c butter sprinkles. Sprinkle the vegetables with $1/2$ c shredded cheddar cheese. Spray the cheese generously with butter-flavored cooking spray. Cover and put the vegetables on a hot pad on the dinner table. The heat from the vegetables will melt the cheese.

2 MINUTES BEFORE DINNER, spoon the rice onto a large serving platter or into a 9 x 13-inch baking dish.

1 MINUTE BEFORE DINNER, remove the vegetables from the oven. Add the meat to the vegetables. Stir in 3 T steak sauce and mix well. Pour the bell peppers, onion, and meat over the rice. Sprinkle 1 t steak seasoning over the top and place on the dinner table.

NOTE: The easiest way to cut the bell peppers is to cut off the top and, using your fingers, pull the seeds out and rinse out the inside of the pepper with water. The easiest way to cut an onion is to cut off the ends and cut in half. Remove the outer layer and then cut into chunks. For kebabs, discard small inner part of onion.

>>> Parmesan-Crusted London Broil

Italian Butter-Herb Potatoes • Seasoned Broccoli

The Parmesan-Crusted London Broil and Italian Butter-Herb Potatoes seasonings in each of these individual recipes are delicious; together they are fantastic!

PARMESAN-CRUSTED LONDON BROIL
Yield: 6 servings
(4 ounces per serving)
Calories: 181 (42% fat); Total Fat: 8g; Cholesterol: 71mg; Carbohydrate: 0g; Dietary Fiber: 0g; Protein 25g; Sodium: 130mg; Diabetic Exchanges: 3 lean meat

ITALIAN BUTTER-HERB POTATOES
Yield: 6 servings ($1/2$ cup per serving)
Calories: 135 (27% fat); Total Fat: 4g; Cholesterol: 10mg; Carbohydrate: 23g; Dietary Fiber: 2g; Protein 2g; Sodium: 585mg; Diabetic Exchanges: $1^1/2$ starch, $1/2$ fat

SEASONED BROCCOLI
Yield: 6 servings ($1/2$ cup per serving)
Calories: 69 (39% fat); Total Fat: 3g; Cholesterol: 4mg; Carbohydrate: 8g; Dietary Fiber: 3g; Protein 4g; Sodium: 343mg; Diabetic Exchanges: $1^1/2$ vegetable, $1/2$ fat

PARMESAN-CRUSTED LONDON BROIL

1	$3/4$ pounds beef top round steak (London broil), cut 1-inch thick	$1/4$	plus $1/4$ teaspoon garlic salt
$1/2$	plus $1/2$ tablespoon Italian seasoning	$3/4$	plus $3/4$ tablespoon reduced-fat Parmesan-style grated topping

ITALIAN BUTTER-HERB POTATOES

2	medium russet potatoes (about 2 cups chopped)	1	teaspoon plus $1/4$ teaspoon garlic salt
2	large red skin potatoes (about 3 cups chopped)	$3^1/2$	tablespoons imitation butter-flavored sprinkles
1	tablespoon Italian seasoning	4	tablespoons light butter

SEASONED BROCCOLI

$1^1/2$	pounds precut fresh broccoli florets	$1/4$	teaspoon ground black pepper
5	tablespoons light ranch salad dressing	$1/2$	teaspoon garlic salt
1	teaspoon ranch salad dressing mix	$1^1/2$	teaspoons reduced-fat Parmesan-style grated topping

Supplies List

Timer
2½-quart saucepan with lid
2 medium serving bowls
Electric grill
Dutch oven with lid
Colander

Grocery List

PACKAGED
Light ranch salad dressing
Ranch salad dressing mix

PRODUCE
2 medium russet potatoes
2 large red skin potatoes
1½ pounds fresh broccoli
    florets

DAIRY
Light butter
Rreduced-fat Parmesan-style
    grated topping

MEAT
1¾ pounds beef top round
    steak

Pantry List

Italian seasoning
Garlic salt
Ground black pepper
Imitation butter-flavored
    sprinkles

Instructions

30 MINUTES BEFORE DINNER, prepare the potatotes. Cut 2 medium russet potatoes and 2 large red skin potatoes into $1/2$-inch-thick pieces. Set aside.

29 MINUTES BEFORE DINNER, in a 2 $1/2$-quart saucepan combine 4 c water, 1 T Italian seasoning, and 1 t garlic salt over high heat. Bring to a boil.

25 MINUTES BEFORE DINNER, add the potatoes to the water.

24 MINUTES BEFORE DINNER, start broccoli. Put 2 c water in a large Dutch oven. Add 1 $1/2$ lb fresh precut broccoli florets. Cover and set aside.

21 MINUTES BEFORE DINNER, turn off the burner under the potatoes. Cover and let sit on the hot burner.

20 MINUTES BEFORE DINNER, prepare the London broil. Trim all visible fat from 1 $3/4$ lb top round steak.

19 MINUTES BEFORE DINNER, preheat the indoor electric grill.

18 MINUTES BEFORE DINNER, sprinkle $1/2$ T of the Italian seasoning and $1/4$ t of the garlic salt on top of the steak. Using a fork, pierce the steak for about 1 to 2 minutes to tenderize and season the meat.

16 MINUTES BEFORE DINNER, turn over the meat and sprinkle the remaining $1/2$ T Italian seasoning and the remaining $1/4$ t garlic salt on top of the steak. Using a fork pierce the steak for 2 minutes to tenderize and season the meat.

14 MINUTES BEFORE DINNER, sprinkle $3/4$ T of the Parmesan topping over the meat. Spray with butter-flavored cooking spray and press into the meat. Turn over the meat sprinkle with the remaining $3/4$ T Parmesan topping. Spray with butter-flavored cooking spray.

Turn on the burner under the broccoli to high heat

9 MINUTES BEFORE DINNER, generously spray the upper and lower grilling surfaces of the electric grill with nonfat butter-flavored cooking spray. Place the meat on the grill. Close lid and cook.

8 MINUTES BEFORE DINNER, drain the potatoes. Put the potatoes in a medium serving bowl. Stir in $3^1/_2$ T butter sprinkles and 4 T butter. Stir in $^1/_4$ t garlic salt until well mixed. Cover and place on the dinner table.

6 MINUTES BEFORE DINNER, rotate the steak 45 degrees to create diamond-shaped grill marks. Close the lid and continue cooking.

Turn off the heat under the broccoli.

3 MINUTES BEFORE DINNER, remove the meat from the grill and place on a cutting board.

2 MINUTES BEFORE DINNER, drain the broccoli and place in a medium serving bowl. Gently toss with 5 T ranch salad dressing, 1 t ranch salad dressing mix, $^1/_4$ t ground black pepper, $^1/_2$ t garlic salt. Sprinkle $1^1/_2$ t Parmesan topping over the top. Place on the dinner table.

1 MINUTE BEFORE DINNER, slice the steak against the grain being careful not to spill the juices. Place on a platter and put on the dinner table.

>>> Cranberry Spiced Pork Medallions

Maple Mashed Sweet Potatoes • French Broccoli

No one could believe I cooked this entire meal in less than 30 minutes. Everything about this menu is high-quality, from the presentation to the flavor combination. This is another first-class menu to use for company.

CRANBERRY SPICED PORK MEDALLIONS

Yield: 6 servings

(4 ounces pork per serving)

Calories: 186 (19% fat); Total Fat: 4g; Cholesterol: 63mg; Carbohydrate: 14g; Dietary Fiber: 1g; Protein 23g; Sodium: 53mg; Diabetic Exchanges: 1 other carbohydrate, 3 lean meat

MAPLE MASHED SWEET POTATOES

Yield: 7 servings ($^1/_2$ cup per serving)

Calories: 155 (0% fat); Total Fat: 0g; Cholesterol: 0mg; Carbohydrate: 36g; Dietary Fiber: 5g; Protein 2g; Sodium: 608mg; Diabetic Exchanges: $2^1/_2$ starch

FRENCH BROCCOLI

Yield: 6 servings ($^2/_3$ cup per serving)

Calories: 78 (10% fat); Total Fat: 1g; Cholesterol: 3mg; Carbohydrate: 15g; Dietary Fiber: 5g; Protein: 5g; Sodium: 365mg; Diabetic Exchanges: $1^1/_2$ vegetable, $^1/_2$ other carbohydrate

CRANBERRY SPICED PORK MEDALLIONS

$1^3/_4$ pounds pork tenderloin	$^1/_2$ teaspoon ground allspice
1 (8-ounce) can cranberry sauce	

MAPLE MASHED SWEET POTATOES

1 teaspoon light salt	3 tablespoons imitation butter-flavored sprinkles
2 large sweet potatoes (about 5 cups chopped)	$^1/_2$ cup sugar-free maple syrup

FRENCH BROCCOLI

2 (16-ounce) packages frozen broccoli	2 tablespoons 30%-less-fat real bacon pieces
$^1/_2$ cup fat-free French salad dressing	$^1/_4$ teaspoon light salt

---

Instructions

30 MINUTES BEFORE DINNER, start the water for the sweet potatoes. Put 4 c water in a $4^1/_2$-quart saucepan and place over high heat on the stove.

Peel 2 large sweet potatoes and cut into 1-inch pieces.

Add the sweet potatoes to the boiling water. Return to a boil and boil for 2 to 3 minutes.

22 MINUTES BEFORE DINNER, start the broccoli. In a 12-inch nonstick saucepan, combine 2 packages frozen broccoli and 1 c water over high heat. Cover and cook for 5 minutes.

19 MINUTES BEFORE DINNER, turn off the boiling water under the potatoes. Cover and let sit on the hot burner.

17 MINUTES BEFORE DINNER, turn off the heat to the broccoli. Keep covered and let sit on the hot burner.

15 MINUTES BEFORE DINNER, preheat the indoor electric grill.

14 MINUTES BEFORE DINNER, prepare the pork. Remove all visible fat from the pork tenderloin. Cut into 12 (2-ounce) medallions, about $1/2$-inch thick.

11 MINUTES BEFORE DINNER, start the sauce for the pork. In a small microwavable bowl, stir together 1 can cranberry sauce with $1/2$ t ground allspice until well mixed; set aside.

10 MINUTES BEFORE DINNER, generously spray the upper and lower grilling surfaces with nonfat cooking spray. Place the pork medallions on the grill and close the lid to cook.

5 MINUTES BEFORE DINNER, rotate the pork medallions 45 degrees to create diamond-shaped grill marks.
   Cover and cook the cranberry sauce in the microwave for 1 minute.

4 MINUTES BEFORE DINNER, drain the broccoli. Put in a large serving bowl and gently stir in $1/2$ c French salad dressing and $1/4$ t salt. Sprinkle 2 T of bacon pieces on top. Cover and place on the dinner table.

3 MINUTES BEFORE DINNER, remove the pork medallions from the grill and place on a serving plate. Spoon the cranberry sauce over the pork medallions. Place on the dinner table.

2 MINUTES BEFORE DINNER, drain the sweet potatoes. Pour the cooked sweet potatoes into a large serving bowl. Gently stir in $1/2$ c maple syrup and $1/2$ t salt. Place on the dinner table.

NOTE: For easier cleanup, I peel my sweet potatoes over the garbage can.

Supplies List

Timer
$4^1/2$-quart saucepan
12-inch nonstick saucepan
   with lid
Small bowl
2 large serving bowls
Serving plate
Indoor electric grill
Colander

Grocery List

PACKAGED

$1/2$ cup sugar-free maple
   syrup
$1/2$ cup fat-free French salad
   dressing
1 (8-ounce) can cranberry
   sauce
30%-less-fat real crumbled
   bacon pieces

PRODUCE

2 large sweet potatoes

FROZEN

2 (16-ounce) packages frozen
   broccoli

MEAT

$1^3/4$ pounds pork tenderloin

Pantry List

Light salt
Ground allspice
Imitation butter-flavored
   sprinkles

>>> Polynesian Chicken with Caramelized Sweet Potatoes

Tropical Garden Salad

Expect this menu to be requested again and again! The Tropical Garden Salad is a deliciously light salad that uses ordinary ingredients in a unique combination for a delightful treat.

POLYNESIAN CHICKEN WITH CARAMELIZED SWEET POTATOES
Yield: 6 servings
(4 ounces chicken; 2 tablespoons pineapple mixture; 4¹/₂ ounces sweet potatoes per serving)

Calories: 297 (5% fat); Total Fat: 1g; Cholesterol: 66mg; Carbohydrate: 41g; Dietary Fiber: 5g; Protein 28g; Sodium: 292mg; Diabetic Exchanges: 2 starch, ¹/₂ fruit, 3 very lean meat

TROPICAL GARDEN SALAD
Yield: 6 servings
(1¹/₂ cup per serving)

Calories: 86 (0% fat); Total Fat: 0g; Cholesterol: 0mg; Carbohydrate: 18g; Dietary Fiber: 3g; Protein 2g; Sodium: 350mg; Diabetic Exchanges: 1 fruit, 1 vegetable

POLYNESIAN CHICKEN WITH CARAMELIZED SWEET POTATOES

1	(20-ounce) can crushed pineapple in juice, drained
6	(4-ounce) frozen boneless, skinless chicken breasts
¹/₂	teaspoon allspice
¹/₂	teaspoon light salt
2	tablespoons dark brown sugar
1³/₄	pounds sweet potatoes, cut into ¹/₂-inch-thick slices

TROPICAL GARDEN SALAD

9	cups chopped romaine or iceberg lettuce (1 large head)
1	(15-ounce) can mandarin orange slices in light juice, drained and chilled
³/₄	cup fat-free poppy seed salad dressing, chilled

Instructions

30 MINUTES BEFORE DINNER, make the salad. Cut 1 large head romaine or iceberg lettuce into bite-size pieces. Place in a large salad bowl. Arrange 1 drained can mandarin oranges on top of the lettuce. Cover and place in the refrigerator until dinner is ready.

25 MINUTES BEFORE DINNER, cut $1^3/_4$ lb sweet potatoes into $^1/_2$-inch-thick slices. Set side.

20 MINUTES BEFORE DINNER, preheat the indoor electric grill.

18 MINUTES BEFORE DINNER, in a medium bowl, stir together 1 can drained crushed pineapple, $^1/_2$ t allspice, $^1/_2$ t salt, and 2 T dark brown sugar until well-mixed.

15 MINUTES BEFORE DINNER, generously spray the upper and lower grilling surfaces of the electric grill with nonfat cooking spray. Put the 6 frozen chicken breasts on the preheated grill and close the grill. Cook for 3 minutes.

12 MINUTES BEFORE DINNER, arrange the potato slices on the grill with the chicken. Top each potato slice with 1 T pineapple mixture. Spray the pineapple mixture with nonfat cooking spray. Place 1 T pineapple mixture on top of each piece of chicken. Spray the pineapple mixture with nonfat cooking spray. Close the grill lid and continue cooking for 4 to 6 more minutes, or until the chicken is completely white in the center, the potatoes are tender when pierced with a fork, and the pineapple is caramelized.

7 MINUTES BEFORE DINNER, remove any cooked pieces of chicken and potato and keep warm while the remaining pieces continue cooking.

6 MINUTES BEFORE DINNER, toss the salad with $^3/_4$ cup salad dressing until the lettuce and oranges are evenly coated. Place the salad on dinner table.

5 MINUTES BEFORE DINNER, remove more pieces of chicken and potato that are fully cooked. Close lid after checking to quicken the cooking process.

2 MINUTES BEFORE DINNER, continue checking the doneness of the chicken and sweet potatoes. Once fully cooked, place them on a serving platter and place on the dinner table.

NOTE: *To cook this dish on an outdoor grill it will take 2 to 3 times longer on medium-high heat and the chicken and potatoes will need to be turned after cooking 5 to 10 minutes, depending on the thickness of the chicken. For easy cleanup, wipe the indoor grill with a damp cloth while still slightly warm.*

Supplies List

Timer
Large salad bowl
Large bowl
Electric grill
Medium bowl
Serving platter

Grocery List

PACKAGED

1 (15-ounce) can mandarin orange slices in light juice
1 (8-ounce) bottle fat-free poppy seed salad dressing
1 (20-ounce) can crushed pineapple in juice

PRODUCE

1 large head romaine or iceberg lettuce
$1^3/_4$ pounds sweet potatoes

FROZEN

6 (4-ounce) frozen boneless, skinless chicken breasts

Pantry List

Dark brown sugar
Allspice
Light salt
Nonfat cooking spray

>>> Chicken Bites over Sweet & Spicy Brown Rice with Vegetables

Sweet & Spicy Brown Rice with Vegetables

When I asked my friends and family what I should title this menu someone quickly replied, "Really good." We all laughed and agreed. The rice has just the right amount of "bite" to be spicy without being too spicy. I especially like the large serving size. This is very filling.

CHICKEN BITES
Yield: 6 servings
(4 ounces per serving)
Calories: 165 (8% fat); Total Fat: 1g; Cholesterol: 66mg; Carbohydrate: 10g; Dietary Fiber: 0g; Protein 27g; Sodium: 437mg; Diabetic Exchanges: 1/2 other carbohydrate, 3 very lean meat

SWEET & SPICY BROWN RICE
WITH VEGETABLES
Yield: 6 servings
(1 1/3 cup per serving)
Calories: 241 (3% fat); Total Fat: 1g; Cholesterol: 0mg; Carbohydrate: 51g; Dietary Fiber: 4g; Protein 4g; Sodium: 126mg; Diabetic Exchanges: 1 starch, 2 vegetable, 1 1/2 fruit

CHICKEN BITES

1/3	cup Teriyaki Baste & Glaze
2	tablespoons pineapple sundae topping or honey
1 1/2	pounds chicken breasts, cut into bite-size pieces
1/4	teaspoon ground red pepper

SWEET & SPICY BROWN RICE WITH VEGETABLES

1	(20-ounce) can crushed pineapple in pineapple juice
1	(14-ounce) can fat-free less-sodium chicken broth
1	(16-ounce) package frozen 3-Pepper & Onion Blend
1	(14-ounce) package frozen Oriental vegetable blend
1/2	teaspoon ground red pepper
1/2	cup Splenda Brown Sugar Blend
1 1/2	cups whole-grain instant brown rice

Instructions

30 MINUTES BEFORE DINNER, start the rice with vegetables. Drain 1 can crushed pineapple.

29 MINUTES BEFORE DINNER, in a 12-inch nonstick saucepan over high heat, combine the drained crushed pineapple, 1 can chicken broth, 1 bag frozen 3-Pepper and Onion Blend, 1 bag frozen Oriental vegetable blend, and $1/2$ t ground red pepper. Bring to a boil.

21 MINUTES BEFORE DINNER, add $1/2$ c Splenda Brown Sugar Blend and $1^1/2$ c whole-grain instant brown rice to the boiling liquid. Reduce the heat to medium-low. Cover and cook for 13 minutes.

14 MINUTES BEFORE DINNER, cut $1^1/2$ lb chicken into bite-size pieces. Pour $1/3$ c Teriyaki Baste & Glaze and 2 T pineapple sundae topping into a 1-gallon zip-top bag. Add the chicken. Using your hands, gently squeeze the bag to mix the ingredients together until the chicken is covered with the sauce. Set aside.

11 MINUTES BEFORE DINNER, preheat the indoor electric grill.

10 MINUTES BEFORE DINNER, stir the rice and vegetables. Cover and continue cooking over medium-low heat.

8 MINUTES BEFORE DINNER, turn off the heat to the rice and vegetables and let sit on the hot burner.

5 MINUTES BEFORE DINNER, spray the upper and lower grilling surfaces of the electric grill with nonfat cooking spray. Add the marinated chicken on the grill in a single layer. Close the lid and cook.

1 MINUTE BEFORE DINNER, pour the juices (from the chicken that cooked and drained) over the rice and vegetables. Place the grilled chicken on top of the rice and vegetables. Lightly sprinkle the chicken with $1/4$ t ground red pepper.
    Place the saucepan on a hot pad on the dinner table.

Supplies List

Timer
12-inch nonstick saucepan
    with lid
1-gallon zip-top bag
Indoor electric grill

Grocery List

PACKAGED

1 (20-ounce) can crushed
    pineapple in pineapple
    juice
Whole-grain instant
    brown rice
Pineapple sundae topping
Splenda Brown Sugar Blend
Teriyaki Baste & Glaze

FROZEN

1 (16-ounce) package
    3-Pepper & Onion Blend
1 (14-ounce) package frozen
    Oriental vegetable blend

POULTRY

$1^1/2$ pounds chicken breasts

Pantry List

1 (14-ounce) can fat-free
    less-sodium chicken broth
Ground red pepper

>>> Canadian Top Sirloin

Buttered Bi-Colored Sweet Corn on the Cob • Seasoned Button Mushrooms

This is an excellent dinner any time of year, but I especially like it when sweet corn is in season! The corn couldn't be any sweeter than when it's prepared in this time-saving manner. Every bit of this juicy steak melts in your mouth. This is a winning menu that I am sure you will make over and over again.

CANADIAN TOP SIRLOIN
Yield: 6 servings
(4 ounces per serving)
Calories: 146 (30% fat); Total Fat: 5g; Cholesterol: 46mg; Carbohydrate: 0g; Dietary Fiber: 0g; Protein 24g; Sodium: 223mg; Diabetic Exchanges: 3 lean meat

BUTTERED BI-COLORED SWEET CORN ON THE COB
Yield: 6 servings (1 ear per serving)
Calories: 94 (25% fat); Total Fat: 3g; Cholesterol: 5mg; Carbohydrate: 17g; Dietary Fiber: 2g; Protein 3g; Sodium: 45mg; Diabetic Exchanges: 1 starch, 1/2 fat

SEASONED BUTTON MUSHROOMS
Yield: 6 servings
(4 to 6 mushrooms per serving)
Calories: 27 (0% fat); Total Fat: 0g; Cholesterol: 0mg; Carbohydrate: 5g; Dietary Fiber: 1g; Protein 3g; Sodium: 333mg; Diabetic Exchanges: 1 vegetable

CANADIAN TOP SIRLOIN

2	pounds boneless top sirloin steak, cut 1-inch thick
1 1/2	teaspoons minced bottled garlic
1 1/2	teaspoons steak seasoning
1	teaspoon liquid smoke

BUTTERED BI-COLORED SWEET CORN ON THE COB

6	ears fresh bi-colored sweet corn
2	tablespoons light butter
	Light popcorn salt
1	hot dog bun

SEASONED BUTTON MUSHROOMS

2	(8 ounce) packages fresh button mushrooms
2	tablespoons Worcestershire sauce
2	tablespoons light soy sauce
2	tablespoons fat-free Italian salad dressing
2	tablespoons water

Instructions

30 MINUTES BEFORE DINNER, preheat the outdoor gas grill on high and start the steak. Remove all visible fat from 2 lb boneless top sirloin steak. Place the steak on a large cutting board. Rub 1 1/2 t minced garlic on top of the steak. Sprinkle with 1 1/2 t steak seasoning and 1 t liquid smoke. Pierce the steak with a fork numerous times to help season the steaks. Set aside.

25 MINUTES BEFORE DINNER, prepare the corn. Remove and discard the husks from 6 ears bi-colored sweet corn. Dampen a dish towel with water. Place the towel in the middle of a carousel microwave plate. Rinse the ears of corn under water. Do not dry. Stack the corn into a pyramid shape in center of the wet towel. Wrap the towel over the corn to help it remain moist while it cooks. Cook for 6 minutes.

20 MINUTES BEFORE DINNER, make the mushrooms. Rinse 2 packages button mushrooms under cold running water. Place the mushrooms in a medium nonstick saucepan, along with the Worcestershire sauce, soy sauce, Italian salad dressing, and 2 t water. Cook over medium heat until boiling. Cover and turn off the heat.

15 MINUTES BEFORE DINNER, rearrange the corn in the microwave and cook an additional 6 minutes. Turn off heat to the mushrooms. Cover and leave the mushrooms in the pan until ready to serve dinner.

Rearrange the ears of corn and microwave another 6 minutes

10 MINUTES BEFORE DINNER, place the steak at a 45-degree angle on the preheated grill. Cook for 2 to 3 minutes, and then press the steak firmly with tongs to create grill marks into the meat. Close the lid of grill and cook the steak over high heat for 2 to 3 minutes. Rotate the steak 45 degrees to create diamond-shaped grill marks. Cook an additional 2 to 3 minutes.

7 MINUTES BEFORE DINNER, rearrange the ears of corn within the pyramid and cook another 6 minutes.

5 MINUTES BEFORE DINNER, turn over the steak and grill the same way, cooking for 4 to 6 minutes for medium rare to medium. Cook longer if you prefer medium-well or well-done steaks.

3 MINUTES BEFORE DINNER, place the mushrooms in serving bowl with a slotted spoon. Place the corn on a serving plate. Place the steak on another serving plate. Spread 2 T butter in the center of the hot dog bun (or a slice of bread) and place on a small plate. Have guests roll their own ear of corn in the buttered bread.

NOTE: A meat thermometer should read 145 degrees for medium rare steaks.

Supplies List

Timer
Medium nonstick saucepan
    with lid
2 serving plates
Small plate
Outdoor gas grill

Grocery List

PACKAGED

1 hot dog bun (or a slice of
    bread)
Fat-free Italian salad dressing
Liquid smoke

PRODUCE

6 ears fresh bi-colored sweet
    corn
2 (8-ounce) packages fresh
    button mushrooms

MEAT

2 pounds boneless top sirloin
    steak

DAIRY

Light butter

Pantry List

Worcestershire sauce
Light soy sauce
Minced garlic
Steak seasoning
Light popcorn salt

>>> Italian Steak Bites

Italian Herb Smashed Potatoes • Bacon & Tomato Cheddar Bread Crisps • Tomato & Mozzarella Tossed Salad

There is no pasta in this Italian inspired menu, but my friends and family all agree: this is an Italian favorite.

ITALIAN STEAK BITES
Yield: 6 servings (4 ounces per serving)

Calories: 160 (29% fat); Total Fat: 5g; Cholesterol: 47mg; Carbohydrate: 3g; Dietary Fiber: 0g; Protein 25g; Sodium: 236mg; Diabetic Exchanges: 1 vegetable, 3 lean meat

ITALIAN HERB SMASHED POTATOES
Yield: 7 servings ($^1/_2$ cup per serving)

Calories: 144 (22% fat); Total Fat: 4g; Cholesterol: 13mg; Carbohydrate: 25g; Dietary Fiber: 2g; Protein 4g; Sodium: 524mg; Diabetic Exchanges: $1^1/_2$ starch, $^1/_2$ fat

BACON & TOMATO CHEDDAR BREAD CRISPS
Yield: 6 servings (1 slice per serving)

Calories: 100 (13% fat); Total Fat: 1g; Cholesterol: 5mg; Carbohydrate: 15g; Dietary Fiber: 1g; Protein 6g; Sodium: 307mg; Diabetic Exchanges: 1 starch, $^1/_2$ very lean meat

TOMATO & MOZZARELLA TOSSED SALAD
Yield: 6 servings ($1^1/_2$ cup per serving)

Calories: 55 (9% fat); Total Fat: 1g; Cholesterol: 3mg; Carbohydrate: 9g; Dietary Fiber: 2g; Protein 5g; Sodium: 555mg; Diabetic Exchanges: 2 vegetable, $^1/_2$ very lean meat

ITALIAN STEAK BITES

$1^3/_4$ pound beef sirloin (1-inch thick)	1 teaspoon steak seasoning
1 tablespoon Italian seasoning	$^1/_2$ cup marinara sauce

ITALIAN HERB SMASHED POTATOES

1 tablespoon Italian seasoning (Durkee)	$3^1/_2$ tablespoons imitation butter-flavored sprinkles
1 plus $^1/_4$ teaspoons garlic salt	4 tablespoons light butter
2 medium russet potatoes (about $2^1/_2$ cups chopped)	$^3/_4$ cup fat-free sour cream
2 large red skin potatoes (about $2^1/_2$ cups chopped)	

BACON & TOMATO CHEDDAR BREAD CRISPS

6 ($^1/_3$-inch-thick) slices French bread	6 teaspoons 30%-less-fat real bacon pieces
6 tablespoons shredded fat-free cheddar cheese	12 grape tomatoes, sliced thin

TOMATO & MOZZARELLA TOSSED SALAD

9 cups precut iceberg lettuce (1 large head)	$^3/_4$ cup fat-free zesty Italian salad dressing
1 cup grape tomatoes	
$^1/_2$ cup shredded fat-free mozzarella cheese	

Instructions

30 MINUTES BEFORE DINNER, start the potatoes. In a $2^1/2$-quart saucepan, combine 4 c water, 1 T Italian seasoning, and 1 t garlic salt over high heat and bring to a boil.

29 MINUTES BEFORE DINNER, cut 2 medium russet potatoes and 2 large red skin potatoes into $^1/2$-inch pieces.

25 MINUTES BEFORE DINNER, add the potatoes to the boiling water and cook for 4 minutes.

24 MINUTES BEFORE DINNER, prepare the steak. Remove all visible fat from $1^3/4$ lb beef sirloin. Cut the meat into $1^1/2$ to 2-inch pieces. Place the meat in a 1-gallon zip-top bag with 1 T Italian seasoning, and 1 t steak seasoning. Squeeze the bag to coat the meat with the seasonings. Set aside.

21 MINUTES BEFORE DINNER, turn off the burner under the potatoes. Cover and let the potatoes sit on the hot burner.

20 MINUTES BEFORE DINNER, start making the bread crisps. Preheat the oven to 425 degrees.

Spray both sides of 6 slices French bread generously with fat-free butter-flavored cooking spray. Arrange the bread on a baking sheet. Sprinkle 1 T Cheddar cheese on each slice of bread. Generously spray the cheese with butter-flavored cooking spray. Add 1 t bacon pieces and 2 sliced grape tomatoes on each slice of bread.

12 MINUTES BEFORE DINNER, preheat the indoor electric grill.

Make the tossed salad. In a large salad bowl, toss together 9 c precut iceberg lettuce, 1 cup grape tomatoes, and $^1/2$ c mozzarella cheese. Set aside.

8 MINUTES BEFORE DINNER, drain the potatoes. Place in a $2^1/2$-quart serving bowl. Using an electric mixer, beat the cooked potatoes with $^1/4$ t garlic salt, $3^1/2$ T butter-flavored sprinkles, 4 T light butter, and $^3/4$ c sour cream until well mixed. (You may need to take a brief break from making these potatoes in order to put the bread in the oven and also preheat the grill. You will have ample time to finish these potatoes later.)

CONTINUED ON NEXT PAGE >>>

Supplies List

Timer
$2^1/2$-quart saucepan with lid
1-gallon zip-top bag
$2^1/2$-quart serving bowl
Large serving bowl
Electric mixer
Indoor electric grill
Baking sheet
Colander

Grocery List

PACKAGED
$^1/2$ cup marinara sauce
2 tablespoons 30%-less-fat real bacon crumbles
French bread
1 (8-ounce) bottle Zesty Italian salad dressing

PRODUCE
2 medium russet potatoes
2 large red skin potatoes
12 grape tomatoes
1 large head iceberg lettuce

MEAT
$1^3/4$ pound beef sirloin

DAIRY
Shredded fat-free Cheddar cheese
$^1/2$ cup shredded fat-free mozzarella cheese
Light butter
$^3/4$ cup fat-free sour cream

Pantry List

Italian seasoning
Garlic salt
Fat-free butter flavored cooking spray
Imitation butter-flavored sprinkles
Steak seasoning

6 **MINUTES BEFORE DINNER,** bake the bread crisps for 5 minutes, or until bottom of bread is crispy and golden brown.

Start cooking the Italian Steak Bites. Generously spray the upper and lower grilling surfaces of the indoor electric grill with nonfat cooking spray. Arrange the pieces of seasoned beef onto the grill in a single layer. Close the lid firmly, pressing down to help sear grill marks into the meat.

Put $1/2$ c marinara sauce in a large serving bowl. Cover with waxed paper and microwave for 1 minute.

5 **MINUTES BEFORE DINNER,** toss the salad with $3/4$ c zesty Italian salad dressing. Put on the dinner table.

4 **MINUTES BEFORE DINNER,** continue making the potatoes. Once the potatoes are completely made, cover to keep warm. Place on the dinner table.

2 **MINUTES BEFORE DINNER,** add the steak bites to the large serving bowl with the preheated marinara sauce. Stir until the steak bites are coated with the marinara sauce. Place on the dinner table.

1 **MINUTE BEFORE DINNER,** place the bread crisps from the oven on a hot pad on the dinner table.

SEAFOOD

>>> Crab Fettuccini Alfredo

Greek-Inspired French Bread • Sesame Broccoli

This meal is very easy to prepare and even easier to eat. This is as good as any fine Italian restaurant at a fraction of the price, fat, and calories. Since it's so easy, I'll be surprised if you ever order this dish at a restaurant again.

CRAB FETTUCCINI ALFREDO
Yield: 7½ servings
(1 cup per serving)

Calories: 312 (6% fat); Total Fat: 2g; Cholesterol: 35mg; Carbohydrate: 54g; Dietary Fiber: 1g; Protein 19g; Sodium: 341mg; Diabetic Exchanges: 3 starch, ½ skim milk, 1 very lean meat

GREEK-INSPIRED FRENCH BREAD
Yield: 6 servings
(1 slice per serving)

Calories: 85 (12% fat); Total Fat: 1g; Cholesterol: 0mg; Carbohydrate: 15g; Dietary Fiber: 1g; Protein 4g; Sodium: 303mg; Diabetic Exchanges: 1 starch

SESAME BROCCOLI
Yield: 6 servings
(¾ cup per serving)

Calories: 55 (16% fat); Total Fat: 1g; Cholesterol: 2mg; Carbohydrate: 9g; Dietary Fiber: 5g; Protein 5g; Sodium: 245mg; Diabetic Exchanges: 2 vegetable

CRAB FETTUCCINI ALFREDO

12 ounces fettuccini, uncooked
1 pint fat-free half-and-half
2 tablespoons flour
1 teaspoon Old Bay seasoning
1 tablespoon imitation butter-flavored sprinkles
$1/3$ cup reduced-fat Parmesan-style grated topping
1 pound imitation crabmeat salad style chunks

GREEK-INSPIRED FRENCH BREAD

6 ($1/3$-inch-thick) slices French bread
1 teaspoon Italian seasoning
4 green olives, finely chopped
3 tablespoon fat-free feta cheese crumbles

SESAME BROCCOLI

2 (16-ounce) packages frozen broccoli
2 tablespoons imitation butter-flavored sprinkles
$1^1/2$ tablespoons reduced-fat Parmesan-style grated topping
$1/2$ teaspoon dried parsley
1 teaspoon toasted sesame seeds

Instructions

30 MINUTES BEFORE DINNER, bring 4 quarts of water to a boil in a Dutch oven.

27 MINUTES BEFORE DINNER, start the French bread. Cut 6 ($^1/_3$-inch-thick) slices French bread at a 45-degree angle; set aside. Finely chop 4 green olives; set aside.

25 MINUTES BEFORE DINNER, start the broccoli. Cut the tops off the 2 bags frozen broccoli and microwave on high for 6 minutes.

Continue making the French bread. Spray both sides of each bread slice with nonfat butter-flavored cooking spray and place on a baking sheet. Sprinkle each bread slice lightly with 1 t Italian seasoning, 4 finely chopped green olives, and 3 T feta cheese crumbles. Set aside.

20 MINUTES BEFORE DINNER, add 12 ounces fettuccini to the boiling water. Return to a boil. Boil for 12 minutes, or until the pasta is tender.

Preheat oven to 350 degrees.

18 MINUTES BEFORE DINNER, remove the 2 bags of broccoli from the microwave and shake them. Cook for another 6 minutes.

17 MINUTES BEFORE DINNER, while the pasta is cooking, start the Alfredo sauce. Pour 1 pint half-and-half into a 12-inch nonstick saucepan. With a whisk, stir in 2 T flour until dissolved.

Turn the heat to the burner under the saucepan to medium. Continue stirring constantly and add 1 t Old Bay seasoning, 1 T butter-flavored sprinkles, and $^1/_3$ c Parmesan topping.

11 MINUTES BEFORE DINNER, remove the broccoli from the microwave and place in a large microwavable bowl. Add 2 T butter-flavored sprinkles, $1^1/_2$ T Parmesan topping, $^1/_2$ t dried parsley, and 1 t toasted sesame seeds mixing well. Cover with waxed paper and cook for 4 minutes.

10 MINUTES BEFORE DINNER, once the Alfredo sauce is thick, gently stir in 1 lb crabmeat. Reduce the heat to low. Cover and continue cooking to heat the crabmeat, stirring frequently.

CONTINUED ON NEXT PAGE >>>

Supplies List

Timer
Dutch oven
Baking sheet
12-inch nonstick saucepan
    with lid
Large microwavable bowl
Serving platter
Colander

Grocery List

PACKAGED

1 (12-ounce) box fettuccini
4 green olives
French bread
Toasted sesame seeds
$^1/_2$ cup reduced-fat
    Parmesan-style grated
    topping

FROZEN

2 (16-ounce) packages frozen
    broccoli

SEAFOOD

1 pound imitation crabmeat
    salad style chunks

DAIRY

1 pint fat-free half-and-half
Fat-free feta cheese crumbles

Pantry List

Nonfat butter-flavored
    cooking spray
Flour
Old Bay seasoning
Italian seasoning
Dried parsley
Imitation butter-flavored
    sprinkles

>>> Crab Fettuccini Alfredo
CONTINUED FROM PREVIOUS PAGE

8 MINUTES BEFORE DINNER, drain the pasta.

6 MINUTES BEFORE DINNER, bake the French bread in the preheated oven for 5 minutes.

4 MINUTES BEFORE DINNER, turn off the heat under the Alfredo sauce. Stir in the cooked fettuccini noodles until well coated with the sauce.

3 MINUTES BEFORE DINNER, test the broccoli to see if it is still hot. If you prefer it warmer, microwave for 1 more minute and place on the dinner table.

2 MINUTES BEFORE DINNER, place the Alfredo on a hot pad on the dinner table.

1 MINUTE BEFORE DINNER, remove the French bread from the oven and place on a serving platter on the dinner table. When making the French bread you will not think you have enough toppings, but the flavor goes a long way.

>>> Honey Mustard & Dill Fish

Herb Smashed Potatoes • Cheesy Ranch Bread Crisps

This marvelous, moist, and tender fish melts in your mouth and is every bit as delicious as any fine restaurant. As with every menu in this book, it is easy enough to make every day; yet the fish, potato, and bread courses are special enough for company.

HONEY MUSTARD & DILL FISH
Yield: 6 servings
(4 ounces per serving)

Calories: 195 (14% fat); Total Fat: 3g; Cholesterol: 57mg; Carbohydrate: 16g; Dietary Fiber: 1g; Protein 24g; Sodium: 489mg; Diabetic Exchanges: 1 other carbohydrate, 3 very lean meat

HERB SMASHED POTATOES
Yield: 7 servings (¹/₂ cup per serving)

Calories: 135 (23% fat); Total Fat: 4g; Cholesterol: 13mg; Carbohydrate: 23g; Dietary Fiber: 1g; Protein 4g; Sodium: 522 mg; Diabetic Exchanges: 1¹/₂ starch, ¹/₂ fat

CHEESY RANCH BREAD CRISPS
Yield: 6 servings (1 slice per serving)

Calories: 136 (25% fat); Total Fat: 4g; Cholesterol: 8mg; Carbohydrate: 18g; Dietary Fiber: 1g; Protein 8g; Sodium: 466mg; Diabetic Exchanges: 1 starch, 1 lean meat

HONEY MUSTARD & DILL FISH

18	reduced-fat butter flavored crackers
³/₄	cup fat-free honey Dijon salad dressing
1	tablespoon lemon juice
1	teaspoon dried dill weed
1¹/₂	pounds fresh or frozen tilapia (if frozen, thawed)

HERB SMASHED POTATOES

4	cups water
4	medium Yukon Gold potatoes
1	tablespoon Italian seasoning
1¹/₄	teaspoons garlic salt
3¹/₂	tablespoons imitation
	butter-flavored sprinkles
¹/₄	cup light butter
³/₄	cup fat-free sour cream

CHEESY RANCH BREAD CRISPS

6	(¹/₃-inch-thick) slices French bread
12	teaspoons light ranch salad dressing
6	tablespoons shredded fat-free cheddar cheese
6	tablespoons shredded fat-free mozzarella cheese
6	teaspoons reduced-fat Parmesan-style grated topping
	Dried parsley

CONTINUED ON NEXT PAGE >>>

Supplies List

Timer
$2^1/_2$-quart saucepan
1-gallon zip top bag
Medium mixing bowl
Large jelly-roll pan
    ($17^1/_4$ x $11^1/_2$ x 1-inch)
Bowl
Electric mixer
Large salad bowl
Colander

Grocery List

PACKAGED
Light ranch salad dressing
Favorite salad dressing
Lemon juice
1 (8-ounce) bottle fat-free
    honey Dijon salad dressing
Reduced-fat butter-flavored
    crackers
French bread
Precut and washed green
    salad mixture

PRODUCE
4 medium Yukon Gold potatoes

FISH
$1^1/_2$ pounds tilapia

DAIRY
1 (8-ounce) container fat-free
    sour cream
Shredded fat-free cheddar
    cheese
Shredded fat-free mozzarella
    cheese
Light butter
Reduced-fat Parmesan-style
    grated topping

Pantry List on page 239

Instructions

30 MINUTES BEFORE DINNER, preheat the oven to 425 degrees. If tilapia is frozen, thaw in cold water in the sink.

29 MINUTES BEFORE DINNER, start the potatoes. In a $2^1/_2$-quart saucepan, combine 4 c water, 1 T Italian seasoning, and 1 t garlic salt over high heat. Bring to a boil.

28 MINUTES BEFORE DINNER, wash the 4 potatoes and cut into $^1/_2$-inch pieces.

25 MINUTES BEFORE DINNER, place the potato pieces into the boiling water. Cook for 4 minutes.

21 MINUTES BEFORE DINNER, turn off the burner under the potatoes. Cover and let sit on the hot burner.

20 MINUTES BEFORE DINNER, start the fish. Crush 18 crackers in a 1-gallon zip-top plastic bag with the palm of your hand. Set the crushed crackers aside.

18 MINUTES BEFORE DINNER, put $^3/_4$ c honey Dijon salad dressing into a medium mixing bowl. Stir in 1 T lemon juice and 1 t dried dill weed until well mixed.

16 MINUTES BEFORE DINNER, spray a large jelly-roll pan with nonfat cooking spray. Dip $1^1/_2$ lb tilapia into the salad dressing mixture and place on the prepared jelly-roll pan. Sprinkle the cracker crumbs on top of the fish, pressing the crumbs into the fish.

12 MINUTES BEFORE DINNER, bake the fish for 10 minutes.

11 MINUTES BEFORE DINNER, start making the bread crisps. Spray both sides of 6 ($^1/_3$-inch-thick) slices French bread generously with butter-flavored cooking spray. Spread 2 t light ranch salad dressing on one side of each bread slice. Place on a baking sheet. Sprinkle 1 T shredded cheddar cheese, 1 T shredded mozzarella cheese, 1 t Parmesan topping, and dried parsley over each slice of bread. Generously spray the cheese with butter-flavored cooking spray.

7 MINUTES BEFORE DINNER, bake the bread crisps in the oven for 5 minutes, or until the bottom of the bread is crispy and golden brown.

5 MINUTES BEFORE DINNER, drain the potatoes and place in a mixing bowl. Using an electric mixer, blend together $3^{1}/_{2}$ T butter sprinkles, $^{1}/_{4}$ cup butter, $^{1}/_{4}$ t garlic salt, and $^{3}/_{4}$ c sour cream until well mixed. Cover and place on the dinner table.

2 MINUTES BEFORE DINNER, remove the fish from the oven and place on a hot pad on the dinner table. Place the bread crisps from the oven on a hot pad on the dinner table.

1 MINUTE BEFORE DINNER, put 2 bags precut and washed green salad mixture into a large salad bowl and place on the dinner table along with your favorite fat-free salad dressing.

NOTE: *If your fish are still frozen, a quick way to thaw them is to soak them in cold water in a plastic zip-top bag or the package they came in.*

Pantry List

Italian seasoning
Garlic salt
Dried dill weed
Dried parsley
Nonfat cooking spray
Fat-free butter-flavored
   cooking spray
Imitation butter-flavored
   sprinkles

>>> Southwestern Bay Scallop Stew

Southwestern Bruschetta Bread • Pepper & Onion Brown Rice Blend

The sweet and spicy bay scallops surround the towering castle of red, yellow, and green bell peppers and brown rice with knights of crispy Southwestern bruschetta bread. This makes a meal presentation fit for your royal family that is every bit as impressive visually as it is tasty.

Bay Scallops

Yield: 6 servings ($^2/_3$ cup per serving)

Calories: 156 (5% fat); Total Fat: 1g; Cholesterol: 37mg; Carbohydrate: 17g; Dietary Fiber: 0g; Protein 19g; Sodium: 719mg; Diabetic Exchanges: 1 other carbohydrate, 3 very lean meat

Southwestern Bruschetta Bread

Yield: 10 servings (1 slice per serving)

Calories: 91 (0% fat); Total Fat: 0g; Cholesterol: 1mg; Carbohydrate: 17g; Dietary Fiber: 2g; Protein 5g; Sodium: 366mg; Diabetic Exchanges: 1 starch

Pepper & Onion Brown Rice Blend

Yield: 6 servings (1 cup per serving)

Calories: 111 (4% fat); Total Fat: 1g; Cholesterol: 0mg; Carbohydrate: 25g; Dietary Fiber: 3g; Protein 2g; Sodium: 31mg; Diabetic Exchanges: 1 starch, 2 vegetable

BAY SCALLOPS

$^1/_4$	cup chili sauce	1	tablespoon cornstarch
$1^1/_2$	teaspoons Old Bay seasoning	1	teaspoon Southwest chipotle seasoning
2	tablespoons honey		
$1^1/_2$	pounds frozen bay scallops	$^1/_2$	cup ketchup

SOUTHWESTERN BRUSCHETTA BREAD

1	($14^1/_2$-ounce) can diced tomato with green pepper, celery and onion, reserve $^1/_2$ cup juice	10	($^1/_2$-inch-thick) slices of multi-grain French bread
		$^1/_2$	cup shredded fat-free mild cheddar cheese

PEPPER & ONION BROWN RICE BLEND

$^1/_2$	cup tomato juice reserved from the bread recipe	1	teaspoon Southwest chipotle seasoning
$^3/_4$	cup apple cider (or apple juice)	2	(16-ounce) packages frozen 3-Pepper & Onion Blend
1	cup whole-grain instant brown rice		

Instructions

30 MINUTES BEFORE DINNER, start the rice. Drain the juice from 1 can diced tomato with onion and green pepper into a $4^1/_2$-quart saucepan, using your hands to squeeze out all of the juice. Add $^3/_4$ c apple cider and 1 c rice.

Place the saucepan over high heat. Stir in 1 t chipotle seasoning.

26 MINUTES BEFORE DINNER, place 2 bags frozen 3-Pepper & Onion Blend on top of the rice. Do not stir. Cover and bring to a boil.

Start preparing the bruschetta. Inside the can of tomatoes, add $^1/_2$ t chipotle seasoning and 1 t Splenda granular stirring well. Set aside.

24 MINUTES BEFORE DINNER, once the rice has come to a boil, reduce the heat to low and continue cooking.

Continue making the bruschetta. Cut 10 ($^1/_2$-inch-thick) slices of multi-grain French bread. Spray both sides of the bread slices with nonfat butter-flavored cooking spray. Place on a baking sheet. Spoon 1 heaping tablespoon of the drained tomatoes on top of each slice of bread. Evenly sprinkle the $^1/_2$ c shredded cheddar cheese over the bread. Spray the cheese with nonfat butter-flavored cooking spray; set aside.

20 MINUTES BEFORE DINNER, start the bay scallops. In a 12-inch nonstick skillet over high heat, combine $^1/_4$ c chili sauce, $1^1/_2$ t Old Bay seasoning, 2 T honey, 1 T cornstarch, and 1 t Southwest chipotle seasoning. Stir until well mixed and the cornstarch is dissolved. Add $1^1/_2$ lb frozen bay scallops and mix well.

14 MINUTES BEFORE DINNER, turn off the rice and stir. Cover and let sit on the warm burner.

12 MINUTES BEFORE DINNER, preheat the oven to 425 degrees.

10 MINUTES BEFORE DINNER, add $^1/_2$ c ketchup to the scallops. Reduce the heat to medium-low and stir. Do not cover so the sauce will thicken.

8 MINUTES BEFORE DINNER, bake the bread for 6 minutes.

4 MINUTES BEFORE DINNER, place 1 c of the 3-Pepper & Onion Rice Blend in the center of each dinner plate or bowl. Spoon $^2/_3$ c of the scallops and sauce around the rice. Place each serving on the dinner table.

2 MINUTES BEFORE DINNER, remove the bread from the oven. Let sit 1 minute to cool.

1 MINUTE BEFORE DINNER, place the bread on the dinner table.

Supplies List

Timer
$4^1/_2$-quart saucepan with lid
Baking sheet
12-inch nonstick skillet

Grocery List

PACKAGED
1 ($14^1/_2$-ounce) can diced
   tomatoes with onion and
   green pepper
Multi-grain French bread
Apple cider
Chili sauce

FROZEN
2 (16-ounce) packages frozen
   3-Pepper & Onion Blend
$1^1/_2$ pounds frozen bay
   scallops

DAIRY
$^1/_2$ cup shredded fat-free mild
   cheddar cheese

SEASONINGS
Southwest chipotle seasoning

Pantry List

Cornstarch
Whole-grain instant brown
   rice
Ketchup
Old Bay seasoning
Honey
Nonfat butter-flavored
   cooking spray

>>> Salmon Florentine

Maple Sweet Potatoes • Always Tender Asparagus Spears

Here's a meal fit for a king that won't make the queen's waist big. Serve this menu for lots of "ooo's" and "ahhs!"

SALMON FLORENTINE
Yield: 6 servings
(1 fillet per serving)
Calories: 236 (31% fat); Total Fat: 8g; Cholesterol: 75mg; Carbohydrate: 14g; Dietary Fiber: 1g; Protein 27g; Sodium: 531mg; Diabetic Exchanges: 1 starch, 3 lean meat

MAPLE SWEET POTATOES
Yield: 6 servings (1/2 cup per serving)
Calories: 123 (0% fat); Total Fat: 0g; Cholesterol: 0mg; Carbohydrate: 29g; Dietary Fiber: 3g; Protein 2g; Sodium: 673mg; Diabetic Exchanges: 2 starch

ALWAYS TENDER ASPARAGUS SPEARS
Yield: 6 servings
(3 to 4 spears per serving)
Calories: 32 (0% fat); Total Fat: 0g; Cholesterol: 0mg; Carbohydrate: 6g; Dietary Fiber: 3g; Protein 3g; Sodium: 90mg; Diabetic Exchanges: 1 vegetable

SALMON FLORENTINE

1   (10-ounce) package frozen creamed spinach
1   tablespoon honey mustard
1/2 cup fat-free mayonnaise
1   tablespoon lemon juice
6   (4-ounce) salmon fillets (no skin)
1   cup corn flakes
1/4 teaspoon lemon pepper

MAPLE SWEET POTATOES

1   teaspoon light salt
2   large sweet potatoes (about 5 cups chopped)
3   tablespoons imitation butter-flavored sprinkles
1/2 cup sugar-free maple syrup

ALWAYS TENDER ASPARAGUS SPEARS

1/4 teaspoon allspice
1   tablespoon Splenda granular
1   tablespoon imitation butter-flavored sprinkles
1 3/4 pound fresh asparagus, trimmed
Popcorn salt (optional)

Instructions

30 MINUTES BEFORE DINNER, start the water for the sweet potatoes. Put 4 c of water in the saucepan and bring to a boil over high heat.

28 MINUTES BEFORE DINNER, microwave 1 package frozen creamed spinach for 2 minutes.
Preheat the oven to 450 degrees.

27 MINUTES BEFORE DINNER, peel 2 large sweet potatoes and cut them into 1-inch pieces.

23 MINUTES BEFORE DINNER, add the sweet potato pieces to the boiling water. Return to a boil and boil for 2 to 3 minutes.

22 MINUTES BEFORE DINNER, start the asparagus spears. Put $^1/_2$-inch of water in a 12-inch nonstick skillet. Stir in $^1/_4$ t allspice and 1 T Splenda until dissolved. Place the asparagus in the water. Cover and bring to a boil over medium-high heat.

19 MINUTES BEFORE DINNER, turn off the boiling water under the sweet potatoes. Cover and let sit on the hot burner.

Turn off the heat under the asparagus. Keep covered and let sit on the hot burner.

18 MINUTES BEFORE DINNER, in a medium bowl stir together until well mixed the thawed creamed spinach, 1 T honey mustard, $^1/_2$ c mayonnaise, and 1 T lemon juice. Set aside.

Spray a 9 x 13-inch casserole dish with nonfat cooking spray. Place 6 salmon fillets in the prepared casserole dish. Spread the creamed spinach mixture over the fish. Sprinkle 1 c crushed corn flakes over the fish. Sprinkle $^1/_4$ t lemon pepper over the corn flakes.

15 MINUTES BEFORE DINNER, bake the salmon on the top rack for 10 to 15 minutes, or until the fish flakes with a fork.

5 MINUTES BEFORE DINNER, test the fish to see if it is fully cooked. If fully cooked, remove from the oven and place on the stove. Cover to keep warm. If the fish does not flake, then continue baking.

4 MINUTES BEFORE DINNER, drain the sweet potatoes and put into a large serving bowl. Drizzle with a $^1/_2$ c maple syrup and $^1/_2$ t light salt. Beat with an electric mixer to make the potatoes soft and creamy. Place on table.

2 MINUTES BEFORE DINNER, drain the asparagus. Lay the spears on a serving plate. Sprinkle with 1 T butter sprinkles and popcorn salt, if desired.

1 MINUTE BEFORE DINNER, check the fish for doneness. Place the salmon on a hot pad on the dinner table.

Supplies List

Timer
$4^1/_2$-quart saucepan
12-inch nonstick skillet
9x13-inch casserole dish
Large serving bowl
Electric mixer
Colander

Grocery List

PACKAGED

Honey mustard
Corn flakes

PRODUCE

2 large sweet potatoes
$1^3/_4$ pound fresh asparagus

FROZEN

1 (10-ounce) package frozen creamed spinach

FISH

6 (4-ounce) salmon fillets

Pantry List

Lemon juice
Light salt
Allspice
Lemon pepper
Nonfat cooking spray
Fat-free mayonnaise
Sugar-free maple syrup
Imitation butter-flavored sprinkles
Splenda granular
Popcorn salt (optional)

>>> Dill-icious Tilapia with Shrimp

Asparagus & Portobello Mushroom Medley • Raspberry Pecan Salad with Cranberries

As the "cookbook lady," using ordinary ingredients to create extraordinary recipes is a gift God uses through me. This dish is one such inspired recipe! The thought of using dill pickle juice to bake the fish and shrimp simply came to me. If you are the least bit hesitant to try this, but you like the flavor of dill, then I want to encourage you to set aside your fears. Without a shadow of a doubt I know you are absolutely going to love it!

DILL-ICIOUS TILAPIA WITH SHRIMP

Yield: 6 servings (5 ounces cooked fish and 3 shrimp per serving)

Calories: 175 (15% fat); Total Fat: 3g; Cholesterol: 132mg; Carbohydrate: 0g; Dietary Fiber: 0g; Protein 36g; Sodium: 326mg; Diabetic Exchanges: 5 very lean meat

ASPARAGUS & PORTOBELLO MUSHROOM MEDLEY

Yield: 6 servings ($1/2$ cup per serving)

Calories: 49 (0% fat); Total Fat: 0g; Cholesterol: 0mg; Carbohydrate: 10g; Dietary Fiber: 4g; Protein 4g; Sodium: 172mg; Diabetic Exchanges: 2 vegetable

RASPBERRY PECAN SALAD WITH CRANBERRIES

Yield: 6 servings ($1 2/3$ cups per serving)

Calories: 93 (19% fat); Total Fat: 2g; Cholesterol: 3mg; Carbohydrate: 16g; Dietary Fiber: 3g; Protein 4g; Sodium: 480mg; Diabetic Exchanges: 1 other carbohydrate, $1/2$ lean meat

DILL-ICIOUS TILAPIA WITH SHRIMP

2 pounds fresh or frozen tilapia (if frozen, thawed)
1 cup dill pickle juice
18 peeled & deveined shrimp (30-40 count)
1 teaspoon Old Bay seasoning
$1/2$ teaspoon dried dill weed

ASPARAGUS & PORTOBELLO MUSHROOM MEDLEY

1 (6-ounce) portobello mushroom, cut into thin slices
2 pounds fresh asparagus, trimmed
$1/2$ large red onion, sliced into rings and separated ($3/4$ cup)
1 tablespoon imitation butter-flavored sprinkles
$1/2$ teaspoon garlic salt

RASPBERRY PECAN SALAD WITH CRANBERRIES

2 (11-ounce) packages spring mix salad greens (about 10 cups chopped)
3 tablespoons fat-free feta cheese crumbles
$1 1/2$ tablespoons 30%-less-fat bacon pieces
$1/4$ cup dried cranberries
3 teaspoons finely chopped pecans
$3/4$ cup fat-free raspberry pecan salad dressing
$1/2$ cup fat-free Italian-flavored croutons

Instructions

30 MINUTES BEFORE DINNER, preheat the oven to 450 degrees.

Coat a jelly-roll pan with nonfat cooking spray. Arrange 2 lb tilapia on the prepared jelly-roll pan. Pour 1 c dill pickle juice over the fish. Arrange 18 shrimp on top of the fish. Sprinkle with 1 t Old Bay seasoning and $1/2$ t dried dill weed. Spray with nonfat cooking spray. Cover with aluminum foil and bake on the middle rack for 25 minutes, or until the fish flakes easily with a fork.

20 MINUTES BEFORE DINNER, start cooking the vegetable medley. Fill a large saucepan with 1-inch of water. Add 1 thinly sliced portobello mushroom, 2 lb trimmed fresh asparagus, and onion slices. Bring the water to a boil. Cover and turn off the heat. Let the vegetables steam in the hot saucepan on the hot burner until dinner is ready.

10 MINUTES BEFORE DINNER, start making the salad. In a large salad bowl, toss together 2 packages spring mix salad greens, 3 T feta cheese crumbles, $1^1/2$ T bacon pieces, $1/4$ c dried cranberries, $1^1/2$ T pecans, and $3/4$ c salad dressing until well mixed. Sprinkle the top of the salad with $1/2$ c croutons. Place the salad on the dinner table.

3 MINUTES BEFORE DINNER, drain the water from the vegetable medley. Sprinkle lightly with 1 T butter sprinkles and $1/2$ t garlic salt. Put on the dinner table.

1 MINUTE BEFORE DINNER, place the fish and shrimp on a serving platter and place on the dinner table.

Supplies List
Timer
Jelly-roll pan
Large saucepan
Large salad bowl
Serving platter
Colander

Grocery List

PACKAGED
1 (8-ounce) bottle fat-free raspberry pecan salad dressing
Fat-free Italian-flavored croutons
30%-less-fat bacon pieces
Dried cranberries

PRODUCE
1 (6-ounce) Portobello mushroom
2 pounds fresh asparagus
1 large red onion
2 (11-ounce) packages spring mix salad greens

FISH/SEAFOOD
2 pounds fresh or frozen tilapia
1 package peeled & deveined shrimp (30-40 count)

DAIRY
Fat-free feta cheese crumbles

Pantry List
Old Bay seasoning
Dried dill weed
Garlic salt
Nonfat cooking spray
Imitation butter-flavored sprinkles
Finely chopped pecans
Dill pickle juice

>>> Really Dilly Tuna Casserole

Apricot Vinaigrette Tossed Salad • Cantaloupe Wedges

I am not a big fan of tuna casseroles, but this one is so delicious that it has become one of my favorites! I can't believe how terrific it tastes. The salad dressing I created to go with this entrée is the perfect complement!

REALLY DILLY TUNA CASSEROLE
Yield: 6 servings (1 cup per serving)

Calories: 252 (17% fat); Total Fat: 5g; Cholesterol: 29mg; Carbohydrate: 30g; Dietary Fiber: 3g; Protein 21g; Sodium: 931mg; Diabetic Exchanges: 2 starch, 2 very lean meat

APRICOT VINAIGRETTE TOSSED SALAD
Yield: 6 servings (1½ cups per serving)

Calories: 61 (0% fat); Total Fat: 0g; Cholesterol: 1mg; Carbohydrate: 13g; Dietary Fiber: 2g; Protein 2g; Sodium: 408mg; Diabetic Exchanges: 1 vegetable, ½ other carbohydrate

REALLY DILLY TUNA CASSEROLE

1 ¼	cups water
1½	cups dill pickle juice
1	($10^3/_4$-ounce) can 98% fat-free condensed cream of mushroom soup
4	cups No-Yolk extra-broad noodles, uncooked
2	slices reduced-fat deli-thin sliced Swiss cheese slices *
2	(6-ounce) cans chunk light tuna in water, drained
1	($8^1/_2$-ounce) can peas and carrots, drained
¼	teaspoon dried dill weed (optional)

APRICOT VINAIGRETTE TOSSED SALAD

²/₃	cup fat-free Italian salad dressing
3	tablespoons apricot preserves
1	large head iceberg lettuce (about 9 cups chopped)
½	cup zesty Italian croutons

Instructions

30 MINUTES BEFORE DINNER, cut the cantaloupe in half. With a spoon remove and discard the seeds. Cut the cantaloupe into wedges. Remove the rind from each cantaloupe wedge. Place the wedges on a serving plate and cover. Place in the refrigerator until dinner time.

25 MINUTES BEFORE DINNER, start the casserole. In a 12-inch nonstick saucepan over high heat, bring $1^1/_4$ c water, $1^1/_2$ c dill pickle juice, and 1 can cream of mushroom soup to a boil. Add 4 c No-Yolk noodles and return to a boil. Reduce the heat to medium and boil for 10 minutes, stirring frequently.

While the pasta is cooking, cut the 2 slices Swiss cheese into very thin strips.

9 MINUTES BEFORE DINNER, stir in 2 cans drained tuna and 1 can drained peas and carrots. Turn off the heat.

Sprinkle the shredded cheese over the casserole.

If desired, sprinkle the cheese with $^1/_4$ t dried dill weed for garnish.

Cover the saucepan and let sit on the warm burner until dinner is ready to be served.

7 MINUTES BEFORE DINNER, prepare the salad. In the bottom of a large salad bowl, use a whisk to combine $^2/_3$ c Italian salad dressing and 3 T apricot preserves.

Remove and discard the core from 1 large head iceberg lettuce.

Cut the lettuce into bite-size pieces and place in the bowl with the dressing.

Toss the lettuce with the dressing until well coated.

Sprinkle $^1/_2$ c zesty Italian croutons on top of the salad and place the salad on the dinner table.

1 MINUTE BEFORE DINNER, place the cantaloupe wedges on the dinner table. Place the tuna casserole on a hot pad on the dinner table as well.

*NOTE: One (6.67-oz) package of reduced-fat Swiss cheese slices (Sargento) has nine thin slices.

Supplies List

Timer
12-inch nonstick saucepan
    with lid
Large salad bowl

Grocery List

PACKAGED

1 ($10^3/_4$-ounce) can 98%
    fat-free condensed cream
    of mushroom soup
1 (12-ounce) bag No-Yolk
    extra broad noodles
2 (6-ounce) cans chunk light
    tuna in water
1 (8-ounce) bottle fat-free
    Italian salad dressing
Zesty Italian croutons
Apricot preserves
1 ($8^1/_2$-ounce) can peas and
    carrots

PRODUCE

Cantaloupe
1 large head iceberg lettuce

DAIRY

2 slices reduced-fat deli thin
    sliced Swiss cheese slices

Pantry List

Dried dill weed (optional)
Dill pickle juice

>>> Crabby Rice Stove-Top Casserole

Sweet Cocktail Salad Dressing • Shrimp Garden Salad • Ranch Bread Crisps

> Everyone agreed . . . we all really like the "bite and zip" the Old Bay seasoning gives this casserole.

CRABBY RICE STOVE-TOP CASSEROLE

Yield: 7 servings (1 cup per serving)

Calories: 162 (6% fat); Total Fat: 1g; Cholesterol: 32mg; Carbohydrate: 26g; Dietary Fiber: 2g; Protein 12g; Sodium: 321mg; Diabetic Exchanges: 1$^1/_2$ starch, 1 vegetable, 1 very lean meat

SWEET COCKTAIL SALAD DRESSING

Yield: 6 servings

(2 tablespoons per serving)

Calories: 46 (0% fat); Total Fat: 0g; Cholesterol: 0mg; Carbohydrate: 11g; Dietary Fiber: 1g; Protein 0g; Sodium: 303mg; Diabetic Exchanges: $^1/_2$ other carbohydrate

SHRIMP GARDEN SALAD

Yield: 6 servings

(1$^1/_3$ cups per serving)

Calories: 101 (26% fat); Total Fat: 3g; Cholesterol: 35mg; Carbohydrate: 7g; Dietary Fiber: 2g; Protein 11g; Sodium: 272mg; Diabetic Exchanges: 1$^1/_2$ vegetable, 1$^1/_2$ lean meat

RANCH BREAD CRISPS

Yield: 6 servings (1 slice per serving)

Calories: 108 (9% fat); Total Fat: 1g; Cholesterol: 2mg; Carbohydrate: 17g; Dietary Fiber: 1g; Protein 7g; Sodium: 398mg; Diabetic Exchanges: 1 starch, $^1/_2$ very lean meat

CRABBY RICE STOVE-TOP CASSEROLE

2$^1/_2$ cups water

2 teaspoons Old Bay seasoning

1$^1/_2$ cups whole-grain instant brown rice

1 (8$^1/_2$-ounce) can peas and carrots, drained

1 (16-ounce) package imitation crabmeat, cut into bite-size pieces

SWEET COCKTAIL SALAD DRESSING

$^3/_4$ cup fat-free French salad dressing

1 teaspoon prepared horseradish

1 teaspoon Splenda granular

SHRIMP GARDEN SALAD

8 cups bagged, washed, and precut iceberg lettuce

1 medium cucumber, peeled and sliced

1 cup grape tomatoes

1 cup shredded fat-free cheddar cheese

6 ounces salad shrimp

$^1/_2$ cup fat-free croutons

RANCH BREAD CRISPS

6 ($^1/_3$-inch-thick) slices French bread

6 teaspoons light ranch salad dressing

$^3/_4$ cup shredded fat-free mozzarella cheese

Dried parsley

Instructions

30 MINUTES BEFORE DINNER, start making the bread crisps. Spray both sides of 6 ($1/3$-inch-thick) slices French bread with butter-flavored cooking spray. Place on a baking sheet. Set aside.

27 MINUTES BEFORE DINNER, start making casserole. In a nonstick 12-inch saucepan, bring $2^1/2$ c water and 2 t Old Bay seasoning to a boil.

23 MINUTES BEFORE DINNER, once liquid is boiling, stir in $1^1/2$ c brown rice. Return to a boil. Reduce the heat to medium low. Cover and simmer for 12 minutes, or until the rice is tender.

20 MINUTES BEFORE DINNER, make the salad dressing. In a small bowl combine $3/4$ c French salad dressing, 1 t horseradish, and 1 t Splenda granular. Cover and refrigerate until dinner time.

15 MINUTES BEFORE DINNER, assemble the salad. In a large bowl combine 8 c precut and washed iceberg lettuce, 1 medium peeled and sliced cucumber, 1 c grape tomatoes, 1 c shredded cheese, and 6 ounces salad shrimp. *Do not put on the croutons yet!* Toss the salad until well mixed. Cover and place in the refrigerator to keep chilled.

10 MINUTES BEFORE DINNER, turn off the heat to the rice. Stir in 1 can drained peas and carrots and 1 package crabmeat, cut into bite size pieces. Cover and let sit on the warm burner until dinner is ready to be served.

9 MINUTES BEFORE DINNER, finish making the bread crisps. Preheat the oven to 425 degrees.

Spread 1 t light ranch salad dressing on one side of each slice of bread. Sprinkle each slice with dried parsley and 2 tablespoons shredded mozzarella. Generously spray the cheese with butter-flavored cooking spray.

6 MINUTES BEFORE DINNER, put the bread crisps in the oven and bake for 5 minutes, or until bottom of bread is crispy and golden brown.

3 MINUTES BEFORE DINNER, sprinkle $1/2$ c croutons over the salad. Place the salad and the dressing on the dinner table.

1 MINUTE BEFORE DINNER, place the casserole and the bread crisps from the oven both on hot pads on the dinner table.

Supplies List

Timer
Baking sheet
Nonstick 12-inch saucepan
Large bowl
Small bowl

Grocery List

PACKAGED

Whole-grain instant brown rice
1 ($8^1/2$-ounce) can peas and carrots
1 (8-ounce) bottle fat-free French salad dressing
French bread
Light ranch salad dressing
Fat-free croutons
Prepared horseradish

PRODUCE

8 cups bagged, washed, and precut iceberg lettuce
1 medium cucumber
1 cup grape tomatoes

SEAFOOD

1 (16 ounce) package imitation crab
6 ounces salad shrimp

DAIRY

1 cup shredded fat-free cheddar cheese
$3/4$ cup shredded fat-free mozzarella cheese

Pantry List

Dried parsley
Fat-free butter-flavored cooking spray
Old Bay seasoning
Splenda granular

>>> Seafood & Shells by the Seaside

Lobster Topped Waves of Lettuce

Even special meals such as this (that are expensive to make) can be made quickly and effortlessly in less than thirty minutes.

SEAFOOD & SHELLS BY THE SEASIDE
Yield: 8 servings
(1½ cups per serving)
Calories: 380 (15% fat); Total Fat: 6g; Cholesterol: 150mg; Carbohydrate: 52g; Dietary Fiber: 2g; Protein 27g; Sodium: 716mg; Diabetic Exchanges: 3½ starch, 3 very lean meat

LOBSTER TOPPED WAVES OF LETTUCE
Yield: 6 salads (1 wedge per serving)
Calories: 109 (8% fat); Total Fat: 1g; Cholesterol: 14mg; Carbohydrate: 20g; Dietary Fiber: 3g; Protein 7g; Sodium: 554mg; Diabetic Exchanges: 2 vegetable, ½ other carbohydrate, 1 very lean meat

SEAFOOD & SHELLS BY THE SEASIDE

1   tablespoon Old Bay seasoning
4½ cups medium pasta shells
6   tablespoons light butter
1   tablespoon bottled minced garlic
2   teaspoons garlic salt with parsley
1   pound small cocktail shrimp, cooked, deveined, and tails removed
1   pound imitation crabmeat
Reduced-fat Parmesan-style grated topping (optional)

LOBSTER TOPPED WAVES OF LETTUCE

1   large head iceberg lettuce
½   cup fat-free French salad dressing
¼   cup cocktail sauce
18 grape tomatoes
1   (8-ounce) package imitation lobster

Instructions

25 MINUTES BEFORE DINNER, start the salad. Remove and discard the core from 1 head iceberg lettuce.

Cut the head of lettuce into 6 wedges. Arrange the wedges down the center of a large serving platter.

In a medium bowl, combine $^1/_2$ cup French salad dressing and $^1/_4$ cup cocktail sauce until well mixed. Pour over the center of the wedges of lettuce.

Arrange 18 grape tomatoes and 1 package imitation lobster over the salad dressing. Cover with plastic wrap and place in the refrigerator until dinner is ready.

17 MINUTES BEFORE DINNER, start the seafood & shells. Add 1 T Old Bay seasoning to 4 quarts of water in a large Dutch oven over high heat. Bring to a boil.

12 MINUTES BEFORE DINNER, once the water comes to a boil, stir in the pasta shells. Return to a boil and cook the pasta for 8 minutes.

In a 12-inch nonstick saucepan, melt 6 T light butter over low heat. Add 1 T minced garlic, 2 t garlic salt with parsley, 1 lb shrimp, and 1 lb imitation crab-meat and cook for 10 minutes.

3 MINUTES BEFORE DINNER, drain the pasta. Gently stir the cooked pasta into the seafood. Place the skillet on a hot pad on the dinner table. For a prettier presentation, pour the cooked pasta dinner into a 9 x 13-inch casserole dish. If desired, sprinkle with Parmesan topping.

1 MINUTE BEFORE DINNER, place the salad on the table.

NOTE: *To save time purchase shrimp already cooked, deveined, and with tails removed*

Supplies List

Timer
Large serving platter
Medium bowl
Large 12-inch nonstick skillet
9 x 13-inch casserole dish
    (optional)
Colander
Dutch oven

Grocery List

PACKAGED

1 (8-ounce) bottle fat-free
    French salad dressing
Cocktail sauce
1 (12-ounce) box
    medium-size pasta shells

PRODUCE

1 large head iceberg lettuce
18 grape tomatoes

SEAFOOD

1 pound imitation lobster
1 pound small cocktail
    shrimp
1 (8-ounce) package
    imitation crab

DAIRY

Light butter
Reduced-fat Parmesan-style
    grated topping (optional)

Pantry List

Old Bay seasoning
Minced garlic
Garlic salt with parsley

>>> Shrimp & Rice Stove-Top Casserole

Crabby Tossed Salad • French Bread Lobster Crisps

My dinner guests really raved about how much they liked this meal! I'm sure your dinner guests will, too! What is so nice about this menu is that it is such a "special treat type of meal," yet it is easy to put together comfortably in 30 minutes or less.

SHRIMP & RICE STOVE-TOP CASSEROLE

Yield: 8 servings (1 cup per serving)

Calories: 154 (8% fat); Total Fat: 1g; Cholesterol: 85mg; Carbohydrate: 22g; Dietary Fiber: 3g; Protein 13g; Sodium: 391mg; Diabetic Exchanges: 1 starch, 1 vegetable, 1¹/₂ very lean meat

CRABBY TOSSED SALAD

Yield: 6 servings (1¹/₂ cups per serving)

Calories: 95 (6% fat); Total Fat: 1g; Cholesterol: 20mg; Carbohydrate: 13g; Dietary Fiber: 3g; Protein 10g; Sodium: 165mg; Diabetic Exchanges: 1¹/₂ vegetable, ¹/₂ other carbohydrate, 1 very lean meat

FRENCH BREAD LOBSTER CRISPS

Yield: 6 servings (1 crisp per serving)

Calories: 105 (9% fat); Total Fat: 1g; Cholesterol: 20mg; Carbohydrate: 15g; Dietary Fiber: 1g; Protein 8g; Sodium: 281mg; Diabetic Exchanges: 1 starch, 1 very lean meat

SHRIMP & RICE STOVE-TOP CASSEROLE

2¹/₂ cups water
1 cup shrimp cocktail sauce
1 (16-ounce) package frozen shrimp
1 (16-ounce) bag frozen 3-Pepper & Onion Blend
1¹/₂ cups whole-grain instant brown rice
¹/₂ cup shredded fat-free mozzarella cheese

CRABBY TOSSED SALAD

1 large head iceberg lettuce (about 9 cups chopped)
1 medium cucumber, peeled and sliced
1 red bell pepper, cut into thin strips
¹/₂ cup grape tomatoes
¹/₂ cup fat-free shredded mozzarella cheese
8 ounces imitation crabmeat
¹/₂ cup fat-free croutons

FRENCH BREAD LOBSTER CRISPS

6 (¹/₃-inch) slices of French bread
Fat-free butter-flavored cooking spray
1 teaspoon Italian seasoning
1 (6-ounce) can lobster meat, drained
Garlic salt

Instructions

25 MINUTES BEFORE DINNER, start the casserole. In a nonstick 12-inch saucepan, combine $2^1/_2$ c water, 1 c shrimp cocktail sauce, 1 package shrimp, and 1 bag frozen peppers and onion and bring to a boil over medium-high heat.

21 MINUTES BEFORE DINNER, once the liquid is boiling, stir in $1^1/_2$ c whole-grain instant brown rice. Return to a boil. Reduce the heat to medium. Cover and simmer for 12 minutes, or until the rice is tender.

19 MINUTES BEFORE DINNER, preheat the oven to 350 degrees.

18 MINUTES BEFORE DINNER, prepare the salad. Cut 1 large head iceberg lettuce into 9 c of bite-size pieces. Peel and cut 1 medium cucumber into thin slices. Slice 1 red bell pepper into thin strips. Place the lettuce, cucumber slices, and red bell pepper strips in a large salad bowl. Top the salad with $^1/_2$ c grape tomatoes, $^1/_2$ c shredded mozzarella cheese, and 8 ounces imitation crabmeat. *Do not put on the croutons yet!* Toss the salad until well mixed. Cover and refrigerate to keep chilled.

13 MINUTES BEFORE DINNER, make the lobster crisps. Cut the French bread at a 45-degree angle into $^1/_3$-inch-thick slices.

Spray both sides of each bread slice generously with butter-flavored cooking spray and place the bread slices on a baking sheet.

Lightly sprinkle 1 t Italian seasoning over the slices of bread. Top with 1 can drained lobster meat. Sprinkle lightly with garlic salt, if desired. Spray the tops of the lobster meat generously with the butter-flavored cooking spray. Set aside.

8 MINUTES BEFORE DINNER, turn off the heat to the rice. Sprinkle $^1/_2$ c shredded mozzarella cheese over the rice. Spray the cheese with butter-flavored cooking spray. Cover and let sit on the warm burner until dinner is ready.

7 MINUTES BEFORE DINNER, bake the lobster crisps for 5 minutes, or until crispy.

2 MINUTES BEFORE DINNER, put favorite salad dressings on the dinner table.
Sprinkle $^1/_2$ c croutons over the salad and place the salad next to the salad dressings on the dinner table.

1 MINUTE BEFORE DINNER, place the casserole on a hot pad on the dinner table. Remove the lobster crisps from the oven, put on a plate, and place on the dinner table.

Supplies List

Timer
Nonstick 12-inch saucepan
    with lid
Large salad bowl
Baking sheet
Plate

Grocery List

PACKAGED

Whole-grain instant
    brown rice
Fat-free croutons
1 (8-ounce) jar shrimp
    cocktail sauce
French bread

PRODUCE

1 large head iceberg lettuce
1 medium cucumber
1 red bell pepper
$^1/_2$ cup grape tomatoes

FROZEN

1 (16-ounce) bag frozen
    3-Pepper and Onion Blend
1 (16-ounce) package shrimp

SEAFOOD

1 (6-ounce) can lobster
8 ounces imitation crab

DAIRY

1 cup shredded fat-free
    mozzarella cheese

Pantry List

Garlic salt
Fat-free butter flavored
    cooking spray
Italian seasoning

>>> Florentine-Stuffed Fish

Honey Mustard Cauliflower • Dilly Green Beans & Sliced Potatoes

Here's a menu simple enough to put together, but impressive for company. The colors are beautiful and the flavors are fantastic. Special thanks to my assistant, Brenda Crosser of Florida, who inspired this fish recipe.

FLORENTINE-STUFFED FISH
Yield: 6 servings
(6 ounces fish; $^2/_3$ cup Florentine stuffing per serving)
Calories: 289 (13% fat); Total Fat: 4g; Cholesterol: 85mg; Carbohydrate: 23g; Dietary Fiber: 2g; Protein 39g; Sodium: 694mg; Diabetic Exchanges: $1^1/_2$ starch, 5 very lean meat

HONEY MUSTARD CAULIFLOWER
Yield: 6 servings ($^2/_3$ cup per serving)
Calories: 74 (0% fat); Total Fat: 0g; Cholesterol: 0mg; Carbohydrate: 16g; Dietary Fiber: 4g; Protein 3g; Sodium: 151mg; Diabetic Exchanges: $1^1/_2$ vegetable, $^1/_2$ other carbohydrate

DILLY GREEN BEANS & SLICED POTATOES
Yield: 6 servings ($^2/_3$ cup per serving)
Calories: 65 (0% fat); Total Fat: 0g; Cholesterol: 0mg; Carbohydrate: 13g; Dietary Fiber: 4g; Protein 2g; Sodium: 731mg; Diabetic Exchanges: $^1/_2$ starch, $1^1/_2$ vegetable

FLORENTINE-STUFFED FISH

1	(10-ounce) package frozen spinach
1	(6-ounce) package corn bread stuffing mix
1	cup hot water
$2^1/_4$	pounds tilapia or any mild fish
1	teaspoon lemon pepper

HONEY MUSTARD CAULIFLOWER

2	(16-ounce) packages frozen cauliflower
1	cup water
$^1/_4$	cup fat-free honey Dijon salad dressing
2	tablespoons honey

DILLY GREEN BEANS & SLICED POTATOES

$^1/_2$	cup dill pickle juice
2	($14^1/_2$ ounce) cans Italian-cut green beans, drained
1	(15- ounce) can sliced white potatoes, drained
$^1/_2$	teaspoon dried dill weed
1	tablespoon imitation butter-flavored sprinkles

Instructions

30 MINUTES BEFORE DINNER, start preparing the fish. Cook 1 package frozen spinach in the microwave for 2 minutes.

While the spinach is cooking, combine 1 package corn bread stuffing mix with 1 c hot water in a medium microwavable bowl.

Preheat the oven to 400 degrees.

27 MINUTES BEFORE DINNER, add the spinach (do not drain moisture from spinach) to the stuffing and knead with your hands.

25 MINUTES BEFORE DINNER, coat a large jelly-roll pan with nonfat cooking spray. Place half the fish fillets on the prepared baking sheet. Divide the stuffing mixture among the fish fillets. Press the stuffing on top of the fish. Place the remaining fish fillets on top of the stuffing. Spray generously with nonfat cooking spray. Sprinkle 1 t lemon pepper seasoning over all the fish. Set aside.

22 MINUTES BEFORE DINNER, start the cauliflower. Combine 2 bags frozen cauliflower with 1 c of water in a 12-inch nonstick saucepan. Cook, covered, over high heat.

15 MINUTES BEFORE DINNER, place the stuffed fish in the oven.

14 MINUTES BEFORE DINNER, start the beans and potatoes. Place $^1/_2$ c dill pickle juice in a $2^1/_2$-quart nonstick saucepan. Drain 2 cans Italian-cut green beans and 1 can sliced white potatoes. Stir the drained green beans and sliced potatoes into the saucepan with the dill pickle juice. Add $^1/_2$ t dried dill weed. Cover and cook over medium-low heat.

7 MINUTES BEFORE DINNER, start the sauce for the cauliflower. In a small bowl, stir together $^1/_4$ c honey Dijon salad dressing with 2 T honey. Microwave the sauce for 15 to 20 seconds.

3 MINUTES BEFORE DINNER, drain the cauliflower. Put the cauliflower into a large serving bowl. Add the honey mustard sauce and gently stir. Place on the dinner table.

2 MINUTES BEFORE DINNER, drain the pickle juice from the beans and potatoes. Put the green beans and potatoes into a medium serving bowl and gently stir with 1 T butter-flavored sprinkles. Place on the dinner table.

1 MINUTE BEFORE DINNER, remove the fish from the oven. Place on hot pads on the dinner table.

Supplies List

Timer
Medium microwavable bowl
Small bowl
Medium serving bowl
Large serving bowl
Large jelly-roll pan
    (17.2 5x 11½ x 1-inch)
12-inch nonstick saucepan
    with lid
2½-quart nonstick saucepan
    with lid
Colander

Grocery List

PACKAGED

1 (6-ounce) package
    cornbread stuffing mix
Fat-free honey Dijon salad
    dressing
2 (14½-ounce) cans
    Italian-cut green beans
1 (15-ounce) can sliced
    white potatoes

FROZEN

1 (10-ounce) package frozen
    spinach
2 (16-ounce) packages frozen
    cauliflower

FISH

2¼ pounds tilapia or any
    mild fish

Pantry List

Honey
Dried dill weed
Lemon pepper
Nonfat cooking spray
Imitation butter-flavored
    sprinkles
Dill pickle juice

>>> Salmon Chowder

Sweet & Sour Tossed Salad • Oyster Crackers

This Salmon Chowder is not fishy at all. It has a rich, creamy, and smooth flavor that will have you asking for more. The Sweet and Sour Tossed Salad is a perfect accompaniment.

SALMON CHOWDER
Yield: 11 servings
(1 cup per serving)

Calories: 166 (7% fat); Total Fat: 1g;
Cholesterol: 13mg; Carbohydrate: 26g;
Dietary Fiber: 2g; Protein 14g;
Sodium: 582mg; Diabetic Exchanges:
1 starch, 1 skim milk, 1 very lean meat

SWEET & SOUR TOSSED SALAD
Yield: 6 servings
(1½ cups per serving)

Calories: 43 (0% fat); Total Fat: 0g;
Cholesterol: 2mg; Carbohydrate: 9g;
Dietary Fiber: 2g; Protein 2g; Sodium:
156mg; Diabetic Exchanges: ½ fruit

SALMON CHOWDER

3 (14-ounce) cans fat-free less-sodium chicken broth
4 cups frozen shredded hash brown potatoes
3 tablespoons cornstarch
2 (7.1-ounce) packages pink salmon *

3 cups fat-free half-and-half
3 teaspoons lemon pepper
1 (8½-ounce) can sweet peas and carrots

SWEET & SOUR TOSSED SALAD

¼ cup fat-free sour cream
3 teaspoons Splenda granular
¼ cup dill pickle juice
1 (11 ounce) can mandarin oranges, drained

½ whole dill pickle
2 small heads romaine lettuce (about 9 cups chopped)

Instructions

30 MINUTES BEFORE DINNER, start the chowder. In a Dutch oven or large saucepan, bring 2 of the cans chicken broth to a boil over high heat. Add 4 c frozen shredded hash browns and cook for 5 minutes. In a small bowl, whisk 3 T cornstarch into the remaining 1 can chicken broth until the cornstarch is dissolved.

25 MINUTES BEFORE DINNER, add the chicken broth and cornstarch mixture to the boiling potatoes. Reduce the heat to medium low and simmer. Stir in 2 packages salmon, 3 c half-and-half, and 3 t lemon pepper. Continue stirring until the salmon chunks are broken into small pieces.

20 MINUTES BEFORE DINNER, stir the salmon chowder. If needed, adjust the heat so the liquid is simmering.

15 MINUTES BEFORE DINNER, start making the salad. In a large salad bowl, whisk together $1/4$ c sour cream, 3 teaspoons Splenda granular, and $1/4$ c dill pickle juice. Set aside.

10 MINUTES BEFORE DINNER, stir the salmon chowder. Continue making the salad. Drain the juice from 1 can mandarin oranges. Place the drained mandarin oranges in the large salad bowl with the salad dressing. Cut $1/2$ whole dill pickle into quarters and then into thin slices to make a $1/2$ c. Add to the salad dressing. Do not stir. Chop 2 small heads romaine lettuce into bite-size pieces to make 9 c. Add the lettuce to the salad bowl. Do not stir. Place the salad bowl in the refrigerator.

7 MINUTES BEFORE DINNER, stir the salmon chowder. Place oyster crackers in a cloth-lined basket and place on the dinner table.

4 MINUTES BEFORE DINNER, drain 1 can sweet peas and carrots. Stir the sweet peas and carrots into the chowder. Turn off the heat and let the salmon chowder sit on the hot burner. The hot chowder will heat the sweet peas and carrots.

3 MINUTES BEFORE DINNER, toss the salad, making sure the lettuce is well coated with the salad dressing. Place the salad on the dinner table.

1 MINUTE BEFORE DINNER, ladle the chowder into individual soup bowls and put on the dinner table.

NOTE: *We tested this recipe with canned salmon and also with foil-packed salmon. Although it cost less to use canned salmon, we agreed that the foil-packed salmon gives this chowder a much better and smoother taste.*

Supplies List

Timer
Dutch oven or large saucepan
Large bowl
Large salad bowl
Individual soup bowls
Basket

Grocery List

PACKAGED
1 ($8^1/2$-ounce) can sweet peas and carrots
Whole dill pickles
1 (11-ounce) can mandarin oranges

PRODUCE
2 small heads romaine lettuce

FROZEN
4 cups frozen shredded hash brown potatoes

FISH
2 (7.1-ounce) packages pink salmon

DAIRY
3 cups fat-free half-and-half
$1/4$ cup fat-free sour cream

Pantry List

Cornstarch
3 (14-ounce) cans fat-free less-sodium chicken broth
Lemon pepper
Oyster crackers
Dill pickle juice
Splenda granular

>>> Fish Tacos

Fish Taco Sauce • Salsa Salad Wedges

This fun menu, served buffet style, is loaded with flavor. What is great about this menu is that everyone gets to assemble his or her own tacos, which saves the cook time. The taco sauce I created adds extra zip and pizzazz. This is a good menu for parties.

FISH TACOS

Yield: 6 servings (4 ounces fish; 2 corn tortillas per serving)

Calories: 190 (12% fat); Total Fat: 3g; Cholesterol: 57mg; Carbohydrate: 17g; Dietary Fiber: 2g; Protein 25g; Sodium: 294mg; Diabetic Exchanges: 1 starch, 3 very lean meat

FISH TACO SAUCE

Yield: 6 servings (2 tablespoons per serving)

Calories: 24 (30% fat); Total Fat: 1g; Cholesterol: 3mg; Carbohydrate: 4g; Dietary Fiber: 1g; Protein 0g; Sodium: 267mg; Diabetic Exchanges: Free

SALSA SALAD WEDGES

Yield: 6 servings (1 wedge per serving)

Calories: 76 (0% fat); Total Fat: 0g; Cholesterol: 2mg; Carbohydrate: 14g; Dietary Fiber: 2g; Protein 4g; Sodium: 467mg; Diabetic Exchanges: 1 1/2 vegetable, 1/2 other carbohydrate

FISH TACOS

3/4	cup corn flakes	12	(6-inch) corn tortillas
1	tablespoon taco seasoning mix	1/2	head iceberg lettuce (optional)
1	tablespoon fat-free imitation cheese-flavored sprinkles*	1	medium tomato (optional)
1 1/2	pounds frozen tilapia, thawed and cut into 1-inch-thick strips	1	cup shredded fat-free cheddar cheese (optional)

FISH TACO SAUCE

3/4	cup fat-free mayonnaise	1	teaspoon lemon juice
1	teaspoon sweet relish	1/4	teaspoon or more Cajun seasoning
1	teaspoon lime juice		

SALSA SALAD WEDGES

1	large head iceberg lettuce	6	teaspoons fat-free sour cream
1 1/2	cups salsa	6	tablespoons fat-free French salad dressing
6	tablespoons shredded fat-free cheddar cheese		

Instructions

30 MINUTES BEFORE DINNER, preheat the oven to 450 degrees.
Spray a 9 x 13-inch baking pan with nonfat cooking spray. Set aside.

29 MINUTES BEFORE DINNER, prepare the fish tacos. In a 1-gallon zip-top bag combine $3/4$ c corn flakes, 1 T taco seasoning, and 1 T cheese-flavored sprinkles. Crush the corn flakes using your hand or a rolling pin.

26 MINUTES BEFORE DINNER, add $1^1/2$ lb tilapia strips to the crushed corn flake mixture. Lightly toss the fish with the corn flake mixture until the fish is evenly coated with the mixture. Place the coated fish on the prepared baking pan in a single layer. Spray the top of the fish generously with nonfat cooking spray. Set aside.

23 MINUTES BEFORE DINNER, make the sauce. In a small bowl, stir together $3/4$ c fat-free mayonnaise, 1 t sweet relish, 1 t lime juice, 1 t lemon juice, and $1/4$ t Cajun seasoning. Add $1/8$ to $1/4$ t more Cajun seasoning if you prefer your fish taco sauce spicier. Place on the dinner table.

16 MINUTES BEFORE DINNER, bake the fish in the preheated oven for 12 to 15 minutes, or until the fish flakes and easily breaks apart.

14 MINUTES BEFORE DINNER, prepare the optional toppings for the fish tacos. Finely cut $1/2$ head iceberg lettuce into thin shreds and place in a medium bowl. Finely chop 1 medium tomato and place in a bowl. Put 1 c shredded cheddar cheese in a bowl. Place the three bowls next to the sauce on the dinner table to make a condiment buffet area.

9 MINUTES BEFORE DINNER, make the salad wedges. Cut 1 large head iceberg lettuce into 6 wedges. Place the wedges on a platter. Pour $1/4$ c salsa on top of each lettuce wedge. Sprinkle each wedge with 1 T shredded cheddar cheese. Top each serving with 1 t sour cream and drizzle 1 T French salad dressing on top. Place the salad wedges on the dinner table.

3 MINUTES BEFORE DINNER, place 12 corn tortillas on a baking sheet. It is okay if the corn tortillas overlap. Bake the corn tortillas for 2 minutes, just long enough to heat the tortillas.

1 MINUTE BEFORE DINNER, remove the fish and the corn tortillas from the oven. Place both on hot pads on the dinner table near the prepared condiments.

*NOTE: Fat-free imitation cheese-flavored sprinkles are found in the spice aisle or popcorn aisle.

Supplies List

Timer
9 x 13-inch pan
1-gallon zip-top plastic bag
Small bowl
Platter
Medium bowl
3 bowls
Baking sheet

Grocery List

PACKAGED

Corn flakes
12 (6-inch) corn tortillas
Lime juice
Sweet relish
1 (16-ounce) jar salsa
Fat-free French salad dressing
Lemon juice

PRODUCE

1 plus $1/2$ head iceberg lettuce
1 medium tomato (optional)

FISH

$1^1/2$ pounds frozen tilapia

DAIRY

1 (8-ounce) package shredded fat-free cheddar cheese
Fat-free sour cream

SEASONINGS

Taco seasoning mix
Fat-free imitation cheese-flavored sprinkles
Cajun seasoning

Pantry List

Fat-free mayonnaise
Nonfat cooking spray

>>> Lobster Pizzas

Sweet & Sour Speckled Wedged Salads

These individual pizzas are a tremendous hit at our home, as are the wedged salads!

LOBSTER PIZZAS

Yield: 8 servings

(1 pizza per serving)

Calories: 356 (14% fat); Total Fat: 5g; Cholesterol: 58mg; Carbohydrate: 44g; Dietary Fiber: 4g; Protein 32g; Sodium: 1932mg; Diabetic Exchanges: 3 starch, 3$^1/_2$ very lean meat

SWEET & SOUR SPECKLED WEDGED SALADS

Yield: 8 servings

(1 wedge per serving)

Calories: 56 (33% fat); Total Fat: 2g; Cholesterol: 4mg; Carbohydrate: 8g; Dietary Fiber 2g; Protein 2g; Sodium: 163mg; Diabetic Exchanges: 1 vegetable, $^1/_2$ other carbohydrate, $^1/_2$ fat

LOBSTER PIZZAS

$^1/_4$ cup light butter	1 cup cocktail sauce
4 (8-ounce) packages imitation lobster pieces	8 (8-inch) soft flour tortillas
$^1/_2$ teaspoon garlic salt with dried parsley	2 cups fat-free mozzarella cheese
8 ounces fat-free cream cheese	Dried parsley (optional)

SWEET & SOUR SPECKLED WEDGED SALADS

1 large head iceberg lettuce	1 tablespoon dried parsley
$^1/_3$ cup light Miracle Whip	2 tablespoons fat-free sour cream
$^1/_3$ cup sweet pickle juice	1 large tomato

Instructions

30 MINUTES BEFORE DINNER, make the salad wedges. Hit the head of lettuce on the counter to loosen the core. Remove and discard the core. Cut the lettuce into 8 pie-shaped wedges. Place the wedges in a circle on a large cake plate. Cover and place in the refrigerator until dinner is ready.

25 MINUTES BEFORE DINNER, prepare the dressing. In a small bowl, combine $1/3$ c light Miracle Whip, $1/3$ c sweet pickle juice, 1 T dried parsley, and 2 T sour cream. Cover and place in the refrigerator.

20 MINUTES BEFORE DINNER, preheat the oven to 450 degrees.

19 MINUTES BEFORE DINNER, start the pizzas. Heat $1/4$ c light butter in the microwave for 20 seconds, or until fully melted.

18 MINUTES BEFORE DINNER, stir 4 packages imitation lobster and $1/2$ t garlic salt with dried parsley into the melted light butter until well mixed.

Spread 2 T cream cheese then 2 T cocktail sauce over each of the 8 soft flour tortillas. Arrange $1/2$ c of the lobster mixture on each soft flour tortilla. Sprinkle $1/4$ c mozzarella cheese over each tortilla. Generously spray the cheese with nonfat cooking spray. If desired for added color, sprinkle with dried parsley.

9 MINUTES BEFORE DINNER, place the pizzas directly on the preheated oven rack (do not use a baking sheet). Bake for 7 minutes, or until the edges of the tortillas are crispy and golden brown.

8 MINUTES BEFORE DINNER, chop 1 large tomato. Set aside.

6 MINUTES BEFORE DINNER, remove the iceberg lettuce wedges and dressing from the refrigerator. Evenly pour the salad dressing over the lettuce wedges. Sprinkle with the chopped tomato. Place the salads on the dinner table.

2 MINUTES BEFORE DINNER, remove the pizzas from the oven. Cut each pizza into quarters.

1 MINUTE BEFORE DINNER, place the pizzas on a serving platter and put on the dinner table.

Supplies List

Timer
Large cake plate
Small bowl
Serving platter

Grocery List

PACKAGED
Sweet pickles
Cocktail sauce
8 (8-inch) soft flour tortillas

PRODUCE
1 large head iceberg lettuce
1 large tomato

FISH
4 (8-ounce) packages
    imitation lobster pieces

DAIRY
Light butter
Fat-free sour cream
8 ounces fat-free cream
    cheese
2 cups fat-free mozzarella
    cheese

Pantry List

Nonfat cooking spray
Dried parsley
Garlic salt with dried parsley
Light Miracle Whip

>>> Shrimp Scampi

California Vegetable Medley • Cheddar Bread Twists

Since this recipe is so simple to make at home and costs a fraction of what it would at any fine restaurant, I doubt I'll ever order shrimp scampi at a restaurant again. The tender vegetables in this meal are the perfect accompaniment to the scampi. The entrée and vegetables are low in calories, so we can afford to splurge on cheesy bread twists, which is a special treat.

SHRIMP SCAMPI
Yield: 6 servings
(4 ounces per serving)
Calories: 123 (36% fat); Total Fat: 5g; Cholesterol: 178mg; Carbohydrate: 2g; Dietary Fiber: 0g; Protein 18g; Sodium: 257mg; Diabetic Exchanges: 3 lean meat

CALIFORNIA VEGETABLE MEDLEY
Yield: 6 servings (1 cup per serving)
Calories: 65 (0% fat); Total Fat: 0g; Cholesterol: 0mg; Carbohydrate: 13g; Dietary Fiber: 4g; Protein 5g; Sodium: 533mg; Diabetic Exchanges: 2 1/2 vegetable

CHEDDAR BREAD TWISTS
Yield: 12 servings
(1 bread twist per serving)
Calories: 85 (15% fat); Total Fat: 1g; Cholesterol: 1mg; Carbohydrate: 13g; Dietary Fiber: 0g; Protein 4g; Sodium: 263mg; Diabetic Exchanges: 1 starch

SHRIMP SCAMPI

1 1/2 pounds frozen small shrimp (41-50 count)
4 tablespoons light butter
2 tablespoons bottled minced garlic

CALIFORNIA VEGETABLE MEDLEY

1 tablespoon bottled minced garlic
1 teaspoon seasoned salt
2 (16-ounce) packages frozen California blend vegetables
1 (8-ounce) package fresh sliced mushrooms
1/4 cup imitation butter-flavored sprinkles

CHEDDAR BREAD TWISTS

1 (11-ounce) can refrigerated bread stick dough
3/4 cup shredded fat-free cheddar cheese
36 plus 36 sprays of fat-free butter spray

Instructions

30 MINUTES BEFORE DINNER, start the vegetable medley. Add 4 c of hot water to a $4^1/_2$-quart saucepan. Stir in 1 T minced garlic and 1 t seasoned salt.

28 MINUTES BEFORE DINNER, turn the heat to high and add 2 packages frozen California blend vegetables. Cover and cook on high for about 10 minutes. Once water has come to a boil, let cook for 1 minute. Turn off the heat and let the vegetables remain, covered, in the hot saucepan.

27 MINUTES BEFORE DINNER, place $1^1/_2$ pounds frozen shrimp in a colander. Run cold water over them until the shrimp are thawed. Leave the shrimp in the colander.

23 MINUTES BEFORE DINNER, preheat the oven to 375 degrees.

22 MINUTES BEFORE DINNER, prepare the bread twists. Coat a baking sheet with cooking spray.

Unroll the dough, and press $^3/_4$ c shredded cheddar cheese into the dough. Spray the cheese with 36 sprays of butter spray.

Making one bread twist at a time, separate the dough at the perforations. Holding both ends of the dough, twist each breadstick into a spiral. Lay the dough twists on the prepared baking sheet. Repeat for all 12 pieces of dough. Press any remaining cheese into the twists.

15 MINUTES BEFORE DINNER, turn off the heat under the vegetables. Add 1 package mushrooms. Cover and let sit on the hot burner.

Continue making the bread twists.

11 MINUTES BEFORE DINNER, bake the bread twists for 10 minutes.

8 MINUTES BEFORE DINNER, start the shrimp scampi. This entrée cooks quickly and needs your undivided attention.

In a large 12-inch nonstick saucepan melt 1 T of the butter over medium-high heat. Add 2 T minced garlic and cook for 1 minute. Add the shrimp and cook, stirring every 30 to 60 seconds. Add the remaining 3 T butter, one tablespoon at a time, every 2 to 3 minutes,. The shrimp will only take 4 to 5 minutes to fully cook.

CONTINUED ON NEXT PAGE >>>

Supplies List

Timer
Baking sheet
Large 12-inch nonstick
    saucepan with lid
Serving bowl
Platter
Colander

Grocery List

PRODUCE
1 (8-ounce) package sliced
    mushrooms

FROZEN
2 (16-ounce) packages frozen
    California blend vegetables
$1^1/_2$ pounds frozen small
    shrimp (41-50 count)

DAIRY
Light butter
$^3/_4$ cup shredded fat-free
    cheddar cheese
Fat-free butter spray
1 (11-ounce) can refrigerated
    bread stick dough

Pantry List

Nonfat cooking spray
Minced garlic
Seasoned salt
Imitation butter-flavored
    sprinkles

Once the shrimp are fully cooked, turn off the heat. Cover and place the saucepan on a hot pad on the diner table.

3 MINUTES BEFORE DINNER, drain the vegetables. Place in a serving bowl and add $1/4$ c butter-flavored sprinkles until well mixed. Put the vegetables on the dinner table.

1 MINUTE BEFORE DINNER, remove the bread twists from the oven. Spray each twists with 3 sprays of butter spray.

Put the bread sticks on a platter and place on the dinner table.

NOTE: It is very important not to overcook the shrimp as they will become chewy. As soon as the shrimp become white and are no longer transparent remove them from the heat.

VEGETARIAN

>>> Vegetarian Goulash

Soft Onion Drop Biscuits • Ranch Salad Wedges Topped with Bell Pepper Confetti

This goulash is so hearty and filling it is a meal in itself. Most meat lovers will never guess this is a vegetarian dish. The deep earthy orange-colored soft biscuits have a wonderful aroma and onion flavor. The secret behind the vibrant color, fragrant aroma, and undistinguishable great taste of the biscuits is tomato sauce.

VEGETARIAN GOULASH
Yield: 8 servings (1 cup per serving)
Calories: 135 (0% fat); Total Fat: 0g; Cholesterol: 0mg; Carbohydrate: 22g; Dietary Fiber: 5g; Protein 12g; Sodium: 776mg; Diabetic Exchanges: 1 starch, 1 1/2 vegetable, 1 very lean meat

SOFT ONION DROP BISCUITS
Yield: 11 servings
(1 biscuit per serving)
Calories: 68 (14% fat); Total Fat: 1g; Cholesterol: 0mg; Carbohydrate: 13g; Dietary Fiber: 0g; Protein 2g; Sodium: 354mg; Diabetic Exchanges: 1 starch

RANCH SALAD WEDGES TOPPED WITH BELL PEPPER CONFETTI
Yield: 6 servings
(1 wedge per serving)
Calories 73 (7% fat); Total Fat: 1g; Cholesterol: 0mg; Carbohydrate: 16g; Dietary Fiber: 2g; Protein 2g; Sodium: 368mg; Diabetic Exchanges: 1 1/2 vegetable, 1/2 other carbohydrate

VEGETARIAN GOULASH

2	cups rotini pasta	3	(14 1/2 -ounce) cans diced tomatoes with chilies
1	cup frozen chopped onions		
1/2	cup chopped green bell pepper	1	(12-ounce) package frozen vegetarian beef-flavored crumbles
1/2	cup chopped celery		

SOFT ONION DROP BISCUITS

1 1/2	cups low-fat baking mix	1	teaspoon dried chopped chives
1	(8-ounce) can tomato sauce	1/2	cup frozen chopped onion
1/2	teaspoon garlic salt		

RANCH SALAD WEDGES TOPPED WITH BELL PEPPER CONFETTI

1/2	cup chopped green bell pepper	1	large head iceberg lettuce
1/2	cup chopped red bell pepper	12	tablespoons fat-free ranch salad dressing
1/2	cup chopped yellow bell pepper		

Instructions

30 MINUTES BEFORE DINNER, bring 3 quarts water in a large Dutch oven over high heat to a boil.

Set aside $^1/_2$ c green bell pepper, $^1/_2$ c red bell pepper, and $^1/_2$ c yellow bell pepper to use as the bell pepper confetti for the salad wedges.

25 MINUTES BEFORE DINNER, start the goulash. Add 2 c rotini pasta to the boiling water. Return the water to a boil and cook for 8 minutes, or until tender.

Coat a 12-inch nonstick saucepan with cooking spray. Add 1 c frozen onions, $^1/_2$ c green bell pepper, and $^1/_2$ c celery. Cook, covered, until crisp and tender, about 5 minutes. Stir frequently.

20 MINUTES BEFORE DINNER, add 3 cans diced tomatoes with chilies and 1 package frozen vegetarian beef-flavored crumbles to the sautéed vegetables. Bring to a boil. Reduce the heat to medium. Simmer, covered, for 5 minutes, stirring occasionally.

15 MINUTES BEFORE DINNER, drain the pasta. Stir the cooked pasta into the saucepan. Reduce the heat to medium low. Cover and cook another 5 minutes.

Preheat the oven to 400 degrees.

12 MINUTES BEFORE DINNER, prepare the biscuits. In a medium bowl, combine $1^1/_2$ c baking mix, 1 can tomato sauce, $^1/_2$ t garlic salt, 1 t chives, and $^1/_2$ c onion until well mixed. Dough will be sticky.

10 MINUTES BEFORE DINNER, turn off the heat under the goulash. Let sit on the warm burner, covered, until time for dinner.

Coat a baking sheet with nonfat cooking spray and set aside.

Drop the biscuit dough by rounded tablespoonfuls onto the prepared baking sheet.

8 MINUTES BEFORE DINNER, bake the biscuits in the oven on the middle rack for 8 minutes.

7 MINUTES BEFORE DINNER, prepare salad wedges. Remove and discard the core of 1 large head iceberg lettuce.

With a large knife, cut the head of lettuce into 6 pie-shaped wedges. Place the wedges on individual salad plates or on a large platter.

Top each wedge of lettuce with 2 T ranch salad dressing. Sprinkle evenly with $^1/_2$ c green bell pepper, $^1/_2$ c red bell pepper, and $^1/_2$ c yellow bell pepper.

Place the salad wedges on the table.

2 MINUTES BEFORE DINNER, put the biscuits in a basket and place on the dinner table. Set the goulash on a hot pad on the table.

Supplies List

Timer
Large Dutch oven
12-inch nonstick saucepan with lid
Baking sheet
Colander

Grocery List

PACKAGED

1 (8-ounce) can tomato sauce
3 (14$^1/_2$-ounce) cans diced tomatoes with chilies
1 (8-ounce) bottle fat-free ranch salad dressing
1 (12-ounce) box rotini pasta

PRODUCE

$^1/_2$ cup chopped celery
1 large head iceberg lettuce
$^1/_2$ cup chopped red bell pepper
$^1/_2$ cup chopped yellow bell pepper
1 cup chopped green bell pepper

FROZEN

1$^1/_2$ cups frozen chopped onions
1 (12-ounce) package frozen vegetarian beef-flavored crumbles

Pantry List

Nonfat cooking spray
Garlic salt
Dried chopped chives
Low-fat baking mix

>>> Angel Hair Pasta Smothered in Vegetarian Sausage Marinara

Italian Seasoned Buttermilk Biscuits • Italian Caesar Salad

For those people who don't know about vegetarian products available at the grocery store, I know the title of this recipe sounds like an oxymoron. You are probably wondering, "How can a sausage entrée be vegetarian?" The secret is the Italian sausage veggie crumbles.

ANGEL HAIR PASTA SMOTHERED IN VEGETARIAN SAUSAGE MARINARA
Yield: 6 servings
(1 1/3 cups per serving)
Calories: 319 (26% fat); Total Fat: 9g; Cholesterol: 6mg; Carbohydrate: 39g; Dietary Fiber: 7g; Protein 19g; Sodium: 1564mg; Diabetic Exchanges: 2 starch, 2 vegetable, 1 1/2 very lean meat, 1 fat

ITALIAN SEASONED BUTTERMILK BISCUITS
Yield: 10 servings
(1 biscuit per serving)
Calories: 55 (24% fat); Total Fat: 2g; Cholesterol: 0mg; Carbohydrate: 9g; Dietary Fiber: 0g; Protein 1g; Sodium: 264mg; Diabetic Exchanges: 1/2 starch, 1/2 fat

ITALIAN CAESAR SALAD
Yield: 6 servings (1 1/2 cups per serving)
Calories: 39 (15% fat); Total Fat: 1g; Cholesterol: 2mg; Carbohydrate: 6g; Dietary Fiber: 2g; Protein: 3g; Sodium: 333mg; Diabetic Exchanges: 1 1/2 vegetable

ANGEL HAIR PASTA SMOTHERED IN VEGETARIAN SAUSAGE MARINARA

- 1   (12-ounce) package vegetarian sausage-flavored crumbles
- 1   (14-ounce) can diced tomatoes with onion, celery, and green peppers
- 1/2 cup frozen chopped onion
- 1   (14-ounce) can fat-free low-sodium beef broth
- 1   (26-ounce) jar Three Cheese pasta sauce
- 1   (4-ounce) can sliced mushrooms, undrained
- 4   ounces angel hair pasta

ITALIAN SEASONED BUTTERMILK BISCUITS

- 1   (7 1/2-ounce) can refrigerated buttermilk biscuits
- 2   tablespoons fat-free Italian salad dressing
- 1/2 teaspoon Italian seasoning
- 1/2 teaspoon garlic salt

ITALIAN CAESAR SALAD

- 1/2 cup fat-free Italian salad dressing
- 1 1/2 teaspoons bottled minced garlic
- 1   tablespoon reduced-fat Parmesan-style grated topping
- 1/4 cup liquid egg substitute
- 1   large head romaine lettuce

Instructions

30 MINUTES BEFORE DINNER, start the marinara. In a 12-inch nonstick saucepan, combine 1 package vegetarian sausage-flavored crumbles, 1 can diced tomatoes with green pepper and onion, $^1/_2$ c frozen chopped onion, 1 can beef broth, 1 jar pasta sauce, and 1 can sliced mushrooms with liquid over medium-high heat. Bring to a low boil. Reduce the heat to medium and simmer, uncover.

20 MINUTES BEFORE DINNER, bring 3 quarts of water to a boil in a Dutch oven over medium-high heat. Add 4 oz angel hair pasta. Return to a boil and cook for 4 minutes.

15 MINUTES BEFORE DINNER, drain the pasta and stir into the sauce. Turn off the heat to the sauce. Cover and let sit on the hot burner until dinner.

13 MINUTES BEFORE DINNER, preheat the oven to 400 degrees.

Coat a baking sheet with nonfat cooking spray.

Prepare 1 can buttermilk biscuits. Put 2 T Italian salad dressing in a small shallow bowl. Dip both sides of each biscuit in the salad dressing and place on the prepared baking sheet. Sprinkle all of the biscuits evenly with $^1/_2$ t Italian seasoning and $^1/_2$ t garlic salt.

10 MINUTES BEFORE DINNER, bake the biscuits for 9 minutes.

Prepare the salad dressing. In a large salad bowl, combine $^1/_2$ c Italian salad dressing, $1^1/_2$ t minced garlic, 1 T Parmesan topping, and $^1/_4$ c liquid egg substitute until well blended. Set aside.

Wash 1 large head romaine lettuce and cut into pieces. Add to the large salad bowl with the dressing and toss until the lettuce is coated with dressing. Set the salad on the dinner table.

1 MINUTE BEFORE DINNER, place the biscuits and the pasta on the dinner table.

NOTE: To simmer at a low boil means small bubbles should be on the surface of the sauce.

Supplies List

Timer
12-inch nonstick saucepan with lid
Small shallow bowl
Large salad bowl
Dutch oven

Grocery List

PACKAGED

1 (14-ounce) can diced tomatoes with green pepper and onion
1 (26-ounce) jar Three Cheese pasta sauce
1 (4-ounce) can sliced mushrooms
4 ounces angel hair pasta
1 (8-ounce) bottle fat-free Italian salad dressing
Reduced-fat Parmesan-style grated topping

PRODUCE

1 large head romaine lettuce

FROZEN

1 (12-ounce) package vegetarian sausage-flavored crumbles
$^1/_2$ cup frozen chopped onions

DAIRY

$^1/_4$ cup liquid egg substitute
1 ($7^1/_2$-ounce) can refrigerated buttermilk biscuits

Pantry List

Nonfat cooking spray
1 (14-ounce) can fat-free less-sodium beef broth
Italian seasoning
Garlic salt
Minced garlic

>>> Little Italy Barley Soup

Vegetarian Sausage Drop Biscuits • Bell Pepper Medley with Italian Dip

This is a wonderful thick soup that is great to enjoy while sitting by the fire after a long day.

LITTLE ITALY BARLEY SOUP

Yield: 7 servings (1 cup per serving)

*Calories: 206 (18% fat); Total Fat: 4g;
Cholesterol: 4mg; Carbohydrate: 31g;
Dietary Fiber: 6g; Protein 12g;
Sodium: 949mg; Diabetic Exchanges:
1 starch, 3 vegetable, 1 lean meat*

VEGETARIAN SAUSAGE DROP BISCUITS

Yield: 8 servings

(1 biscuit per serving)

*Calories: 74 (17% fat); Total Fat: 1g;
Cholesterol: 1mg; Carbohydrate: 12g;
Dietary Fiber: 0g; Protein 4g; Sodium:
247mg; Diabetic Exchanges: 1 starch*

**BELL PEPPER MEDLEY
WITH ITALIAN DIP**

Yield: 6 servings

*Calories: 53 (0% fat); Total Fat: 0g;
Cholesterol: 6mg; Carbohydrate: 10g;
Dietary Fiber: 1g; Protein 3g; Sodium:
178mg; Diabetic Exchanges: 2 vegetable*

LITTLE ITALY BARLEY SOUP

1   (12-ounce) package frozen vegetarian sausage-flavored crumbles, reserve $1/2$ cup for the biscuits

1   (14-ounce) can diced tomatoes with onion, celery, and green peppers

$1/2$ cup frozen chopped onion

1   (14-ounce) can fat-free less-sodium beef broth

1   (26-ounce) jar Three Cheese pasta sauce

1   (4-ounce) can sliced mushrooms, undrained

$1/2$ cup quick pearl barley

VEGETARIAN SAUSAGE DROP BISCUITS

1   cup reduced-fat baking mix

$1/4$ cup plus 2 tablespoons water

$1/2$ cup vegetarian sausage-flavored crumbles

$1/4$ cup shredded fat-free mozzarella cheese

BELL PEPPER MEDLEY WITH ITALIAN DIP

1   medium green pepper

1   medium red pepper

1   medium yellow pepper

1   (8-ounce) container fat-free sour cream

1   teaspoon fat-free Italian dressing mix

$1/2$ teaspoon Italian seasoning

2   tablespoons fat-free mayonnaise

Instructions

30 MINUTES BEFORE DINNER, set aside $1/2$ c vegetarian sausage-flavored crumbles to use in the drop biscuits recipe.

Make the soup. In a 12-inch nonstick saucepan, combine the remaining vegetarian sausage-flavored crumbles, 1 can diced tomatoes $1/2$ c onion, 1 can beef broth, 1 jar pasta sauce, and 1 can sliced mushrooms with liquid over medium-high heat. Bring to a boil.

22 MINUTES BEFORE DINNER, stir in $1/2$ c barley. Reduce the heat to medium. Cover and simmer for 12 minutes.

20 MINUTES BEFORE DINNER, cut 1 green bell pepper, 1 red bell pepper, and 1 yellow bell pepper into strips.

15 MINUTES BEFORE DINNER, preheat the oven to 350 degrees.

Spray a baking sheet with nonfat cooking spray.

Prepare the biscuits. In a medium bowl combine 1 c baking mix, $1/4$ c plus 2 T water, the reserved $1/2$ c vegetarian sausage, and $1/4$ c shredded mozzarella. Mix well. Drop the dough by heaping tablespoonfuls onto the prepared baking sheet; set aside.

10 MINUTES BEFORE DINNER, turn off the heat to the soup and stir. Cover and let sit on the hot burner until dinner.

Bake the biscuits for 8 minutes.

8 MINUTES BEFORE DINNER, prepare the Italian Dip. In a small bowl, mix together 1 container sour cream, 1 t Italian dressing mix, $1/2$ t Italian seasoning, and 2 T mayonnaise until well blended.

Place the bell pepper strips on a serving tray with the Italian Dip and place on the dinner table.

2 MINUTES BEFORE DINNER, remove the biscuits from the oven and arrange on a serving plate. Put the biscuits on the dinner table.

1 MINUTE BEFORE DINNER, transfer the soup to a large bowl and place on the dinner table.

Supplies List

Timer
12-inch nonstick saucepan with lid
Baking sheet
Medium bowl
Small bowl
Large bowl
Serving plate
Serving tray

Grocery List

PACKAGED

1 (14-ounce) can diced tomatoes with green pepper and onion
1 (26-ounce) jar Three Cheese pasta sauce
1 (4-ounce) can sliced mushrooms
Quick pearl barley

PRODUCE

1 medium green bell pepper
1 medium red bell pepper
1 medium yellow bell pepper

FROZEN

1 (12-ounce) package plus $1/2$ cup vegetarian sausage-flavored crumbles
$1/2$ cup frozen chopped onions

DAIRY

$1/4$ cup shredded fat-free mozzarella cheese
1 (8-ounce) container fat-free sour cream

Pantry List

Nonfat cooking spray
1 (14-ounce) can fat-free low-sodium beef broth
Fat-free Italian dressing mix
Italian seasoning
Reduced-fat baking mix
Fat-free mayonnaise

>>> Whole Wheat Penne & Broccoli with Creamy Alfredo Sauce

Simple Dinner Salad • French Bread

> The serving size of this meal is large and very filling. If you want you can also serve a tossed salad and French bread, but my friends and I couldn't even eat the entire entrée without having the extra salad or bread.

WHOLE WHEAT PENNE & BROCCOLI
Yield: 6 servings (2 cups penne and vegetables per serving)

Calories: 271 (5% fat); Total Fat: 2g; Cholesterol: 0mg; Carbohydrate: 52g; Dietary Fiber: 10g; Protein 14g; Sodium: 917mg; Diabetic Exchanges: 3 starch, 1^1/$_2$ vegetable

CREAMY ALFREDO SAUCE
Yield: 7 servings (^{1}/$_2$ cup per serving)

Calories: 146 (10% fat); Total Fat: 2g; Cholesterol: 9mg; Carbohydrate: 26g; Dietary Fiber: 0g; Protein 11g; Sodium: 694mg; Diabetic Exchanges: 1 starch, 1 skim milk

WHOLE WHEAT PENNE & BROCCOLI

1	(12-ounce) box whole wheat penne pasta, uncooked
2	(16-ounce) bags frozen broccoli cuts
1	tablespoon bottled minced garlic
1	teaspoon light salt
^{1}/$_4$	cup imitation butter-flavored sprinkles
1	(8^1/$_4$-ounce) can sliced carrots, drained
1	(7-ounce) can sliced mushrooms, drained

CREAMY ALFREDO SAUCE

1	quart fat-free half-and-half
^{1}/$_4$	cup flour
2	tablespoons imitation butter-flavored sprinkles
2	teaspoons garlic salt
^{1}/$_2$	cup reduced-fat Parmesan-style grated topping

Instructions

30 MINUTES BEFORE DINNER, bring 4 quart water to a boil in a Dutch oven. Make a simple dinner salad. Put 1 (11-ounce) bag washed salad greens into a large bowl. Place the salad in the refrigerator to keep chilled until dinner time.

24 MINUTES BEFORE DINNER, slice a loaf of French bread and put the slices in a basket on the dinner table, if desired. Cover the bread with a towel to prevent it from drying out.

23 MINUTES BEFORE DINNER, cook the broccoli. In a medium microwave-safe bowl, place 2 bags frozen broccoli cuts. Cover with waxed paper and microwave for 8 minutes.

21 MINUTES BEFORE DINNER, add 1 box whole wheat penne pasta to the boiling water and cook for 12 minutes, or until tender.

15 MINUTES BEFORE DINNER, stir the broccoli. Cover and cook 6 minutes longer.

14 MINUTES BEFORE DINNER, prepare the Alfredo sauce. Pour 1 quart fat-free half-and-half into a 12-inch nonstick saucepan. Using a whisk, stir $1/4$ c flour into the half-and-half until dissolved. Heat the saucepan to medium. Stir in 2 t garlic salt, 2 T butter-flavored sprinkles, and $1/2$ c Parmesan topping. Continue stirring constantly until thick and creamy.

9 MINUTES BEFORE DINNER, turn off the burner under the Alfredo sauce and let the pan sit on the warm burner. The sauce will thicken as it cools.

8 MINUTES BEFORE DINNER, drain the pasta. Return the pasta to the Dutch oven and cover to keep warm.

6 MINUTES BEFORE DINNER, add 1 T minced garlic, $1/4$ c butter sprinkles, 1 t light salt, 1 can carrots, and 1 can mushrooms to the cooked broccoli. Cover with waxed paper and cook 2 to 3 more minutes, or until fully heated.

3 MINUTES BEFORE DINNER, stir the cooked vegetables into the cooked penne.
   Spoon 2 c of the penne onto each dinner plate. Pour $1/2$ c of the Alfredo sauce over each serving of pasta.

1 MINUTE BEFORE DINNER, place the dinner plates on the table. If having a salad, place the salad and salad dressing on the table.

Supplies List

Timer
Dutch oven
Medium microwavable bowl
12-inch nonstick saucepan
Colander

Grocery List

PACKAGED

Salad dressing (optional)
French bread (optional)
1 (12-ounce) box whole
   wheat penne pasta
1 (8¼-ounce) can sliced
   carrots
1 (7-ounce) can sliced
   mushrooms
½ cup reduced-fat
   Parmesan-style grated
   topping

PRODUCE

Lettuce (optional)

FROZEN

2 (16-ounce) bags frozen
   broccoli cuts

DAIRY

1 quart fat-free half-and-half

Pantry List

Flour
Minced garlic
Light salt
Garlic salt
Imitation butter-flavored
   sprinkles

>>> Vegetarian Chili with Corn Bread Dumplings

Corn Bread Dumplings ● Celery Sticks with Fat-Free Blue Cheese Dip

This hearty dinner sticks to your bones and is so satisfying and filling that you'll forget it is vegetarian.

VEGETARIAN CHILI
Yield: 6 servings (1 cup per serving)

Calories: 171 (3% fat); Total Fat: 1g; Cholesterol: 0mg; Carbohydrate: 25g; Dietary Fiber: 9g; Protein 16g; Sodium: 1181mg; Diabetic Exchanges: 1 starch, 2 vegetable, 1 1/2 very lean meat

CORN BREAD DUMPLINGS
Yield: 6 servings (2 dumplings per serving)

Calories: 156 (18% fat); Total Fat: 3g; Cholesterol: 0mg; Carbohydrate: 29g; Dietary Fiber: 1g; Protein 4g; Sodium: 383mg; Diabetic Exchanges: 2 starch

CELERY STICKS WITH BLUE CHEESE DIP
Yield: 6 (4-elery stick and 1 1/2-tablespoon dip) servings

Calories 35 (0% fat); Total Fat: 0g; Cholesterol: 1mg; Carbohydrate: 8g; Dietary Fiber: 2g; Protein 1g; Sodium: 232mg; Diabetic Exchanges: 1/2 other carbohydrate

VEGETARIAN CHILI

1	(12-ounce) package vegetarian beef-flavored crumbles	1	(15-ounce) can chili beans with seasoning
1/2	cup frozen chopped onion	1	teaspoon Splenda granular
2	(14 1/2 -ounce) cans diced chili-style tomatoes	1/2	teaspoon chili powder

CORN BREAD DUMPLINGS

1	(8 1/2 -ounce) box corn muffin mix	2	egg whites
		1/3	cup water

CELERY STICKS WITH BLUE CHEESE DIP

6	large ribs celery	1/2	cup fat-free blue cheese

Instructions

30 MINUTES BEFORE DINNER, start the chili. In a 12-inch nonstick saucepan over medium heat, combine 1 package vegetarian beef-flavored crumbles, $^1/_2$ c onion, 2 cans diced tomatoes, 1 can chili beans with seasoning, 1 t Splenda granular, and $^1/_2$ t chili powder and bring to a low boil.

25 MINUTES BEFORE DINNER, start the dumplings. In a medium bowl, mix together 1 box corn muffin mix, 2 egg whites, and $^1/_3$ c water until well blended. The batter will be thin.

22 MINUTES BEFORE DINNER, make 12 dumplings by dropping the corn bread batter by heaping tablespoonfuls into the chili. Each dumpling will be $1^1/_2$ T.

20 MINUTES BEFORE DINNER, cover the chili and dumplings and cook for 15 minutes.

5 MINUTES BEFORE DINNER, turn off the heat under the chili and let sit on the warm burner until time for dinner.

4 MINUTES BEFORE DINNER, cut 6 large celery ribs vertically into 4 sticks. Arrange on a plate around a small bowl filled with $^1/_2$ c blue cheese salad dressing.

1 MINUTE BEFORE DINNER, place the chili and dumplings on a hot pad on the dinner table.

Supplies List

Timer
12-inch nonstick saucepan
with lid
Medium bowl
Plate
Small bowl

Grocery List

PACKAGED

2 ($14^1/_2$-ounce) cans diced
chili-style tomatoes
1 ($8^1/_2$-ounce) box corn
muffin mix
Fat-free blue cheese salad
dressing
1 (15-ounce) can chili beans
with seasoning

PRODUCE

Celery

FROZEN

1 (12-ounce) package
vegetarian beef-flavored
crumbles
$^1/_2$ cup frozen chopped
onions

DAIRY

2 eggs

Pantry List

Chili powder
Splenda granular

>>> Aztec Vegetarian Dinner

Fiesta Tossed Salad

Thank you to Brenda Crosser who sent in this idea. She uses this as a filling for soft corn tortillas. We liked it as a meal in itself without the extra calories of the soft corn tortillas. Whatever way you choose to eat it, you'll never miss the meat.

AZTEC VEGETARIAN DINNER

Yield: 6 servings ($^3/_4$ cup per serving)

Calories: 245 (4% fat); Total Fat: 1g; Cholesterol: 0mg; Carbohydrate: 41g; Dietary Fiber: 10g; Protein 18g; Sodium: 1119mg; Diabetic Exchanges: $3^1/_2$ starch, $1^1/_2$ very lean meat

FIESTA TOSSED SALAD

Yield: 6 servings ($1^1/_2$ cup per serving)

Calories: 47 (0% fat); Total Fat: 0g; Cholesterol: 0mg; Carbohydrate: 11g; Dietary Fiber: 2g; Protein 1g; Sodium: 247mg; Diabetic Exchanges: 1 vegetable, $^1/_2$ other carbohydrate

AZTEC VEGETARIAN DINNER

1   (12-ounce) package vegetarian beef-flavored crumbles
1   ($1^1/_4$-ounce) package taco seasoning mix
$1^1/_2$ cups water
1   (15-ounce) can black beans, drained
1   ($15^1/_4$-ounce) can corn, drained
1   ($14^1/_2$-ounce) can diced potatoes, drained

FIESTA TOSSED SALAD

$^1/_2$ cup fat-free French salad dressing
$^1/_4$ cup mild chunky salsa
$^1/_2$ cup frozen 3-Pepper & Onion Blend
1   large head iceburg lettuce (about 9 cups chopped)

Instructions

30 MINUTES BEFORE DINNER, prepare the Aztec dinner. Spray a 12-inch nonstick saucepan with nonfat cooking spray. Add 1 package vegetarian beef-flavored crumbles, 1 package taco seasoning mix, and $1^1/_2$ c water to the prepared skillet. Bring to a boil over medium heat.

25 MINUTES BEFORE DINNER, stir in 1 can drained black beans, 1 can drained corn, and 1 can drained diced potatoes. Bring to a boil.

20 MINUTES BEFORE DINNER, reduce the heat to low and simmer for 15 minutes, stirring occasionally.

15 MINUTES BEFORE DINNER, prepare the salad. Finely chop $^1/_2$ c frozen vegetable blend.

10 MINUTES BEFORE DINNER, in a small bowl combine $^1/_2$ c French salad dressing and $^1/_4$ c salsa until well blended. Add the chopped vegetable blend to the dressing and mix well.

3 MINUTES BEFORE DINNER, toss the salad dressing with 1 large head chopped iceberg lettuce and place on the dinner table.

1 MINUTES BEFORE DINNER, put the Aztec dinner on a hot pad and place on the dinner table.

Supplies List

Timer
12-inch nonstick skillet
Small bowl

Grocery List

PACKAGED

1 (15-ounce) can black beans
1 ($15^1/_4$-ounce) can corn
1 ($14^1/_2$-ounce) can diced
    potatoes
1 (8-ounce) bottle fat-free
    French salad dressing
Mild chunky salsa

FROZEN

$^1/_2$ cup frozen 3-Pepper &
    Onion vegetable blend
1 (12-ounce) package
    vegetarian beef-flavored
    crumbles

PRODUCE

1 large head iceberg lettuce

SEASONINGS

1 ($1^1/_4$-ounce) package taco
    seasoning mix

Pantry List

Nonfat cooking spray

>>> Southwestern Chili

Corn Bread Mini Muffins • Celery Sticks with Cool & Creamy Fiery Dip

From the very first bite, you will think this meal was delivered from an authentic Mexican restaurant.

SOUTHWESTERN CHILI

Yield: 6 servings (1 cup per serving)

Calories: 202 (2% fat); Total Fat: 1g; Cholesterol: 0mg; Carbohydrate: 32g; Dietary Fiber: 9g; Protein 17g; Sodium: 1499mg; Diabetic Exchanges: 1^1/$_2$ starch, 2 vegetable, 2 very lean meat

CORN BREAD MINI MUFFINS

Yield: 6 servings

(4 mini muffins per serving)

Calories: 177 (16% fat); Total Fat: 3g; Cholesterol: 0mg; Carbohydrate: 34g; Dietary Fiber: 1g; Protein 4g; Sodium: 555mg; Diabetic Exchanges: 2^1/$_2$ starch

CELERY STICKS WITH COOL & CREAMY FIERY DIP

Yield: 6 servings (4 celery sticks; 2 tablespoons dip per serving)

Calories: 33 (0% fat); Total Fat: 0g; Cholesterol: 3mg; Carbohydrate: 5g; Dietary Fiber: 1g; Protein 2g; Sodium: 94mg; Diabetic Exchanges: ^{1}/$_2$ other carbohydrate

SOUTHWESTERN CHILI

1	(12-ounce) package vegetarian beef-flavored crumbles
1	cup mild chunky salsa
^{1}/$_2$	cup Mexicorn, drained
2	(14^1/$_2$-ounce) cans diced chili-style tomatoes
1	(15-ounce) can chili beans with seasoning
1	teaspoon Splenda granular
1	teaspoon taco seasoning

CORN BREAD MINI MUFFINS

1	(8^1/$_2$-ounce) box corn muffin mix
1	egg white
^{1}/$_4$	cup mild chunky salsa
^{1}/$_2$	cup Mexicorn, drained

CELERY STICKS WITH COOL & CREAMY FIERY DIP

6	large celery ribs
^{1}/$_2$	cup fat-free sour cream
^{1}/$_4$	cup taco sauce
^{1}/$_2$	teaspoon Splenda granular

Instructions

30 MINUTES BEFORE DINNER, start the chili. In a 12-inch nonstick saucepan, stir together 1 bag vegetarian beef crumbles, 1 c salsa, $1/2$ cup Mexicorn, 2 cans tomatoes, 1 can chili beans, 1 t Splenda granular, and 1 t taco seasoning. Bring to a low boil over medium heat.

25 MINUTES BEFORE DINNER, start the muffins. In a medium bowl, mix together 1 box corn muffin mix, 1 egg white, $1/4$ c salsa, and the remaining Mexicorn (about $1/2$ cup) until well blended.

22 MINUTES BEFORE DINNER, coat a 24-cup mini-muffin pan with nonfat cooking spray. Carefully drop the muffin batter by rounded tablespoonfuls into the prepared mini-muffin pan.

20 MINUTES BEFORE DINNER, stir and cover the chili. Reduce the heat to low and cook for 15 minutes.

Preheat the oven to 400 degrees.

18 MINUTES BEFORE DINNER, vertically slice 6 large celery ribs into 24 sticks. Arrange on a serving plate.

Make the vegetable dip. In a small bowl, stir together $1/2$ c sour cream, $1/4$ c taco sauce, and 1 t Splenda granular until well blended. Place the bowl in the center of the celery sticks. Cover and refrigerate until dinner is ready.

15 MINUTES BEFORE DINNER, bake the muffins on the middle rack of the oven for 8 to 10 minutes.

8 MINUTES BEFORE DINNER, remove the lid from the chili and continue cooking at a low boil.

5 MINUTES BEFORE DINNER, remove the muffins from the oven and let cool.

3 MINUTES BEFORE DINNER, turn off the heat under the chili and let sit for 3 minutes.

Place the celery and dip on the dinner table.

2 MINUTES BEFORE DINNER, put the mini muffins in a basket and place on the dinner table.

1 MINUTE BEFORE DINNER, place the chili on a hot pad on the dinner table.

Supplies List

Timer
12-inch nonstick skillet
Medium bowl
24-cup mini muffin pan
Serving plate
Small bowl
Basket

Grocery List

PACKAGED

$1 1/4$ cup mild chunky salsa
1 cup Mexicorn
2 ($14 1/2$-ounce) cans diced chili-style tomatoes
1 ($8 1/2$-ounce) box corn muffin mix
Splenda granular
1 (15-ounce) cans chili beans with seasoning

PRODUCE

1 bunch celery

FROZEN

1 (12-ounce) package vegetarian beef crumbles

DAIRY

$1/2$ cup fat-free sour cream
1 egg

Pantry List

Nonfat cooking spray
Taco seasoning
Taco sauce

>>> Creamy Sausage & Bean Chowder

Little Dilly Corn Muffins • Celery Bites with Zesty Cheddar Dip

Rich Northern flavors of Italy and smooth Southern flavors from America unite for an absolutely delicious and hearty vegetarian meal. If you don't tell them that you used vegetarian sausage in this chowder, most likely they will never know.

CREAMY SAUSAGE & BEAN CHOWDER

Yield: 6 servings (1 cup per serving)

Calories: 205 (26% fat); Total Fat: 6g; Cholesterol: 4mg; Carbohydrate: 22g; Dietary Fiber: 7g; Protein 16g; Sodium: 1258mg; Diabetic Exchanges: 1 1/2 starch, 2 lean meat

LITTLE DILLY CORN MUFFINS

Yield: 6 servings (3 mini muffins per serving)

Calories: 157 (18% fat); Total Fat: 3g; Cholesterol: 0mg; Carbohydrate: 29g; Dietary Fiber: 1g; Protein 4g; Sodium: 452mg; Diabetic Exchanges: 2 starch

CELERY BITES WITH ZESTY CHEDDAR DIP

Yield: 6 servings (1/2 cup per serving)

Calories: 44 (0% fat); Total Fat: 0g; Cholesterol: 3mg; Carbohydrate: 9g; Dietary Fiber: 1g; Protein 2g; Sodium: 394mg; Diabetic Exchanges: 1/2 other carbohydrate

CREAMY SAUSAGE & BEAN CHOWDER

1   (15 1/2 -ounce) can great Northern beans, undrained
1   (12-ounce) package vegetarian sausage-flavored crumbles
1/4   teaspoon sage
2   (10 3/4 -ounce) cans 98% fat-free cream of celery soup
2   cups water

LITTLE DILLY CORN MUFFINS

1   (8 1/2 -ounce) box corn muffin mix
2   egg whites
1/3   cup dill pickle juice
1/4   dill pickle spear, finely chopped
1/4   teaspoon dried dill weed

CELERY BITES WITH ZESTY CHEDDAR DIP

1/2   cup chili sauce, chilled
2   teaspoons Splenda granular
1/4   cup fat-free sour cream
1/4   cup shredded fat-free cheddar cheese
6   celery ribs

Instructions

25 MINUTES BEFORE DINNER, start making the chowder. In a 12-inch non-stick saucepan, mash 1 can great Northern beans with a potato masher or back of a spoon until half the beans are mashed. Turn the heat to medium. Stir in 1 package vegetarian sausage-flavored crumbles, $1/4$ t sage, 2 cans cream of celery soup, and 2 c water. Continue stirring until well mixed. Bring to a low boil.

20 MINUTES BEFORE DINNER, preheat the oven to 400 degrees.

Coat 18 mini-muffin cups with nonstick cooking spray. Set aside.

Reduce the heat under the chowder to medium-low and simmer for 15 minutes.

15 MINUTES BEFORE DINNER, start making the corn muffins. In a medium bowl stir together 1 box corn muffin mix, 2 egg whites, $1/3$ c dill pickle juice, $1/4$ of a finely chopped dill pickle spear, and $1/4$ t dried dill. Mix well.

12 MINUTES BEFORE DINNER, drop the batter by rounded tablespoonfuls into the prepared mini-muffin cups. Bake the muffins for 8 to 9 minutes, or until golden brown.

9 MINUTES BEFORE DINNER, make the dip. In a medium bowl, add $1/2$ c chilled chili sauce, 2 t Splenda granular, $1/4$ cup sour cream, and $1/4$ c cheddar cheese. Mix until well blended.

Cut the 6 celery ribs into 1-inch pieces. Place next to the dip on the dinner table.

3 MINUTES BEFORE DINNER, remove the muffins from the oven.

Put the chowder on a hot pad and place on the dinner table.

2 MINUTES BEFORE DINNER, put the muffins in a basket and place on the dinner table.

Supplies List

Timer
12-inch nonstick saucepan with lid
Potato masher or spoon
Mini-muffin pan
Medium bowl

Grocery List

PACKAGED

1 ($15^{1}/_{2}$-ounce) can great Northern beans
2 ($10^{3}/_{4}$-ounce) cans 98% fat-free cream of celery soup
Chili sauce
Dill pickle spears
1 ($8^{1}/_{2}$-ounce) box corn muffin mix

PRODUCE

1 bunch celery

FROZEN

1 (12-ounce) package vegetarian sausage-flavored crumbles

DAIRY

$1/4$ cup fat-free sour cream
$1/4$ cup shredded fat-free cheddar cheese
2 eggs

Pantry List

Dried dill
Sage
Nonstick cooking spray
Dill pickle juice
Splenda granular

>>> Fettuccini Alfredo

Italian Herb Bread Twists • Garlic-Buttered Broccoli

Your family and friends will not believe that this Alfredo sauce is low-fat. Once you see how super easy this sauce is to make, you'll never want to buy the high-fat Alfredo sauce again. My friends were surprised at how well they liked the whole-wheat fettuccini. You can substitute regular fettuccini in this recipe if you'd prefer.

FETTUCCINI ALFREDO

Yield: 6 servings (1 cup per serving)

Calories: 308 (9% fat); Total Fat: 3g; Cholesterol: 10mg; Carbohydrate: 56g; Dietary Fiber: 4g; Protein 18g; Sodium: 505mg; Diabetic Exchanges: 3 starch, 1 skim milk

ITALIAN HERB BREAD TWISTS

Yield: 12 servings (1 bread twist per serving)

Calories: 73 (17% fat); Total Fat: 1g; Cholesterol: 0mg; Carbohydrate: 13g; Dietary Fiber: 0g; Protein 2g; Sodium: 233mg; Diabetic Exchanges: 1 starch

Garlic-Buttered Broccoli

Yield: 6 servings (³/₄ cup per serving)

Calories: 49 (0% fat); Total Fat: 0g; Cholesterol: 0mg; Carbohydrate: 9g; Dietary Fiber: 5g; Protein: 4g; Sodium: 582mg; Diabetic Exchanges: 2 vegetable

FETTUCCINI ALFREDO

12	ounces whole wheat fettuccini, uncooked	1	tablespoon imitation butter-flavored sprinkles
1	pint fat-free half-and-half	¹/₂	cup reduced-fat Parmesan-style grated topping
2	tablespoons flour		
1	teaspoon garlic salt		

ITALIAN HERB BREAD TWISTS

1	(11-ounce) can refrigerated bread stick dough	¹/₂	teaspoon garlic salt
1	tablespoon Italian seasoning	36	plus 36 sprays of fat-free butter spray

GARLIC-BUTTERED BROCCOLI

2	(16-ounce) bag frozen broccoli cuts	3	tablespoons imitation butter-flavored sprinkles
1	tablespoon bottled minced garlic	1	teaspoon light salt

Instructions

30 MINUTES BEFORE DINNER, start the bread twists. Preheat the oven to 375 degrees.

Coat 1 baking sheet with nonfat cooking spray. Unroll 1 can refrigerated breadsticks, but do not separate the dough. Sprinkle the dough with 1 T Italian seasoning and $^1/_2$ t garlic salt. Press the seasonings into the dough. Making one bread twist at a time, separate the dough at the perforations. Holding both ends of the dough, twist each breadstick into a spiral. Lay the dough twists on the prepared baking sheet. Repeat for all 12 pieces of dough.

Spray each dough twist with 3 sprays fat-free butter spray. Set aside.

24 MINUTES BEFORE DINNER, start making the broccoli. In a medium microwavable bowl, put 2 bags frozen broccoli cuts. Cover with waxed paper and cook for 8 minutes in the microwave.

20 MINUTES BEFORE DINNER, bring 4 quarts of water to a boil in a Dutch oven.

15 MINUTES BEFORE DINNER, stir the partially cooked broccoli. Cover with waxed paper and cook for 6 minutes in the microwave. Let the broccoli remain in the microwave once fully cooked.

11 MINUTES BEFORE DINNER, bake the bread twists for 11 minutes at 375 degrees.

10 MINUTES BEFORE DINNER, add 12 ounces fettuccini to the boiling water and cook for 8 to 9 minutes, or until the pasta is tender.

While pasta is cooking, start Alfredo sauce. In a 12-inch nonstick saucepan, put 1 pint fat-free half-and-half. Using a whisk, stir in 2 T flour until dissolved. Turn on the heat to the burner under the saucepan to medium. Continue stirring and add 1 t garlic salt, 1 T butter sprinkles, and $^1/_2$ c Parmesan topping. Reduce heat to medium low and stir frequently.

3 MINUTES BEFORE DINNER, stir 1 T minced garlic, 3 T butter sprinkles, and 1 t salt into the cooked broccoli. Microwave the broccoli for 2 more minutes to heat through.

2 MINUTES BEFORE DINNER, remove the bread twists from the oven and let cool on the baking sheet.

Drain the pasta. Stir the cooked pasta into the Alfredo sauce.

1 MINUTE BEFORE DINNER, put the Fettuccini Alfredo on a hot pad and place on the dinner table along with the broccoli. Put the bread sticks on a platter and place on the dinner table.

Supplies List

Timer
Baking sheet
Medium microwavable bowl
Dutch oven
12-inch nonstick saucepan with lid
Colander

Grocery List

PACKAGED

1 (12-ounce) box whole wheat fettuccini
$^1/_2$ cup reduced-fat Parmesan-style grated topping

FROZEN

2 (16-ounce) bag frozen broccoli cuts

DAIRY

1 pint fat-free half-and-half
1 (11-ounce) can refrigerated bread dough

Pantry List

Flour
Italian Seasoning
Garlic salt
Minced garlic
Imitation butter-flavored sprinkles
Light salt
Fat-free butter spray
Nonfat cooking spray

>>> Oriental Vegetarian Chili

Crunchy Wonton Strips ● Sesame Seed Spinach Salad ● Fortune Cookies

Oriental vegetables unite with an all-time American favorite for a unique recipe that's every bit as delicious as it is unique.

ORIENTAL VEGETARIAN CHILI
Yield: 7¹/₂ servings
(1 cup per serving)
Calories: 146 (0% fat); Total Fat: 0g; Cholesterol: 0mg; Carbohydrate: 31g; Dietary Fiber: 7g; Protein 6g; Sodium: 906mg; Diabetic Exchanges: 1¹/₂ starch, 1¹/₂ vegetable

CRUNCHY WONTON STRIPS
Yield: 7 servings
(14 strips per serving)
Calories: 67 (0% fat); Total Fat: 0g; Cholesterol: 2mg; Carbohydrate: 13g; Dietary Fiber: 0g; Protein 2g; Sodium: 14mg; Diabetic Exchanges: 1 starch

SESAME SEED SPINACH SALAD
Yield: 6 servings (1 cup per serving)
Calories: 38 (14% fat); Total Fat: 1g; Cholesterol: 0mg; Carbohydrate: 8g; Dietary Fiber: 1g; Protein 2g; Sodium: 38mg; Diabetic Exchanges: ¹/₂ other carbohydrate

ORIENTAL VEGETARIAN CHILI

2   (16-ounce) bags frozen Oriental stir-fry vegetables
1   (15-ounce) can spicy chili beans
2   (14¹/₂-ounce) cans diced chili-style tomatoes
¹/₂ cup plum sauce

CRUNCHY WONTON STRIPS

20 wonton wrappers
Fat-free butter spray
Light salt
Toasted sesame seeds

SESAME SEED SPINACH SALAD

2   tablespoons honey
1   tablespoon apple cider vinegar
1   (10-ounce) bag washed and ready-to-use fresh spinach
1   plus ¹/₂ teaspoon toasted sesame seeds*

Instructions

25 MINUTES BEFORE DINNER, start making the chili. In a 12-inch nonstick saucepan over medium-high heat, combine 2 bags vegetables, 1 can chili beans, 2 cans tomatoes, and $1/2$ c plum sauce. Bring to a low boil.

Preheat the oven to 350 degrees.

20 MINUTES BEFORE DINNER, prepare the wonton strips. Coat both sides of 20 wonton wrappers with fat-free butter spray. Place on 2 jelly-roll pans. Slice each wonton wrapper into 5 strips. Sprinkle with light salt and sesame seeds.

12 MINUTES BEFORE DINNER, put the fortune cookies on the dinner table.

11 MINUTES BEFORE DINNER, reduce the heat to medium-low under the chili. Cover and cook for 10 minutes.

10 MINUTES BEFORE DINNER, bake the wonton strips for 7 minutes.

9 MINUTES BEFORE DINNER, start the salad. In a small microwavable bowl, combine 2 T honey and 1 T apple cider vinegar. Microwave for 15 to 20 seconds, or until it comes to a boil. Stir until the honey is dissolved. Set aside.

Remove any large stems from the spinach and place in a large salad bowl.

Toss the spinach with the salad dressing and 1 t of the toasted sesame seeds until leaves are shiny and coated with the salad dressing. Sprinkle the top of the salad with the remaining $1/2$ t toasted sesame seeds. Place the salad on the dinner table.

3 MINUTES BEFORE DINNER, remove the wonton strips from the oven and place on a plate. Put on the dinner table. These are great crumbled into the chili.

1 MINUTE BEFORE DINNER, place the chili on a hot pad on the dinner table.

NOTE: You can save time by buying sesame seeds that are already toasted.

Supplies List

Timer
12-inch nonstick skillet
Jelly-roll pans
Small microwavable bowl
Large salad bowl
Plate

Grocery List

PACKAGED

1 (15-ounce) can spicy chili
   beans
2 (14½-ounce) cans diced
   chili-style tomatoes
Plum sauce (found in Chinese
   food aisle)
20 wonton wrappers
Toasted sesame seeds*
Fortune cookies

PRODUCE

1 (10-ounce) bag washed and
   ready-to-use fresh spinach

FROZEN

2 (16-ounce) bags Oriental
   stir-fry vegetables

Pantry List

Light salt
Honey
Apple cider vinegar
Fat-free butter spray

>>> Spinach, Sausage & Rice Stove-Top Casserole

Greek-Inspired Wedged Salads • Tomato & Mozzarella Bread Crisps

If you like spinach pie and Greek food, then you'll love the flavors of this Greek-inspired menu that is fit for a king.

SPINACH, SAUSAGE, & RICE STOVE-TOP CASSEROLE

Yield: 8 servings (1 cup per serving)

Calories: 191 (14% fat); Total Fat: 3g; Cholesterol: 0mg; Carbohydrate: 25g; Dietary Fiber: 4g; Protein 15g; Sodium: 788mg; Diabetic Exchanges: 1^1/$_2$ starch, 1 vegetable, 1^1/$_2$ very lean meat

GREEK-INSPIRED WEDGED SALADS

Yield: 6 servings (1 wedge per serving)

Calories: 65 (11% fat); Total Fat: 1g; Cholesterol: 1mg; Carbohydrate: 12g; Dietary Fiber: 3g; Protein 4g; Sodium: 716mg; Diabetic Exchanges: 2^1/$_2$ vegetable

TOMATO & MOZZARELLA BREAD CRISPS

Yield: 6 servings (1 slice per serving)

Calories: 104 (8% fat); Total Fat: 1g; Cholesterol: 2mg; Carbohydrate: 18g; Dietary Fiber: 2g; Protein 6g; Sodium: 420mg; Diabetic Exchanges: 1 starch, 1^1/$_2$ very lean meat

SPINACH, SAUSAGE & RICE STOVE-TOP CASSEROLE

4   cups water

1   (12-ounce) bag vegetarian sausage-flavored crumbles

^{1}/$_3$ cup tabbouleh

1^1/$_2$ cups instant whole-grain brown rice

2   (14-ounce) cans spinach, drained

^{1}/$_2$ cup fat-free feta cheese

GREEK-INSPIRED WEDGED SALADS

^{1}/$_2$ (14^1/$_2$-ounce) can diced tomatoes with green pepper and onion, drained

^{1}/$_2$ cup fat-free Italian salad dressing

1   teaspoon dried parsley

6   green olives, cut into thin slices

3   mild cherry peppers, cut into thin slices

^{1}/$_3$ cup fat-free feta cheese

1   large head iceberg lettuce (about 9 cups chopped)

TOMATO & MOZZARELLA BREAD CRISPS

^{1}/$_2$ (14 ^{1}/$_2$-ounce) can diced tomato with green pepper and onion, drained

4   teaspoons olive juice

6   (^{1}/$_3$-inch) slices French bread

1   teaspoon Italian seasoning

^{1}/$_2$ cup shredded fat-free mozzarella cheese

1   teaspoon dried parsley

Instructions

30 MINUTES BEFORE DINNER, start the casserole. In a 12-inch nonstick saucepan over high heat, bring 4 c water, 1 bag vegetarian sausage-flavored crumbles, and $1/3$ c Tabbouleh to a boil.

26 MINUTES BEFORE DINNER, once the liquid is boiling, stir in $1^1/2$ c instant brown rice. Return to a boil and reduce the heat to medium. Cover and simmer for 12 minutes, or until the rice is tender.

24 MINUTES BEFORE DINNER, prepare the salads. Set aside $3/4$ c of 1 can drained diced tomatoes with green pepper and onion.

In a medium bowl, combine $1/2$ c Italian salad dressing, 1 t parsley, 6 green olives, 3 mild cherry peppers, and $1/3$ c feta cheese until well mixed. Set side.

Cut 1 large head iceberg lettuce into 6 wedges. Place each wedge on individual salad plates. Pour $1/4$ c dressing on each wedge of lettuce. Place in the refrigerator to keep chilled.

14 MINUTES BEFORE DINNER, start making the bread crisps.

Preheat oven to 375 degrees.

Cut the French bread into 6 ($1/3$-inch-thick) slices. Coat both sides of each bread slice with nonfat butter-flavored cooking spray and place on a baking sheet.

In a small bowl, mix together the reserved $3/4$ c tomatoes with green pepper and onion, 4 t olive juice, and 1 t Italian seasoning until well blended. Place 2 T of the tomato mixture on top of each bread slice. Evenly sprinkle with $1/2$ c shredded mozzarella cheese. Spray the cheese with nonfat butter-flavored cooking spray to help it melt smoothly. Sprinkle $1/2$ t dried parsley evenly on top of the cheese. Set aside.

8 MINUTES BEFORE DINNER, turn off the heat to the rice and stir in the 2 cans spinach. Sprinkle $1/2$ c fat-free feta cheese on top of the casserole. Cover and let sit on the warm burner for 6 to 7 minutes.

6 MINUTES BEFORE DINNER, bake the bread crisps for 5 minutes.

2 MINUTES BEFORE DINNER, put the casserole on a hot pad on the dinner table. Put the salads on the table.

1 MINUTE BEFORE DINNER, place bread crisps on hot pads on the dinner table.

Supplies List

Timer
12-inch nonstick saucepan
  with lid
Medium bowl
Individual salad plates
Small bowl

Grocery List

PACKAGED

Green olives
3 mild cherry peppers
Tabbouleh
Whole-grain instant
  brown rice
2 (14-ounce) cans spinach
1 (14$1/2$-ounce) can diced
  tomatoes with green
  pepper and onion
$1/2$ cup fat-free Italian salad
  dressing
French bread

PRODUCE

1 large head iceberg lettuce

FROZEN

1 (12-ounce) bag vegetarian
  sausage-flavored crumbles

DAIRY

Fat-free feta cheese
$1/2$ cup shredded fat-free
  mozzarella cheese

Pantry List

Dried parsley
Italian seasoning

>>> Creamy Sausage & Spinach Soup

Vegetable Tray with Dilly Red French Dip • Rye Bread Bowls (optional)

Here's a "makes you feel all warm and cozy" soup that'll make even the chilliest of days not seem so cold.

CREAMY SAUSAGE & SPINACH SOUP

Yield: 7 servings (1 cup per serving)

Calories: 203 (14% fat); Total Fat: 3g; Cholesterol: 2mg; Carbohydrate: 26g; Dietary Fiber: 5g; Protein 19g; Sodium: 1485mg; Diabetic Exchanges: $1/2$ starch, 1 skim milk, 1 vegetable, $1^1/2$ very lean meat

VEGETABLE TRAY WITH DILLY RED FRENCH DIP

Yield 6 servings ($1/2$ bell pepper; 4 teaspoons salad dressing per serving)

Calories 51 (0% fat); Total Fat: 0g; Cholesterol: 0mg; Carbohydrate: 12g; Dietary Fiber: 2g; Protein 1g; Sodium: 202mg; Diabetic Exchanges: 1 vegetable, $1/2$ other carbohydrate

CREAMY SAUSAGE & SPINACH SOUP

1	Gala apple, finely chopped ($1^1/2$ cups)	1	teaspoon seasoned salt
$1/2$	cup frozen chopped onion	1	($10^3/4$-ounce) can 98% fat-free broccoli cheese soup
1	(12 ounce) package vegetarian sausage-flavored crumbles	2	cups fat-free half-and-half
3	(14-ounce) cans spinach, drained		

VEGETABLE TRAY WITH DILLY RED FRENCH DIP

$1/4$	teaspoon dried dill	1	yellow bell pepper
$1/2$	cup fat-free red French salad dressing	1	orange bell pepper
		1	red bell pepper

Instructions

20 MINUTES BEFORE DINNER, make the dip. Combine $1/4$ t dill and $1/2$ c French salad dressing and place in a small bowl in the center of a serving platter. Slice 1 yellow bell pepper, 1 orange bell pepper, and 1 red bell pepper into strips and place on the serving platter around the dip. Cover and refrigerate until time for dinner.

12 MINUTES BEFORE DINNER, start making the soup. Heat 1 finely chopped apple in the microwave for 1 minute.

Combine $1/2$ c onion and 1 package vegetarian sausage-flavored crumbles in a 12-inch nonstick saucepan and cook over medium-low heat for 2 to 3 minutes, or until the onion is tender.

Add the apple, 3 cans spinach, and 1 t seasoned salt to the saucepan. Reduce the heat to low and simmer for 3 to 4 minutes.

Stir in 1 can broccoli cheese soup and 2 c half-and-half. Bring to a low boil, stirring constantly, about 4 to 5 minutes.

1 MINUTE BEFORE DINNER, ladle the soup into bowls and place on the dinner table along with the bell peppers strips and French salad dressing.

NOTE: *A nice optional presentation is to serve the soup in Kaiser roll bowls. If making the bread bowls, start them 30 minutes before dinner. Using a sharp serrated knife, cut $1/2$ inch off the top of 6 rye Kaiser rolls, reserving the top. Hollow out the bread, leaving a $1/2$-inch-thick shell. Place the bread bowl and the reserved lid on a dinner plate. The bread will add the following to the meal: Calories 125 (13% fat); Total Fat: 2g; Cholesterol: 0mg; Carbohydrate: 23g; Dietary Fiber: 1g; Protein 4g; Sodium: 233mg; Diabetic Exchanges: $1^1/2$ starch.*

Supplies List

Timer
Serving platter
12-inch nonstick saucepan with lid
Small bowl

Grocery List

PACKAGED
Rye Kaiser rolls (optional)
3 (14-ounce) cans spinach
$1/2$ cup fat-free Red French salad dressing
1 ($10^3/4$-ounce) can 98% fat-free broccoli cheese soup

PRODUCE
1 Gala apple
1 yellow bell pepper
1 orange bell pepper
1 red bell pepper

FROZEN
$1/2$ cup frozen chopped onion
1 (12-ounce) package vegetarian sausage-flavored crumbles

DAIRY
1 pint fat-free half-and-half

Pantry List

Seasoned salt
Dried dill

>>> Three-Alarm Chili

Hose-It-Down Cool & Creamy Cucumber Salad • Captain's Hat Whole Wheat & Green Chiles Mini Biscuits

Firefighters everywhere will like this spicy chili, and if they like it hotter, simply add Tabasco sauce one teaspoon at a time. The salad is cool and refreshing, and the biscuits have just enough bite to keep even the most tired firefighters (or hungry parents, after a long day) on his or her toes.

THREE-ALARM CHILI

Yield: 6 servings (1 cup per serving)

Calories: 170 (3% fat); Total Fat: 1g;
Cholesterol: 1mg; Carbohydrate: 21g;
Dietary Fiber: 8g; Protein 18g;
Sodium: 1062mg; Diabetic Exchanges:
1 starch, 1 vegetable, 2 very lean meat

HOSE-IT-DOWN COOL & CREAMY CUCUMBER SALAD

Yield: 7 servings (1/2 cup per serving)

Calories: 46 (0% fat); Total Fat: 0g;
Cholesterol: 6mg; Carbohydrate: 8g;
Dietary Fiber: 0g; Protein 3g; Sodium:
193mg; Diabetic Exchanges:
1/2 other carbohydrate

CAPTAIN'S HAT WHOLE WHEAT & GREEN CHILIES MINI BISCUITS

Yield: 6 servings
(2 mini biscuits per serving)

Calories: 75 (0% fat); Total Fat: 0g;
Cholesterol: 0mg; Carbohydrate: 15g;
Dietary Fiber: 3g; Protein 4g; Sodium:
206mg; Diabetic Exchanges: 1 starch

THREE-ALARM CHILI

1 (4 1/2 -ounce) can chopped green chilies
1 cup bold & spicy bloody Mary mix
1 (12-ounce) bag frozen vegetarian beef-flavored crumbles
1 (15 1/2 -ounce) can hot and spicy chili beans in chili sauce
1 (14 1/2 -ounce) can diced tomatoes with mild green chilies
6 tablespoons shredded fat-free cheddar cheese

HOSE-IT-DOWN COOL & CREAMY CUCUMBER SALAD

2 medium cucumbers
1 cup fat-free sour cream
1/2 cup chopped fresh chives
2 teaspoons ranch salad dressing mix
1/8 teaspoon ground black pepper
1/8 teaspoon light salt

CAPTAIN'S HAT WHOLE WHEAT & GREEN CHILIES MINI BISCUITS

2 tablespoons chopped green chilies
1 cup whole wheat flour
2 egg whites
1 tablespoon Splenda granular
1/2 teaspoon baking soda
1/4 teaspoon seasoned salt

Instructions

30 MINUTES BEFORE DINNER, set aside 2 T canned chopped green chilies.

29 MINUTES BEFORE DINNER, in a 12-inch nonstick saucepan over medium-high heat, begin the chili. Combine the remaining 1 can chopped green chilies, 1 c Bloody Mary mix, 1 package frozen vegetarian beef-flavored crumbles, 1 can chili beans, and 1 can diced tomatoes. Stir until well mixed. Bring to a boil.

26 MINUTES BEFORE DINNER, once the chili comes to a boil, reduce the heat to low. Cover and simmer until dinner is ready.

25 MINUTES BEFORE DINNER, start making the salad. Cut 2 medium cucumbers in half lengthwise. Using a tablespoon, remove and discard the seeds. Chop the seeded cucumber and put in a medium bowl. Add 1 c sour cream, $^1/_2$ c chopped chives, 2 t ranch salad dressing mix, $^1/_8$ t ground black pepper, and $^1/_8$ t light salt and stir until well mixed.

14 MINUTES BEFORE DINNER, preheat the oven to 350 degrees.

13 MINUTES BEFORE DINNER, start making the mini biscuits. In a medium bowl, stir together the reserved 2 T chopped green chilies, 1 c whole wheat flour, 2 egg whites, 1 T Splenda granular, $^1/_2$ t baking soda, and $^1/_4$ t seasoned salt.
   Coat a baking sheet with nonfat butter-flavored cooking spray.
   Drop the biscuit dough by rounded tablespoonfuls onto the prepared baking sheet. Spray the dough with nonfat butter-flavored cooking spray.

8 MINUTES BEFORE DINNER, bake the biscuits for 5 to 7 minutes.

3 MINUTES BEFORE DINNER, check the biscuits. If they are done, take them out of the oven. Let them remain on the baking sheet to cool.

2 MINUTES BEFORE DINNER, ladle 1 c of chili in individual serving bowls. Top each serving with 1 T shredded cheddar cheese. Spray the cheese with nonfat cooking spray. Cover each bowl with a plate to help retain the heat of the chili, which will melt the cheese. Take each serving of chili to the dinner table.

1 MINUTE BEFORE DINNER, if the biscuits are still in the oven take them out. Let cool on the baking sheet for 1 minute. Put the mini biscuits in a basket and place on the dinner table.

Supplies List

Timer
12-inch nonstick saucepan
Medium bowl
Baking sheet
Basket

Grocery List

PACKAGED

1 ($4^1/_2$-ounce) can chopped green chilies
Bold & spicy Bloody Mary mix (nonalcoholic)
1 ($15^1/_2$-ounce) can hot & spicy chili beans in chili sauce
1 ($14^1/_2$-ounce) can diced tomatoes with mild green chilies
Ranch salad dressing mix

PRODUCE

$^1/_2$ cup chopped fresh chives
2 medium cucumbers

FROZEN

1 (12-ounce) bag vegetarian beef-flavored crumbles

DAIRY

Shredded fat-free cheddar cheese
1 (8-ounce) container fat-free sour cream
2 eggs

Pantry List

Ground black pepper
Light salt
Seasoned salt
Baking soda
Whole wheat flour
Nonfat butter-flavored cooking spray
Splenda granular

>>> One-Pan Lasagna Stove-Top Dinner

Italian Squash Medley • Garlic & Chive Bread Knots

You will never want to serve store-bought lasagna again. This is so much more satisfying and delicious. With the simplicity of this easy timeline, you will have your entire homemade meal completed in less than 30 minutes.

ONE-PAN LASAGNA STOVE-TOP DINNER

Yield: 7 servings (1 cup per serving)

Calories: 251 (14% fat); Total Fat: 4g; Cholesterol: 7mg; Carbohydrate: 34g; Dietary Fiber: 5g; Protein 19g; Sodium: 795mg; Diabetic Exchanges: 2 starch, 1 vegetable, 2 very lean meat

ITALIAN SQUASH MEDLEY

Yield: 6 servings (2/3 cup per serving)

Calories: 22 (0% fat); Total Fat: 0g; Cholesterol: 0mg; Carbohydrate: 4g; Dietary Fiber: 1g; Protein 1g; Sodium: 331mg; Diabetic Exchanges: 1 vegetable

GARLIC & CHIVE BREAD KNOTS

Yield: 10 knots

(1 to 2 knots per serving)

Calories: 59 (31% fat); Total Fat: 2g; Cholesterol: 2mg; Carbohydrate: 9g; Dietary Fiber: 0g; Protein 1g; Sodium: 278mg; Diabetic Exchanges: 1/2 starch, 1/2 fat

ONE-PAN LASAGNA STOVE-TOP DINNER

1 (26-ounce) jar garlic and herb pasta sauce
1 cup hot water
1 (12-ounce) package vegetarian sausage-flavored crumbles
4 cups No-Yolk brand extra-broad noodles, uncooked
1/2 cup low-fat ricotta cheese
1/2 cup shredded fat-free mozzarella cheese
1 tablespoon reduced-fat Parmesan-style grated topping

ITALIAN SQUASH MEDLEY

2 small green zucchini
2 small yellow squash
10 grape tomatoes
1/4 cup fat-free Italian salad dressing
1 teaspoon steak seasoning
1/4 teaspoon seasoned salt

GARLIC & CHIVE BREAD KNOTS

1 (7 1/2-ounce) can refrigerated buttermilk biscuits
1 tablespoon light butter
1 tablespoon bottled minced garlic
1 teaspoon garlic salt, divided
2 teaspoons dried chives

Instructions

30 MINUTES BEFORE DINNER, start the squash medley. Cut 2 small green zucchini and 2 small yellow squash into thin slices. Place in a 12-inch non-stick saucepan. Add 10 grape tomatoes, $1/4$ c Italian salad dressing, 1 t steak seasoning, and $1/4$ teaspoon seasoned salt. Cover with a lid and set aside.

23 MINUTES BEFORE DINNER, start the lasagna. In a 12-inch nonstick saucepan over medium heat, combine 1 jar pasta sauce, 1 cup hot water, and 1 package frozen vegetarian sausage-flavored crumbles until well mixed. Bring to a boil, keeping the sauce covered to avoid splattering.

18 MINUTES BEFORE DINNER, add the noodles to the sauce and cook for 10 minutes, stirring occasionally.

16 MINUTES BEFORE DINNER, start the bread knots. Separate 1 can refrigerated buttermilk biscuits into 10 biscuits. Roll each biscuit into a long strip and tie into a knot.

In a 1-gallon size zip-top bag melt, 1 T light butter in the microwave for 5 to 8 seconds, or until melted. Add 1 T minced garlic, $1/2$ t garlic salt, and 2 t dried chives. Place the biscuit knots in the zip-top bag and shake until the knots are well coated.

10 MINUTES BEFORE DINNER, preheat the oven to 400 degrees. Coat a baking sheet with nonfat cooking spray and place the knots on the baking sheet.

8 MINUTES BEFORE DINNER, add $1/2$ c ricotta cheese to the lasagna and mix well.

Turn off the heat under the lasagna. Sprinkle $1/2$ c shredded mozzarella cheese and 1 T grated Parmesan topping over the lasagna. Cover and let the lasagna sit on the warm burner until dinner time.

Place the Italian Squash Medley over medium heat.

Put the bread knots in the preheated oven.

5 MINUTES BEFORE DINNER, stir the squash medley, cover, and continue to cook. Place the lasagna on a hot pad on the table.

2 MINUTES BEFORE DINNER, transfer the squash to a serving bowl and plac on the table. Remove the bread knots from the oven, place them in a basket, and put on the table.

Supplies List

Timer
12-inch nonstick saucepan with lid
12-inch nonstick skillet
1-gallon zip-top bag
Baking sheet

Grocery List

PACKAGED

1 (26-ounce) jar garlic & herb pasta sauce
1 (12-ounce) bag No-Yolk extra broad pasta
Fat-free Italian salad dressing

PRODUCE

2 small green zucchini
2 small yellow squash
10 grape tomatoes

FROZEN

1 (12-ounce) package vegetarian sausage-flavored crumbles

DAIRY

Light butter
Low-fat ricotta cheese
$1/2$ cup shredded fat-free mozzarella cheese
Reduced-fat Parmesan-style grated topping
1 ($7^1/2$-ounce) can refrigerated buttermilk biscuits

Panrty List

Steak seasoning
Seasoned salt
Minced garlic
Nonfat cooking spray
Garlic salt
Dried chives

>>> Little Italy Chili Topped with Italian Biscuit Bites

Italian Biscuit Bites • Taste of Italy Garden Salad

The aromatic flavors of Italy unite with the robust seasonings of hearty chili for a unique and distinguished flavor the whole family will love and most likely keep asking for again and again.

LITTLE ITALY CHILI

Yield: 6 servings (1 cup per serving)

Calories: 215 (16% fat); Total Fat: 4g; Cholesterol: 0mg; Carbohydrate: 28g; Dietary Fiber: 7g; Protein 17g; Sodium: 1353mg; Diabetic Exchanges: 1 starch, 3 vegetable, 1 lean meat

ITALIAN BISCUIT BITES

Yield: 6 servings
(6$^1/_2$ biscuit bites per serving)

Calories: 89 (25% fat); Total Fat: 2g; Cholesterol: 0mg; Carbohydrate: 15g; Dietary Fiber: 0g; Protein 2g; Sodium: 368mg; Diabetic Exchanges: 1 starch, $^1/_2$ fat

TASTE OF ITALY GARDEN SALAD

Yield: 6 servings
(1$^1/_2$ cups per serving)

Calories: 61 (9% fat); Total Fat: 1g; Cholesterol: 3mg; Carbohydrate: 9g; Dietary Fiber: 3g; Protein 5g; Sodium: 569mg; Diabetic Exchanges: 2 vegetable

LITTLE ITALY CHILI

1	package (12-ounce) package vegetarian sausage-flavored crumbles	1	teaspoon Splenda granular
1	(15-ounce) can chili beans	$^1/_2$	teaspoon chili powder
2	(14$^1/_2$-ounce) cans diced tomatoes with basil, garlic, and oregano	1	teaspoon cumin
		$^1/_2$	cup water

ITALIAN BISCUIT BITES

1	(7$^1/_2$-ounce) can refrigerated buttermilk biscuits	2	teaspoons Italian seasoning
15	sprays fat-free butter spray	$^1/_2$	teaspoon garlic salt

TASTE OF ITALY GARDEN SALAD

1	large head romaine lettuce (about 9 cups chopped)	18	grape tomatoes
$^1/_2$	cup shredded fat-free mozzarella cheese	$^3/_4$	cup fat-free Italian salad dressing
$^1/_2$	cucumber, sliced	$^1/_2$	cup fat-free Italian croutons

Instructions

30 MINUTES BEFORE DINNER, start making the Little Italy Chili. In a 12-inch nonstick saucepan over medium-high heat, bring to a low boil 1 package vegetarian sausage-flavored crumbles, 1 can chili beans, 2 cans diced tomatoes, 1 t Splenda , $^1/_2$ t chili powder, 1 t cumin, and $^1/_2$ cup water.

20 MINUTES BEFORE DINNER, prepare the biscuits. Separate 1 can refrigerated buttermilk biscuits into 10 biscuits. Using scissors, cut each biscuit into quarters. Drop the biscuit quarters into the low boiling chili. Spray the dough with 15 sprays fat-free butter spray. Sprinkle 2 t Italian seasoning and $^1/_2$ t garlic salt on top. Reduce the heat to medium low. Cover and cook for 10 minutes.

10 MINUTES BEFORE DINNER, start assembling the salad. In a large salad bowl, combine 9 c romaine lettuce, $^1/_2$ c shredded mozzarella cheese, $^1/_2$ sliced cucumber, and 18 grape tomatoes.

7 MINUTES BEFORE DINNER, turn off the heat to the chili, keep covered and let sit until dinner. Continue making the salad.

2 MINUTES BEFORE DINNER, toss the salad with $^3/_4$ c Italian salad dressing and $^1/_2$ c Italian croutons. Place the salad on the dinner table.

1 MINUTE BEFORE DINNER, place chili on a hot pad on the dinner table.

Supplies List

Timer
12-inch nonstick skillet with lid
Scissors
Large salad bowl

Grocery List

PACKAGED

1 (15-ounce) can chili beans
2 (14½-ounce) cans diced tomatoes with basil, garlic, and oregano
Fat-free Italian croutons
1 (8-ounce) bottle fat-free Italian salad dressing

PRODUCE

1 large head romaine lettuce
1 cucumber
18 grape tomatoes

FROZEN

1 (12-ounce) package vegetarian sausage-flavored crumbles

DAIRY

½ cup shredded fat-free mozzarella cheese
1 (7½-ounce) can refrigerated buttermilk biscuits

Pantry List

Fat-free butter spray
Chili powder
Cumin
Italian seasoning
Garlic salt
Splenda granular

>>> Tamale Pie Casserole

Cool & Creamy South of the Border Dip with Assorted Bell Pepper Strips

My friend, Hercules (nicknamed because of his strength), is a big meat and potatoes eater and doesn't care for vegetarian entrées. He told me with great enthusiasm that this Tamale Pie Casserole was a "killer!" I wish you could have seen the look of shock on his face when I told him it was vegetarian. His jaw practically hit the floor. He loved it, as did the rest of my family and friends. I know you will too. My sombrero goes off to my assistant, Brenda Crosser, for this *muy bueno* recipe!

TAMALE PIE CASSEROLE

Yield: 7 servings

(1½ cups per serving)

Calories: 370 (10% fat); Total Fat: 4g; Cholesterol: 20mg; Carbohydrate: 55g; Dietary Fiber: 9g; Protein 30g; Sodium: 1966mg; Diabetic Exchanges: 3 starch, 2 vegetable, 3 very lean meat

COOL & CREAMY SOUTH OF THE BORDER DIP

Yield: 6 servings (2 tablespoons dip; ½ bell pepper per serving)

Calories: 54 (0% fat); Total Fat: 0g; Cholesterol: 3mg; Carbohydrate: 11g; Dietary Fiber: 2g; Protein 2g; Sodium: 99mg; Diabetic Exchanges: ½ other carbohydrate, 1 vegetable

TAMALE PIE CASSEROLE

2	(14½-ounce) cans diced tomatoes with chilies	1	(8½-ounce) box corn muffin mix
2	(15-ounce) cans vegetarian chili	¼	cup pasteurized southwestern liquid egg substitute
1	(11-ounce) can Mexicorn*	1	cup shredded fat-free cheddar cheese
1	(12-ounce) package frozen vegetarian beef-flavored crumbles		

COOL & CREAMY SOUTH OF THE BORDER DIP

½	cup fat-free sour cream	1	large fresh yellow bell pepper
3	tablespoons taco sauce	1	large fresh red bell pepper
2	tablespoons fat-free French salad dressing	1	large fresh green bell pepper

Instructions

30 MINUTES BEFORE DINNER, drain 1 of the cans diced tomatoes with chilies, reserving $1/3$ cup juice; set the tomatoes and juice aside.

29 MINUTES BEFORE DINNER, preheat the oven to 450 degrees.

28 MINUTES BEFORE DINNER, start the casserole. In an ovenproof 12-inch nonstick saucepan over medium-high heat, combine the remaining 1 can diced tomatoes with chilies, the reserved can diced tomatoes with chilies, 2 cans vegetarian chili, 1 can Mexicorn, and 1 package frozen vegetarian beef crumbles. Bring to a boil. Reduce the heat to medium-low. Cover and cook at a low boil.

25 MINUTES BEFORE DINNER, in a medium bowl, stir together the reserved $1/3$ c tomato juice, 1 box corn muffin mix, and $1/4$ c Southwestern liquid egg substitute until well mixed. Set aside.

18 MINUTES BEFORE DINNER, stir the chili in the saucepan.

17 MINUTES BEFORE DINNER, spread the corn muffin batter over the chili. Cover and continue cooking the chili at a low boil.

15 MINUTES BEFORE DINNER, start the dip. In a small bowl, stir together until well mixed $1/2$ c sour cream, 3 T taco sauce, and 2 T French salad dressing.

12 MINUTES BEFORE DINNER, cut 1 large fresh yellow bell pepper, 1 large fresh red bell pepper, and 1 large fresh green bell pepper into strips. Place the bell pepper strips on a large serving platter to serve with the dip. Place on the dinner table along with the dip.

6 MINUTES BEFORE DINNER, remove the lid from the chili. Sprinkle the chili with 1 c shredded cheddar cheese. Spray the cheese generously with nonfat cooking spray. Put the casserole in the oven on the top rack and bake for 4 minutes.

1 MINUTE BEFORE DINNER, remove the casserole from the oven and place on a hot pad on the dinner table.

NOTE: Mexicorn is sweet corn with chopped red bell pepper.

Supplies List

Timer
Ovenproof 12-inch nonstick saucepan with lid
Medium bowl
Small bowl
Large serving platter

Grocery List

PACKAGED
2 ($14^{1}/_{2}$-ounce) cans diced tomatoes with chilies
2 (15-ounce) cans vegetarian chili
Fat-free French salad dressing
1 ($8^{1}/_{2}$-ounce) box corn muffin mix
1 (11-ounce) can Mexicorn*

PRODUCE
1 large yellow bell pepper
1 large red bell pepper
1 large green bell pepper

FROZEN
1 (12-ounce) package frozen vegetarian beef-flavored crumbles

DAIRY
1 cup shredded fat-free cheddar cheese
$1/2$ cup fat-free sour cream
1 small container Southwestern liquid egg substitute

Pantry List

Nonfat cooking spray
Taco sauce

>>> Oven-Baked Stuffed Portobello Mushrooms

Always Tender Asparagus Spears • Pineapple Tidbit Salad

Although this is a mushroom dish, it is as good as any steak you've ever had.

**OVEN-BAKED STUFFED
PORTOBELLO MUSHROOMS**
**Yield: 6 servings (1 mushroom and
²/₃ cup stuffing per serving)**

*Calories: 228 (26% fat); Total Fat: 7g;
Cholesterol: 7mg; Carbohydrate: 24g;
Dietary Fiber: 6g; Protein 22g;
Sodium: 553mg; Diabetic Exchanges: 1
starch, 2 vegetable, 2¹/₂ lean meat*

ALWAYS TENDER ASPARAGUS SPEARS
**Yield: 6 servings
(3 to 4 spears per serving)**

*Calories: 29 (0% fat); Total Fat: 0g;
Cholesterol: 0mg; Carbohydrate: 6g;
Dietary Fiber: 2g; Protein 2g; Sodium:
135mg; Diabetic Exchanges:
1 vegetable*

PINEAPPLE TIDBIT SALAD
Yield: 6 servings (¹/₂ cup per serving)

*Calories: 110 (7% fat); Total Fat: 1g;
Cholesterol: 3mg; Carbohydrate: 22g;
Dietary Fiber: 1g; Protein 3g; Sodium:
108mg; Diabetic Exchanges: 1¹/₂ fruit*

OVEN-BAKED STUFFED PORTOBELLO MUSHROOMS

3	slices rye bread
6	(7-ounce) portobello mushrooms
¹/₃	cup chopped celery
¹/₃	cup frozen chopped onion
¹/₂	cup chicken broth
¹/₄	teaspoon ground sage (optional)
1	(12-ounce) package vegetarian sausage-flavored crumbles, or 1 pound low-fat Italian turkey sausage cooked, drained, and crumbled
4	slices reduced-fat deli-thin Swiss cheese

ALWAYS TENDER ASPARAGUS SPEARS

¹/₄	teaspoon allspice
1	tablespoon Splenda granular
1¹/₂	tablespoons plus 1¹/₂ teaspoons imitation butter-flavored sprinkles
1¹/₂	pounds fresh asparagus, trimmed
	Popcorn salt (optional)

PINEAPPLE TIDBIT SALAD

4	ounces fat-free cream cheese, softened
1	(30-ounce) can pineapple tidbits in pineapple juice, chilled
1	cup fat-free frozen whipped topping, thawed
2	tablespoons Splenda Brown Sugar Blend
1	tablespoon finely chopped walnuts

Instructions

30 MINUTES BEFORE DINNER, preheat the oven to 350 degrees.

Toast 3 slices rye bread in the toaster and cut into $1/2$-inch pieces. Set aside.

27 MINUTES BEFORE DINNER, start the mushrooms. Clean 6 portobello mushrooms with a dry cloth. Remove the stems from the mushrooms and discard. Spray the tops of each mushroom with nonfat cooking spray. Place the portobello mushroom caps top side down on 2 jelly-roll pans, not baking sheets, as liquid will be released in cooking and the pan needs $1/4$-inch sides to hold the liquid. Cover the pans with aluminum foil and bake for 10 to 13 minutes, or until the stuffing is prepared.

25 MINUTES BEFORE DINNER, prepare the stuffing. In a large saucepan over high heat, bring $1/3$ c celery, $1/3$ c onion, $1/2$ c chicken broth, $1/4$ t ground sage, and 1 package vegetarian sausage-flavored crumbles to a boil. Stir in the toasted bread pieces. Turn off the heat. Cover and let the stuffing sit on the hot burner. The process of preparing the stuffing and bringing the liquid to a boil happens quickly, so make sure you have all of your ingredients ready.

20 MINUTES BEFORE DINNER, prepare the asparagus. Add $1/2$ inch of water to a 12-inch nonstick saucepan. Add $1/4$ t allspice, 1 T Splenda granular, $1^1/_2$ T butter-flavored sprinkles and stir until dissolved. Add $1^1/_2$ lb trimmed asparagus to the water. Cook over medium-high heat until boiling. Once the water comes to a boil, turn off the heat. Let sit on the hot burner, covered, until dinner is ready to be served.

15 MINUTES BEFORE DINNER, make the salad. Using your hands, drain the pineapple. Set the pineapple aside.

In a medium bowl, combine 4 oz cream cheese, 1 c thawed whipped topping, and 2 T Splenda Brown Sugar Blend until smooth and creamy. Add the drained pineapple tidbits to the cream mixture and stir until well mixed. Sprinkle the top of the salad with 1 T walnuts. Cover and refrigerate until dinner is ready.

Supplies List

Timer
Toaster
2 jelly-roll pans (baking sheets with $1/4$-inch sides)
Foil
Large saucepan
12-inch nonstick saucepan
Medium bowl
Platter
Colander

Grocery List

PACKAGED
Rye bread
$1/2$ cup chicken broth
1 (30-ounce) can pineapple tidbits in juice

PRODUCE
$1/3$ cup chopped celery
$1^1/_2$ pounds fresh asparagus
6 (7-ounce) portobello mushrooms

FROZEN
$1/3$ cup frozen chopped onion
1 (12-ounce) package vegetarian sausage-flavored crumbles or 1 pound low-fat Italian turkey sausage
1 cup frozen fat-free whipped topping

DAIRY
4 slices reduced-fat deli-thin sliced Swiss cheese
4 ounces fat-free cream cheese

Pantry List on page 300

CONTINUED ON NEXT PAGE >>>

Pantry List

Allspice
Popcorn salt (optional)
Ground sage (optional)
Imitation butter-flavored
   sprinkles
Finely chopped walnuts
Nonfat cooking spray
Splenda Brown Sugar Blend
Splenda granular

10 MINUTES BEFORE DINNER, remove the mushroom caps from the oven and drain the liquid from the jelly-roll pans. Spoon $^2/_3$ c of the prepared stuffing into each mushroom cap.

Cut 4 Swiss cheese slices into thin strips. Arrange the cheese on top of the stuffing and spray with cooking spray. Return to the oven and bake for an additional 5 minutes, or until the cheese is melted.

2 MINUTES BEFORE DINNER, place the salad on the dinner table.

Drain the asparagus and arrange the spears on a serving plate. Sprinkle with $1^1/_2$ t butter-flavored sprinkles and lightly with popcorn salt, if desired.

1 MINUTE BEFORE DINNER, place the stuffed mushrooms on a platter and place on the dinner table.

NOTE: When you let the asparagus come to a boil and then turn the heat off right away, you don't have to worry about overcooking them and they remain warm until the rest of the dinner is complete

DESSERTS

>>> Double-Chocolate Cherry Snack Squares

Preparation time: 10 minutes **Baking time:** 15 minutes **Total time:** 25 minutes

These babies are great for curing your sweet tooth without using a lot of calories and fats.

Yield: 20 servings

(1 square per serving)

Calories: 135 (21% fat); Total Fat: 3g; Cholesterol: 1mg; Carbohydrate: 25g; Dietary Fiber: 1g; Protein 2g; Sodium: 279mg; Diabetic Exchanges: $1^1/_2$ other carbohydrate, $^1/_2$ fat

Supplies List

Timer
10 x 15-inch jelly-roll pan
Medium bowl

Grocery List

PACKAGED

1 (18.25-ounce) box chocolate cake mix
1 (10-ounce) jar maraschino cherries

DAIRY

3 eggs

Pantry List

Chocolate chips
1 cup fat-free mayonnaise
Nonfat cooking spray

1   ($18^1/_4$-ounce) box chocolate cake mix, dry
3   egg whites
1   cup fat-free mayonnaise
$^1/_4$ cup finely chopped chocolate chips
$^1/_2$ cup finely chopped maraschino cherries

Instructions

> Preheat the oven to 350 degrees.
> Spray a jelly-roll pan with nonfat cooking spray. Set aside.
> In a medium bowl, stir together the cake mix, egg whites, and mayonnaise until well mixed. The batter will be sticky.
> Spray your hands with nonfat cooking spray and press the dough into the prepared jelly-roll pan to the edges of the pan.
> Press the chocolate chips and maraschino cherries onto the top of the batter.
> Bake on the middle rack for 15 minutes, or until a toothpick inserted in the center comes out clean.
> Let cool for 5 to 10 minutes before cutting.

>>> Chocolate Raspberry Four-Layer Cake

Preparation time: 18 minutes **Baking time:** 12 minutes **Total time:** 30 minutes

My friend thinks that this tastes like a dessert you would order at a fancy restaurant.

Yield: 16 servings

(1 slice per serving)

Calories: 216 (12% fat); Total Fat: 3g; Cholesterol: 2mg; Carbohydrate: 46g; Dietary Fiber: 1g; Protein 3g; Sodium: 375mg; Diabetic Exchanges: 3 other carbohydrate, $^1/_2$ fat

Supplies List

Timer
Four (9-inch) round cake pans
Large bowl
Electric mixer
Glass measuring cup
Cake plate

Grocery List

PACKAGED
1 cup fat-free mayonnaise
1 small jar fat-free hot fudge topping

DAIRY
6 eggs

BAKING ITEMS
1 (12-ounce) can raspberry filling
1 (18.25-ounce) box Super Moist chocolate fudge cake mix
Chocolate sprinkles

Pantry List

$^1/_2$ cup applesauce
Nonfat cooking spray

6	egg whites
$^1/_2$	cup applesauce
1	cup fat-free mayonnaise
$^1/_2$	cup fat-free hot fudge topping
1	(12-ounce) can raspberry filling
1	tablespoon chocolate sprinkles
1	(18$^1/_4$-ounce) Super Moist chocolate fudge cake mix, dry

Instructions

> Preheat the oven to 350 degrees.
> Spray four (9-inch) round cake pans with nonfat cooking spray. Set aside.
> In a large mixing bowl with a mixer at medium speed, beat egg whites until soft peaks form.
> Add the applesauce, mayonnaise, and cake mix. Beat with a mixer until well blended.
> Spoon 1$^1/_3$ cup batter into each prepared cake pan.
> Bake for 12 minutes, or until a toothpick inserted in the center comes out clean.
> Microwave the raspberry filling for 30 seconds in a glass measuring cup.
> Place one cake layer on a cake plate. Spread $^1/_4$ cup raspberry filling over the cake. Top with another cake layer. Spread $^1/_4$ cup raspberry filling on top of the second layer. Repeat for the remaining 2 cake layers and spread the remaining raspberry filling on top.
> Heat the hot fudge in the microwave for 40 to 50 seconds, or until hot and bubbly. Stir until smooth and creamy, removing all lumps.
> Spoon 1 tablespoon of hot fudge in the center of the cake. Drizzle the remaining hot fudge with a spoon around the top edge of the cake allowing it to run the down sides of the cake. Sprinkle the top of the entire cake with the chocolate sprinkles. Slice and serve. It's good with a dollop of Cool Whip.

>>> Stuffed Almond Cupcakes

Preparation time: 10 minutes or less   **Baking time:** 17 minutes   **Total time:** 27 minutes or less

The wonderful almond filling in these babies is a nice surprise that makes them an extra special treat to eat. Expect rave reviews!

Yield: 18 servings
(1 muffin per serving)
Calories: 161 (21% fat); Total Fat: 4g; Cholesterol: 0mg; Carbohydrate: 29g; Dietary Fiber: 1g; Protein 2g; Sodium: 216mg; Diabetic Exchanges: 2 other carbohydrate, 1 fat

Supplies List
Timer
Nonstick muffin pan
Medium bowl

Grocery List
PACKAGED
1 (18.25-ounce) box white cake mix
1 (12.5-ounce) can almond cake and pastry filling

DAIRY
Egg whites

Pantry List
Almond extract
Sliced almonds
Nonfat cooking spray

1   (18$^1/_4$-ounce) box white cake mix, dry
3   egg whites
1   cup water
1   teaspoon almond extract
$^1/_2$ (12$^1/_2$-ounce) can almond filling
2   tablespoons sliced almonds, finely chopped

Instructions

> Preheat the oven to 350 degrees.
> Coat 18 nonstick muffin cups with nonfat cooking spray. Set aside.
> In a medium bowl, combine the cake mix, egg whites, water, and almond extract. Mix until well blended.
> Spoon 3 tablespoon of batter into each of the 18 muffin cups. Place 1 tablespoon almond filling in the center of the batter in each muffin cup. Spoon 1 tablespoon of batter over the almond filling. Evenly sprinkle the tops of the cupcakes with 2 tablespoons finely chopped almonds.
> Place the muffin cups in the oven on the middle rack and bake for 17 minutes, or until a toothpick inserted in the center of 1 cupcake comes out clean.
> Let cool 3 to 4 minutes before removing from the muffin pan.

>>> Cherry Surprise-Filled Chocolate Cupcakes

Preparation time: 13 minutes **Baking time:** 17 minutes **Total time:** 30 minutes

The cherry centers in the middle of these delightful cupcakes are a surprise that both children and adults welcome.

Yield: 18 servings

(1 cupcake per serving)

Calories: 143 (12% fat); Total Fat: 2g; Cholesterol: 0mg; Carbohydrate: 29g; Dietary Fiber: 2g; Protein 3g; Sodium: 257mg; Diabetic Exchanges: 2 other carbohydrate, $^1/_2$ fat

Supplies List

Timer
Muffin pan
Medium mixing bowl

Grocery List

PACKAGED

1 (21-ounce) can light cherry pie filling
1 small jar fat-free hot fudge topping
1 (18.25-ounce) box devil's food cake mix

DAIRY

6 eggs

Pantry List

Almond extract
Unsweetened applesauce
Nonfat cooking spray

1 teaspoon almond extract
1 (18$^1/_4$-ounce) box devil's food cake mix, dry
1 $^1/_3$ cups water
2 tablespoons unsweetened applesauce
6 egg whites
$^1/_2$ (21-ounce) can light cherry pie filling
18 teaspoons fat-free hot fudge topping

Instructions

> Preheat the oven to 350 degrees.
> Coat 18 muffin cups with nonfat cooking spray. Set aside.
> In a medium mixing bowl, combine the almond extract, cake mix, water, applesauce, and egg whites. Mix with a wire whisk or a large spoon for 1 minute.
> Spoon 3 tablespoons of batter into each of the muffin cups. Place 2 teaspoons pie filling in the center of the batter of each muffin cup. Spoon 1 tablespoon of batter over the cherry pie filling.
> Bake the cupcakes for 17 minutes, or until a toothpick inserted in the center of a cupcake comes out clean.
> Let the cupcakes cool 3 to 4 minutes. Remove the cupcakes from the muffin pan. Spread 1 teaspoon of hot fudge topping on top.

>>> Pumpkin Spice Cookies

Preparation time: 10 minutes **Baking time:** 7 to 8 minutes **Total time:** 18 minutes or less

This soft cookie is a special treat for pumpkin pie lovers.

Yield: 42 servings

(1 cookie per serving)

Calories: 59 (14% fat); Total Fat: 1g; Cholesterol: 0mg; Carbohydrate: 12g; Dietary Fiber: 0g; Protein 1g; Sodium: 92mg; Diabetic Exchanges: 1 other carbohydrate

Supplies List

Timer
4 baking sheets
Large bowl
Large platter

Grocery List

PACKAGED

1 (18.25-ounce) box spice cake mix
1 (15-ounce) can pumpkin pie mix

FROZEN

1 (8-ounce) container fat-free dessert whipped topping

DAIRY

2 eggs

Pantry List

Nonfat butter-flavored cooking spray

1   cup frozen fat-free dessert whipped topping, thawed

2   egg whites

1   ($18^1/4$-ounce) box spice cake mix, dry

1   cup pumpkin pie mix*

Instructions

> Preheat the oven to 350 degrees.
> Spray four baking sheets with nonfat butter-flavored cooking spray. Set aside.
> In a large bowl, combine the whipped topping, egg whites, cake mix, and pumpkin pie. Mix and stir together until well mixed.
> Drop the cookie dough by rounded tablespoonfuls onto the prepared baking sheets.
> Bake for 7 to 8 minutes. Cool on the baking sheets for 2 to 3 minutes before removing to a large platter.
> For an extra treat, serve these cookies with Sweet Cream Cheese Spread (see page 307).

__NOTE:__ There is a huge difference in taste between pumpkin pie mix and 100% pumpkin. Pumpkin pie mix has sugar and spices already in it, whereas pumpkin is pure pumpkin with no added sugar or spices. For this recipe make sure you purchase pumpkin pie mix.

>>> Sweet Cream Cheese Spread

Total preparation time: 3 minutes or less

For an added extra treat make this sweet cream cheese spread and put a bowl of it with a butter-knife in the center of a large platter of the pumpkin cookies so guests can spread some cream cheese spread on their cookies. My friends loved them this way. The spread is also good on graham crackers.

Yield: 42 servings
(1 teaspoon per serving)
Calories: 8 (0% fat); Total Fat: 0g;
Cholesterol: 1mg; Carbohydrate: 1g;
Dietary Fiber: 0g; Protein 1g; Sodium:
27mg; Diabetic Exchanges: Free

Supplies List
Medium bowl
Electric mixer

Grocery List

DAIRY
1 (8-ounce) package fat-free
cream cheese

Pantry List
Splenda granular
Vanilla extract

1   (8-ounce) package fat-free
cream cheese, softened

$3/4$ cup Splenda granular
$1/2$ teaspoon vanilla extract

Instructions

> In a medium bowl with an electric mixer on medium speed, beat together the cream cheese, $3/4$ cup granular Splenda, and vanilla extract until well blended. Serve at room temperature.

>>> Cherry Delight Four-Layer Cake

Preparation time: 18 minutes **Baking time:** 12 minutes **Total time:** 30 minutes

This cake is light and airy. The pretty red and white colors would make this an excellent dessert for Christmas or Valentine's Day.

Yield: 16 servings

(1 slice per serving)

Calories: 155 (13% fat); Total Fat: 2g; Cholesterol: 0mg; Carbohydrate: 31g; Dietary Fiber: 1g; Protein 2g; Sodium: 229mg; Diabetic Exchanges: 2 other carbohydrate, 1/2 fat

Supplies List

Timer
4 (9-inch) round cake pans
Large bowl
Electric mixer
Food processor

Grocery List

PACKAGED

1 (20-ounce) can light cherry pie filling
1 (18.25-ounce) box Super Moist butter recipe white cake mix

DAIRY

6 eggs

Pantry List

1/2 cup unsweetened applesauce
Almond extract
Nonstick cooking spray

6	egg whites
1/2	cup unsweetened applesauce
1 1/4	cups water
1	tablespoon almond extract
1	(18 1/4 -ounce) box Super Moist butter recipe white cake mix, dry
1	(20-ounce) can light cherry pie filling

Instructions

> Preheat the oven to 350 degrees.
> Spray four (9-inch) round cake pans with nonfat cooking spray. Set aside.
> In a large bowl with an electric mixer on medium speed, beat 6 egg whites until soft peaks form.
> Add the applesauce, water, cake mix, and almond extract. Mix with an electric mixer on medium until well blended.
> Put 1 1/2 cups batter into each prepared cake pan.
> Bake for 12 minutes, or until a toothpick inserted in the center of one layer comes out clean.
> While the cakes are baking, place the cherry pie filling in a food processor. Pulse for 30 seconds, or until finely chopped.
> Remove the cakes from the oven and assemble while still warm. Place one cake layer on a cake plate. Spread with 1/4 cup cherry filling. Top with another cake layer. Spread with 1/4 cup cherry filling. Repeat for the remaining two cake layers and the remaining 1/2 cup cherry filling. You will have 1/2 cup cherry pie filling left over.

NOTE: This cake is even better served with a dollop of frozen fat-free dessert whipped topping and cherry filling.

>>> Butter Pecan Cookies

Preparation time: 15 minutes **Baking time:** 10 minutes per baking sheet
Total time: 25 minutes or less

These delicious butter pecan cookies are sure to treat your sweet tooth.

**YIELD: 58 SERVINGS
(1 COOKIE PER SERVING)**
*Calories: 48 (19% fat); Total Fat: 1g;
Cholesterol: 0mg; Carbohydrate: 9g;
Dietary Fiber: 0g; Protein 0g; Sodium:
60mg; Diabetic Exchanges:
$1/2$ other carbohydrate*

Supplies List

Timer
Cookie sheets
Medium bowl
Electric mixer

Grocery List

PACKAGED
1 (18.25-ounce) box Super
Moist butter pecan cake mix

DAIRY
2 eggs

FROZEN
1 (8-ounce) container fat-free
dessert whipped topping

Pantry List

Whole wheat flour
Pecans
Nonfat cooking spray

1   (8-ounce) container
    fat-free dessert whipped
    topping, thawed
2   egg whites

1   ($18^1/4$-ounce) box Super Moist
    butter pecan cake mix, dry
$1/4$ cup whole wheat flour
$1/4$ cup finely chopped pecans

Instructions

> Preheat oven to 350 degrees.
> Coat 2 cookie sheets with nonfat cooking spray. Set aside.
> In a medium bowl with an electric mixer on medium speed, beat the fat-free whipped topping until smooth.
> In a large bowl with an electric mixer on medium speed, beat 2 egg whites until soft peaks form. Combine the whites with the whipped topping.
> Add the cake mix and flour and beat on medium speed until well blended.
> Drop by rounded teaspoonfuls onto the prepared cookie sheets. Sprinkle with the finely chopped pecans.
> Bake for 10 minutes.

>>> Freckled Lemon Sunshine Cake

Preparation time: 18 minutes **Baking time:** 12 minutes **Total time:** 30 minutes

Just looking at this cheerful cake will brighten anybody's day.

Yield: 16 servings
(1 slice per serving)
Calories: 195 (14% fat); Total Fat: 3g;
Cholesterol: 1mg; Carbohydrate: 39g;
Dietary Fiber: 0g; Protein 3g; Sodium:
287mg; Diabetic Exchanges:
$2^1/_2$ *other carbohydrate*

Supplies List
Timer
Four (9-inch) round cake pans
Large bowl
Electric mixer
Cake plate

Grocery List
PACKAGED
1 (18.25-ounce) box lemon
supreme cake mix
1 (21-ounce) can lemon cream
pie filling

PRODUCE
1 lemon

DAIRY
6 eggs
$1/_2$ cup fat-free sour cream

Pantry List
Poppy seeds
Nonfat cooking spray

6	egg whites
$1/_2$	cup fat-free sour cream
$1^1/_4$	cups water
1	box lemon supreme cake mix, dry
1	(21-ounce) can lemon cream pie filling
$1/_2$	teaspoon poppy seeds
1	medium fresh lemon

Instructions

> Preheat the oven to 350 degrees.
> Spray four (9-inch) round cake pans with nonfat cooking spray. Set aside.
> In a large bowl with an electric mixer, beat 6 egg whites on medium speed until soft peaks form.
> Add the sour cream, water, and cake mix. Beat until well blended.
> Spoon $1^3/_4$ cups batter into each prepared cake pan.
> Bake for 12 minutes, or until a knife inserted in the center comes out clean.
> Remove the cake layers from the oven and assemble while still warm.
> Place one cake layer on a cake plate. Spread with $1/_2$ c lemon cream pie filling. Top with another cake layer. Spread with $1/_2$ cup lemon cream pie filling. Repeat for the remaining 2 cake layers and 1 cup lemon cream pie filling.
> Sprinkle the poppy seeds over the top of the cake.
> Cut the lemon in half lengthwise and then into $1/_8$-inch-thick slices. Arrange the lemon slices around the bottom edge of the cake on the cake plate so that the cake looks like it is surrounded with flower petals. Slice and serve.

>>> Harvest Snack Cake Squares

Preparation time 5 minutes **Baking time:** 25 minutes **Total time:** 30 minutes

Here's a great snack for autumn treats and after-school snacks.

YIELD: 20 SERVINGS

(1 SQUARE PER SERVING)

*Calories: 138 (17% fat); Total Fat: 3g;
Cholesterol: 0mg; Carbohydrate: 27g;
Dietary Fiber: 1g; Protein 2g; Sodium:
193mg; Diabetic Exchanges:
2 other carbohydrate*

Supplies List
Timer
11x17-inch jelly-roll pan
Large bowl
Electric mixer

Grocery List
PACKAGED
1 (18.25-ounce) box Super Moist
carrot cake mix
1 (15-ounce) can pumpkin pie mix

DAIRY
4 eggs

FROZEN
Fat-free dessert whipped
topping (optional)

Pantry List
Cinnamon (optional)
Nonfat cooking spray

2	cups pumpkin pie mix
4	egg whites
$^1/_2$	cup water
1	(18$^1/_4$-ounce) box Super Moist carrot cake mix, dry

Fat-free dessert whipped topping (optional)

Cinnamon (optional)

Instructions

> Preheat the oven to 350 degrees.
> Coat a jelly-roll pan with nonfat cooking spray. Set aside.
> In a large mixing bowl combine the pumpkin pie mix, egg whites, water, and cake mix. Beat with an electric mixer on medium speed for 2 to 3 minutes, or until well blended.
> Spread the batter into the prepared jelly-roll pan.
> Bake for 25 minutes, or until a knife inserted in the center comes out clean. Cut into 20 squares.

NOTE: If desired, serve warm with a dollop of frozen fat-free dessert whipped topping and sprinkled with cinnamon.

>>> Apple Spice Four-Layer Cake

Preparation time: 10 minutes **Baking time:** 13 to 15 minutes
Total time: 23 to 25 minutes

This delicious cake is sure to add a spicy sweet ending to your dinner.

Yield: 16 servings

(1 slice per serving)

Calories: 201 (11% fat); Total Fat: 3g; Cholesterol: 3mg; Carbohydrate: 42g; Dietary Fiber: 0g; Protein 3g; Sodium: 280mg; Diabetic Exchanges: 3 other carbohydrate, $^1/_2$ fat

Supplies List

Timer
4 (8-inch) round cake pans
Large bowl
Electric mixer
Cake plate

Grocery List

PACKAGED
1 (20-ounce) can apple pie filling
1 (18.25-ounce) box spice cake mix

DAIRY
6 eggs
1 (8-ounce) container
fat-free sour cream

Pantry List

Ground allspice
Unsweetened applesauce
Nonfat cooking spray

$^1/_2$ cup unsweetened applesauce
1 (18.25-ounce) box spice cake, dry
6 egg whites

1 cup fat-free sour cream
1 (20-ounce) can apple pie filling
1 teaspoon ground allspice

Instructions

> Preheat the oven to 350 degrees.
> Spray four (8-inch) round cake pans with nonfat cooking spray. Set aside.
> In a large bowl, combine the applesauce, cake mix, egg whites, and sour cream. With an electric mixer beat until well blended.
> Pour $1^1/4$ cups batter into each of the four prepared cake pans.
> Bake for 13 to 15 minutes, or until a knife inserted in center comes out clean.
> While the cakes are baking, prepare the filling. Combine the apple pie filling and allspice in a food processor and process for 1 minute, or until well blended.
> Assemble the cakes by placing one cake layer on a cake plate. Spread with $^1/_2$ cup spiced apple pie filling. Top with another cake layer. Spread with $^1/_2$ cup apple pie filling. Repeat for the remaining two cake layers and 1 cup apple pie filling. Sprinkle the top layer lightly with ground allspice.

>>> Frozen Pumpkin Yogurt

Total Time: 5 minutes or less

I love pumpkin ice cream, but I can't handle all of the calories. So, I created this healthier version of the frozen treat that is every bit as delicious.

YIELD: 6 SERVINGS

(1/2 CUP PER SERVING)

Calories: 121 (0% fat); Total Fat: 0g; Cholesterol: 0mg; Carbohydrate: 27g; Dietary Fiber: 2g; Protein 3g; Sodium: 114mg; Diabetic Exchanges: 2 other carbohydrate

Supplies List

Blender
Dessert cups

Grocery List

PACKAGED

1 (15-ounce) can pumpkin pie mix

FROZEN

1 pint fat-free sugar-free vanilla frozen yogurt

2 cups fat-free sugar-free vanilla frozen yogurt, softened   1 1/2 cups pumpkin pie mix

Instructions

> In a blender combine the vanilla frozen yogurt and the pumpkin pie mix and process on high speed until well blended.
> Spoon 1/2 cup frozen yogurt into individual dessert cups.
> Cover and keep chilled in the freezer until ready to eat.

>>> Peppermint Candy Blizzard

Total time: 5 minutes or less

My friends and family went nuts over these. I have a feeling yours will, too.

Yield: 5 servings (1 cup per serving)

Calories: 182 (0% fat); Total Fat: 0g; Cholesterol: 2mg; Carbohydrate: 39g; Dietary Fiber: 0g; Protein 7g; Sodium: 110mg; Diabetic Exchanges: 1 skim milk, 2 other carbohydrate

Supplies List

Timer
Blender
5 serving cups or tall-stemmed glasses

Grocery List

PACKAGED
5 miniature peppermint candy canes

FROZEN
1 quart low-fat frozen vanilla yogurt

DAIRY
1 cup fat-free low-carb milk

Pantry List

Mint extract
Red food coloring

5	miniature peppermint candy canes
1	cup ice
4	cups low-fat frozen vanilla yogurt
1	cup fat-free low-carb milk
$1/4$	teaspoon mint extract
4	drops red food coloring

Instructions

> In a blender, combine 4 of the miniature peppermint candy canes with the ice, yogurt, milk, mint extract, and food coloring. Cover and process on high speed until well blended.

> Spoon into individual serving cups. This is exceptionally pretty in tall-stemmed glasses.

> Place the remaining 1 candy cane in a sealed zip-top bag and crush with either a rolling pin or can. Sprinkle evenly on top of all desserts.

>>> Apricot Cranberry Bake

Preparation time: 5 minutes **Baking time:** 25 minutes **Total time:** 30 minutes

This fruity combination has just the right amount of sweetness and tartness for a dessert worth making over and over again.

Yield: 9 servings (1 square per serving)

Calories: 134 (11% fat); Total Fat: 2g; Cholesterol: 2mg; Carbohydrate: 29g; Dietary Fiber: 2g; Protein 2g; Sodium: 134mg; Diabetic Exchanges: 2 other carbohydrate, $^1/_2$ fat

Supplies List

Timer
9 x 9-inch baking dish
or a 9-inch pie pan
Bowl

Grocery List

PACKAGED
2 (15-ounce) cans apricots
1 (8-ounce) can jellied cranberry sauce

FROZEN
1 (8-ounce) container fat-free dessert whipped topping (optional)

DAIRY
Light butter

Pantry List

$^1/_2$ cup oats
$^3/_4$ cup reduced-fat baking mix
Ground cinnamon
Nonfat cooking spray

1	tablespoon light butter
$^3/_4$	cup reduced-fat baking mix
$^1/_2$	cup oats
2	(15-ounce) cans apricots, drained
1	(8-ounce) can jellied cranberry sauce
1	teaspoon ground cinnamon
	Fat-free dessert whipped topping (optional)

Instructions

> Preheat the oven to 400 degrees.
> Spray a 9 x 9-inch baking dish or a 9-inch pie pan with nonfat cooking spray. Set aside.
> In a bowl using a fork, mix together the butter, baking mix, and oats until well mixed. Set aside.
> Chop the 2 cans drained apricots into bite-size pieces.
> Combine the cranberry sauce, cinnamon, and chopped apricots together in the bottom of the prepared baking dish until well mixed.
> Sprinkle the crumbled oat mixture on top.
> Bake for 25 minutes, or until the fruit is hot and bubbly.
> Let cool for 4 to 5 minutes before serving.

NOTE: *If desired, serve with a dollop of fat-free whipped topping.*

>>> Very Cherry Cookies

Preparation time: 15 minutes **Baking time:** 8 minutes **Total time:** 23 minutes

These cookies have a wonderful flavor of cherry with a very pretty, decorative look to them. The beautiful, cheerful, bright red color is perfect for Christmas or Valentine's Day.

Yield: 40 servings

(1 cookie per serving)

Calories: 66 (17% fat); Total Fat: 1g; Cholesterol: 0mg; Carbohydrate: 13g; Dietary Fiber: 0g; Protein 1g; Sodium: 84mg; Diabetic Exchanges: 1 other carbohydrate

Supplies List

Timer
Medium bowl
Cookie sheets

Grocery List

PACKAGED
1 (18.25-ounce) box Super Moist cherry chip cake mix

FROZEN
1 (8-ounce) container fat-free dessert whipped topping

DAIRY
2 eggs

OTHER
1 (10-ounce) jar maraschino cherries
Red sugar crystals

Pantry List

Nonfat cooking spray

20	maraschino cherries
1	cup dessert fat-free whipped topping, thawed
2	egg whites
1	(18$^1/_4$-ounce) box Super Moist cherry chip cake mix, dry
1	tablespoon red sugar crystals

Instructions

> Preheat the oven to 350 degrees.
> Drain the cherries and set them in a single layer on a paper towel to dry.
> Spray 2 cookie sheets with nonfat cooking spray. Set aside.
> Slice the maraschino cherries in half and set aside.
> In a medium bowl, using a spatula, stir together the whipped topping, egg whites, and cake mix until well mixed.
> Drop dough by rounded teaspoonfuls onto the prepared cookie sheets.
> Evenly sprinkle each mound of cookie dough with red sugar crystals. Top each cookie with half a maraschino cherry.
> Bake for 7 to 8 minutes.
> Let the cookies cool on the cookie sheets for 2 to 3 minutes to finish cooking.

>>> Cherry Crumb Squares

Preparation time: 10 minutes **Baking time:** 15 minutes **Total time:** 25 minutes

This dessert is sure to be a sweet ending to your meal or a great snack by itself.

Yield: 20 servings

(1 square per serving)

Calories: 106 (24% fat); Total Fat: 3g; Cholesterol: 3mg; Carbohydrate: 16g; Dietary Fiber: 1g; Protein 3g; Sodium: 162mg; Diabetic Exchanges: 1 other carbohydrate, 1/2 fat

Supplies List

Timer
10x15-inch jelly-roll pan
Small mixing bowl
Food processor

Grocery List

PACKAGED
1 (20-ounce) can
light cherry pie filling

DAIRY
Light butter
1 (8-ounce) package
fat-free cream cheese
1 (8-ounce) can refrigerated
reduced-fat crescent rolls

Pantry List

Nonfat butter-flavored cooking spray
1/2 cup Splenda Brown Sugar Blend
1/2 cup quick-cooking oats
All-purpose flour

1	(8-ounce) can refrigerated reduced-fat crescent rolls
1	(8-ounce) package fat-free cream cheese
1/2	cup Splenda Brown Sugar Blend
1/2	cup quick-cooking oats
1/4	cup all-purpose flour
2	tablespoons light butter
1	(20-ounce) light cherry pie filling

Instructions

> Preheat the oven to 375 degrees.
> Spray a jelly roll pan with nonfat cooking spray. Set aside.
> Spread 1 can refrigerated crescent rolls over the prepared jelly-roll pan. You will need to pull and press the dough to cover the entire jelly-roll pan.
> Place the dough in the oven and bake for 5 minutes.
> While the dough is baking, mix the cream cheese and 1/4 cup of the Splenda Brown Sugar Blend in a small mixing bowl.
> Remove the dough from oven and increase the temperature to 425 degrees.
> In a small mixing bowl, combine the oats, flour, remaining 1/4 cup Splenda, and butter. Mix with a fork until crumbly.
> Pour 1 can light cherry pie filling into a food processor and process for 15 to 20 seconds, or until the cherries are finely chopped.
> Spread the cream cheese mixture, the cherry pie filling, and the crumb mixture over the warm crust in that order. Spray with nonfat butter-flavored cooking spray.
> Bake for 10 minutes on the top rack of the oven.
> Let cool before cutting into 20 squares.

>>> Hot Fudge Cranberry Sundae

Total time: 5 minutes or less

Here's a creative twist to an old favorite. It's delicious and a wonderful quick dessert to put together at the last minute when you are in a pinch. It's also just the answer to those "gotta have chocolate" cravings during the holidays. It's very chocolaty and satisfying. Women especially like this one.

Yield: 1 serving ($^1/_2$ cup yogurt and 2$^1/_2$ tablespoons topping per serving)

Calories: 135 (0% fat); Total Fat: 0g; Cholesterol: 0mg; Carbohydrate: 32g; Dietary Fiber: 1g; Protein 4g; Sodium: 70mg; Diabetic Exchanges: 2 other carbohydrate

Supplies List

Microwaveable bowl
Dessert cup

Grocery List

PACKAGED

Whole-berry cranberry sauce
Fat-free hot fudge

FROZEN

Fat-free dessert whipped topping
$^1/_2$ cup fat-free no-sugar-added vanilla frozen yogurt

$^1/_2$ tablespoon fat-free hot fudge
1   tablespoon whole-berry cranberry sauce
$^1/_2$ cup fat-free no-sugar-added vanilla frozen yogurt
1   tablespoon fat-free dessert whipped topping

Instructions

> Combine the hot fudge and cranberry sauce in a microwavable bowl. Heat for 15 to 20 seconds, or until well melted. Stir until well mixed.
> Place the vanilla frozen yogurt in a dessert cup.
> Spoon the heated hot fudge-cranberry mixture over the frozen yogurt. Top with whipped topping.

>>> Triple Berry Trifle

Total time: 10 minutes or less

The simplicity of this pretty and light dessert is a gift in itself. I like the fact that it is very impressive visually. The layers of red and white dress up any table or buffet. Another bonus is that diabetics can enjoy this too!

Yield: 10 servings
(²/₃ cup per serving)
Calories: 167 (3% fat); Total Fat: 1g; Cholesterol: 0mg; Carbohydrate: 38g; Dietary Fiber: 4g; Protein 2g; Sodium: 226mg; Diabetic Exchanges: 1 fruit, 1¹/₂ other carbohydrate

Supplies List

Large mixing bowl
Glass trifle bowl

Grocery List

PACKAGED
²/₃ cup sugar-free strawberry glaze
1 (10-ounce) box angel food cake

FROZEN
1 (16-ounce) bag
frozen strawberries
1 (16-ounce) bag
frozen blackberries
¹/₂ cup frozen blueberries
Fat-free dessert whipped topping

1	(8-ounce) fat-free dessert whipped topping
1	(16-ounce) bag frozen strawberries
1	(10-ounce) angel food cake
1	(16-ounce) bag frozen blackberries
¹/₂	cup frozen blueberries
²/₃	cup sugar-free strawberry glaze

Instructions

> Slice 1 angel food cake into thirds horizontally. Set aside.
> In a large mixing bowl, gently stir together the frozen strawberries, frozen blackberries, frozen blueberries, and strawberry glaze until well mixed. Set aside 3 blackberries for later use.
> Place one angel food cake layer into the bottom of a glass trifle bowl. Cut one layer into 1-inch pieces. Place half the pieces in the bowl to fill in any empty spaces. Spoon half the mixed berries evenly over the angel food cake. Pour any juice over the fruit and cake. Spread ²/₃ of the whipped topping over the berries. Place the remaining one cake layer over the whipped topping. Place the remaining one-half of the angel food cake pieces in the bowl to fill in any empty spaces. Spoon the remaining berries over the cake. Spread the remaining ¹/₃ of the whipped topping in the center of the dessert, letting most of the berries be exposed.
> Garnish with the 3 reserved blackberries in the center of the whipped topping.
> Cover and keep refrigerated until ready to serve.

NOTE: *This dessert is made while the berries are still frozen so that while the berries defrost, their juices will drain into the layers of angel food cake.*

>>> Angel Snack Cake

Preparation time: 5 minutes **Baking time:** 12 to 15 minutes **Total time:** 20 minutes or less

I believe angels in heaven rejoice when good things happen. Earth "angels" watching their weight will rejoice while eating this sweet low-calorie delight. The base of this cake is derived from an angel food cake mix, thus its name, "Angel Snack Cake."

Yield: 24 servings
(1 square per serving)
Calories: 97 (0% fat); Total Fat: 0g; Cholesterol: 0mg; Carbohydrate: 22g; Dietary Fiber: 0g; Protein 1g; Sodium: 168mg; Diabetic Exchanges: 1$^1/_2$ other carbohydrate

Supplies List
19x13-inch jelly-roll pan
Large mixing bowl
Electric mixer

Grocery List
PACKAGED
1 (16-ounce) box
angel food cake mix
1 (16-ounce) can
whole cranberry sauce

Pantry List
Nonfat cooking spray

1   (16-ounce) box angel food cake mix, dry

1   (16-ounce) can whole cranberry sauce

Instructions

> Preheat oven 350 degrees.
> Coat a jelly-roll pan with nonfat cooking spray. Set aside.
> In a large mixing bowl, combine the angel food cake mix with the cranberry sauce.
> With an electric mixer on low speed, beat for 30 seconds. Increase the speed to medium and beat for another 30 seconds.
> Spread into the prepared jelly-roll pan.
> Bake for 12 to 15 minutes.
> Let cool before cutting into 24 squares.

>>> Chocolate Cherry Snow-Capped Cake

Preparation time: 20 minutes   **Baking time:** 7 to 8 minutes
Total time: 27 to 28 minutes or less

This recipe could not be any better! Every time I turned around, someone in my family was getting another piece.

Yield: 12 servings
(1 frosted slice per serving)
Calories: 268 (12% fat); Total Fat: 4g;
Cholesterol: 0mg; Carbohydrate: 56g;
Dietary Fiber: 1g; Protein 5g;
Sodium: 331mg; Diabetic Exchanges:
4 other carbohydrate, 1 fat

Supplies List
Timer
6 (8-inch) round cake pans
Electric mixer
Medium glass bowl
Large mixing bowl
Small saucepan

Grocery List
PACKAGED
1 (18.25-ounce) box
chocolate cake mix
1 (20-ounce) can cherry pie filling

DAIRY
8 eggs

Pantry List
$1/2$ cup unsweeteened applesauce
1 cup sugar
Cream of tartar
Vanilla extract
Nonfat cooking spray

CHOCOLATE CHERRY CAKE
6   egg whites
1   ($18^1/4$-ounce) box chocolate
     cake mix, dry
$1^1/4$ cup water

$1/2$ cup unsweetened applesauce
$1/2$ (20-ounce) can cherry pie
       filling

SNOW FROSTING
1   cup sugar
$1/4$ teaspoon cream of tartar
$1/3$ cup water

2   egg whites
1   teaspoon vanilla extract

Instructions
> Preheat the oven to 350 degrees.
> Line six (8-inch) round cake pans with waxed paper and coat with nonfat cooking spray. Set aside.
> In a medium glass bowl, beat the egg whites with an electric mixer on high speed until soft peaks form. Set aside.
> In a large mixing bowl, combine the cake mix, water, and applesauce. Stir until well mixed.
> Gently fold the egg whites into the batter.
> Pour the batter evenly into the six prepared cake pans. Each cake should be thin.
> Bake for 7 to 8 minutes, or until a toothpick inserted into the center of each cake comes out clean.

>>> Chocolate Cherry
Snow-Capped Cake
CONTINUED FROM PREVIOUS PAGE

> While the cakes are baking, prepare the Snow Frosting.
> In a small saucepan over medium heat, combine the sugar, cream of tartar, and water. Stir and cook until bubbly and the sugar is dissolved.
> In a medium glass mixing bowl combine the egg whites and vanilla.
> Slowly pour the sugar syrup into the egg whites while beating with an electric mixer on high speed until soft peaks form, about 7 minutes.
> Once the cakes are finished baking, put them in the freezer to cool for 5 minutes.
> Remove the cakes from the freezer and place one cake layer on a cake plate. Spread 2 tablespoons of the cherry pie filling over the cake layer. Spread $1/2$ cup of the frosting over the cherry pie filling. Top with another cake layer. Repeat for the remaining cherry pie filling, frosting, and cake layers.
> On the top layer place your spatula flat on the frosting and lift straight up to create snowy peaks on the top of the torte.

NOTE: If you only have two (8-inch) cake pans, you can bake two layers at a time and repeat. This cake does not travel well. The movement in the car can make the frosting deflate.

BOOKS BY DAWN HALL

Published by Harvest House Publishers 2006
Seven Simple Steps to a Healthier You

Published by Thomas Nelson Publishers
Busy People's Slow Cooker Cookbook
Busy People's Low-Fat Cookbook
Busy People's Down-Home Cooking without the Down-Home Fat
Busy People's Diabetic Cookbook
Busy People's Low-Carb Cookbook
Busy People's Fun, Fast, Festive Christmas Cookbook

All of the recipes in the Busy People's cookbooks are low in fat
and made with seven or fewer easy-to-find ingredients.

All of Busy People's cookbooks are available for fund-raising,
special sales incentives, donor gifts, and promotional purposes.
For more information please e-mail SpecialMarkets@ThomasNelson.com.

AUTHOR CONTACT INFORMATION

Dawn Hall
P.O. Box 53
Swanton, Ohio 43558
Office Phone: (419) 826-2665
Web site: DawnHallCookbooks.com
E-mail: Dawn@DawnHallCookbooks.com

>>> Index

Casseroles cont.

Swiss Ranch Beef Pasta Casserole, 58–59
Tamale Pie Casserole, 296–297
Tuna Tabbouleh Rice Casserole, 34–35

Cauliflower

Cheesy Cheddar Cauliflower, 52–53
French Cauliflower, 32–33
Garlic-Buttered Broccoli, Cauliflower & Carrot Medley, 46–47
Honey Mustard Cauliflower, 254–255

Celery

Celery Bites with Zesty Cheddar Dip, 280–281
Celery Sticks with Blue Cheese Dip, 274–275
Celery Sticks with Cool & Creamy Fiery Dip, 278–279
Celery Stuffed with Creamy Blue Cheese, 90–91
Chunky Celery Salad, 196–197
Cool & Creamy Zesty Vegetable Dip with Celery Sticks, 136–137

Cheese. *See also* Blue cheese; Feta cheese; Parmesan cheese

Bacon & Cheddar Broccoli, 210–212
Bacon & Green Onion Cheese Spread, 18–19
Bacon & Tomato American Bread Crisps, 196–197
Bacon & Tomato Cheddar Bread Crisps, 152–153
Bacon Swiss Bread Crisps, 154–155
Cheddar & Chive Buttermilk Biscuits, 114–115
Cheddar Bread Twists, 262–264
Cheesy California Vegetable Medley, 216–218
Cheesy Cheddar Broccoli, 62–63
Cheesy Cheddar Cauliflower, 52–53
Cheesy Ham & Cheddar Pasta Casserole, 76–77
Cheesy Hot Potatoes, 180–181
Cheesy Ranch Bread Crisps, 237–239
Cheesy-Stuffed Portobello Mushrooms, 54–55
Cheesy Turnip Green Casserole, 190–191
Grilled Chicken Cordon Bleu, 194–195
Grilled Pepperoni & Cheesy Chicken, 170–171

Ham & Cheese Corn Bread Dumplings, 142–143
Ham & Swiss Broccoli, 213–215
Ham & Swiss Pasta Casserole, 78–79
Ham & Swiss Tomato Bread Crisps, 96–97
Hickory Smoked Sausage with Cheddar Cheese, 198–199
Hot Ham & Swiss Chicken Sandwiches, 110–111
Mushroom & Swiss Chicken, 82–83
Philly Cheese Steak Macaroni Casserole, 39–41
Swiss Ranch Beef Pasta Casserole, 58–59
Swiss-Stuffed Kielbasa & Rye Sandwiches, 130–131
Three-Pepper, Four Cheese Chicken Pasta, 36–38
Tomato & Mozzarella Bread Crisps, 286–287
Tomato & Mozzarella Salad, 142–143
Tomato & Mozzarella Tossed Salad, 230–232
Vegetarian Sausage & Cheddar Broccoli, 74–75

Cherries

Cherry Crumb Squares, 317
Cherry Delight Four-Layer Cake, 308
Cherry Surprise-Filled Chocolate Cupcakes, 305
Chocolate Cherry Snow-Capped Torte, 320–321
Double-Chocolate Cherry Snack Squares, 302
Very Cherry Cookies, 316

Chicken

Buffalo Chicken Chili, 148–149
Buffalo Chicken Pieces, 196–197
Caesar Chicken Pasta Casserole, 54–55
Chicken & Broccoli Pasta Casserole, 64–65
Chicken Barley Soup, 90–91
Chicken Bites over Sweet & Spicy Brown Rice with Vegetables, 226–227
Chicken Dijon Pasta Casserole, 62–63
Chicken in the Clouds Chowder, 150–151
Chipotle Chicken Pasta, 80–81
Coconut Chicken, 200–201
Creamed Chicken, 102–103
Grilled Chicken Cordon Bleu, 194–195
Grilled Pepperoni & Cheesy Chicken, 170–171

Fish. *See also* Salmon; Tuna
    Dill-icious Tilapia with Shrimp, 244–245
    Fish Tacos, 258–259
    Florentine-Stuffed Fish, 254–255
    Honey Mustard & Dill Fish, 237–239
    Mild & Light Mahi-Mahi, 182–184

Fruit salads & sides
    Brown Sugar & Cinnamon Apple Salad, 198–199
    Citrus Salad, 150–151
    Creamy Blueberry & Pineapple Salad, 182–184
    Creamy Spiced Apricot Salad, 176–177
    Crunchy Crab Salad, 20–21
    Fresh Strawberry Cream Salad, 84–85
    Frosted Watermelon Wedges with Fresh Blueberries, 4–5
    Grape Salad, 12–13
    Harvey Sliced Apple Salad, 130–131
    Melon Medley Kebabs, 6–7
    Pineapple Tidbit Salad, 298–300
    Ruby Fruit Salad, 10–11
    Spiced Peaches & Cream Salad, 100–101
    Tangy Watermelon Wedges, 24–25
    Watermelon Sandwiches, 8–9

Grapefruit
    Citrus Salad, 150–151

Grapes
    Grape Salad, 12–13

Gravies & sauces
    Creamy Alfredo Sauce, 272–273
    Fettuccini Alfredo, 282–283
    Fish Taco Sauce, 258–259
    Kielbasa Alfredo Sauce, 156–158
    Mushroom Gravy, 210–212
    Savory Peach Chutney Gravy, 112–113
    Savory Turkey Gravy, 120–121
    Steak Tips with Onions & Gravy, 207–209
    Turkey Gravy with Chive Dumplings, 122–123
    Vegetarian Sausage Marinara, 268–269
    World's Easiest Mushroom Gravy, 140–141

Green beans
    Buttered Bean Medley, 94–95
    Citrus Green Beans, 180–181
    Country Green Beans, 102–103
    Dilly Green Beans & Sliced Potatoes, 254–255
    Garlic Green Beans, 108–109
    Green Jean Beans, 176–177
    Seasoned Green Beans with Bacon & Onion, 76–77

Green chilies
    Captain's Hat Whole Wheat & Green Chilies Mini Biscuits, 290–291
    Green Chili Salsa Salad, 104–105
    Three-Alarm Chili, 290–291

Greens. *See also* Turnip greens
    Southern-Style Mixed Greens, 118–119

Grocery lists, ix, xiii

Ham
    Cheesy Ham & Cheddar Pasta Casserole, 76–77
    Crabby Ham & Potato Au Gratin Chowder, 96–97
    Freckled Cucumber & Ham Salad, 10–11
    Grilled Chicken Cordon Bleu, 194–195
    Grilled Ham Steak, 185–187
    Ham & Cheese Corn Bread Dumplings, 142–143
    Ham & Swiss Broccoli, 213–215
    Ham & Swiss Pasta Casserole, 78–79
    Ham & Swiss Tomato Bread Crisps, 96–97
    Ham & Yam Casserole, 32–33
    Ham with Fried Cabbage, 185–187
    Hot Ham & Swiss Chicken Sandwiches, 110–111
    Turnip Greens with Ham & Apple, 92–93

Honeydew melon
    Melon Medley Kebabs, 6–7

Hot dogs
    Chili Dog Chili with Whole Wheat Corn Bread Dumplings, 136–137
    Corn Dog Dumplings, 126–127
    Whole Wheat Corn Dog Dumplings, 138–139

Kielbasa
    Kielbasa Alfredo Sauce, 156–158
    Swiss-Stuffed Kielbasa & Rye Sandwiches, 130–131

INDEX   331

Sausage cont.

Kielbasa Alfredo Sauce, 156–158
Smoked Sausage, Potatoes & Sauerkraut, 92–93
Smoked Sausage & Sauerkraut, 100–101
Spinach, Barley & Italian Sausage Soup, 154–155
Swiss-Stuffed Kielbasa & Rye Sandwiches, 130–131

Sausage, vegetarian
Angel Hair Pasta Smothered in Vegetarian Sausage Marinara, 268–269
Creamy Sausage & Bean Chowder, 280–281
Creamy Sausage & Spinach Soup, 288–289
Little Italy Barley Soup, 270–271
Little Italy Chili Topped with Italian Biscuit Bites, 294–295
One-Pan Lasagna Stove-Top Dinner, 292–293
Oven-Baked Stuffed Portobello Mushrooms, 298–300
Spinach, Sausage & Rice Stove-Top Casserole, 286–287
Vegetarian Sausage & Cheddar Broccoli, 74–75
Vegetarian Sausage Drop Biscuits, 270–271

Scallops
Southwestern Bay Scallop Stew, 240–241

Shrimp
Dill-icious Tilapia with Shrimp, 244–245
Seafood & Shells by the Seaside, 250–251
Shrimp & Rice Stove-Top Casserole, 252–253
Shrimp Garden Salad, 248–249
Shrimp Scampi, 262–264
Spicy Shrimp Soup, 2–3
Sweet & Succulent Shrimp Kebabs, 188–189

Soups, stews & chowders. *See also* Chili
Bold & Spicy Gazpacho, 16–17
Chicken Barley Soup, 90–91
Chicken in the Clouds Chowder, 150–151
Chilled Tex-Mex Black Bean Soup, 14–15
Crabby Ham & Potato Au Gratin Chowder, 96–97
Cream of Greens Soup, 134–135
Creamy Northern Bean Soup with Dumplings, 142–143
Creamy Sausage & Bean Chowder, 280–281
Creamy Sausage & Spinach Soup, 288–289

Hickory Smoked Chicken & Bean Chowder, 152–153
Little Italy Barley Soup, 270–271
Salmon Chowder, 256–257
Southwestern Bay Scallop Stew, 240–241
Southwestern Beef & Barley Soup, 88–89
Spicy Shrimp Soup, 2–3
Spinach, Barley & Italian Sausage Soup, 154–155
Vegetarian Goulash, 266–267

Spinach
Bacon & Onion Spinach Salad, 148–149
Beef & Spinach Salad with Sweet Lime Dressing, 18–19
Creamy Sausage & Spinach Soup, 288–289
Excellent Spinach Salad, 64–65
Florentine-Stuffed Fish, 254–255
Fresh Mushroom & Baby Spinach Salad with Sweet Italian Salad Dressing, 170–171
Fresh Strawberry Spinach Salad with Sweet Bacon & Blue Cheese Vinaigrette, 39–41
Mandarin Orange Spinach Salad with Sweet Bacon & Blue Cheese Vinaigrette, 44–45
Salmon Florentine, 242–243
Sesame Seed Spinach Salad, 284–285
Simple Spinach Salad with Honey Salad Dressing, 72–73
Spinach, Barley & Italian Sausage Soup, 154–155
Spinach, Sausage & Rice Stove-Top Casserole, 286–287
Spinach Salad with French Bacon Salad Dressing, 84–85
Super Simple Spinach Salad with Sweet Homemade Dressing, 36–38

Spreads. *See* Dips & spreads

Squash
Italian Squash Medley, 42–43, 292–293

Stews. *See* Soups, stews & chowders

Strawberries
Fresh Strawberry Cream Salad, 84–85
Fresh Strawberry Spinach Salad with Sweet Bacon & Blue Cheese Vinaigrette, 39–41
Triple Berry Trifle, 319